Islamic Homosexualities

Islamic Homosexualities

Culture, History, and Literature

Stephen O. Murray and Will Roscoe

with additional contributions by
Eric Allyn, Louis Crompton,
Mildred Dickemann, Badruddin Khan,
Hasan Mujtaba, Nauman Naqvi,
Jim Wafer, and Sigrid Westphal-Hellbusch

NEW YORK UNIVERSITY PRESS
New York and London

NEW YORK UNIVERSITY PRESS
New York and London

Library of Congress Cataloging-in-Publication Data

Murray, Stephen O.
    Islamic homosexualities : culture, history, and literature /
Stephen O. Murray and Will Roscoe ; with additional contributions by
Eric Allyn . . . [et al.].
        p.   cm.
    Includes bibliographical references (p.) and index.
    ISBN 0-8147-7467-9 (cloth : acid-free paper). — ISBN
0-8147-7468-7 (pbk. : acid-free paper)
    1. Homosexuality—Islamic countries.   2. Homosexuality—Islamic
countries—History.   3. Homosexuality, Male—Islamic countries.
4. Gays in popular culture—Islamic countries.   I. Roscoe, Will.
II. Title.
HQ76.3.I75M87   1997
306'.62'0917671—dc20   96-35677
                              CIP

New York University Press books are printed on acid-free paper,
and their binding materials are chosen for strength and durability.

Manufactured in the United States of America

10 9 8 7 6 5 4 3 2 1

For Shivananda Khan and the Naz Foundation,
articulating the needs of men who have sex with men
in Muslim societies

Contents

PART III: HISTORICAL STUDIES

PART IV: ANTHROPOLOGICAL STUDIES

PART I

Introduction to Islamic Homosexualities

CHAPTER 1

Introduction

Will Roscoe and Stephen O. Murray

While the study of sexuality may no longer be a "virgin field," as historian Vern Bullough (1976) once described it, our knowledge concerning homosexuality in most periods of history remains uneven and few attempts have been made to create historical or cross-cultural syntheses of the evidence on homosexuality that does exist. We know something about homosexual patterns among the elite men of classical Athens (Dover 1978; Halperin 1990; Winkler 1990), in the Roman Empire (Richlin 1993; Lilja 1983), among medieval clerics (Boswell 1980) and some victims of the Inquisition, in certain locales of Renaissance Europe (Monter 1981; Murray and Gerard 1983; Ruggiero 1985; Smith 1991), and in the early modern era of northwestern Europe, Holland and London in particular (Gerard and Hekma 1989; Trumbach 1977, 1991; Bray 1982). We do not yet know how these patterns are related through time or social structure. While there are models explaining such large-scale transformations as the emergence of feudalism, nothing comparable exists to account for equally epochal transformations in human sexuality.

Cross-cultural research is equally spotty. The North American "berdache" has earned the distinction of being anthropology's most famous example of a "queer" social role among non-Western peoples, while comparable roles throughout Oceania, Africa, and Asia have been barely studied. Herdt has done pioneering work on age-stratified homosexuality in Melanesia, but

Asian and Pacific homosexual traditions are only beginning to receive attention (Murray 1992; Jackson 1995; Leupp 1995). Islamic homosexualities (and
those of sub-Saharan Africa) have been almost completely overlooked (with
the exception of the occasional mention of Islamic boy-love in orientalist discourse). The first goal of this collection, therefore, is to correct this oversight
by offering historical, anthropological, and literary studies and texts docu-
menting the conceptions and organizations of homosexual desire and conduct in Islamic societies.[1] Only one chapter ("Muhammad and Male
Homosexuality") focuses on the treatment of homosexuality in the religion
of Islam and its written guide, the *Qur'ān*.

Despite important regularities across both time and space, there are multi-
ple Islamic societies. Some even speak of Islams, rather than a single, timeless
Islamic tradition transparently derived from the *Qur'ān*.[2] As anthropologist
Lloyd Fallers notes, "Islam has held quite different meanings for Arabs,
Persians, Southeast Asians, and Africans, and within these regional groups,
for various segments of society. It has meant different things to particular
Muslim communities at different points in their histories" (1974:xv).
Without anything like the papacy's centralization of authority over definition of God's will and sacred book, various interpretations have co-existed.
Away from the Sunni/Shi'a borders, however, Muslims often have believed
that there is a singular Islam that is a macrocosm, the "Islamic world," which
is presumed to share familiar interpretations and arrangements that are not
recognized by the locals as being local variants.[3] Variations over space or time
in acceptance of unpublicized homosexualities are central in this volume.

A second goal of this collection is to counter the pronounced Eurocentrism
of recent research on homosexuality and gender difference. Since the 1970s,
most work in lesbian/gay history has focused exclusively on the modern
period of western Europe and North America—a shortcoming each of us has
commented on (Roscoe 1987; Murray 1984, 1992, 1995). Based on the evidence from this period, constructionists have developed an account of the
emergence of "homosexual" as a category of personhood that credits this
development to social factors (e.g., urbanization and industrialization) and to
specialist discourse, especially that of forensic psychiatry, which recodified
gender and, then, sexuality from moral to medical discourse.[4] Although
details of the social constructionist model can be criticized and the actual historical processes involved need to be much better documented (e.g., the dis-
semination of the "homosexual" category from elite medical discourse to
popular consciousness), most scholars today agree that the current predomi-
nance of egalitarian homosexuality, in which both partners define themselves as "gay," is a recent modern development. It first appeared in cities of

Europe and North America tentatively at the beginning of the early twentieth century and more dramatically following the Second World War.[5]

The thrust of this collection is to challenge the dominant, Eurocentric model of gay/lesbian history and the implicit, occasionally explicit, assertion in many social constructionist accounts that contemporary homosexuality is somehow incomparable to any other pattern (or that there are no other patterns). The implication is that nothing at all preceded modern homosexuality or that whatever homosexual behavior occurred earlier was too disorganized, spontaneous, and insignificant to compare with modern homosexuality. "Pre-modern" societies are assumed to be more hostile toward same-sex relations or lacking the conditions necessary for social roles and identities incorporating homosexuality to develop. Despite their pessimistic post-humanist disavowals, social constructionist accounts still evoke a history of homosexuality as a progressive, even teleological, evolution from pre-modern repression, silence, and invisibility to modern visibility and social freedom. Certainly the distinctions between age- and status-differentiated homosexuality, gender-variant social roles, and modern gay identity are important, but this collection questions the assumption that the practitioners of pre-modern homosexualities never formulated identities based on their practices and never created networks among themselves that might have achieved sufficient density and localization to be noticed, that "identity" and "subculture" are uniquely modern and western inventions.

Western exceptionalism—the practice of viewing the history of western Europe as representing the culmination of all human progress—has been subject to criticism for some time. Even before Edward Said deconstructed orientalism, scholars like Marshall Hodgson consistently advocated an inter-regional perspective to offset Eurocentrism. As Hodgson argues:

The peculiarly eccentric character of the West—it was so long a dependent frontier, so suddenly a center of world transformation, but almost never developed in and for itself alone—has meant that the human significance of Western history is more than usually tied in with a wider setting. . . . One would suppose a primary interest in a history of the West would be precisely to trace our weird role in the world at large. (1993:265–66).

The long history and broad distribution of Islamic societies provides an opportunity for placing the emergence of modern homosexual identity in northern Europe within a broader context and testing the assumptions of recent work in lesbian/gay history. The contributions in this collection reveal consistent patterns of Islamic homosexualities that can be traced over the course of centuries, from age-differentiated relations (whether the idealized love of boys found in Persian, Turkish, Urdu, and Arabic poetry or the sexual use of young male entertainers, dancers, and military cadets) to alternative gender statuses represented by the male *khanith* of Oman, the female *mustergil* of southern Iraq, and the sworn virgins of the Balkans. To say that male homosexuality flourished in Islamic societies would be an overstatement typical of orientalist discourse, but it would be no exaggeration to say that, before the twentieth century, the region of the world with the most visible and diverse homosexualities was not northwestern Europe but northern Africa and southwestern Asia. Indeed, the contrast between "Western" and "Islamic" homosexualities is not so much one of visibility versus invisibility or modern freedom versus traditional repression, but of containment versus elaboration, of a single pattern of homosexuality defined and delimited by institutions and discourses closely linked to the modern nation-state versus the variety, distribution, and longevity of same-sex patterns in Islamic societies.

Above all the great variety of Islamic homosexual patterns warns us that overly simple, unilinear models will be inadequate. There is nothing inevitable about the development of modern homosexual identity. Both status-differentiated and gender-variant homosexual patterns, as Islamic examples suggest, are capable of long-term development and elaboration, of adapting to changing social contexts. Urbanization, for example, is often cited as an important social factor in the emergence of modern homosexuality and subculture. But Islamic societies were characterized by their cosmopolitanism throughout northern Europe's dark and middle ages, when that region remained, in relation to the Islamic world, a predominantly rural backwater. Why, then, did gay identity not develop in the context of Islamic cosmopolitanism, and why has egalitarian rather than status-differentiated or gender-defined homosexuality become the predominant form of same-sex relations in late-twentieth-century Western societies? Answering questions like these (to which we will return in the Conclusion) should provide a much clearer understanding of the precise relationship between social structures, ideology and belief systems, and factors like urbanization, family structure, and so forth as they impact on the expression and forms of homosexuality.

Contemporary Western homosexual identity may represent a singular configuration of identity, lifestyle, and group formation, but as the essays in this collection show, none of these elements are unique to the modern homosexual. In fact, as Trumbach (1991), Chauncey (1994), and Roscoe (1995) have argued, the original "modern homosexual" (whether we take the early-eighteenth-century Molly or the late-nineteenth-century Uranian to be that figure) was in fact a highly gendered social role and identity. Further, individuals such as Ulrichs, Symonds, Carpenter, and Ellis, who have been credited with constructing the "modern homosexual," knew of and frequently drew upon records of non-European gender-defined and status-differentiated homosexualities (see Roscoe 1995). The separation of gender variance and sexual object choice did not occur in medical-psychiatric discourse until the early twentieth century, and it did not become a widespread basis of self-identification until after the Second World War. Until that watershed, to be homosexual was to be a nonmasculine man or a non-feminine woman, while (by convention at least) the "masculine" men and "feminine" women with whom one had sex were defined and defined themselves as "normal."

In fact, there have been two modern homosexualities: the gender-variant (if not third-gendered) Mollies and Uranians, and the "sexed being" represented by the homosexual, who is defined strictly on the basis of the anatomical sex of his or her partners, regardless of who penetrates whom or who might be considered more or less "masculine" or "feminine." It is identities of the latter type (that is, Western gay sexual identity) that are unrepresented (or undeveloped) in Islamic history. However, identities based on gender difference comparable to Mollies and Uranians are amply attested. The nonmasculine male entertainers called *mukhannath* (see chapters 2 and 3) certainly had "identities" in the sense of occupying social roles with a specific name, and they arguably participated in a "subculture" as well (Rowson 1991). Balkan sworn virgins and southern Iraq *mustergil* had identities too, while Persian and Arabic poets who drew their inspiration from beautiful youth and speculated on the spiritual dimensions of same-sex love developed a self-conscious homoerotic literary genre unrivaled until quite recent times.

Undoubtedly, the traditional paradigm of status-differentiation, which always places sexual partners in distinct categories depending on who penetrates whom, mitigates any of these patterns from developing into an identity in the modern sense. But treating the patterns of homosexuality we find in Islamic societies as categorically distinct from all aspects of modern homosexual identity and lifestyles reinforces the conceits of Eurocentrism. The possibilities for expressing homosexual desire, pursuing homosexual relations, adopting "non-heterosexual" identities, and joining networks of those similarly inclined or employed existed in various times and places in the Islamic world. As the examples documented in this collection suggest, there is a continuum from gay identity to its absence, not a sharp break.

OVERVIEW

Contributions to this volume has been organized into four sections—introduction to Islamic homosexualities, literary studies, historical studies and texts, and anthropological contributions. The resulting sequence is partly historical (going forward through time) and partly geographic (going from west to east).

In addition to this Introduction, Part I includes a chapter by Roscoe with an overview of status-differentiated and gender-defined homosexuality in the "Oikoumene"—the broad region of citied societies depending on intensive agriculture from the Mediterranean to South Asia—before the rise of Islam. As this review shows, Islamic conquerors and missionaries encountered well-established patterns of homosexuality in most of the regions they entered. The following chapter by Wafer reviews the brief references to homosexuality in the *Qur'ān* and in *hadīths* about the Prophet, and argues for a homology between submission to the will of Allah and the sexual submission of young males to older males. In the third chapter Murray shows how the apparent tolerance for homosexuality in Islamic societies depends upon a widespread and enduring pattern of collective denial in which the condition for pursuing either age-stratified or gender-defined homosexuality is that the behavior never be publicly acknowledged. Even so, he demonstrates that homosexual conduct was not so covert that there were no labels for homosexual roles.

Most of the existing literature about homosexuality in Muslim societies deals with males. In the final chapter of Part I, Murray reviews the few and scattered references to lesbianism (see also the appendix to his chapter on the mamlūks). Subsequent chapters by Dickemann and Westphal-Helsbusch describe female gender-crossing roles, although the sexual behavior and cultural expectations of sexual behavior for women in these roles are less than clear.

Part II, Literary Studies, includes three chapters that examine medieval Persian, Arabic, and Turkish writings, mostly poetry, to disentangle the corporeal from the ethereal in their extensive invocations of and discourse on love. Studies of poetry are useful, because individual feelings about loved ones (of any age or sex) were not recorded in Islamic fiction or non-fiction. As Grunebaum (who finds even poetry "unrevealing and discreet") notes:

Even after the weakening of the classical ideal in the later Middle Ages, the biographer and especially the autobiographer dealt frankly and realistically only with religious development and to some extent with sensual enjoyment. Private experience is neither objectivized in action through novel or drama nor presented indirectly through the personification of virtues and ideas or through the casting of figures of history and legend to represent and express personal attitudes. There is abundant evidence for the Arab's keen understanding of man; but this is not to be found . . . outside the religious sphere, in his confessional writing. (1952:332)[6]

Part III, Historical Studies, begins with Murray's discussion of the military elites of medieval Egypt and Syria and of the Ottoman Empire, the latter continuing into the twentieth century. These troops of sultans and other "slaves" were used in an attempt to fashion a one-generation elite far removed from their natal families, unable to pass on office to their descendants. In theory this promoted loyalty exclusively to the sultan. However, bonds within the elite, including sexual ones, became important. Motivation shifted from advancing family members, to advancing favorites, contrary to the intended atomization of the "slave" elites. Eventually, these systems weakened and family influences increased. Murray argues that proscription of inheritance correlates to the acceptance of pederasty in these institutions and, in the case of mamlūk wives, enhanced women's status.

The following two chapters deal with the northeastern reaches of the Ottoman Empire, the Balkans. Murray reviews nineteenth-century descriptions of Ali Pasha's court, and Mildred Dickemann discusses nineteenth- and twentieth-century Muslim and Christian women who resisted marriage and adopted a male gender identity. The final chapters in Part III excavate some nineteenth- and early-twentieth-century Western accounts of pederasty and male entertainers/prostitutes in Morocco, Iraq, and Uzbekistan, and Richard Burton's survey of age- and gender-defined homosexuality from the "Terminal Essay" of his translation of *A Thousand Nights and a Night* (first published in 1885). Part III concludes with a review of diverse studies like Burton's, but dealing with the region south of Burton's "sotadic zone," the east and west coasts of Africa along which Islam spread.

The chapters in Part III are more comparative (ethnological) than those in Part IV, Anthropological Studies, although the boundary is fuzzy. The chapters in Part IV are based on more contemporary and direct observation (with varying degrees of participation). Especially those by Pakistanis are more experience-near than those by sympathetic European ethnographers (Westphal-Hellbusch and Wikan) and less-sympathetic American ones (Geertz and Peacock). Gender-crossing roles (particularly male dancers and actors who perform as women) in Iraq, Oman, Pakistan, Indonesia, and the southern Philippines are also examined. Prostitution is often a cultural corollary of these roles, although Mujtaba discusses male prostitutes in Pakistan who are not public entertainers. Next, Badruddin Khan discusses the overwhelming family pressure in Pakistan that keeps personal desires trivial and forecloses any alternative organization. Incorporating two other Karachi natives' responses to his analysis, he also discusses the rising tide of urban violence in Karachi and the erosion of "traditional" sexual opportunities, even within the sphere of private pleasure. The final chapter provides a brief look at an incipient "modern gay" organization of homosexuality in Malaysia and attempts by Pink Triangle and the Naz Project from within Islamic assumptions to reduce

HIV-transmission in homosexual sex and to provide nonjudgmental care for persons with AIDS there and in South Asia.

In the Conclusion we review the dominant idioms of Islamic homosexualities and discuss the social, historical, and religious factors that account for their presence, form, and longevity. We argue that the comparative perspective afforded by the study of Islamic homosexualities can help scholars develop more complex and multifactorial models to explain why identities based on same-sex desire first emerged in the industrialized, urban societies of northwestern Europe and North America.

STYLISTIC MATTERS

Quotations and citations include various romanizations of Arabic, Farsi, and Turkish words. We have endeavored to standardize written representations in our own writing, but have not imposed it on quotations from others (so that, for instance, although we write *Qur'ān, Koran* appears in quotations).

Although many contributions of necessity draw from a predominantly Western discourse about an Other with whom there is a long history of religious antagonism, territorial rivalry, and shifting feelings of considerable cultural inferiority and superiority, we have sought to maximize polyvocality in writing and compiling this collection by quoting earlier observers, Islamic authors, and, wherever possible, Islamic informants (see Kluckhohn 1943: 268; Murray 1986). The compilation of previous discourse is a venerable tradition among Muslim authors (e.g., "necklaces"; see Grunebaum 1948, 1952; Giffen 1971:60–61). In the present collection, lengthy quotations are meant to minimize distortion of what earlier writers wrote, not just to emulate Arabic tradition. There has been so much misrepresentation of what both natives and scholars have said about homosexuality in Islamic societies that lengthy quotations, especially from members of contemporary Islamic societies, are invaluable. Readers should not have to seek hard-to-find but critical sources to find out exactly what an author wrote. We endeavor clearly to distinguish what the original observers said from our (sometimes skeptical) interpretations.

Notes

1. The only previous work in this area, a collection edited by Schmitt and Sofer (1992), deals exclusively with male homosexuality and consists primarily of personal accounts by recent Western travelers relating their disappointing sexual encounters with Arabs and Iranians.

2. For example, Fallers (1974:xvi), el-Zein (1977:242–43). Contemporary American anthropologists (e.g., Geertz 1968, 1995; Eickelman 1981, 1982) tend to write of differ-

ent "local contexts"; earlier ones of Redfield's "little traditions" (see the application by Grunebaum 1955), or "subtraditions" (e.g., Geertz 1960), or "indigenization," which Geertz (1995:56) characterizes as "attempt[s] to deal with the problem posed to quranic orthodoxy by plurality of belief and diversity of practices" in various Islamic societies.

3. This is not to deny that there is knowledge of regional and national differences— or that the belief in a universal shared Islam in the singular has real consequences!

4. In fact, two types of social constructionism can be distinguished. Sociologists and social historians such as Barry Adam, John D'Emilio, and David Greenberg, although crediting medical-psychiatric discourse and labeling practices with playing an important role in the formation of modern homosexual roles, also pay attention to broader social and economic forces, while scholars influenced by Michel Foucault, such as David Halperin, Jonathan Ned Katz, and Lillian Faderman, focus almost exclusively on the role of discourse in constructing not only linguistic categories, but identities, roles, and desires. The latter might be better described as "discourse creationism" (Murray 1995, 1996).

5. As Murray has long stressed, "the modern Western notion that everyone who engages in homosexual behavior is 'a homosexual,' a distinct species with unique features . . . does not very well explain life and categorization even in the society for which the model has been elaborated, since, on the one hand, not everyone involved in homosexual behavior is defined (by self or by others) as homosexual, and, on the other hand, no single type with a unique set of features exists" (Murray 1984:45). Even in the self-proclaimed "gay Mecca" in which we both live, age-stratified, gender-stratified, and other status-structured homosexualities exist, even though the most visible organization of homosexuality is the "modern gay" one. Similarly, the rise of a gay subculture in Bangkok has not eliminated the effeminate *kathoey* role or patron-client sexual relations (Jackson 1995:268).

6. One should not infer from the absence of discourse and late development of the novel that there was no conception of a self. See Spiro (1993) on the general error of concluding that non-Westerners do not conceive of selves, and Wikan (1990) for a refutation of the mistake in a specific place (predominantly Muslim north Bali).

References

Adam, Barry D. 1987. *The rise of a gay and lesbian movement.* Boston: Twayne. (2nd edition, 1995).

Boswell, John. 1980. *Christianity, social tolerance, and homosexuality: Gay people in western Europe from the beginning of the Christian era to the fourteenth century.* Chicago: University of Chicago Press.

Bray, Alan. 1982. *Homosexuality in renaissance England.* London: Gay Men's Press.

Bullough, Vern L. 1976. *Sex, society, and history.* New York: Science History Publications.

Chauncey, George, Jr. 1994. *Gay New York: Gender, urban culture, and the making of the gay male world, 1890–1940.* New York: Basic.

D'Emilio, John. 1983. *Sexual politics, sexual communities.* Chicago: University of Chicago Press.

Dover, Kenneth J. 1978. *Greek homosexuality.* Cambridge: Harvard University Press.

Eickelman, Dale F. 1981. *The Middle East: An anthropological approach.* Englewood Cliffs, NJ: Prentice-Hall.

———.1982. "The study of Islam in local contexts." *Contributions to Asian Studies* 17:171–75.

el-Zein, Abdul Hamid M. 1977. "Beyond ideology and theology: The search for an anthropology of Islam." *Annual Review of Anthropology* 6:227–54.

Faderman, Lillian. 1981. *Surpassing the love of men*. New York: Morrow.

———— 1991. *Odd girls and twilight lovers: A history of lesbian life in twentieth-century America*. New York: Columbia University Press.

Fallers, Lloyd A. 1974. Foreword to *The sacred meadow* by Abdul Hamid el-Zein, xv–xvii. Evanston, IL: Northwestern University Press.

Foucault, Michel. 1978. *The history of sexuality*. New York: Pantheon.

Geertz, Clifford. 1960. *The religion of Java*. New York: Free Press.

————.1968. *Islam observed*. New Haven: Yale University Press.

————. 1995. *After the fact: Two countries, four decades, one anthropologist*. Cambridge: Harvard University Press.

Gerard, Kent, and Gert Hekma, eds. 1989. *The pursuit of sodomy: Male homosexuality in renaissance and enlightenment Europe*. Binghamton, NY: Haworth.

Giffen, Lois Anita. 1971. *Theory of profane love among the Arabs: The development of the genre*. New York: New York University Press.

Greenberg, David F. 1988. *The construction of homosexuality*. Chicago: University of Chicago Press.

Grunebaum, Gustave E. von. 1948. "The nature of the Arabic literary effort." *Journal of Near Eastern Studies* 4:116–21.

————. 1952. "The aesthetic foundation of Arabic literature." *Comparative Literature* 4:323–40.

————. 1955. *Unity and variety in Muslim civilization*. Chicago: University of Chicago Press.

Halperin, David M. 1990. *One hundred years of homosexuality and other essays on Greek love*. New York: Routledge.

Hodgson, Marshall G. 1993. *Rethinking world history: Essays on Europe, Islam, and world history*, ed. Edmund Burke. Cambridge: Cambridge University Press.

Jackson, Peter A. 1995. *Dear Uncle Go: Male homosexuality in Thailand*. Bangkok: Bua Luang.

Kluckhohn, Clyde. 1943. Review of *Sun Chief* by Leo Simmons. *American Anthropologist* 45:267–70.

Leupp, Gary P. 1995. *Nanshoku*. Berkeley: University of California Press.

Lilja, Saara. 1983. *Homosexuality in republican and Augustan Rome, Commentationes Humanarum Litterarum* 74. Helsinki: Finnish Society of Sciences and Letters.

Monter, William E. 1981. "Sodomy and heresy in early modern Switzerland." *Journal of Homosexuality* 6:41–55.

Murray, Stephen O. 1984. *Social theory, homosexual realities*. New York: Gay Academic Union.

————. 1986. "A note on variability." In *New perspective in language, culture, and personality*, ed. W. Cowan, M. Foster, and K. Koerner, 265–66. Amsterdam: John Benjamins.

————. 1992. *Oceanic homosexualities*. New York: Garland.

————. 1995. "Discourse creationism." *Journal of Sex Research* 32:263–65.

————. 1996. *American gay*. Chicago: University of Chicago Press.

Murray, Stephen O., and Kent Gerard. 1983. "Renaissance sodomite subcultures?" *Onder Vrouwen, Onder Mannen* 1:182–96.

Richlin, Amy. 1993. "Not before homosexuality: The materiality of the *cinaedus* and the Roman law against love between men." *Journal of the History of Sexuality* 3(3):523–73.

Roscoe, Will. 1987. "Bibliography of berdache and alternative gender roles among North American Indians." *Journal of Homosexuality* 14:81–171.

————. 1995. "Was We'wha a homosexual? Native American survivance and the two-spirit tradition." *GLQ: A Journal of Lesbian/Gay Studies* 2(3):193–235.

Rowson, Everett K. 1991. "The effeminates of early Medina." *Journal of the American Oriental Society* 111:671–93.

Ruggiero, Guido. 1985. *The boundaries of eros.* New York: Oxford University Press.

Schmitt, Arno, and Jehoeda Sofer. 1992. *Sexuality and eroticism among males in Moslem societies.* Binghamton, NY: Harrington Park Press.

Smith, Bruce R. 1991. *Homosexual desire in Shakespeare's England: A cultural poetics.* Chicago: University of Chicago Press.

Spiro, Melford E. 1993. "Is the Western conception of the self 'peculiar' within the context of world cultures?" *Ethos* 21:107–53.

Trumbach, Randolph. 1977. "London's sodomites." *Journal of Social History* 11:1–33.

———. 1991. "London's Sapphists: From three sexes to four genders in the making of modern culture." In *Body guards: The cultural politics of gender ambiguity,* ed. Julia Epstein and Kristina Straub, 112–41. New York: Routledge.

Wikan, Unni. 1990. *Managing turbulent hearts.* Chicago: University of Chicago Press.

Winkler, John J. 1990. *The constraints of desire: The anthropology of sex and gender in ancient Greece.* New York: Routledge.

CHAPTER 2

The Will Not to Know

Islamic Accommodations of Male Homosexuality

Stephen O. Murray

Although, clearly, waves of puritanism rose and fell before contemporary "Islamism" (more commonly mislabeled "fundamentalism"),[1] traditional and modern Arab states (and non-Arab Islamic ones, with the exception of contemporary Iran) have not attempted to remove homosexual behavior or its recurrent practitioners from society.[2] Variations over space or time in acceptance of unpublicized homosexualities are important—and central to this volume.[3] Although in theory the *Qur'ān* legislates every aspect of social life, interpretations and applications of that fixed and authoritative guide have differed widely,[4] though not without limit. Recognizing the existence of variance should not preclude examining similarities that do exist across space and time, however.[5]

In this chapter, I will argue that there is a common Islamic ethos of avoidance in acknowledging sex and sexualities. This argument is not intended to justify viewing urban and rural, past and present Islamic societies as indistinguishable or uninfluenced by undisguised European repugnance for visible pederasty. Nor do I wish to minimize the extent to which current strictures are reactions to earlier Western contempt more than products of indigenous traditions (including Islam). As AbuKhalil writes:

What passes in present-day Saudi Arabia, for example, as sexual conservatism is due more to Victorian puritanism than to Islamic mores. It is quite inaccurate to attribute prevailing sexual mores in present-day Arab society to Islam. Originally, Islam did not have the same harsh Biblical judgment about homosexuality as Christianity. Homophobia, as an ideology of hostility toward people who are homosexual, was produced by the Christian West. Homophobic influences in Arab cultures are relatively new, and many were introduced . . . from Western sources. (1993:32)

While it is important to note the invention of tradition for this and much else in what passes for "Islamic fundamentalism" (see Lewis 1993:90–92), the dialectic is more complicated. Some of the medieval Christian animus for homosexuality was probably a product of culturally backward Europeans searching for reasons to feel superior to Muslim civilizations. Christian animus seems to have increased (even if it did not arrive "out of the blue" as Boswell [1980] imagined) after failed Crusades. As a marker of the Muslim enemy, homosexuality became a part of antagonistic acculturation, an oft-underlined-by-Christians "moral superiority" to Muslims (and, eventually, to a larger Sotadic zone of depravity, especially "prostitution").

Usually in Arab and other Islamic societies, everyone successfully avoids public recognition (let alone discussion!) of deviations from normative standards—sexual or other. Under Islamic law, as Jehoeda Sofer notes, "The rules of penal procedure are extremely strict. Only oral testimony by eye witnesses is admitted. Four trustworthy Muslim men must testify that they have seen 'the key entering the key hole' or the culprit must confess four times. Since there is severe punishment for unproven accusation, the punishment was rarely carried out" (1992a:132). This will not to know extends beyond official procedures to everyday practice, as historian Maarten Schild observes:

The established societal norms and morals of Islam are accepted as unchangeable and respected by the majority of Muslims, which does not imply however that they will or can conform to them in practice. . . . In practice it is only public transgression of Islamic morals that is condemned, and therefore Islamic law stresses the role of eyewitnesses to an offence. The police are not allowed to go in search of possible sinners, who can only be caught red-handed, and not behind the "veil of secrecy" of closed doors. In a way, concealment is advised, because to disclose a dreadful sin would be a sin in itself. It is not only condemnation by the law which can be avoided by secrecy, the same can be said of shame.[6] . . .

This emphasis on externals in Islamic law as well as in the social concept of shame, with its connivance in theoretically forbidden and shameful behavior, could be deemed hypocritical. But such a judgment would be beside the point, missing the essence of the entire matter, which is that in principle the validity of Islamic morals and of the social role pattern is confirmed by not openly resisting it, and it is just that which maintains the system as it is. (1990:617–18)

Norwegian anthropologist Unni Wikan has described this general circum-Mediterranean preference for avoiding direct confrontation of other people's failings:

The world is imperfect; people are created with dissimilar natures, and are likewise imperfect. It is up to every person to behave as correctly—i.e., tactfully, politely, hospitably, morally, and amicably—as possible in all the different encounters in which he engages, rather than to demand such things of others. To blame, criticise, or sanction those who fall short of such ideas is to be tactless and leads to loss of esteem. . . . Even the party who has been [directly] offended will have difficulties imposing compliance on his rights. For human nature is strong and unbending, and not easily broken. . . . Desires, drives, longings and propensities force their way to the surface despite all constraints. The best way for man is to accept others as they are, while training himself to virtue and gracefulness. That is the way to win esteem.[7] (1977:311–12; 1982:179)

Since men are not reproached in public for even flagrant violations of norms, no matter how much they may be discussed when they are not within earshot, it is difficult for them to be able to distinguish with any certainty what is genuinely secret from what is politely not mentioned, and to be sure what others think about them:

To be a man in a society where sanctions are discreetly expressed, if at all, and everyone is provided with a "public" that in a sense "honours" him, does not make life all that easy. The man must steer a deft and elegant course with very few signals from that public who are his judges. He can never be sure that his value is what he thinks it is, as he observes his bland reflection in his polite spectators. (Wikan 1984:646)

This also insulates both the local and the overarching social system from direct challenge. As Khan explains in this volume, even frequent and recurrent homosexual behavior does not matter in Islamic societies as long as a man continues his family line and does not throw away property indulging in his vices. Trig Tarazi, a Palestinian born in Kuwait and now living in Boston, told Wockner:

The Arab world is very much into the family unit and men must fulfill their family role. But as long as they do that, they are free to do whatever they want and this is not questioned. And since nobody talks about homosexuality, they don't have to fear somebody is going to say this—or even think this about them. It's very strange to have men come up to you in bars and show you pictures of their kids and then say, "OK, let's go [have sex] now." To them, being gay is a sexual thing. It's not emotional. And the tiny minority who do see themselves as gay in the Western sense—as loving men—are frustrated; they feel oppressed the most. The rest of the men are very comfortable. They think it's the best of all possible worlds. Since nobody recognized homosexuality as even existing, they can get away with things we cannot get away with here. But if you start talking about homosexuality, they get very uncomfortable. (1992:106)

The Spanish formula "Todos hecho, nada dicho" (everything is done, nothing is said) seems to be a circum-Mediterranean strategy for maintaining absolute moral prescriptions in principle by keeping silent about the vagaries of "human nature" in an imperfect world in which "shameful acts [are] an inherent part of life" (Wikan 1977:314; cf. Murray 1987:195–97, 1995a:49–70). Even if "everyone knows," it is still possible that no one will say anything about what is known.

Discussion of the "don't ask, don't tell, don't pursue" approach to "homosexuals" in the U.S. military mandated by senators and President Clinton in mid-1993 helped me to understand both the will not to know that I had also encountered in Latin America and how this protection of the public sphere from acknowledgment of even (or of especially?) rampant homoeroticism actually sustains stigmatization, strangling any possible challenge to conventional contempt. Relatively blatant homosexual behavior has at times been ignored by U.S. military authorities. What is different (both from the U.S. military and from the usual Mediterranean/Islamic status quo) is announcing and demanding respect for identities based on homosexuality (demanding respect for being gay or lesbian, distinguished from "committing sodomy"). Claims of an identity and demands of respect for it challenge the accommodation of discrete homosexual behavior.[8] Except for a few urban Turks, Malaysians, and emigrants very recently, no such challenge has been made in any Islamic society. As the German Islamicist Arno Schmitt describes the trans-Islamic norm:

A man should not allow others to bugger him. Otherwise he loses his name, his honor, that is, if others know it and are known to know. The decisive line is not between the act kept secret and the act known by many, but between only talking behind one's back and saying it in your presence, between rumors and public knowledge. There is always room for maneuver, you can always ignore what everybody knows. As long as nobody draws public attention to something everybody knows, one ignores what might disrupt important social relations. There is a clear rule: You cannot be fucked. But what this really comes down to is: Saying of somebody that he has been fucked disturbs social relations. (1992:7)

This is not inconsistent with sodomy being very common, as the Italian editor/author Gianni De Martino notes for Morocco:

One does it, but does not talk about it; men and boys make jokes and puns about it, allude to it, do it, but never talk about it in a serious manner. . . . After the act the 'impure object' is thrown away. . . . The Maghribian man eliminates the fucked one after the act; he denies all importance to the act and declares it to be free of sentiment. At once he rushes to the shower. . . . To talk about it is something else, not because one feels guilty making it, but because it would be shameful to denounce somebody as having been fucked. Done discreetly, one is able to pretend that nothing has happened. (1992:25, 27)

Similarly, in a novel filled with male sexual assaults of younger males, Larbi Layachi explains that it is forbidden for "a man to make love to boys. Of course, they all do it, but when someone gets caught it is disgraceful" (1986:64).[9] "Mansour," a Tehran native, also reports the disjunction between (allegedly universal) homosexual behavior and (nearly impossible) "modern" gay identity:

Every man in Iran is involved in male-to-male sex, because premarital [heterosexual] sex and sex outside marriage are not only a sin, but are also very difficult [to find]. But being gay and having a gay identity is a Western phenomenon. Iranian men act in a very cliché[d] male/female role. One is either the active or the passive partner, but all men are involved in male sex. (Quoted by Wockner 1992:110; see also Kafi 1985)

As noted, having been sodomized damages someone's reputation only if the behavior becomes known (Schmitt 1985:55). If one starts to like being sodomized, the behavior is almost certain to become known, and "some say that one penetration—whether by force, for money, or in play by an older cousin—might be enough to become addicted." The danger of starting to enjoy being penetrated and then desiring and seeking it is a part of transcontinental Islamic cosmology: "To most Muslims anal lust is not really unnatural. One has to avoid getting buggered precisely in order not to acquire a taste for it and thus become addicted. It is like an infectious disease: once infected it is difficult to get rid of it" (Schmitt 1992:8). Young Latin American men have given me the same reason—fear that they would like it too much—for not being anally receptive. "If I let him fuck me," a young Guatemalteco told Erskine Lane, "I'd probably like it and then I'd do it again, and then I'd be queer" (1978:56). Latin American conceptions of sexuality seem to be based on the same circum-Mediterranean complex of male honor with its fear of the abyss of debauchery that follows sexual receptivity.[10]

Once a boy is known to have been fucked, whatever his own reactions to the experience, he is fair game for others. (See Figure 2.1.) The Dutch psychologist Andreas Eppink reported from his fieldwork in Morocco that

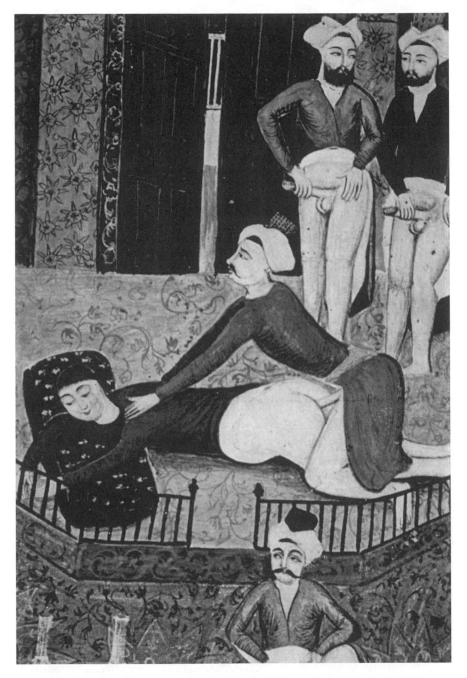

2.1 Lining up to use a boy. From *Sawaqub al-Manaqib* (copies in the Morgan
Library, the Topkapi Palace Museum, etc.).

boys look for younger boys (7–13 years old) who are "fit" for this. Persuasion is effected by nice words, money or force. From my conversations it is clear that tips are exchanged about boys/young men/men who could be/are "fit." Usually one cannot claim somebody for oneself. . . . This "informing" has as a consequence that some boys get the reputation of *zāmel* (someone submitting to anal intercourse). If a boy has this image it will be most difficult for him to submit [i.e., mount] another from his own circle; he will be forced to fulfill the passive role until he goes outside his circle or gets married. (1992:36)

He also quotes Tony Duvert:

A penetrated anus attracts the bachelors of the community like a pot of honey draws flies. One is known to be available (coupable) and talked about. Everyone goes to him to relieve their need, sometimes by force. It would be shocking if he refused once he had been breached. . . . A proper (obéissant) boy keeps his asshole sealed tight. The one whose is open[ed] becomes the whore (le putain) of the other boys and thereby helps save theirs. It is like an educational game: one will be the bottom for all). The first who relaxes (his guard) is fucked (pédé). (1976:77–78)[11]

In some sense, one's honor can only be lost once (even though males do not have a hymen that is either intact or not). These Moroccan observations suggest that it is less a matter of the *pédé* becoming addicted than that he lacks choice once others know that he has been (and therefore can be) penetrated— at least until he becomes a hairy adolescent and, therefore, no longer attractive. Without indicating the extent of the sample on which it is based, Schmitt makes the interesting observation, "I never met a first-born youth willing to take the submissive position of being penetrated, whereas many younger brothers viewed it as inevitable" (1992:3). According to De Martino, the cultural expectation is that those who have been used anally will outgrow being desirable and stop getting fucked (despite the dangers of addiction to it): "By the age of 15 or 16 a *zāmel* loses his admirers or he starts refusing advances: becomes a 'man,' i.e., he fucks boys and courts girls" (1992:26).

For a beloved to "become a man" may be more a gradual process than a clean break. Fictional representations of Turkish man-boy relations by Istrati (1926:155, 168) and Kazantzakis (1953:299 and passim) show that before being ready to let go of their "boytoys," patrons were willing to arrange for the boys to have sexual relations with women. Pierre Loti's Turkish boatman/ravisher also aided him in his quest for a woman.[12] In his contribution to this volume, Crompton mentions an Andalusian boy-lover who allowed his beloved access to his harem. And Walters (1991:46) alluded to a 16-year-old Yemeni neighbor who was reputed to be the passive partner of other young adult males, and who refused to wear pants to school as other adolescent males did, making advances to a foreign woman (Walters's lover).

Some boys who have been regularly used for sex are fated (or traumatized or addicted or choose) to continue being penetrated, and may, therefore, also seek to preserve an androgynous appeal.[13] In Morocco those who depilate and otherwise emulate female appearance are called hassās, in Turkey köçek, in Oman khanith, in Pakistan khusra, and so forth. I have been unable to find any data on the relative proportion of sexually used boys in any Islamic society who grow up as proper men or as gender variant.[14] Whatever the behavioral frequencies, the cultural conception seems to be that a boy who gets fucked is more likely to grow into a man who gets fucked, and who also will dress in a way to advertise his sexual availability, although he should outgrow getting fucked. If he does, no one, not even those who remember it from personal experience, will mention his pre-adult sexual behavior in his presence (and probably not at all). His male honor depends on his conduct as an adult. In contemporary Oman, this extends even to those who openly practiced transvestitic homosexual prostitution as adults (Wikan 1977:308–9, 312). The sarcastic maxim of the Persian wit 'Obeyd-e Zakani (ca. 1300–ca. 1370), "Do not withhold your posterior favors from friends and foes when young, so that in old age you can attain the status of a sheik, a preacher or a man of fame and dignity" ([1350]1985:65), surely is an exaggeration—but one does not exaggerate what does not exist, nor satirize what has no relation to what the audience recognizes as reality (see Javadi 1988).

'Obeyd relates an anecdote that seems to provide a counter-example of youthful receptivity being overlooked, but it actually reveals the general refusal to publicly acknowledge adolescent sexual receptivity:

Sultan Mahmud [reigned from Ghazna, 988–1030], accompanied by Talhak, the jester, attended the sermon of a certain preacher. When they arrived the preacher was saying that whoever had made love to a young boy, on the day of judgment would be made to carry him across the narrow bridge of Sirat, which leads to heaven. Sultan Mahmud was terrified and began to weep. Talhak told him: "O Sultan, do not weep. Be happy that on that day you will not be left on foot either." (1985:78)

The court jester has a special license to say what is generally unsaid, extending to remembering what has been obliterated from social memory. Another of 'Obeyd's Persian anecdotes even more directly contrasts clerical castigation of male sexual receptivity with its ubiquity in the society:

A preacher was saying in Kashan that on the day of Resurrection the custody of the holy well of Kothar [in Paradise] will be with Imam 'Ali [the cousin of the Prophet], and he will give its water to the man of anal integrity. A man from the audience got up and said, "Your reverence, if this is the case, he will have to put it back in the pitcher and drink it all himself." (p. 82)

Ideal Norms . . . and Variability from Them

As will be discussed in subsequent chapters, there was also a quasi-religious sanction for pederasty in medieval mystic writing, especially Sufi.[15] Persian and Arab poets' descriptions of the beloved, especially from the high tide of Arabic civilization in Andalusia, were based on models in pre-Islamic Arabic, Egyptian, and Greek poetry, and were highly stereotyped, according to Marc Daniel:

The beloved of whom the Arab poets write is always a young boy, at most an adolescent. . . . The boy is always brown and slender; his waist is supple and thin like a willow branch or like a lance; his hair, black as scorpions, traces on his forehead the letters of the Arabic alphabet; his eyes are arcs which hurl arrows; his cheeks are roses; his saliva has the sweetness of honey; his buttocks resemble a dune of moving sand. When he walks, you could call him a young faun; when he is motionless, he eclipses the brightness of the moon. (1977:5)

Daniel mentions a number of examples. Others appear in *Gay Sunshine* 29/30; Lane (1975); and Leyland (1977). For instance, the ninth-century Syrian poet Abu Tamman's appetites were excited by a boy

when his plump cheeks glow
with health and the slender
plumes of his mustache, tender,
are just beginning to grow. (Lacey 1988:89)

Annemarie Schimmel summarizes the ideal for Hafiz and other Persians "with his round, light-coloured moon face, a mouth like a *mim* or a dot, and slightly slanting eyes—an ideal that appeared in Persian miniatures" (1979b:30). Wickens adds, "The so-called 'apple' of the chin-pits (i.e., a cleft or dimple) is one of the several stereotyped tokens of beauty in Persian poetry; tall and slender youths are likewise commonly referred to as 'cypresses'" (1974:296).

As for ancient Greeks with a similar conception of the most desirable characteristics in a partner, the ideal of sexual dreams should not be confused with the bounds of tastes, let alone with those of actual daily behavior. Despite the normative stress on age-stratified relationships, homosexual behavior was not entirely age-defined. Marc Daniel relates examples of adults from all social stations who wished to be penetrated (1977:9). *A Thousand and*

One Nights includes two stories (216 and 326, the former the framing story in Pasolini's film "Arabian Nights") in which women disguised as men become rulers and command their husbands to submit their buttocks for penetration. Albeit reluctantly, these adult males lie face down before their wives gleefully reveal their true identities.

Recognition of real variety occasionally found its way even into poetry, as in the lines from the eighth-century Baghdad poet Bachar ibn Baurdi: "Take your friend just as he is, for if you refuse to drink the water of the oasis pool with its little bit of straw,[16] you risk dying of thirst" (M. Daniel 1977:7). Al-Tīfāshī's purportedly thirteenth-century compilation includes a number of instances of preferences for postpubescent males and the unequivocal statement that many men "are attracted by adult men, whose beard has already grown" (Lacey 1988:79, 80, 82, 84). The Persian writer Jāmī asked, "Is it not the same youth as last year? He has the same eyes, the same brows, the same lips, the same teeth. It is true that he has increased in stature, and that his body is more vigorous. What impudence, what shame, what irreverence to cease to visit him and to desire his company!" (Surieu 1967:174).[17]

Indeed, defense of continuing love for postpubescent males became a genre.[18] Al-Hariri (1054–1122) explained that he dared to love a boy whose beard has sprouted, with an analogy that values the transformation: "If you love a sterile and barren garden at a time of bitter drought, will you abandon it when the grass starts to grow?"[19] Similarly, Ibn Sara (1095–1123) wrote, "With the sprouting beard his loveliness merely grew subtler, finer, and my love for him followed suit. For us, the beard was not some vile darkness creeping cross his cheeks, but only a trickling down of the beautiful blackness of his eyes" (both quoted by Schild 1988:44). The Urdu poet Najmuddīn Shāh Mubārak Ābrū (1692–1747) wrote:

There is no pleasure in kissing that lip
On which there is no "verdure of down"

and

The bloom of his face shown forth when the down appeared.
Before the verdure came, it was merely a wasteland of beauty. (Naim 1979:142, 141)

In one of 'Obeyd-e Zakani's stories, at least one old man must have been sexually receptive if the two had sex at the top of a minaret in the holy city of Qom.[20]

Just as there was variation from the age-differentiated norm, so were there departures from normative bisexuality, for example, al-Hakam II, the Khalif of Cordoba from 961 to 976, who was "so exclusively committed to boy-love that in order to please him, his wife Subh had to dress like a boy and bear the masculine name Djafar" (M. Daniel 1977:9). Earlier, the Khalif of Baghdad, al-Amin (787–813, ruled 809–13) "gave himself over wholly to dissipated pleasure in the company of his eunuchs,"[21] to the extent that it became a major scandal, first in the capital city and later throughout the empire. His mother Zubaidah (Zubayda)

sought to wean him from his young eunuchs by a novel counter-attraction. She selected some of her most gifted and attractive maidens with beauty of form and of face and dressed them up in the current elegant costume of page boys. She then displayed these, in large numbers, before her son in the hope of winning him away from his unnatural life. Amin was quite amused with the sight. Some of these girls did indeed touch a normal spring in his heart, which they now shared with his eunuchs. Hence Zubaidah's aim was but partially accomplished. Thereafter, society, high and low, made these boy-attired girls the popular fad of the day. (Abbott 1946:210–12)

The vogue lasted at least a century.

It should be remembered that Islam replaced religions with sacred sexually receptive—often gender-variant—functionaries, as Roscoe shows (see also Roscoe 1996). Transvestitic homosexuality has occurred and continues to occur in addition to (and mixed with) pederasty. After all, *berdache,* the word European colonists applied to sexual and gender variances around the world, derives from the Persian *bardash* through Arabic.[22] To take some scattered examples, in 1810 Byron and John Hobhouse saw transvestite boys dancing at coffeehouses in Galata, a Constantinople suburb (Crompton 1985:143–44). Figure 2.2 shows a performance for an Ottoman sultan. Flaubert's 1849–50 letters from Egypt include a vivid description of cross-dressing dancing boys, and document sodomy in the baths, as well.[23] (See Figure 2.3.) Another late-nineteenth-century traveler, C. B. Klunzinger, reported from Egypt:

The performance of the *chauel* or male dancer is not much of an improvement on that of the female dancer. Clothed and tricked out like a dancing girl, he goes through the same kind of motions on another evening to the delight of the spectators. Sometimes he also plays on some instrument, and sings as well; he blows the bagpipe full of wind, and while it escapes melodiously from the holes of the tubes, under the play of his fingers he strikes up his ear-piercing song, which is followed by the hip-dance—a threefold artistic effect produced all at once. This class of hermaphrodites, the product of the luxurious East, also resembles the dancing-girls in their abandoned morals. (1878:190–91)

A few decades later, Edward Lane attributed Egyptian transvestite dancers with functions similar to those of the South Asian *hijra*:

2.2 A Sultan watches a köçek. From Tokpaki Palace Museum.

Many of the people of Cairo, affecting, or persuading themselves, to consider that there is nothing improper in the dancing of the Ghawázee but the fact of its being performed by females, who ought not thus to expose themselves, employ men to dance in the same manner; but the number of these male performers, who are mostly young men, and who are called "Khäwals," is very small. They are Muslims and natives of Egypt. As they personate women, their dances are exactly of the same description as those of the Ghawázee; and are, in like manner, accompanied by the sound of castanets: but, as if to prevent their being thought of be really females, their dress is suited to their unnatural profession; being partly male, and partly female: it chiefly consists of a tight vest, a girdle, and a kind of petticoat. This general appearance, however, is more feminine than masculine: they suffer the hair of the head to grow long, and generally braid it, in the manner of the women; the hair on the face, when it begins to grow, they pluck out; and they imitate the women also in applying kohl and henna to their eyes and hands. In the streets, when not engaged in dancing, they often even veil their faces; not from shame, but merely to affect the manners of women. They are often employed, in preference to the Ghawázee, to dance before a house, or in its court, on the occasion of a marriage-fête, or the birth of a child, or a circumcision; and frequently perform at public festivals.

There is, in Cairo, another class of male dancers, young men and boys, whose performances, dress, and general appearance are almost exactly similar to those of the Khäwals; but who are distinguished by a different appellation, which is "Gink;" a term that is Turkish, and has a vulgar signification which aptly describes their character. They are generally Jews, Armenians, Greeks, and Turks. (1908:389)[24]

Chapter 13 quotes mid-nineteenth-century accounts by Schuyler and Buckingham of Uzbeki and Iraqi dancing boy catamites, along with some recent accounts of Indonesian and Filipino analogs. In Persia, ca. 1907, there were fourteen troupes of nine to fourteen male dancers and about forty groups of female dancers.

Notwithstanding the great number of female groups, boys were preferred. These kids, orphans mostly, were entrusted to the care of a leader of a theatrical group. . . . The kids started at an age of 8 to 10 years and would perform until they became too old, i.e. at an age of 16 to 18 years. While dancing, the boys wore long tunics of brocade. Their long hair and suggestive movements, which roused the feelings of the male spectator, made them hard to distinguish from female dancers. A special kind of dancers were the *raqqas-i chehel band push*, which were young boys who wore long silken skirts, sewn with ribbons.

The dancers, who also did acrobatic tricks, were fed and clothed by the leader of the group. He also was obliged to pay for their baths and to take care of them when they were ill. Ordinary dancers earned 20 to 40 tomans yearly, whilst handsome boys with fine voices, on whose popularity the success of a group depended, earned up to 100 tomans. These starboys were known as *jan*. The services of a group were rather expensive, 20 to 30 tomans per evening. (Floor 1971:105–6)[25]

2.3 Turkish bath. From *Sawaqub al-Manaqib* (copies in the Morgan library, the Topkapi Palace Museum, etc.).

Both natives and foreign observers assumed that "boy dancers" were sexually available. Coon wrote more specifically of boy sex slaves in northwestern Morocco in the 1920s:

In the Jebala, markets were formerly held in which boys stolen from their families were sold. They were and still are kept by their purchasers for the purpose of sodomy, and other uses [i.e., apprenticeship] are made secondary to it. When they have grown to an age at which they cease to interest their purchasers sexually, they are released and allowed to earn their own living. The market el Had Ikauen of Ktama was a famous boy market and was not closed until the advent of the Spanish forces of occupation [1910] who have been trying to prevent such sales, although it is difficult to stamp out private transactions. Boy markets are found in the Western Arabaphone Senhaja, Ghomara, and Ktama [tribes], also, of course, in the rest of the so-called Jebala and centered at Sheshawen and in the tribes of Beni Zerwal. (1931:110–11)[26]

Thesiger also noted male prostitutes and transvestite dancers and discreet peer homosexual relations in southern Iraqi towns (1964:123–24).[27] Wikan (1977) asserts that 2 percent of the adult male population in the town of Sohar in contemporary Oman dressed in the neither-male-nor-female garb of the *khanith* and engaged in homosexual prostitution.[28]

A more monogamous role for effeminate youths was that of camp wife among the Afghan Pathan:

Zune-e-suffuree (traveling wives) were the essential part of any camel caravan or other company of travelers passing through the forbidding Khyber [Pass] and into the fertile Punjaub. But these so-called "wives," not only the ideals of Afghan traders but of Pathan troops going into battle on the Frontier, were in fact catamites. Hidden from strangers and the evil eye in camel panniers (*kejawahs*), these youths, ranging in age from five to twenty years, were scented, depilated, rouged hennaed, and adorned with long silken pomaded hair and kohl-rimmed provocative eyes. In a word, no one could have distinguished them from women or girls unless they stripped them of their costly gowns. (Edwardes 1959:249)

According to Zaidi, truck drivers in contemporary Pakistan, not unlike earlier camel drivers, "always have younger boys or *chelas* with them" (1994:29). (*Chela* is the term for disciple of a guru: the role includes being younger as well as being obedient to a master.)

ROLE LABELS

Boswell cited Pérès (1953:341) for his assertion, "The Arabic language contains a huge vocabulary of gay erotic terminology, with dozens of words just to describe types of male prostitutes" (1980:195).[29] Although elaboration of terms for prostitutes does not comprise the best kind of evidence for proto-gay pride and identity, it does indicate recognition of at least one role, not just an act or a succession of acts. Boswell also claimed that *lūtī* (which he derives from *lāta*, "to stick," whereas most scholars take it as an allusion to Lot of Sodom) was "used by gay [*sic*] Muslim writers themselves with defiance, if not pride" (1980:195).[30] Unfortunately, he supplied no examples of such self-reference.[31]

At the other extreme from Boswell—and in ferocious polemics against him—Arno Schmitt ardently defends the dogma that there was no cultural conception of homosexual types before late-nineteenth-century medical discourse created one in northern Europe (1985:58; 1987:176, 179–82; 1992:8, 13–19). I see this as a northern European and American will not to know that anyone else anywhere else ever noticed recurrent homosexual desire; I have termed the postulated invention of "homosexual" by medical discourse "special creationism" (i.e., by medical writing) (see Murray 1995c).

Despite the attested use of *fā'īl/maf'ūl, lūtī/ghulām, liwāt/ma'būn*, and *nākih/mankūhi* for complementary insertor/insertee roles and, especially, the folk Arabic etymology of *liwāt* as one of Lot's people—surely a kind of person (specifically, a microcosm of the national character of those from Sodom), not an act (of sodomy)—Schmitt denies that *liwāt* is a kind of person.[32] Similarly, *ubnah* is "a much-used [Arabic] term for passive male homosexuality, and *ma'būn* is the individual affected by it" (Rosenthal 1978:45). In the view of the fourteenth-century medical writer Muhammad, born Zakarīyā' al-Rāzī (850–923),

If the *ubnah* is prolonged, the person affected by it cannot be cured, in particular, if he is obviously feminine and effeminate (*ta'nīth-takhnīth*) and loves very much to be like a woman. If it is in its beginning stages and the person affected by it is not obviously effeminate and not strongly inclined to pleasure but rather ashamed (of it) and would like to be free from it, it is possible for him to be treated. (translated by Rosenthal 1978:56–57; cf. Lacey 1988:231)[33]

The influential Arab medical theorist Ibn Sīna (980–1037, known in the West as Avicenna and translated into Latin in the twelfth century) also saw *ubnah* as a state of being, not just a behavior.[34]

Continuing in orthodox Foucaultian/Weeksian fashion to claim that there are only acts, not roles, nor even inclinations, Schmitt claims, "There are no homosexuals, there is no word meaning homosexual" (1992:4). He glosses the Northwest African Arabic *mamhūn*, Turkish *ibne*, and Farsi *obnai* as someone who "needs to be fucked" or "is addicted to being buggered," deriving the latter two from *ma'būn*, "somebody who wants to be fucked" (1992:11–12). There is also (in Persian/Farsi, Arabic, and in Urdu, which also has *istānī*, "anuser") the *malūt*, "someone upon whom *liwat* is done" (Schmitt 1992:13), which also appears cognate to these other terms. The role complement to the *maf'ūl* is the *fāʿīl*—"doer" (Southgate 1984:434). AbuKhalil glosses *ahl al-liwāt* as "advocate of *at-talawwut*" (engaging in *liwāt*) and *ghulat al-latah* as "ultra-homosexual," while stressing that the discussions of the comparative advantages of sex with boys and of women required not just consciousness of homosexual tastes but systematic reflection and celebration of a pattern of behavior (1993:33).

There are Moroccan terms, including *ail* for boy-lover (Maxwell 1983:286), *louat* for penetrators (Remlinger 1913:104), *pédé* (from the French *pédéraste*, but applied to the insertee: Schmitt 1992:18), *mezlough* for pretty pre-pubescent boys (Remlinger 1913:104), and *zāmel* for those aged nine to seventeen "who get fucked by their cousins, teachers, and neighbors—whether they like it or not," and "those continuing to get fucked [who] are called *hassās*" (De Martino 1992:26),[35] or, more pejoratively, *attaï* (literally, "the giver": Chebel 1988:59; 1995:316). In Moorish Spain, unbearded ephebes were called *ghūlām* or *wasūm*. After their beards began to grow they were called *mu'addi*, while "effeminacy was expressed with the word *muhannāt* and *hāwī*, pl. *hiwa* (catamite)" (Pérès 1953:341).

Zarit glosses the Farsi *kuni* as "somebody who gives his ass (*kun*)" and adds that "Farsi has two complementary words for 'pimp,' one meaning a procurer of vagina (*koskesh*) and the other of ass (*kunkesh*)" (1992:56). The Azarbaijani poet and critic Reza Baraheni notes that in his native Tabriz, as well as in Esphahan and Qazvin, the people refer to those known or suspected of being penetrated by another male as that man's anus, for example. "The young man is the anus of the older man" (1977:60). In Urdu, Punjabi, and also in Hindi and other South Asian languages *launda-baz* is applied to men drawn to penetrating young boys, while *gandu* is applied to those boys and men offering their anuses to penetration.[36] Pakistani-Canadian Badruddin Khan provides the following explication of the terms:

Both *gandu* and *launda-baz* are "kinds of people" to Pakistanis. *Gandu* refers to a man attracted through the *gand* (anus). Lower-class boys may refer to friends as *gandu*; it is a commonly accepted form of pleasure among pre-married males. Pejoratively, the *gandu* is passive. However, the *gandu* may also be active, with the *gand* as the object of his affection. Many insertees grow up to become insertors, so the label must incorporate a certain flexibility so as not to besmirch the reputation of a boy destined to become an insertive man. The equivalent for a man who fancies vaginas is *chutiya*.

Launda-baz refers to an adult man who fancies boys. *Gandu* is subsumed within the label. However, *launde-baz* also covers affection and poetry, cuddling and lovemaking. The key difference between it and *gandu* is that *launde-baz* transcends mere genital discourse. It is pejorative, but less so since it may be used to explain feelings. It is closer to the North American sense of *gay* (except that no sense of community is implied). It is broader than *gandu*, in that it references the entire person (*launda*, boy) and not just the anal cavity.

After marriage (which is virtually universal, because Islam instructs all men to marry, and because an unmarried man is of little consequence in an Islamic society) a man may still be considered to be a launde-baz. He is less likely to be considered a gandu (since presumably he can satisfy himself carnally at will with his wife). (Personal communication, 26 April 1994)

Other terms for a kind of person engaging in recurrent homosexual love and/or sex include *amrad* (beardless) in Farsi and Turkish (Schmitt 1987:178; Southgate 1984:434), *moghlim* which Edwardes (1959:212) glosses as "sodomist" in discussing soliciting fellatio in Istanbul, and *mukhannath/mukhannas* (effeminate, often to the point of transvestism) in Arabic and Farsi (Pérès 1953:341; Southgate 1984:434; Rowson 1991a). In Turkish, *köçek* "used to denote 'a young dancer dressed like a woman,' but now covers both transvestites and transsexuals" (Janssen 1992:83). Masters added the Kurdish *hatiw bas*, which he glossed only as "homosexual" (1953).

Schmitt attests *halaqī* as "somebody having a pathological desire to get buggered" (1992:12),[37] and nineteen more terms from Arabic, Farsi, and Turkish for those who are penetrated (*halaqī, bagā, sarmūt, gulām, oglan, maf'ūl asfal, madbub 'alaihi, mault bihi, manyak, siktiren, ibme/obnai, koni, hulaq, ata'ī, hassās, mamhūn, zāmel*), to which Pellat (1983:776) adds *mulawit*, and Rowson (1990:21; 1991b:686) adds *baghghā'un, 'ilq*, and (for a male prostitute) *mu'ajir*. Schmitt also lists six terms for "buggerer: *lūtī (man from Sodom), fā'īl (doer), sāni' (doer), 'alā (one on top), dabbāb (crawler-over), bitul 'iyal (buggerer), ragel/ragel (buggerer)*, Farsi *shāhid-bazī* (witness of boys' beauty), along with the Farsi/Turkish *gulām-pare/kulampare* (boy ravisher), and the Turkish *keskin* (penetrator)."[38] Chebel adds *nièk* as the insertive complement in Moroccan Arabic to *'attaī*, and elsewhere contrasts *niyāk* (literally, "the kisser") for "the active homosexual" with *manilouk* (literally, "the kissed") for his passive partner (1988:59; 1995:314–15). In contemporary Turkish, Tapinc reports *laço/lubunya*, which he says is derived from Gypsy slang, for the active and passive roles respectively (1992:42). Yüzgün adds *gulampare/kullanpara* as a term of self-reference for Iranian and Turkish boy-lovers he calls "active homosexuals (1993:163).[39]

In one of the many hostile characterizations that Edwardes (1959) takes as sound descriptions,

one sect in particular, the Barmecides of Baghdad, was frequently associated with perversion by medieval Arabs. In the characteristic punning style of the Turks, an adherent of the Abassides, a rival cult, translated Barmecide (*Bermekkee*) as follows: *ber* (up) and *mekke* (to suck), thereby allying the Barmecides with a distinct tribe of fellators and claiming that Ja'afer-bin Yahyeh-bin Khalid-el-Bermekkee, founder of the sect, was a *raud-dheh-ez-zubb* (pintle-sucker).

Although it is not clear where Edwardes found this material, defining a group, not just individuals, by sexual practice (a tribe of fellators) is an interesting example of conceiving a recurrent pattern of sexual conduct defining others (albeit not appreciatively). Similarly, in Iran, Baraheni notes the reputation of the men of particular cities, including, "All the men of Ardebil are supposed to be passive homosexuals, those of Qazvin and Esphahan, active homosexuals" (1977:61).

In short, homosexual roles, both age- and gender-stratified, were and are lexicalized and written about in Arabic, Farsi, Turkish, Urdu, et al. Some terms conflate gender and sexual patterns. Vernacular terminologies, especially for derogatory terms, do not distinguish sex, gender, and sexuality as carefully as Western elite discourses do (Murray 1994). Given the expected sexual availability for a price (in gifts or cash) of dancing boys, the various terms for that occupation (e.g., the Egyptian *khäwal* or the Uzbeki *batcha*), might also be included as terms for young men sexually receptive to older, more affluent, and more masculine men. Patron roles may also be lexicalized, as in *bacabaozlik* and *bacaboyi*, terms for those playing the boy-game in Uzbeki and Farsi, respectively (Baldauf 1990:12). These are role terms. The terms for address between a Uzbeki dancing boy and his patron are *uka* (younger brother) and *aka* (older brother), according to Baldauf (1990:15).[40]

LESS ROLE-DEMARCATED PAIRINGS

Schmitt claims that the many terms he listed "refer either to an action or a preference, not to a character trait" (1992:11). He does not explain, however, how "preference" is orthogonal to "character" in his own mind or in those of the natives of Islamic cultures who apply these labels to particular individuals (under what Schmitt considers the delusion that such words characterize those referred to by them). One of his more peculiar arguments against any Arab conception of homosexual persons is that Arabic verbs for fucking

2.4 Male youth penetrating adult male, nineteenth-century Turkey. Museum of Turkish and Islamic art, Istanbul.

"have no forms of reciprocity" (1992:10).[41] This is hardly surprising. I do not know of such a verb in English or any other language. To fuck and be fucked requires more than two persons, or sequential acts, or use of a dildo: human anatomy precludes A's penis being in B's anus while B's penis is in A's.

If what is supposedly al-Tīfāshī's thirteenth-century compilation is authentic, role versatility was recognized long ago—for example, "Others prefer teenage boys, whom they can fuck and be fucked by" (translated in Lacey 1988:180), and "Young boys can perform equally well on top or on the bottom, whereas women are limited to the role for which nature destined them: they're good for only one thing" (1988:74; see also 77, 180–81, 210, 224). Even if this is not genuinely thirteenth-century, it is unquestionably an Arabic manuscript. Figure 2.4 provides a nineteenth-century Turkish illustration of role reversal, that is, insertive youth and receptive adult. Similarly, Edwardes notes terms for the practice of reciprocity, whether or not the Persian *ulish-tukish* (turn-by-turn) and Arabic *meroof-mejhool* (active-passive) were labels used for persons as well as for practices (1959:232; both taking turns at anal penetration of the other, and mutual fellatio in the case of *ulish-tukish* [p. 233]).

Even absence of terms does not prove the absence of a phenomenon (see Arboleda and Murray 1985). Cultures frequently contain covert categories (Berlin, Breedlove, and Raven 1968; Williams 1993:25). Perhaps the third recurrent organization of homoeroticism, egalitarian relations, was such a covert category. It may even have been overt (lexicalized): *bidal* who would agree to be penetrated first on the basis of the promise then to penetrate his penetrator may be such a term. Rowson quotes al-Rāghib: "If you're empty-handed and out of cash, it seems to me the best course is to buy a fuck with a fuck" (*mubādala*) (1991b:66). Some ostensible *lūtī* were suspected of seeking to penetrate rather than to be penetrated (Rowson 1991b:64 quotes two examples in verse). Wanting to undertake both roles appears not to have been conceived. Upon their reunion in Konya, the legendarily blunt dervish Shamsi Tabrīz (d. 1248) and the poet Mawlānā Jalālu'd-Dīn Rūmī (1207–73) "embraced each other and fell at each other's feet, so that one did not know who was lover and who was beloved" (quoted by Schimmel 1975:313; see Schimmel 1978).[42] Lover and beloved are generally fused in Rūmī's poetry (much of which he published in Shamsüddin's name). For instance,

What am I to do
If love throws its arms around me?
I too put my arms around it
And take it to my heart. (Translated by Halman 1983:36)

Similarly, 'Obeyd-e Zakani's parodic hero Rostam engages in reciprocal sex with Human, his usual antagonist and rival.

Even without any name in general use for the phenomenon, twentieth-century representations of Arab egalitarian homosexuality include the relations between T. E. Lawrence's escorts and between Ridwan and Hilmi in Naguib Mahfouz's novel *Sugar Street* ([1957]1992b).[43] Schmitt (1992:19) attests some loanwords from European languages used in contemporary North Africa for sexually versatile men: *dublifas* (double-faced) in Cairo, *crêpe* and *disque* (done on both sides, played on both sides) in Algiers.

Now, the internationally diffused loanword *gay* is available as a term for men not differing in age or in gender presentation from male sexual partners (Murray 1995b). At least in Turkey, an overtly masculine, urban, young, educated "new sexually conscious stratum of the homosexual population has introduced the word 'gay' with which to identify themselves" (Tapinc 1992: 46; also see Necef 1992; Sofer 1992b). Whether or not egalitarian/"gay" homosexuality existed as a covert category earlier and/or elsewhere, terms for homosexual types—that is, labels for persons,[44] not just acts—have long been lexicalized in a range of Islamic societies.

Feuerstein and al-Marzooq report the "existence of private homosexual ties based on friendship" in Oman (simultaneous with the ready availability of transvestite prostitutes that Wikan [1977] noted), and add that "Omani expatriates in Kuwait and certain other Gulf states are well known for their custom of contractual marriages between men" (1978:666).[45] According to Crapanzano, young Moroccans "sleep with one another, the older mounting the younger," and practice mutual masturbation as well as anal penetration (1980:34, 48).[46] In recalling adolescent "comparative masturbation" the Algerian writer Ali Ghanem mentions the belief that this strengthened (i.e., virilized) youths' penises (1986:78).

In 1952, 38 percent of male Arab students in advanced psychology classes at the American University in Beirut acknowledged homosexual experience, with a median age of first experience of 14 years (the range was 6 to 19; Melikian and Prothro 1954:60).[47] In a 1963 replication Melikian found 44 percent with a mean age at the time of first experience of 12.4 (the range was again 6 to 19; 1967:173).[48] Oraison noted that in 1952 Moroccan male students of the Islamic University openly engaged in homosexual relationships (1975:96). A more recent (but still far from current) survey reported that in Iraq

the previously almost complete acceptance of homosexual practices is now undergoing some change. Some students who had been brought up in the old traditional pattern have expressed anxiety to the authors about their homosexual practices in the University student hostels in Baghdad. (al-Issa and al-Issa 1969:20; also see al-Issa and al-Issa 1971)

These authors assert that (in the late 1960s) homosexuality

is still widely practiced in Iraq, and in the traditional village milieu there is commonly found a gradual and subtle initiation into this practice. At the early stages of development, the child lives in a world of women and children in their part of the household. However, at the age of seven or eight, he starts joining the exclusive society of men. The boys' strong need to belong to this male world is exploited by older adult males to induce them to homosexual practices. As the culture looks down at this passive sexual role, these young boys soon assert their virility in their turn, start playing the role of active homosexuals. In addition to this general pattern of homosexuality, there are also professional homosexuals from the lower class of the village or among individuals who may have been kidnapped as young boys from other parts of Iraq and used for homosexual practices. The widespread homosexuality among men has its counterpart among women and it is not unusual, even among married women, to have an intimate female homosexual partner (*baji'ia*). (al-Issa and al-Issa 1969:19–20)

Noting that the beloved in the Pukhtun folklore of Swat (in northern Pakistan) "is quite often a boy or handsome young man," Lindholm describes the familiar ambivalent combination of age- and gender-stratified homosexuality alongside the reproductive mandate:

Homoerotic relationships were much more common a generation ago than they are now, since Western influence has brought a sense of shame about homosexuality, at least among the more educated. . . . Formerly, guests in the *hujera* were entertained and sexually serviced by dancing boys, and a powerful man might keep several passive homosexuals (*bedagh*) in his retinue. No aspersions were cast on men who had sexual intercourse with a *bedagh* and, in fact, anal sex with a passive homosexual is still considered by some men to be the most satisfying form of congress. . . . Even those men who prefer sex with a *bedagh* are still expected to father children. . . . Men who are *bedaghs* are laughingstocks, but [like the Omani *khanith*] they also marry and are not socially ostracized. . . . In 1977, homosexuality was very much less in evidence in Swat than it had been. Dancing girls had replaced dancing boys, and transvestites had become rare. Nonetheless, the first sexual experiences of many, if not most boys, is with one of their passively inclined peers, or with an older man who is a confirmed *bedagh*. Older men still may cultivate a handsome young protégé who will accompany them everywhere, though the practice is hardly universal. (1982:224–25)[49]

According to Zaidi, "homosexual activity is also common among men in barracks" in contemporary Pakistan (1994:28). Sex between males that occurs away from home is often dismissed as "situational" without considering that to some extent men *choose* occupations that take them recurrently away from home for a long time, so that the "situation" in "situational homosexuality" is not entirely happenstance. Even when the choice of an all-male environment is conscious, it is unlikely to be self-defining. This in turn keeps AIDS from seeming to be a risk, as the Pakistani journalist Talat Aslam notes:

In a vast swathe of Pakistan's rural areas, the Western concept of "being" gay simply does not apply, despite the widespread homosexuality prevalent. In place of the Western notion of homosexuality as a state of being, homosexuality is viewed as an activity which does not in any way "make" you "a homosexual." It is this crucial distinction—between homosexuality as a state and homosexuality as an activity— that escapes those who look at sexual mores through pre-conceived models imported from elsewhere.

This fact has several repercussions for any AIDS-prevention programme. For one, it suggests that homosexual activity is widespread in Pakistan but is much more difficult to pin down as a category. Most of its practitioners, for example, tend to be married or eventually get married, and many of them continue to have both homosexual and heterosexual encounters as the occasion arises. . . . The sheer diversity and scale, not to mention fluidity, of homosexual activity in the country offers a challenge to the AIDS control programme, drawing into the high risk net groups that comprise a far larger category than [a conventional, narrow] one imagines. (1994:32)

His compatriot Asir Ajmal adds, "For a society that hasn't learned to talk publicly about sex, talking about AIDS is not going to be easy" (1994:36; see also Zaidi 1994).

In the early 1980s, Arslan Yüzgün, a Turkish economist conducted a survey of 223 male "homosexuals" in Beyoglu, Istanbul's red-light district (Yüzgün 1986; 1993). Although it seems unlikely that these figures can be taken as a sample of the society as a whole,[50] Yüzgün himself was quite ready to say that 15.7 percent of "Turkish homosexuals" are married, 23.8 percent are university graduates, 56.1 percent are both active and passive, 30.9 percent are only passive, and 13 percent are active. Most of the Turkish men who fuck boys and/or homosexuals are not classified by Yüzgün (and quite likely also not by themselves) as "homosexuals," and Yüzgün avers that there are millions who boast they are *kulampara*, which he translates as "loving a boy" and says "distinguishes an active homosexual" (1993:163). That is, the term that meant boy-lover is now applied to males who penetrate males of whatever age.

PARENTALLY ENFORCED OBLIGATIONS OF MALE LOVERS IN TWO PERIPHERIES OF ISLAM

The pair of chapters at the beginning of Part II show that some (usually Christian) parents sought to have their male children selected by Turkish and Arab officials for military training or as dancing boys and pages. Figure 2.5 shows a Persian father giving his son to the use of others. Here I will note two other exceptions to the will not to know, albeit from peripheral locations.

About the oasis town of Siwa, the site of an ancient oracle temple of Ammon, located in the Libyan desert of western Egypt (see Figure 2.6), anthropologist Walter Cline noted,

All normal Siwan men and boys practice sodomy. . . . Among themselves the natives are not ashamed of this; they talk about it as openly as they talk about love of women, and many, if not most of their fights arise from homosexual competition.[51] In the warrior caste (zaggalah) there was formal brideprice given for a boy. (1936:43)

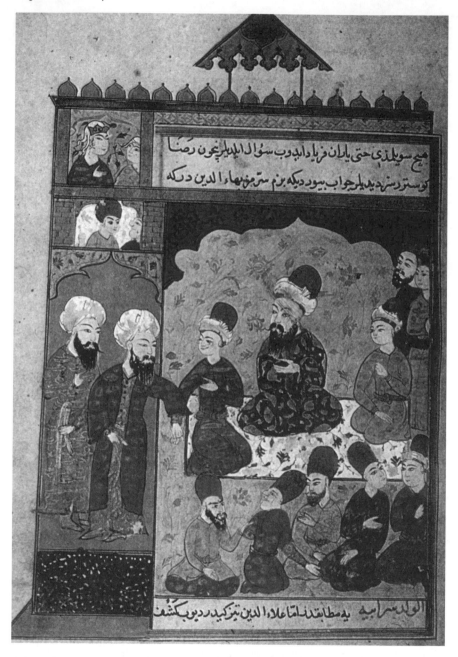

2.5 Father giving son to the use of others. From *Sawaqub al-Manaqib* (copies in the Morgan library, the Topkapi Palace Museum, etc.).

2.6 In the western quarter of El-Siwa; painting by General Reginal Wingate Bart in 1920, from Bart's *Siwa: The oasis of Jupiter Ammon,* London, 1923.

Following his expedition there, archaeologist Count Byron de Prorok also reported an "enthusiasm [that] could not have been approached even in Sodom. . . . Homosexuality was not only rampant, it was raging. . . . Every dancer had his boy friend . . . [and] chiefs had harems of boys" (1936:64). A Siwan merchant told British novelist Robin Maugham that Siwan men "will kill each other for a boy. Never for a woman," although marriage to a boy had by the late 1940s become illegal (1950:80). Brideprice for boys was a feature of a number of tribes in the Sudan. Earlier, 'Abd Allah had reported that Siwan men could take as many as four wives, but that "Siwan customs allow a man but one boy to whom he is bound by a stringent code of obligations" (1917:20). According to Steindorff:

The feast of marrying a boy was celebrated with great pomp, and the money paid for a boy sometimes amounted to fifteen pounds, while the money paid for a woman was a little over one pound besides the clothes which do not exceed two or three pounds for this abnormal marriage. (1904:111; translated by Maugham 1950:80)

This is not to say that boys were not offered for the night, as in Maugham's "The Senussi soldier" (1982:76), which is set in Siwa (although the story is primarily about a liaison with a Bedouin, not a Siwan boy). There was and probably is male prostitution in Siwa, as in most North African cities, but this should be distinguished from long-term relationships with boys for whom brideprice was paid. Such relations should not be called "prostituting their sons to wealthy men," unless brideprice elsewhere is called "prostituting their daughters." The provision of brideprice is properly considered within the cross-cultural category of "marriage," not "prostitution."

Parental enforcement of homosexual obligations has also been reported from another peripheral locale. South African social workers Isaacs and McKendrick mention an interesting instance of contemporary Muslim parents (and the rest of the Muslim community) pressing their sons to repair and sustain their relationship:

Two Muslim men who had been in a relationship for 12 years needed therapy to mediate a domestic conflict. Part of this conflict arose from the concern of their families and friends (all of whom were Muslim) about a potential rift in the relationship, highlighting the sacredness of a union between two people, irrespective of their gender. Furthermore, the older of the two partners was a devotee of the Faith and had unconditional support from his spiritual community. The crisis was in effect exacerbated by the pressure of families and friends who believed that the relationship was cemented by a sacred and legitimate union, and that the commitment had to continue. (1992:163–64)

Chetty (1995:123–26), Gevisser (1995:28), Lewis and Loots (1995:142–43) all report acceptance of homosexuality and cross-dressing as long-established and openly discussed among Western Cape Muslims in South Africa. Lewis and Loots provide a particularly interesting example of pragmatic acceptance by a Muslim family of a son's husband (1995:142, 148–49). On being introduced to two men, not knowing which was her son's partner, a Cape Muslim mother asked, "Nou wie van julle naai my dogter?" (Now which one of you is fucking my daughter?)—so she would know which one to place beside her son at the dining table.[52]

CONCLUSION

The dominant Arabic and southwestern Asian pederastic discourse has co-existed with attested instances of gender-variant homosexuality, and of at least some relatively egalitarian relationships as well. As in other cultures, the major norm or cultural script of homosexual roles does not define the extent of homosexual behavior, relations, or even organizations. At least from the outside, it is possible to think of a great (pederastic) tradition and a little (effeminate) tradition of homosexuality in Islam.[53] Pederasty is the "great tradition" both in being the subject of considerable elite discourse and in seeming to be the statistically most prevalent form in Muslim societies. Men who seek to get fucked are both less written about and seemingly less numerous than men who seek to fuck pretty boys. I have seen no indication that these two patterns of homosexuality (and such "gay" homosexuality as exists) are considered aspects of a single phenomenon, that is, a sexuality defined by object choice. A domain "homosexuality" that includes age-stratified, gender-stratified, and egalitarian same-sex behavior is an etic, not an emic classification. Indeed, I have elicited specific statements that "they're not the same thing" (albeit not from a random sample of persons living in any one Islamic society).

My hypothesized model of the trans-Islamic native domain is that "sexuality" is distinguished not between "homosexual" and "heterosexual" but between taking pleasure and submitting to someone (being used for pleasure). I do not think the implications are fully thought through, but it does seem to me that a male servicing an eager insertee who is rich and promises to do something for him is in the latter category along with the attractive boy who feels he has no alternative but to allow an elder to penetrate him.[54] As Omar, a cosmopolitan Saudi studying in the United States, explained to me,

We assume that every man wants to fuck the most attractive thing he can from among what is available to him [that he can afford]. And I do mean thing!—whether the thing is a wife, a prostitute, a pretty boy, or a pretty mare.[55] The man doesn't much care whether the wife or the prostitute or the boy or the mare wants to be fucked. He doesn't concern himself about whether they enjoy it, though they may. Sometimes some of those getting fucked may enjoy it, but they don't tell anyone, including the man who fucked them, you know? Especially they make sure not to tell the man who fucked them!

A man who wants cock and looks for men to fuck him is an entirely different thing from a man who pushes his cock in the hole of the prettiest thing he can manage to get into, even one who especially likes boys. If the thing he fucks is human, the one who has provided the hole can try to get some kind of reward, some favors, in exchange for having served as the man's desire's receptacle. But, see, if the one who gets fucked obviously enjoys it, there's no need to give them anything else. I think you could say that the Arab view is that the one who gets pleasure should later have to give something for it and the one who puts up with it should get some kind of reward, often some kind of support, sometimes money or a gift. Even the mare gets some reward of special food or a new blanket, or something.

But the wantons—whether they are women or men—they have already gotten what they want, just by getting fucked. I don't know if such men see themselves as being the same as boy-fuckers, I mean the ones who prefer boys. I don't think they see any commonality, they don't define themselves as both wanting males, because what they want from the males they seek is very different, what they get is very different. And one [the boy-fucker] is expected, taken-for-granted, even if not much talked about. The boys' status is not enhanced by getting fucked and it's assumed they will grow up and stop being wanted and that most of the ones who have been penetrated as children won't get to liking it and wanting to keep on. Those who grow up wanting more can't talk about it, and don't gain any status by their desires and trysts becoming known to others. The mares, and prostitutes, and wives, too: none of them brag about it, either. And none of them get together to protest or to raise the price to men, you know?

The respect for the norms evidenced by discretion and covertness keep even acted-upon desires from challenging the public norms or from becoming the basis for mobilizing those with similar experiences and similar desires that might lead to public challenge. With females segregated and tightly controlled, young and/or effeminate males available for sexual penetration are tacitly accepted—and very carefully ignored in Muslim societies, past and present.

Notes

1. Badruddin Khan's and Will Roscoe's comments on successive versions of this chapter have helped to clarify my interpretations, and to lessen the essentializing of a single "Islam" (too often equated with "Arab"). I am grateful to Malek Chebel for clarifying some Moroccan Arabic usages and to David Greenberg for suggesting various materials. I am grateful for Wayne Dynes's erudition without which I would not have known of many of the sources I have used in trying to make sense of ambivalence for the objects of love and lust in Islamic societies across space and time. I am also grateful for his encouragement and patient correctives over the course of many years of my rooting through material on homosexualities in various places and times.

I use "homosexuality" as an etic (cross-cultural comparative) label for recurrent same-sex sexual behavior and pederasty for age-differentiated (but by no means necessarily trans-generational) male-male love and/or sex. I use native labels for roles and personages, and do not use the nouns "homosexual" or "pederast" or "gay" except when/where these terms have been borrowed in native discourses (or in direct quotation of alien observers).

2. For a review of current legislation see Sofer 1992a. On Turkish police harassment that is very similar to the Latin American pattern (including the absence of sodomy laws), see Sofer 1992b:77–78 and Yüzgün 1993:164,166–67. Heribert Murmann, a leader of the Turkish Homosexual Organization, "insists that these are activities of the past" (Judell 1993:23). The first gay and lesbian pride conference in Turkey was scheduled for July 2–6,1993. On 2 July, however, the Governor of Istanbul banned the Christopher Street Day celebration, allegedly faxing all hotels in the city instructing them not to accept foreign celebrants. The next day, 3 July, Turkish authorities arrested and expelled twenty-eight foreign delegates. In addition, three Turkish men were arrested and briefly jailed for their efforts to organize the event. On the recent Iranian exception to traditional canons of evidence and the unprecedentedly active attempt to ferret out and punish those deviating from prescriptive sexual norms, see Danna 1992 and Wockner 1992:107–11.

3. A relatively short-term change is visible within the work of Najib Mahfouz. In his early novel *Midaq Alley*, Kirsha and his wife evidence quite different norms for male homosexual behavior. Kirsha is not much of a patron for his favorite, whereas Abdal-Rahim Pasha Isa in the later novel *Sugar Street* is very helpful to the beautiful young male couple whose presence he enjoys. These Cairo characters share the view that once a man has fulfilled his public and familial duties, he should be free to do whatever he chooses with whomever he chooses, so long as he exercises some discretion ([1947] 1992a:76; [1957]1992b:62–63, 279–84). Dunne suggests the 1940s were a crucial time of social change (and unusual social freedom) in Egypt (1990:75). In Albert Cossery's *Proud Beggars*, which is set in the Cairo of the 1940s, everyone realizes that the police inspector Nour El Dine is a "pederast" (interested in smart, masculine young men rather than the "professional inverts" he has used but not loved), although he endeavors to meet his beloved where they will "escape all gazes" of his acquaintances ([1955]1981:102–5). In Cossery's earlier novel *The Lazy Ones*, Serag is not in the least judgmental about the painter Mimi's obvious ardor for Serag's older brother Rafik, though Rafik rejects Mimi's invitation to go to Mimi's home to see his canvasses, and questions whether Mimi is really an "invert" ([1948]1950:67–69, 117).

4. Most anthropological publication dealing with Islamic societies during the past two decades has focused on local practices, including gendered difference (e.g., Holy 1991; Fernea and Bezirgan 1977; Wikan 1982). Even within Islamic societies, most anthropologists in the preceding half century also emphasized differences (Murray 1981), especially hunting for "pre-Islamic survivals" and "chtonic residues." The texts

of recent text-centric anthropology have remained what their folk say (and occasionally do), not assessment of conformity to the *Qur'ān*.

5. Reticence about socially acknowledging (talking about) sex is far from unique to Islamic societies. See Murray (1995a) on Mexicans and Guatemalans. Cartoonist Al Capp recalled that in the United States during the 1920s, "You never talked about sex. It simply wasn't mentioned. The whole point was to have sex, but never to admit to the other one that you'd had it. Even while you were buttoning up your fly, you just didn't admit it. Nice people simply never talked about it at all" (Fleming and Fleming 1975:39).

6. Williams (1993:72–85, 100–102) makes a strong case for internalization of honor (as self-regard) and other conventional standards within a "shame culture." He was writing specifically about Homeric Greece, but the notion has long been widely generalized to other cultures, e.g., by Barth (1959:82) describing the Swat Pathan view that lacking honor is equivalent to being a woman.

7. She was contrasting coastal Omani reticence to Cairo gossiping, but it seems to me that most of this quotation applies as well to the situation in Latin America (former Iberian colonies that in a real sense are part of the circum-Mediterranean culture complex; see Murray 1987 and 1995a).

8. Another American analog of compulsive reticence about homosexuality (in an elite law firm) is provided by Stewart (1993) and also represented in "Philadelphia," Jonathan Demme's film about a closeted gay lawyer who gets sick and is terminated.

9. In *The Jealous Lover,* the punishment for a thirty-five-year-old man who had paid a young boy for sex was to have his twenty-year-old "lover" repeatedly fucked by other prisoners.

10. See Murray 1987:192–99; 1995a. Also see Winkler 1990:67–69 on ancient Greece. Another similarity is that the cult of virginity and experience of the pleasures of insertive anal sex seems to lead to frequent heterosexual anal intercourse, especially but not exclusively premarital (see Baraheni 1977:47–49).

11. I have retranslated the French text that was quoted and very systematically mistranslated (avoiding nominalizations of kinds of persons) in Eppink (1992:40).

12. See Blanch 1983:110–11; a photograph of the male couple appears facing p. 128 in that volume.

13. "He wanted it" is not always a rationalization of force. Ahmad al-Tīfāshī (or his Syrian translator into French) recounts a teenage boy of well-to-do family complaining that "when he was a child he had never found anybody to break him in and train him suitably, to help him breach his dam and widen its narrow opening" (Lacey 1988:197). A more complex quest for transgression (specifically against his father) motivated the young Algerian protagonist to accept a sexual proposition in Ghanem's autobiographical novel *The Seven-Headed Serpent* (1986:109–10). Blackmail is yet another motivation, as discussed in chapters in this volume about contemporary Pakistan and by Bouhdiba (1985:200–201).

14. American research (e.g., Tindall 1978) about the lack of long-term effects on boys who had been involved sexually with adults cannot just be extrapolated, not only because of differences in cultural expectations, but also because the American boys were not necessarily the insertees, and because they were in relationships, not open to all comers. Wikan overstates (or passes on idealizations of) the amity and equity of relationships "whereby older men seek sexual satisfaction with younger boys" in Islamic societies as "part of a deep friendship or love relationship between two men" in which "both parties play both the active and the passive sexual role—either simultaneously or through time" (1977:310). As discussion below of various labels for the lower status in gender-stratified homosexual relationships will show, the Omani *khanith* may be more flagrant and more numerous than those providing a sexual outlet in other Islamic soci-

eties, but he differs only in degree, not in kind. I know of no estimates of rates of mobility from the role of the fucked to that of the fucker in any Islamic society, only statements like Crapanzano's that "adolescent boys who play the passive role are teased and are expected when they are older to assume the active role" (1973:52n17).

15. See Paret 1927; Pérès 1953; Ritter 1955; Surieu 1967; Wagner 1965; Schimmel 1975:287–343; 1979a,b; Continente Ferrer 1978; N. Daniel 1979; Wormhoudt 1980; Southgate 1984:428–33; Bouhdiba 1985:119; Lacey 1988:25, and my chapter on medieval Persian poetry in this volume.

16. Marc Daniel interpreted straw in the pool as a metaphor for general imperfection rather than for the specific variance from the ideal of having sprouted a beard (indicating post-adolescence, as for the Greeks). Such coming to maturity was sometimes celebrated by lovers not ceasing to love a boy when (or as) he became a man (see Leyland 1977; Wormhoudt 1980:24).

17. The former admirers felt otherwise:

> When the rose in the garden has faded, what use are the thorns and stem?
> . . . When the beauteous bird has flown, what value has the cage? (Surieu
>   1967:175)

18. One that has reached a European language is 'Obeyd's from the fourteenth century (Bausani 1964). Greek debates about loving boys or women were almost certainly models, not just predecessors of discussions of whether *liwāt* or *zinā'* was better. The Arabic progenitor was part of the *Kitāb al-kinayat* by al-Tha'alibi, who died in 1038. Rowson notes that practical advantages (such as pregnancy) are the main concern, "while the rarer appeals to aesthetic considerations suggest rather the similarities between the two sexes as objects of sexual desire (slim waist and ample hips in particular)" (1991b:59). Advocates of *zinā'* occasionally called attention to "full breasts; the advocates of boys make no corresponding counter-arguments on the basis of physical attributes." In particular, the penis of the boy was of no interest (functional or aesthetic).

19. Rather than the autumn of boyhood, the sprouting of a beard is metaphorically spring in Persian and Urdu (*sabza-e-xat*), literally, the verdure of the beard (Naim 1979: 136n20).

20. One says: "This city is full of corruption." His friend replies: "What do you expect from a city where we are the blessed old men?" ('Obeyd-e Zakani [1350] 1985:24).

21. In addition to being a patron of the boy-love poet Abū Nuwās (ca. 756–ca. 810, on whom see Ingrams 1933; Wagner 1965; Bey 1993), Amin organized a group of black eunuchs whom he called "The Ravens" and a group of white ones whom he called "The Grasshoppers." He had a favorite: "Particularly obnoxious was his infatuation for the eunuch Kauthar" (Abbott 1946:211). When Amin attempted to flee the siege of Baghdad in 813, he was accompanied by Kauthar (Kawthar).

22. The Old Persian word *bardag*, which is the basis of *berdache*, was a kind of person, that is, a slave (Sterngass 1892:172, who also notes that it is a village near Shiraz). Thomas Barfield notes that "*bardak* is diminutive form of captive/slave; its gender in Persian is ambiguous. The plural *bardagan* refers to slaves in general" (personal communication, March 24, 1995). Slaves could be sexually used with some impunity in Islamic (and other Mediterranean) societies, but the sense of effeminacy and sexual receptivity does not seem to have been primary originally (Dynes 1985:20). Although clearly a term for a homosexual role used by French observers of Arab (and other) societies, its status as a native term for a homosexual role is uncertain.

23. See Flaubert (1973:567–74 on Egypt; also pp. 638, 669 on Constantinople), the early-sixteenth-century observations by Leo Africanus ([1550]1956:385), mid-eight-

eenth-century ones by Chénier (1788:73–74), and late-twentieth-century ones by Herve and Kurest (1980) of young and or cross-dressed male prostitutes in Fez, Sanger (1858:181) on Algiers. In 1819 Byron referred to the Turkish baths as "marble palaces of sherbet and sodomy" (Crompton 1985:142) and in an 1810 letter wrote that "in England the vices in fashion are whoring & drinking, in Turkey, Sodomy & smoking. We prefer a girl and a bottle, they a pipe and a pathic" (p. 143). Joseph Pitts, visiting Alexandria in the 1680s, was shocked that soldiers "openly bragged about" sodomizing boys (quoted in Dunne 1990:61).

24. If it were not for the qualifier "generally," I would think the Khäwal/Gink distinction was ethnic. It may, however, instead differentiate explicitness of availability for sexual hire rather than shared "tribal" background.

25. Floor was distinguishing *naqqarachis* from *lūtīs*, classes of entertainers supervised by different government officials. The *naqqarachis*, including young boy dancers, bath attendants, masseurs, barbers, corpse-washers, and storytellers (a set of "homosexual occupations" in a number of societies!) were supervised by the Mehtar of the Naqara Khana. His account is based on Aubin (1908:230–33) and Mustawfi (1947, 1:188, 208, 239, 354–57).

26. Coon claimed that "the whole Jebalan area is permeated with this type of sexual depravity, which is practiced without mutual shame or any attempt at concealment. In the Rif, persons sometimes live and die without knowledge of its existence, and those who have traveled and seen it cannot mention it at home without falling into disfavor. It was punished during the recent [First World] war in at least two known instances, by soaking the culprits in gasoline and burning them alive" (1931:111). However, Maxwell notes that Moroccan men "considered sexual relationships with boys a normal and harmless convenience. . . . Homosexuality between man and boy was never considered in any way abnormal or shameful in Morocco until the infiltration of European opinion with the French. . . . *Harkas* were continually on the move, and boys were easier to take into battle than women. All the *harkas* . . . were accompanied by numerous boys for the satisfaction of sexual needs, and no shame attached to the practice on either side" (1983:287, 286). Pellat cautions, "It is not known how much credence should be attached to an allegation by Ibn Hawkal, reiterated in part by al-Idrisi [ca. 1164] (1957:269–70), according to which the Kutama Berbers "offer themselves to their guests as a token of hospitality, without any sense of shame," while at Sētif, they are content to offer their male children (1983:778).

27. Thesiger emphasized that T. E. Lawrence's "escorts [who] made use of each other to slake their needs" were "villagers from the oasis, not Bedu" (1959:110).

28. This case is examined in detail in a later chapter. Also see Greenberg's survey of male prostitution across the Islamic world (1988:177–81).

29. An earlier version of this and part of the following sections was published in the *Archives of Sexual Behavior* 24 (1995):623–29 (© 1995, Plenum Publishing Corporation).

30. Elwell-Sutton suggests that "another less likely source is the Persian word *lūtī,* meaning 'victuals,' whence *lūtī*='greedy'" (1983:839). He continues, "One of the earliest recorded uses of the term in Persian is by the 4th/10th century poet Kisā'ī, who associates it with the words *tāz* and *makyāz*, both meaning 'catamite.'" More recently, *lūtī* and *lātī* have referred to Iranian court jesters and itinerant entertainers, as note 31 details.

31. Although it is very polysemous a term and whatever its original meaning, *lūtī* retains a sense as pederast in contemporary Farsi (Persian), and had primarily that sense in the thirteenth- and fourteenth-century writers Rūmī and 'Obeyd-e Zakani (Elwell-Sutton 1983:839). Floor, in a quite opaque attempt to distinguish among kinds of entertainers called *lūtī* in early twentieth-century Iran (as well as to distinguish them

THE WILL NOT TO KNOW 47

from "hooligans" also called *lūtī*), mentioned that professional wrestlers (*pahlavans*) still at the time of his writing avoided "sexual intercourse with women, believing that this would sap their strength" (1971:114). He did not actually attest anyone referring to himself either as *lūtī* or as *Ahl-i lūt,* the latter term alluding to homosexual relationships among *'ayyars* (whom Floor treats as spiritual predecessors of *lūtīgars* in general and *pahlavans* in particular).

32. To take other stereotypes/synecdoches of national character, Cretans were defined as liars, and Spartans as warriors. They were not regarded (by ancient Athenians) as happening to engage in acts of lying or warfare. The equation of New York with rudeness or Paris with arrogance are not quite so well established, though these are seen as attributes of the populaces of those cities.

33. "The best treatment consists of frequently massaging penis and testicles and drawing them downward. Maids and servants with nice faces and much practice in this matter should be put in charge of the patient, in order to rub and massage that place and apply themselves to it and kiss it and fondle it. This should be done as much as possible" (translated by Rosenthal 1978:57).

34. In addition to rejecting physiological causes for *ubnah,* in his chapter in *Al-Qanun* (The Canon [of Medicine]) Ibn Sīna wrote that it could not be treated, though lust might be broken by punishment. See the translation in Nathan (1994). Ibn Manjli (1984 [ca. 1370]:84) warned that sitting on a panther's skin might incite a man to *ubnah* (1984:84).

35. Westermarck also recorded *zāmel* and *hassās,* but glossed *zāmel* as "boy prostitute" (1926:463), while Remlinger used *zāmel* as a term for male prostitute and *hassās* for anally receptive pubescent boys (1913:104). Moroccan male prostitutes are also called *kahba* (Chebel 1988:62), and men judged insufficiently masculine/phallic are called *mokhsī* (castrated), *bou-terme* (big-assed), and *bāred* (lacking heat), while an exceptionally virile one is a "man and a half," *rajel ou neçf.* Analogies are also frequently made between she-goats (*ātroūs'*) and he-goats (*ma'za*) (Chebel 1988:58–61).

36. Burton noted this in the mid-nineteenth century as quoted in chapter 13 below.

37. Rowson notes that this post-classical term (based on *hulaq,* an Umayyad-period synonym for *ubnah*) was gradually supplemented by *baghghā* (from *bigha,* which originally referred to fornication or prostitution) (1991b:77n37).

38. Perhaps realizing how it subverts his argument, Schmitt (1992:14) only refers to but does not repeat the quotation from the *Hidaya,* written by the Transoxian Hanafite jurist al-Morginani (d. 1197) that he had quoted in an earlier version of the paper (Schmitt 1987:180):

> The phrase *wati' ad-dakarain* confirms this view; it means the "fucking of two males" and as at-Tabari shows in his commentary of the Qur'ān concerning the sura IV, verse 16, the dual is only used when the two persons have different roles, do different things—the plural and the singular being used for general roles. So, as in at-Tabari's case, "the two" refers to *zānī* and *zānīya,* in al-Hilli's to *lūtī* and malūt. (emphasis added)

Zānī, therefore, can be added to the list of insertor role terms.

39. Schmitt derives the term from Arabic *gulīm* meaning "boy" and *pāre* meaning "one who tears apart" (1992:10).

40. See Schuyler's nineteenth-century account reproduced in the chapter, "Nineteenth Century Texts." More recently, a transvestite dancer from the middle of Turkey reported that he was "hired by men who want to drink together one evening. If I dance, they get sexually attracted to me, they touch me and kiss me, but because the towns are small and the men are afraid of gossip, it never ends in sex" (Shimshek 1988:157).

41. Peter T. Daniels (personal communication, October 1995) contends that a grammatical reciprocal form can be generated for any Arabic verb. Since these are derivative, they are not listed separately in dictionaries. Whether such forms are used cannot be resolved merely by their non-inclusion in dictionaries (see Arboleda and Murray 1985).

42. It was "in the experience of this consuming love [that] Rūmī became a poet" (p. 314)—a poet considered by many of the faithful to be heretical and/or obscene, though even what some consider obscene metamorphoses into mystical allegories. This couple provide the best-known Persian expressions of skepticism about the spiritual guise for the worship of beauty: Shamsi in asking. "Why look at the reflection [of the moon in a bowl of water], when you can look at the thing itself [in the sky]?"; Rūmī exclaiming, upon being told that Awhadu'd-Din sought the company of the beautiful with purity of purpose, "Would rather that his desires had been carnal, and that he had outgrown them!" (E. Browne 1920:140). Rūmī also said, "The road is far from lust to love" (translated by Halman 1983:26). It is tempting to read autobiographical reference into these statements (and indeed to most of his oeuvre, since a personal God and Love and Shamsi are so regularly and inextricably wrapped together).

43. The two young men often sleep together ([1957]1992b:55–56). Ridwan and the couple's patron, Abdal-Rahim Pasha both state their lack of sexual interest in women (119, 284;.59, 279). There is no explicit sex, heterosexual or homosexual, in the novel.

44. Taking the stage metaphor, some actors of the sexually receptive part are typecast. And, as with child stars (however beloved), adult careers do not necessarily follow.

45. They failed to make the ethnic and regional distinctions that they vigorously faulted Wikan for failing to make. AbuKhalil reports that "in some Arab countries, like the United Arab Emirates, marriages between males take place regularly" (1993:34).

46. "Moroccans of his [Tuhami's] background do not have oral intercourse," according to Crapanzano (1980:104). "They talk about it a lot; they say the French do it all the time." The accounts of intercultural sexual contact in Schmitt and Sofer (1992) show a shared Arab and Persian repugnance for performing fellatio. Khan (infra) also mentions this for Pakistanis.

47. In contrast, 69 percent reported some heterosexual experience (with a median age of first experience of 17 years of age with a range of 8–21). When asked how many of their ten best friends had engaged in homosexuality, those who reported homosexual experience said that (a mean of) 4.4 of their friends had also. Those who reported never having engaged in homosexual activity estimated only (a mean of) 0.9 of their friends had. When asked what percentage of men over the age of 18 had, the magnitude of difference was still considerable: 43 percent versus 14 percent. These disparities may reflect some degree of association among those more interested in homosexuality, although Melikian and Protho termed it a "conspiracy of silence about sex" (1954:64). Projection also surely accounts for some of the differences. Based on a questionnaire to "about twenty boys" Eppink concluded that a Moroccan "boy scarcely dares to do something of which he is not sure that his friends approve. . . . What a Westerner might take as lack of privacy is seen by Moroccans as security: as long as one sees that others do the same as you do, there is no need to be afraid or to feel shame" (1992:35).

48. In contrast, 75 percent had had heterosexual intercourse (with a mean age of 17.2 and an age range of 8–21). The heterosexual mean age increased from 16.9 to 17.2, while the homosexual one decreased from 13.2 to 12.4 in contrast to the earlier study.

49. Also see p. 244 on the jealousy of seventh- and eighth-grade boys for those who were in exclusive and "passionate (though not sexual, at least to my knowledge)" relationships.

50. According to Sofer (1992b:79), when Yüzgün was asked about his sampling criteria (at a 1987 Amsterdam Free University conference in a discussion of the English synopsis of his 1993 book), he could manage no more substantial a claim than "I knew they were homosexual."

51. A strong substratum of pre-Islamic culture may explain the unusual openness (presuming that the phenomenon was accurately reported, so that there is something to explain). Siwa was the site of an important ancient oracle. Language, non-Islamic rites and beliefs persisted along with a notably libertine sexual lifestyle (Cline 1936:43; Maugham 1950; Prorok 1936:64). I have not been able to guess what the empirical (or logical) basis is for Edwardes and Master's account (or fantasy?) of "Hamite" males in Siwa alternating "active and passive roles" while

> their womenfolk are allowed complete freedom and equality, suffer no social or sexual suppression, and are in fact very promiscuous. . . . All [males] marry at the age of puberty, and all of them experience marital as well as premarital coitus, but most of them seem to prefer homoerotic activities. . . . Consequently, females are obliged to have all their sex fun in girlhood, before the boys become overly attached to their older companions. The married but neglected women traditionally prostitute themselves to outsiders, travelers, and the like. (1963:247)

52. Lewis and Loots (1995) contrast this couple's acceptance to the difficulties a lesbian Muslim-Christian relationship (also in Cape Town) has. Achmat's memoir shows that acceptance of sons' homosexuality is not universal among Cape Muslims (1995:337).

53. Adam (1986) borrowed Robert Redfield's distinction between "the great tradition" and "little traditions" (the great tradition being scriptural, the little ones being practices of illiterate believers within complex civilizations with "religions of the book"). I have resisted applying Redfield's distinction between texts and everyday practices, because I am not sure that what Western scholars consider "folk Islam" is seen by Muslims as an aspect especially of Islam. Fireworks on the Fourth of July, drinking on New Year's Eve, and the tooth fairy are not seen by anyone as intrinsically "Christian," even by those who consider the United States to be the home of God's chosen people. Not every recurrent pattern in a Christian society has anything to do with Christianity, and I do not see why everything in an Islamic society should be seen to derive from Islam. Paradoxically, the distinction may work better for homosexuality than for its original locus, religion.

54. I am mindful that this interpretation may be overly colored by the modern gay conception that the "active" one is the one who does what [s/]he wants (gets his/her way), while the "passive" one is the one who does whatever it is that the other one wants.

55. I do not regard this as instancing what I have elsewhere called "the blind phallus fantasy." The Arab Omar is describing his preferences ("heterosexual" ones if the order of mention is taken as a hierachy of choice). Taking what he can get is not the same as not caring what he fucks. In reading what I proposed to quote, Omar added "at a low cost" and then changed that to "at a price he can afford" and then deleted "price" because he thought Americans would read "price" as a fixed amount, whereas the cost he meant might be an obligation to help in some way. He added that boys are generally viewed as demanding less than wives or female prostitutes, and as being safer than prostitutes (with regard to venereal diseases).

References

Abbott, Nabia. 1946. *Two queens of Baghdad: Mother and wife of Harun al-Rashid.* Chicago: University of Chicago Press.

'Abd Allah. 1917. *Siwan customs.* Harvard African Studies, Vol. 7. Cambridge: Peabody Museum of Harvard University.

AbuKhalil, As'ad. 1993. "A note on the study of homosexuality in the Arab/Islamic civilization." *Arab Studies Journal* 1(2):32–34, 48.

Achmat, Zackie. 1995. "My childhood as an adult molester: A Salt River moffie." In *Defiant desire: Gay and lesbian lives in South Africa*, ed. Mark Gevisser and Edwin Cameron, 325–41. New York: Routledge.

Adam, Barry D. 1986. "Age, structure, and sexuality." *Journal of Homosexuality* 11: 19–33.

Ajmal, Asir. 1994. "Testing the waters." *Herald* (Karachi) 25, 3 (March):36.

al-Idrisi. Vol. 3. 1957. *Description de l'Afrique septentrionale et saharienne: Texte arabe extrait du Kitab nuzhat al-mushtaq fi ikhtiraq al-afaq*. Algiers: La Maison des livres.

al-Issa, Ihsan, and Brigitta al-Issa. 1969. "Psychiatric problems in a developing country: Iraq." *International Journal of Social Psychiatry* 16:15–24.

———. 1971. "Psychiatric problems in a developing country." *Transcultural Psychiatric Review* 8:59–61.

Arboleda Grieve, Manuel A., and Stephen O. Murray. 1985. "Lexical inferences and Maori homosexuality." *Journal of Homosexuality* 12:121–29.

Aslam, Talat. 1994. "Out of focus." *Herald* (Karachi) 25, 3 (March):32.

Aubin, Eugene. 1908. *La Perse d'aujour d'hui*. Paris: Librairie Armand Colin.

Baldauf, Ineborg. 1990. "*Bacabozlik*: Boylove, folksong and literature in Central Asia." *Paidika* 2(2):12–31.

Baraheni, Reza. 1977. *The crowned cannibals: Writings on repression in Iran*. New York: Vintage.

Barth, Fredrik. 1959. *Political leadership among Swat Pathans*. London: Athlone Press.

Bausani, A. 1964. "Il Libro della Barba di 'Obeid Zakani." In *Studi Orientalistici*, ed. A. F. Gabrieli, 1–19. Rome: G. Bardi.

Berlin, Brent, Dennis Breedlove, and Peter H. Raven. 1968. "Covert categories and folk taxonomies." *American Anthropologist* 70:290–99.

Bey, Hakim. 1993. *O tribe that loves boys: The poetry of Abu Nuwas*. Amsterdam: Entimos Press.

Blanch, Lesley. 1983. *Pierre Loti: Portrait of an escapist*. London: Collins.

Boswell, John. 1980. *Christianity, social tolerance, and homosexuality*. Chicago: University of Chicago Press.

Bouhdiba, Abdelwahab. 1985. *Sexuality in Islam*. London: Kegan Paul.

Browne, Edward G. 1920, 1956. *A history of Persian literature: under Tartar dominion, 1265–1502*. Cambridge: Cambridge University Press.

Chebel, Malek. 1988. *L'esprit de sérail*. Paris: Lieu Commun.

———. 1995. *Encyclopédie de l'amour en Islam*. Paris: Payot.

Chénier, Louis de. 1788. *The present state of the empire of Morocco*. London: Robinson.

Chetty, Dhianaraj. 1995. "A drag at Madame Costello's: Cape moffie life and the popular press in the 1950s and 1960s." In *Defiant desire: Gay and lesbian lives in South Africa*, ed. Mark Gevisser and Edwin Cameron, 115–27. New York: Routledge.

Cline, Walter. 1936. *Notes on the people of Siwah and El Garah in the Libyan desert*. Menasha, WI: George Banta.

Continente Ferrer, J. M. 1978. "Aproximación al estudio del tema del amor en la poesía hispano-árabe en los siglos XII y XIII." *Awraq* 1:12–28.

Coon, Carleton S. 1931. *Tribes of the Rif*. Harvard African Studies 9.

Cossery, Albert. [1948] 1950. *The lazy ones*. Norfolk, CT: New Directions. Translation of *Les faineants dans la vallée fertile*. Paris: Domat.

———. [1955] 1981. *Proud beggars*. Santa Barbara, CA: Black Sparrow Press. Translation of *Mendiants et orgueilleux*. Paris: Julliard.

Crapanzano, Vincent. 1973. *The Hamadsha*. Berkeley: University of California Press.

———. 1980. *Tuhami: Portrait of a Moroccan*. University of Chicago Press.

Crompton, Louis. 1985. *Byron and Greek love*. Berkeley: University of California Press.

Daniel, Marc. 1977. "Arab civilization and male love." *Gay Sunshine* 21:1–11, 27.

———. 1979. "L'Ayatolla et les pelotons de l'exécution." *Arcadie* 305:388–9.

Daniel, Norman. 1979. *The Arabs and medieval Europe.* London: Longman.

Danna, Daniela. 1992. "Punishable by death: An Iranian refugee talks about life under Islamic law." *Advocate* 618 (15 December):59–60.

De Martino, Gianni. 1992. "An Italian in Morocco." In *Sexuality and eroticism among males in Moslem societies,* ed. Arno Schmitt and Jehoeda Sofer, 25–32. Binghamton, NY: Harrington Park Press.

Dunne, Bruce W. 1990. "Homosexuality in the Middle East." *Arab Studies Quarterly* 12(3):55–82.

Duvert, Tony. 1976. *Journal d'un innocent.* Paris: Éditions de Minuit.

Dynes, Wayne R. 1985. *Homolexis.* New York: Gay Academic Union.

Edwardes, Allen. 1959. *The jewel in the lotus: A historical survey of the sexual culture of the East.* New York: Julian Press.

Edwardes, Allen, and R. E. L. Masters. 1963. *The cradle of erotica.* New York: Julian Press.

Elwell-Sutton, L. P. 1983. "Lūṭī." *Encyclopedia of Islam* 5:839. Leiden: Brill.

Eppink, Andreas. [1977] 1992. "Moroccan boys and sex." In *Sexuality and eroticism among males in Moslem societies,* ed. Arno Schmitt and Jehoeda Sofer, 33–41. Binghamton, NY: Harrington Park Press.

Fernea, Elizabeth Warnock, and Basima Qattan Bezirgan. 1977. *Middle Eastern Muslim women speak.* Austin: University of Texas Press.

Flaubert, Gustave. 1973. *Correspondence I, 1830–1851.* Paris: Gallimard.

Feuerstein, G., and S. al-Marzooq. 1978. "Omani xanith." *Man* 13:665–67.

Fleming, Karl, and Anne Taylor Fleming. 1975. *The first time.* New York: Simon and Schuster.

Floor, Willem M. 1971. "The Lutis: A social phenomenon in Qajar Persia." *Die Weld des Islams* 13:103–21.

Gevisser, Mark. 1995. "A different fight for freedom: A history of South African lesbian and gay organisation from the 1950s to the 1990s." In *Defiant desire: Gay and lesbian lives in South Africa,* ed. Mark Gevisser and Edwin Cameron, 14–86. New York: Routledge.

Ghanem, Ali. 1986. *The seven-headed serpent.* New York: Harcourt Brace Jovanovich.

Greenberg, David F. 1988. *The construction of homosexuality.* Chicago: University of Chicago Press.

Halman, Talat Sait. 1983. "Love is all: Mevlana's poetry and philosophy." In *Mevlana Celaleddin Rumi and the whirling dervishes,* 9–46. Istanbul: Dost.

Herve, Guy, and Theirry Kurest. 1980. *Les enfants de Fez.* Paris: Libres-Hallier.

Holy, Ladislav. 1991. *Religion and custom in a Muslim society: The Berti of Sudan.* New York: Cambridge University Press.

Ibn Manjli, Muhammad. 1984. *De la chasse: Commerce des grands de ce monde avec les bêtes sauvages des déserts sans onde.* Paris: Sindbad.

Ingrams, W. H. 1933. *Abu Nuwas in life and in legend.* London: Witherby.

Isaacs, Gordon, and Brian McKendrick. 1992. *Male Homosexuality in South Africa.* Cape Town: Oxford University Press.

Istrati, Panaït. 1926. *Kyra Kyralina.* New York: Knopf.

Janssen, Thijs. 1992. "Transvestites and transsexuals in Turkey." In *Sexuality and eroticism among males in Moslem societies,* ed. Arno Schmitt and Jehoeda Sofer, 83–91. Binghamton, NY: Harrington Park Press.

Javadi, Hasan. 1988. *Satire in Persian literature.* Rutherford, NJ: Fairleigh Dickinson University Press.

Judell, Brandon. 1993. "Gays talk Turkey, and vice versa." *Bay Area Reporter* (24 June): 23–24.

Kafi, Hélène. 1985. "Téhéran: L'amour à jet de pierres." *Gai Pied* 190:44–47.

Kazantzakis, Nikos. 1953. *The Greek passion.* New York: Simon and Schuster.

Klunzinger, C. B. 1878. *Upper Egypt.* New York: Scribner's and Armstrong & Co.

Lacey, Edward A. 1988. *The delight of hearts: Or what you will not find in any book* (introduction to and partial translation of *Les délices de coeurs* by René Khawam, which was presented as a miscellany, *Nuzhat al-albab fima la yujadu fi kitab,* comp. Ahmad al-Tīfāshī). San Francisco: Gay Sunshine Press.

Lane, Edward. 1908. *Manners and customs of the modern Egyptians.* New York: Dutton.

Lane, Erskine. 1975. *In praise of boys: Moorish poems from Al-Andalus.* San Francisco: Gay Sunshine Press.

———. 1978. *Game-texts: A Guatemalan journal.* San Francisco: Gay Sunshine Press.

Layachi, Larbi. 1986. *The jealous lover.* Bolinas, CA: Tombouctou Books.

Leo Africanus. [1550] 1956. *Description de l'Afrique.* Paris: Adrien-Maisonneuve.

Lewis, Bernard. 1993. "Islam and liberal democracy." *Atlantic* 271, 2 (Feb.):89–98.

Lewis, Jack, and Francois Loots. 1995. "'Moffies en manvroue': Gay and lesbian life histories in contemporary Cape Town." In *Defiant desire: Gay and lesbian lives in South Africa,* ed. Mark Gevisser and Edwin Cameron, 140–57. New York: Routledge.

Leyland, Winston. 1977. *Orgasms of light.* San Francisco: Gay Sunshine Press.

Lindholm, Charles. 1982. *Generosity and jealousy: The Swat Pukhtun of northern Pakistan.* New York: Columbia University Press.

Lings, Martin. 1975. *What is Sufism?* Berkeley: University of California Press.

Mahfouz, Naguib [Najib]. [1947] 1992a. *Midaq alley (Zuqaq al-Midaqq).* New York: Doubleday.

———. [1957] 1992b. *Sugar street (al-Sukkariyah; al-Qahirah: Maktabat Misr).* New York: Doubleday.

Masters, William M. 1953. "Rowanduz: A Kurdish administrative and mercantile center." Ph. D. dissertation, University of Michigan.

Matar, Nabil I. 1994. "Homosexuality in the early novels of Nageeb Mahfouz." *Journal of Homosexuality* 26(4):77–90.

Maugham, Robin. 1950. *Journey to Siwa.* London: Chapman and Hall.

———. 1982. "The Senussi soldier." In *The boy from Beirut and other stories,* 75–83. San Francisco: Gay Sunshine Press.

Maxwell, Gavin. 1983. *The lords of the Atlas.* London: Century.

Melikian, Levon H. 1967. "Social change and sexual behavior of Arab university students." *Journal of Social Psychology* 73:169–75.

Melikian, Levon H., and Edwin T. Prothro. 1954. "Sexual behavior of university students in the Arab Near East." *Journal of Abnormal and Social Psychology* 49:59–64.

Murray, Stephen O. 1981. "Die ethnoromantische Versuchung." *Der Wissenschaftler und das Irrationale* 1:377–85.

———. 1987. *Male homosexuality in Central and South America.* New York: Gay Academic Union.

———. 1994. "Subordinating native cosmologies to the Empire of Gender." *Current Anthropology* 35:59–61.

———. 1995a. *Latin American male homosexualities.* Albuquerque: University of New Mexico Press.

———. 1995b. "Stigma transformation and relexification in the international diffusion of 'gay.'" In *Beyond the lavender lexicon: Gay and lesbian language,* ed. William Leap, 297–315. New York: Gordon and Breach.

———. 1995c. "Discourse creationism." *Journal of Sex Research* 32:263–65.

Mustawfi, 'Abd Allah. 1947. *Sharh-i zindagani-i man.* Tehran: Chap-i Tehran-i Musavvar.

Naim, C. M. 1979. "The theme of homosexual (pederastic) love in pre-modern Urdu poetry." In *Studies in Urdu gazal and prose fiction,* ed. Umar Memon, 120–42. Madison: University of Wisconsin Press.

Nathan, Bassem. 1994. "Medieval Arabic medical views on male homosexuality." *Journal of Homosexuality* 26(4):37–39.

Necef, Mehmet Ümit. [1985] 1992. "Turkey on the brink of modernity." In *Sexuality and eroticism among males in Moslem societies*, ed. Arno Schmitt and Jehoeda Sofer, 71–75. Binghamton, NY: Harrington Park Press.

'Obeyd-e Zakani, Nezam al-Din. [1350] 1985. *The ethics of the aristocrats and other satirical works*, trans. and ed. Hasan Javadi. Piedmont, CA: Jahan Books.

Oraison, Marc. 1975. *La question homosexuelle*. Paris: Seuil.

Paret, Rudi. 1927. *Früharbische Liebesgeschichten*. Bern: Haupt.

Pellat, Charles. 1983. "Liwāt." *Encyclopedia of Islam* 5:776–79. Leiden: Brill.

Pérès, Henri. 1953. *La poésie andalouse en arabe classique au XIe siècle*, 2d ed. Paris: Adrien-Maisonneuve.

Prorok, Byron Khun de. 1936. *In quest of lost worlds*. New York: Dutton.

Remlinger, Pierre. 1913. *Annales d'Hygiene Publique et de Medecine Legale* 19:97–105.

Ritter, Hellmut. 1955. *Das Meer der Seele*. Leiden: Brill.

Roscoe, Will. 1996. "Priests of the goddess: Gender transgression in ancient religion." *History of Religions* 35(3):295–330.

Rosenthal, Franz. 1978. "Ar-Rāzī on the hidden illness." *Bulletin of the History of Medicine* 52:45–60.

Rowson, Evertt K. 1990. "Gender irregularity as entertainment: Transvestism at the early 'Abbāsid court." Unpublished ms.

———. 1991a. "The effeminates of early Medina." *Journal of the American Oriental Society* 111:671–93.

———. 1991b. "The categorization of gender and sexual irregularity in medieval Arab vice lists." In *Body guards*, ed. J. Epstein and K. Straub, 50–79. New York: Routledge.

Sanger, W. W. 1858. *The history of prostitution*. New York: Harper and Brothers.

Schild, Maarten. 1988. "The irresistible beauty of boys: Middle Eastern attitudes about boy-love." *Paidika* 1,3:37–48.

———. 1990. "Islam." In *Encyclopedia of homosexuality*, ed. W. Dynes, 615–20. New York: Garland.

Schimmel, Annemarie. 1975. *Mystical dimensions of Islam*. Chapel Hill: University of North Carolina Press.

———. 1978. *The triumphal sun: A study of the works of Jalaloddin Rumi*. London: Fine Books.

———. 1979a. "Eros—heavenly and not-so-heavenly—in Sufi literature and life." In *Society and the sexes in medieval Islam*, ed. Afaf Lutfi Al-Sayyid Marsot, 119–42. Malibu, CA: Udenda.

———. 1979b. "Hafiz and his critics." *Studies in Islam* 16:1–33.

Schmitt, Arno. 1985. "Some reflections on male-male sexuality in Muslim society." In *Klein Schriften zu zwischmeannlicker sexualitat und Erotik in der muslimischen Gesellschaft*, by G. De Martino and A. Schmitt, 54–58. Berlin: Schmitt.

———. 1987. "Arab terminology for male-male sex acts and actors." In *Homosexuality, which homosexuality? Social sciences*, 175–83. Amsterdam: Free University.

———. 1992. "Different approaches to male-male sexuality/eroticism from Morocco to Uzbekistan." In *Sexuality and eroticism among males in Moslem societies*, ed. Arno Schmitt and Jehoeda Sofer, 1–24. Binghamton, NY: Harrington Park Press.

Schmitt, Arno, and Jehoeda Sofer. 1992. *Sexuality and eroticism among males in Moslem societies*. Binghamton, NY: Harrington Park Press.

Sergent, Bernard. 1986. *Homosexuality in Greek myth*. Boston: Beacon Press.

Shimshek, Jale. 1988. "Turkey." In *The Second ILGA Pink Book*, 153–62. Utrecht: International Lesbian and Gay Association.

Sofer, Jehoeda. 1992a. "Sodomy in the law of Muslim states." In *Sexuality and eroticism among males in Moslem societies,* ed. Arno Schmitt and Jehoeda Sofer, 131–49. Binghamton, NY: Harrington Park Press.

———. 1992b. "The dawn of a gay movement in Turkey." In *Sexuality and eroticism among males in Moslem societies,* ed. Arno Schmitt and Jehoeda Sofer, 77–81. Binghamton, NY: Harrington Park Press.

Southgate, Minoo S. 1984. "Men, women, and boys: Love and sex in the works of Sa'dī." *Iranian Studies* 17:413–52.

Steindorff, George. 1904. *Durch die Libysche Wuste Zur Amonsoase.* Leipzig: Velohgen and Klasing.

Sterngass, Francis Joseph. [1892] 1970. *A comprehensive Persian-English dictionary.* Beirut: Librairic du Liban.

Stewart, James B. 1993. "Death of a partner." *New Yorker* (21 June):54–71.

Surieu, Robert. 1967. *Sarve naz: An essay on love and the representation of erotic themes in ancient Iran.* Geneva: Nagel.

Tapinc, Huseyin. 1992. "Masculinity, femininity, and Turkish male homosexuality." In *Modern homosexualities,* ed. Kenneth Plummer, 39–49. London: Routledge.

Thesiger, Wilfred. 1959. *Arabian sands.* New York: Dutton.

———. 1964. *The marsh Arabs.* London: Longmans.

Tindall, Ralph H. 1978. "The male adolescent involved with a pederast becomes an adult." *Journal of Homosexuality* 3:373–82.

Wagner, Ewald. 1965. *Abu Nuwas.* Wiesbaden: Franz Steiner.

Walters, Delores M. 1991. "Cast among the outcastes: Interpreting sexual orientation, racial, and gender identity in Yemen." *Society of Lesbian and Gay Anthropologists' Newsletter* 13:43–45.

Westermarck, Edward. 1926. *Ritual and belief in Morocco.* London: Macmillan.

Wickens, G. M., trans. 1974. *Morals pointed and tales adorned* (Sa'dī's *Bustan*). Toronto: University of Toronto Press.

Wikan, Unni. 1977. "Man becomes woman: Transsexualism in Oman as a key to gender roles." *Man* 13: 304–19.

———. 1982. *Behind the veil in Arabia: Women in Oman.* Baltimore: Johns Hopkins University Press.

———. 1984. "Shame and honour: A contestable pair." *Man* 19:635–52.

Williams, Bernard. 1993. *Shame and necessity.* Berkeley: University of California Press.

Winkler, John J. 1990. *The constraints of desire: The anthropology of sex and gender in ancient Greece.* New York: Routledge.

Wockner, Rex. 1992. "Homosexuality in the Arab and Moslem world." In *Coming out,* ed. S. Likosky, 103–16. New York: Pantheon.

Wormhoudt, Arthur. 1980. "Classic Arabic poetry." *Gay Books Bulletin* 4:23–25.

Yüzgün, Arslan. 1986. *Turkiyede escinselik, dün bügün.* Istanbul: Hüryüz.

———. 1993. "Homosexuality and police terror in Turkey." *Journal of Homosexuality* 24(3/4):159–69.

Zaidi, Hasan. 1994. "AIDS: The horror strikes home." *Herald* (Karachi) 25, 3 (March):-24–37.

Zarit, Jerry. [1979] 1992. "An intimate look of the Iranian male." In *Sexuality and eroticism among males in Moslem societies,* ed. Arno Schmitt and Jehoeda Sofer, 55–60. Binghamton, NY: Harrington Park Press.

CHAPTER 3

Precursors of Islamic Male Homosexualities

Will Roscoe

INTRODUCTION

As the religion of Islam spread outward from Arabia—first under the banner of Mohammed's armies, then more slowly in the trail of Muslim traders and missionaries, until the greater part of the region from northwestern Africa to insular southeast Asia came under its influence—it encountered societies with ancient roots. In contrast to Judeo-Christian monotheism, however, Islam proved more capable of accommodating diverse cultural practices and even other religions. The capacity to adapt to and sometimes adopt local customs extended to sexuality as well. Any attempt to understand Islamic homosexualities, therefore, needs to begin with a survey of the sexual patterns of the societies it encountered. These societies, occupying the region from the Mediterranean to insular southeast Asia, have consisted largely of agrarian-based cities interconnected through trade, cultural exchange, and sometimes empires for millennia—hence Toynbee's designation of the region as a single culture area he termed the Oikoumene, the classical Greek term for the inhabited or "civilized" world.

Islam inherited from the civilizations of this region both *status-differentiated* patterns of male homosexuality and *gender-defined* alternative roles for non-masculine males whose sexual partners were usually other males. (This typology is based on Adam 1986 and S. Murray 1992). What follows is

55

an ethnohistorical review of the evidence concerning these patterns of homosexuality that traces their development (to the extent possible) up to late antiquity and the eve of the Muslim conquests.

The category of status-differentiated homosexuality, includes not only *paiderastia*, relations between adult men and youths such as flourished at Athens, but all relations between individuals socially defined as male in which one partner is of higher status than the other (thus encompassing Greenberg's "class-structured" homosexuality [1988:25, 117]). This hierarchical model of sexuality, which applied to heterosexual as well as homosexual relations, was based on a distinction between the inserting (high status) role and the penetrated (low status) role in sexual intercourse—what Boswell terms the "penetration code" (1990:72).[1]

Gender-defined patterns of homosexuality in the Oikoumene culture area included alternative gender statuses and distinct third-gender roles. For purposes of this discussion, this category is further subdivided into *state third-gender* roles, in which gender difference was linked to specific positions in state and civic institutions, and *folk third-gender* roles, exemplified by the devotees of popular goddess cults.[2] These roles were unattached (or only loosely attached) to state institutions. Both state and folk third-gender roles were part of the ancient cultures in all the regions that Muslims eventually contacted, while institutionalized, status-differentiated homosexuality appears to have been more limited to the Mediterranean basin and areas of southwest Asia influenced by Greek and Roman culture.

STATUS-DIFFERENTIATED HOMOSEXUALITY

Greece

There is little evidence of religious or magical beliefs in classical Greek homosexuality. Only by a stretch of imagination can myths like that of Zeus and Ganymede, or the metaphysical treatment of homosexuality by Plato, be compared to the beliefs associated with semen and its transfer between men in the tribal societies of New Guinea (see Herdt 1993). On the other hand, elements of initiation or rites of passage are not entirely missing. On ancient Crete, according to Ephoros, youths were whisked off in staged abductions and sequestered in all-male company in the mountains where they engaged in hunting and other masculine pursuits for two months (Strabo 10.4.21). This culminated in a presentation of symbolic gifts to the initiate and his return to the town as one who was *kleinos*, celebrated (see Koehl 1986). At Sparta, relations between men and youth occurred in the context of universal military training and served the function of transferring the loyalties of the young from their families to the state (Greenberg 1988:107; Cartledge 1981). The sacred band of Thebes, an army of sworn lovers, represented yet another form of institutionalized same-sex relations in a military context (Crompton 1994). As Greek cities increasingly relied on mercenary armies from the fourth century on, however, payment superseded love, honor, and citizenship as the reason men fought wars, and the rationale for military homosexuality lapsed.

In classical Athens, the city about which we have the most information, *paiderastia* was the pastime of young adult citizens in their twenties, who wooed youths "between the onset of puberty and the arrival of the beard" (Halperin 1990:90; Winkler 1990:53). The sexual dimension of such relationships, if we are to believe Plato, was sublimated. If the younger man (the *erōmenos*) did agree to gratify the passions of his lover (the *erastēs*), intercrural intercourse was the only acceptable mode of doing so. Vase paintings almost never depict anal intercourse or fellatio in pederastic scenes. They typically show an older man merely tickling the genitals, or chucking the chin, or, at most, performing intercrural intercourse with a boy or youth (Sutton 1992:14).

Nonetheless, as Dover observes, "A system which encourages something called 'eros' but treats its bodily consummation as incest is all very well as a philosophical construction, such as we encounter in the picture of ideal eros in Plato's *Phaedrus*, but its operation is likely to open a gulf between what is said and what is done" (1978:191). Aristophanic comedy found fertile ground for humor in this gulf between the ideal and the real (Henderson 1975). The male-centered penetration code created other contradictions. Neither heterosexual nor homosexual relations were viewed in terms of a reciprocal exchange of sentiments between equals but rather as a pursuit and/or use of individuals of lower status by men of higher status (Dover 1978:84). By the very fact of being used by them, men's sexual partners were always-already social inferiors. Combined with their economic dependence on men, the result was (and is in present-day patriarchal cultures) a blurring of the distinction between romantic love and commercial sex. Patriarchal values, by inciting male desire while restricting female (and/or younger male) sexual availability, make prostitution inevitable. This, in turn, requires social controls and a discourse that asserts the difference between sex for love and sex for sale.

In classical Athens, both male and female prostitution flourished (see Halperin 1990:88–112; Greenberg 1988:117–20). Some Athenians argued that prostitution was essential to democracy because it provided a way of "insuring that there would always be a category of persons for every citizen to dominate, both socially and sexually," regardless of economic standing (Halperin

1990:100). Equally important was the need to ensure that Athenian citizens themselves did not become common prostitutes and that the status of free-born youth who were the objects of men's desire remained distinct from that of a slave (Golden 1984). In the case of men, renting one's body to another for sexual use was inimical to the definition of citizenship as a brotherhood of equals. A man who did so, as Timarkhos was accused of doing in his youth by Aeschines, could lose all rights to participate in politics and public office.

Nonetheless, the presence of prostitution in Athens appears to have influenced the forms and practices of same-sex relations in general. Male prostitutes, like their female counterparts, have an economic incentive for extending their careers as long as possible. In ancient Athens this meant retaining adolescent youthfulness, the cultural ideal of male beauty, which could be done by wearing one's hair long and removing facial and body hair. Another strategy, more effective in the long term, was to assume a feminine appearance and even cross-dress. Such a practice would confirm another deeply held belief among Greek males—that any man who engaged in excessive sexuality, including (but not limited to) those who were penetrated by other men, would be physically feminized (Brown 1988:10–11, 18–19). Both strategies—appearing young or appearing feminine—avoided the cultural taboo against sexual relations between socially equal adult men.

In fact, non-masculinity appears to have been a personal style of at least some male prostitutes at Athens—if the use of the term *kinaidos* (Latin *cinae-dus*) in texts of this period is any guide (Winkler 1990:45–70). *Kinaidos* originally referred to male dancers and entertainers who were often prostitutes (Kroll 1921:459–62; Richlin 1993:530, 549; Henderson 1975:219–20). However, the term acquired a broader meaning, describing a social type that epitomized deviant male behavior in the eyes of Greek men: the non-masculine, passive homosexual (Richlin 1993). (By Roman times *cinaedus* was synonymous with "male prostitute.") Ensuring that the amorous pursuit of the sons of one's fellow citizens remained distinguishable from prostitution required both *erastēs* and *erōmenos* to avoid not only the sexual acts of the *kinaidos* (anal intercourse and fellatio) but his manners as well. As Winkler notes, "a variety of conventions combined to protect the junior partner from the stigma of effeminacy, of being a *kinaidos*" (1990:53). This pejorative use of *kinaidos* marked and regulated the boundary between acceptable and unacceptable homosexuality. In Aristophanic comedy it is always the penetrated male who is subjected to ridicule, never the man who penetrates (see Henderson 1975:204–22).

Nonetheless, by Hellenistic times a shift in tastes had occurred toward a preference for more effeminate *erōmenoi* (Dover 1978:69,79).[3] Similarly, anal intercourse appears to have replaced intercrural intercourse as the preferred form of male-male sexual contact (Clarke 1993:284). A strictly defined and municipally regulated practice of age-differentiated relations among elite males gave way to a more generic and pliable principle of differentiation based on social status.

Rome

Idealistic claims for male homosexuality are largely absent in Latin literature. Nonetheless, ample evidence indicates that status-differentiated male homosexuality was indigenous among the Romans and, indeed, the Etruscans before them. Valerius Maximus relates several accounts of homosexual affairs going back to the fourth century B.C.E. (6.1.6,7,9–12; cf. 1.5; Bremmer 1980:287; Boswell 1980:63), and the plays of Plautus (d. 184 B.C.E.) provide numerous allusions to homosexuality long before the Roman craze for things Greek (Lilja 1983:16–33, 102–3; Veyne 1985:28–29; Verstraete 1980:232). Homosexual prostitution appears to have been commonplace in the Republic, especially after the Second Punic War (218–201 B.C.E.), when wealth and large numbers of slaves and displaced laborers poured into Italy. In the second century B.C.E., Cato complained that the value of male prostitutes exceeded that of farm lands (Polybius 31.25.5; Athenaeus 6.275). In Augustan Rome, male and female prostitutes were taxed (Boswell 1980:70). The *Fasti Praenestini*, April 25 in the Roman calendar, was a holiday for male prostitutes (Veyne 1985:29; Boswell 1980:70).

There is no indication in any of this of pedagogically rationalized, age-defined relations like those of classical Athens. The normative form of male homosexuality in imperial times involved relations between masters and slaves (Verstraete 1980; Lilja 1983:85, 102–3,112). Accounts of the young Roman male's transition from affairs with male concubines to the role of husband in a heterosexual marriage never suggest that he took anything but the active role in sex in all cases (Richlin 1993:534–35; Fantham 1991:289). Indeed, Romans were scandalized by the Greek practice of wooing freeborn youth. For them, the problem of a citizen youth crossing the line between accepting favors from a lover and exchanging sex for money was circumvented by discouraging all sexual contact by adults with youth, male and female (although voluntary relations were lawful), and by the proliferation of other outlets—slaves, prostitutes, and non-citizens (Boswell 1980:78, 81). Consistent with this practice, freeborn youth of both sexes were rigorously chaperoned, their attendants and teachers carefully screened, and legal safeguards established. The obscure *Lex Scantinia*, for example, is believed to have been adopted to protect freeborn minors from sexual assault or seduction (Veyne 1985:29; Boswell 1980:122; but see Lilja 1983:121). Both acts were legally defined as *stuprum*, a term best translated as "sexual disgrace" or "defilement," a violation of the *pudicitia*, or sexual integrity, of a fellow citizen (Boswell 1980:122; Fantham 1991).

These differences aside, the Roman construction of male sexuality conformed to the same phallocentric/penetration model as the Greeks'. Adult males "took" pleasure from a receptive social inferior, who in return received payment, gifts, protection, and sometimes even wisdom, but not pleasure. This pattern structured sexual relations among the non-elite levels of Roman society as well, judging from the homosexual graffiti of Pompei and elsewhere (Lilja 1983:97–102, 131). The morality of a Roman man who had sex with a male slave or prostitute was rarely questioned. It was the freeborn man who was passive in sexual relations with other men who was the subject of malicious gossip, if not public censure and ridicule, while those who engaged in prostitution received special opprobrium.[4] Also like the Greeks, Romans abhorred non-masculinity in adult men (see Tracy 1976). Accusing one's political opponents of being *mollis* ("soft, feminine") was a common slander (Boswell 1980:69; Richlin 1993:538; Fantham 1991:289). In popular Roman belief, non-masculinity was caused by *impudicitia*, allowing oneself to be penetrated by other men, as surely "as blood flows from murder," to use Quintilian's infelicitous phrase (quoted in Richlin 1993:542). Unlike classical Greeks, however, Romans appear to have always preferred youth who were *mollis*. In Horace, for example, desirable youth always have long, flowing hair, a trait considered synonymous with non-masculinity (Lilja 1983:74).

Thus, the Roman construction of same-sex relations continued the transition from the principle of age-differentiation to a more general principle of status-differentiation, in which age was just one way the status criterion could be met (Boswell 1980:81). Plautus's formulation of the guidelines for male sexuality in the early first century B.C.E. remained current through imperial times and late antiquity: "No one prohibits anyone from going down the public way [i.e., visiting prostitutes]; as long as you do not make a path through posted land, as long as you hold off from brides, single women, maidens, the youth and free boys, love whatever you want" (*Curculio*, 35–38; Richlin 1993:562). Within these bounds (which were quite flexible in practice) homosexuality for male citizens was a matter of individual preference (Boswell 1990:72; cf. MacMullen 1982).

Southwest and South Asia

Southwest Asia. While evidence of alternative gender statuses is abundant for ancient Mesopotamia as early as Sumerian times, there is no indication of institutionalized *paiderastia* in those societies (Bottéro and Petschow 1975; Lambert

1992:153). The *Epic of Gilgamesh*, for example, focuses on the relationship between two male figures who are weakly differentiated in terms of status and age (much like Achilles and Patroclus [Halperin 1990:75–87]). At the same time, none of the early legal codes prohibit homosexual relations (Greenberg 1988:124). Only with the Middle Assyrian laws (1250 B.C.E.) do provisions deal with homosexuality, specifying rather severe punishment for falsely accusing another man of (presumably passive) homosexuality and punishing men who rape their companions (i.e., social equals) (§19–20; Bottéro and Petschow 1975: 461–62; cf. Lambert 1992:146–47). The prognostications of Babylonian omen texts indirectly suggest that the insertive role brought little or no stigma, while the receptive role was viewed ambivalently (*Šumma ālu* 104.13, 31–34). Astrological texts parallel a generic category of "love of a man for a man" with "love of a man for a woman" and "love of a woman for a man"; lesbianism is not mentioned (Lambert 1992:146). It would seem that same-sex love was known in ancient Mesopotamian societies and organized generally, but less strictly than in the Mediterranean world, by a penetration model.

Nor can the classical Greek model of *paederastia* be mapped onto the relationship between David and Jonathan in the Hebrew Bible—there are too many inconsistencies with the status-differentiated model, and there is no hint that such a relationship reflected an institution in Semitic society. Even less is known concerning the status of same-sex relations in Hittite society. Laws dating from the second millennium B.C.E. deal only with homosexual incest (Hoffner 1973:83, 85; Greenberg 1988:124–25).

Persia. The evidence concerning age- or status-defined homosexuality among ancient Persians is conflicting. Herodotus claims that the Persians learned *paiderastia* from the Greeks, and that it was well-established in the fifth century B.C.E. (1.135, 8.104–6; cf. Sextus Empiricus, *Pyrrhoniæ Hypotyposes* 1:152; Quintus Curtius 10.1.26; Ammianus Marcellinus 23.6.76). In *The Schoolmaster*, al-Jāhiz asserts that pederastic customs came to the Muslim world in the mid-eighth century from northeastern Persia (i.e., Khorasan), when the 'Abbāsid general Abu Muslim forbade his soldiers to have contact with women (Daniel 1991:36; Pellat 1992:154; Mez 1937:358n2; also see Ritter 1955:351).[5] The ancient laws of Zoroastrianism, however, severely condemned homosexuality (see Introduction; Bremmer 1980:282; Greenberg 1988:186), although it also bears noting that the *Gathas,* the early texts which might be attributable to Zoroaster (ca. 629–551 B.C.E.), contain no references to homosexuality.[6]

Egypt. Very few references to homosexuality appear in Egyptian texts and inscriptions. The myth in which Horus rapes Seth links the active role to aggression against an enemy and the receptive role to servility and debilitation (Grayson and Redford 1973:75–76; cf. Griffith 1898:4)—a motif that can be found in all the ancient cultures of the Mediterranean basin (Greenberg 1988:127–35; Richlin 1992). The *Book of the Dead* evinces a negative attitude toward sexual relations between males (Manniche 1977:14–15; Greenberg 1988:132–33). In the early first century B.C.E., however, marriage contracts in Egypt often forbade husbands from keeping either concubines or boy-lovers (Hopkins 1980:341).

South Asia. There is little evidence of status-differentiated homosexuality in ancient India (Bremmer 1980:282). Several early Indian law books prescribe penalties for homosexual acts (a fine, according to the fourth century B.C.E. *Arthaśāstra*, 4.13.236). In the influential *Manusmṛti*, homosexual relations are a source of ritual pollution (11.175; ca. 185–149 B.C.E.). A third-gender pattern seems to be the locus for all homosexual expression from Vedic times until the arrival of the Muslims (see below). In Sanskrit literature male figures who engage in homosexual relations do so under the guise of the third-gender figure—that is, by becoming temporary androgynes (O'Flaherty 1980:88–89).

TRANSMISSION

Although Egypt and southwest Asia (including Persia) seem to have lacked institutionalized age-differentiated same-sex patterns, these areas were extensively Hellenized in the wake of Alexander's conquests and exposed to Greek sexual patterns. Intensive cultural exchange continued in the far-flung Roman Empire. Egyptian, Syrian, and Carthaginian cultures mixed indigenous traditions with Greek and Roman influences, homosexual and other. By late antiquity it is safe to say that what could be found at Rome could be found in any number of cities and towns throughout the Mediterranean basin.

With the exceptions concerning rape and relations with freeborn minors described above, homosexuality remained legal until the sixth century (Boswell 1980:71; Greenberg 1988:228). However, a gradual increase in the scope and severity of Roman laws regulating same-sex relations is apparent (Richlin 1993:567–71; Greenberg 1988:228–34). Prostitution was officially banned in the western empire under Philip (244–49 C.E., renewed in 390) and homosexual marriages were banned in 342 (Boswell 1980:123), although in the east prostitutes were still taxed until the early sixth century (Greenberg 1988:228–30; Lilja 1983:120). In 529 and 533 C.E., Justinian placed all homosexual relations under the same category as adultery, subject to the death penalty. In so doing, he followed what had been church opinion since the fourth century and a trend in pagan society toward sexual puritanism

(Greenberg 1988:231–32). Enforcement was sporadic, however, and usually politically motivated. The severest legislation was adopted in Spain, where the Visigoths enacted the first civil law against homosexuality in 650 C.E. with a punishment of castration (Boswell 1980:170ff).

That homosexual patterns continued in areas nominally converted to Christianity is apparent from the writings of early Christians themselves. In Antioch, at the beginning of the fourth century C.E., Chrysostom admitted that even Christian men were pursuing relations with youth (*Adversus oppougnatores vitae monasticae* 3.8–9, 16). His pagan contemporary, Libanius, reported widespread homosexual practices in the eastern empire (*Oration* 25.26–27). In the early fifth century, Salvian, a Christian author, claimed that same-sex relations were common in Carthage (*De gubernatione Dei* 7.15,16,19), while Augustine confessed his own deep passion for a friend, apparently his own age, which he "contaminated" with the "dirt of lust" (*Confessions* 3.1). Early Christians continued to conceptualize male desire in terms of the circum-Mediterranean penetration model, centered on drive rather than object choice. Christian men were assumed to be just as susceptible to temptation by the sight of a beautiful boy as that of a young maid—as the strict regulations for preventing contact between monks promulgated by Pachomius and Horsiesius attest (Rousselle 1988:147–49; 155–56; Brown 1988:245–46). All lust was sinful; homosexuality was rarely singled out (Boswell 1990:73–74).

There appear to have been two modes by which status-differentiated homosexual patterns were transmitted to Islamic societies. One is the more or less unbroken continuation of such relations from ancient times. As contributions in this collection report, institutionalized, age-differentiated homosexual relations have been described among various Islamicized groups in areas that were once part of the Roman Empire—for example, the Balkans, the Middle East, and North Africa. The question for future researchers is whether these traditions have a continuous history back to ancient and pre-Islamic times or whether they developed later, in imitation of Muslims, who by the time they entered these areas had already adopted status-differentiated same-sex patterns. A second mode of transmission is represented by the poetry of those literate Muslims who began extolling the virtues of boy-love in the mid-eighth century. These authors were clearly influenced by models they found in Greek literature (Daniel 1991:44; Wafer and Crompton infra).

GENDER-DEFINED ROLES

Cinaedi appear in most Greek and Latin texts as sexual bogeymen, "the unreal, but dreaded, anti-type of masculinity behind every man's back"

(Winkler 1990:46). Whether or not there was a class of individuals in Greek or Roman society who called themselves *cinaedi* (the debate of Winkler 1990, Halperin 1990, and Richlin 1993), there were certainly real males who functioned as prostitutes and entertainers in the ancient world, and there is sufficient evidence to conclude that many fulfilled the stereotype of being nonmasculine and sexually receptive. Further, the set of psychological, behavioral, and sexual characteristics attributed to *cinaedi* are the same kind that are used to define male and female genders (Winkler 1990:46; Gleason 1990:411). However, as the term *semivir*, used synonymously with *cinaedus*, suggests, it may be more accurate to think of *cinaedi* as occupying a subdivision of the male gender role rather than a third gender as such.[7]

Other instances of gender variance in the ancient world come closer to qualifying as separate genders. The discussion that follows distinguishes two types of these roles. The first I term "state" third genders because their existence is linked to civic and state institutions. Typically defined as "eunuchs," they were an ubiquitous, sometimes influential feature of agrarian societies throughout the Oikoumene region.

As Pellat notes regarding eunuchs in early Islamic society, they "did not mingle much with the population, especially as they were easily recognisable" (1978:1091a). What made them identifiable, however, was more a function of their social role than their castration. The actual procedures termed castration in ancient and Islamic times ranged from severing of the seminal ducts to complete ablation of penis and testicles, and their effects varied considerably. Men castrated after the age of puberty are still able to derive pleasure from sex, achieving erection and orgasm (Brown 1988:169, 268; Rousselle 1988:122–27; Saletore 1974:206–7; Pellat 1978:1090b). Nonetheless, the ancients made a variety of assumptions about the bodies and behavior of those termed eunuchs, attributing to them both secondary sex characteristics and psychological traits, and labeling them in ways that distinguished them from both men and women (Ringrose 1994; Stevenson 1995:510; Saletore 1974:206–7). In the case of ancient Mesopotamia, despite the conventional translation of terms for these roles as "eunuch," there is little or no evidence that the individuals so called were actually castrated.

Ancient authors also assumed that eunuchs were passive homosexuals, if sexual at all, and many clearly did have sex with men. However, the connection between eunuchism and homosexuality is not always a direct one. Both types of individuals fulfill the need of dynastic rulers for retainers who lack competing familial loyalties—eunuchs cannot marry and have children, committed homosexuals do not want to. This places both, by default, outside the patriarchal kinship system, making them less likely to entertain dynastic aspirations. Different societies have taken advantage of both eunuchs and homosexuality for this reason, and this is why the two statuses are sometimes conflated or appear together (see also Murray's chapter on mamlūks). Throughout Eurasia, the appointment of socially defined third-gender males to run state bureaucracies provided rulers with a means of effectively limiting the power of hereditary nobility. (Medieval European rulers used the celibate clergy for the same purpose.) Hence the aristocracy is often the source of the most virulent denunciations of eunuchs (Hopkins 1978:195; Coser 1964).

The second type of alternative gender role found in the ancient world includes "folk" third genders. These roles were not formally linked to city-state institutions. Rather the individuals occupying these statuses lived and functioned at the non-elite levels of their societies in both urban and rural settings. Further, in distinction to state-based third genders, entry to these roles was by self-selection. (Eunuchs and others in state third-gender statuses were in effect a class of elite slaves, often purchased or captured aliens, although occasionally parents or individuals sought castration to take advantage of the social opportunities of that status.)

State Third Gender

Mesopotamia. From Sumerian times on, significant numbers of the personnel of both temples and palaces—the central institutions of Mesopotamian city-states—were individuals with neither male nor female gender identities. The oldest of these roles is that of the Sumerian *gala* priest. Originally a specialist in singing lamentations, *gala* appear in temple records dating back to the middle of the third millennium B.C.E.[8] According to an Old Babylonian text, Enki created the *gala* specifically to sing "heart-soothing laments" for the goddess Inanna (Kramer 1981a:2). Cuneiform references indicate the gendered character of the role (see also Gelb 1975:73; Lambert 1992:150–51). Lamentation and wailing originally may have been female professions, so that men who entered the role adopted its forms. Their hymns were sung in a Sumerian dialect known as *eme-sal*, normally used to render the speech of female gods (Hartmann 1960:138; Krecher 1966; Cohen 1974:11, 32), and some *gala* took female names (Bottéro and Petschow 1975:465). Homosexual proclivities are clearly implied by the Sumerian proverb that reads, "When the *gala* wiped off his ass [he said], 'I must not arouse that which belongs to my mistress [i.e., Inanna]'" (Gordon 1959, no. 2.100). In fact, the word *gala* was written using the signs "penis+anus" (Steinkeller 1992:37).

A related role appearing in Sumerian mythology and liturgical texts from 2000 B.C.E. on was that of the *kur-gar-ra* (Akkadian *kurgarrū*). *Kur-gar-ra* occur in the myth of Enki and Inanna, among the *me*'s (cultural practices and institutions) stolen by Inanna (2.5.21; Farber-Flügge 1973:54), and in the "Descent of Inanna" (Wolkstein and Kramer 1983:64–67). In Akkadian (i.e., Assyrian and Babylonian) texts, *kurgarrū* usually appear in conjunction with the closely related *assinnu* (see Menzel 1981; Henshaw 1994:284–306). *Gala* also appear in Akkadian texts as *kalū* (also *kulu'u* and *kulū*), and their role in Babylonian and Assyrian ritual is, if anything, greater than that of their Sumerian predecessors (Hartmann 1960:143; Henshaw 1994:95).[9] All these priests continue to appear in cuneiform records up to Seleucid times (312 B.C.E. and later; Henshaw 1994:89,95).

Kurgarrū and *assinnu* are most often identified as servants of Inanna/Ishtar, whom they sometimes portrayed by wearing masks and cross-dressing (Civil s.v. A/2:341; cf. Henshaw 1994:285, 292–95). In the neo-Sumerian sacred marriage hymn of Iddin-Dagan, the *sag-ur-sag* dress one side of their bodies as male, the other as female (li. 57–58, 60–63, Römer 1965:130,138; Reisman 1973:187; Sjöberg 1975:224). Like the *galli* (see below), they perform a kind of war dance, perhaps while in a trance state, involving swords, clubs, and blood-letting accompanied by the music of flutes, drums, and cymbals (Römer 1965:131, li. 76; Reisman 1973:188, li. 76–78; Jacobsen 1987:117; Groneberg 1986:39; Henshaw 1994:289-91).[10] In the Erra myth, Ishtar changes the "masculinity" of the *kurgarrū* and *assinnu* into femininity (4.55–56). Although this has been interpreted as evidence of a physical transformation, namely, castration, it could as easily refer to a *psychological* transformation, the result of divine possession or visitation. Many texts attest the importance of dreams and omens in Mesopotamian cultures (see Oppenheim 1956), and there is no clear evidence that any of these priests were eunuchs (Gelb 1975:68; Renger 1969:192–93; Bottéro and Petschow 1975:464–65; Henshaw 1994:126, 285; but see Lambert 1992:150–51). At the same time, the *kurgarrū* and *assinnu*, like *gala*, appear to have practiced some form of homosexuality. Akkadian omen texts instruct men to have intercourse with *assinnu* to obtain luck and refer to the desire of *assinnu* for intercourse with men (Civil s.v. A/2:341; Bottéro and Petschow 1975:463–64; Meissner 1907:9–13; Lambert 1960:279, li. 11–12; see also Lambert 1992:151–53).

In addition to gender-defined religious roles, significant numbers of palace attendants appear to have occupied an alternative gender status. Court officials were collectively designated as being either *ša ziqni*, "bearded," or *ša reš*, a term usually translated as "eunuch" (Civil s.v., *ziqnu* in *ša ziqni*). An important group of *ša reš* were the *girseqû*, who in texts from the Sumerian Ur III period (ca. 2100 B.C.E.–2000 B.C.E.) appear as domestics of palaces, temples, and other large estates and are frequently mentioned as attached to kings, gods, etc. (Civil s.v.; Lambert 1992). The exact nature of their status remains unclear, however. The imputation of beardlessness could refer to an age-group as well as to eunuchs. On the other hand, the beardless figures that frequently appear as musicians and royal attendants in Assyrian reliefs rarely look like youth; they are generally the same size as bearded figures. More importantly, *girseqû* appear in dream omen texts in the same context as *assinnu*, as sexual objects for men (Civil s.v.).

Both linguistic and mythological evidence attests to the antiquity of alternative genders in Mesopotamia. The element -ar in the Sumerian term *kur-garrû*, for example, may date it as far back as the pre-Sumerian, early Chalcolithic period (ca. 5600–5000 B.C.E.; Salonen 1970:6–7; Henshaw 1994: 284). The Sumerian myth known as "The Creation of Man" (ca. 2000 B.C.E.) relates how Ninma̱h fashioned seven types of physically challenged persons, including "the woman who cannot give birth" and "the one who has no male organ, no female organ." Enki finds each one an occupation and position in society: The sexless one "stands before the king" (the role of the *girseqû*), while the barren woman becomes the prototype for the *nadītu* priestesses (Jacobsen 1987:151–66; Jacobsen 1976:113-14; Kramer 1981b:-107). These proceedings are echoed in the Akkadian myth of Atrahasis (ca. 1700 B.C.E.), in which Enki instructs Nintu, Lady of Birth, to establish a "third-category among the people" that includes women unable to give birth, an infant-stealing demon, and priestesses who are barred from childbearing (3.7; trans. in Kilmer 1972:171; cf. Dalley 1991:34–35; Foster 1993:-183; Jacobsen 1976:120; Lambert 1992:139–40).

All this suggests that the link between alternative genders and administrative and religious specialization in Mesopotamian societies was established in prehistoric times in the context of a gender-based division of labor. At the same time, such roles appear closely tied to the social needs of an urban society. Following this hypothesis, as early cities grew so did the number and kind of religious and bureaucratic specialists needed to administer temples that were economic as well as religious centers. In a similar way, when rulers sought to link cities into kingdoms and empires, they created the apparatus for ruling these domains by expanding and extending the administrative structure of their private households. The result was what Max Weber termed patrimonial bureaucracies, staffed predominantly with slaves and former slaves. Although the division of labor at this point was no longer gender-based, many of these specialists continued to be defined in gendered terms.

The practice of castrating captives and slaves to fill these roles, however, does not seem to have become routine in Mesopotamia until Assyrian times (see, for example, Isa. 39:7; Hellanicus fr. 163b; Gray 1912:580; Greenberg

1988:121; Lambert 1992:147–48). It was also adopted by the Persians. According to Xenophon, Cyrus the Great (sixth century B.C.E.) preferred eunuch military officers because their loyalties were not divided between their sovereign and their families, and because they could not harbor dynastic ambitions by fathering children (*Cyropaedia* 7.60–65). His successor, Darius (ruled 521–486 B.C.E.), placed eunuchs in nearly all the chief offices of state, military and administrative (Greenberg 1988:122).

Western Semites. The western Semitic counterparts of the *gala, kurgarrū,* and *assinnu* were the *qedeshīm* (sg. *qedesh*), the male "temple prostitutes" mentioned in Ugaritic texts of the late second millennium (Henshaw 1994: 222–25) and denounced in the Hebrew Bible (Deut. 23:17; 1 Kings 14:24, 15:12, 22:46; 2 Kings 23:7; Job 36:14). The *qedeshīm* seem to have lived within temple precincts, kept busy with sacrifices, cared for sacred objects— and, if we are to believe ancient Hebrew rhetoric, engaged in some form of religious sexual acts (see Brooks 1941).[11] Another such role may have been the *keleb,* a term appearing in Deut. 23.18 as a synonym for *qedesh,* and at Kition on Cyprus in reference to priests of Astarte (D. Thomas 1960). Gender-variant religious roles continued in Syria well into Roman times (see Lucian's *Dea Syria*). Hebrew law, on the other hand, forbade castration, and there is no evidence that Israelites practiced it on humans. Even so, Isaiah 56:3–5 suggests that sufficient numbers of Hebrew men had been subjected to this treatment at the hands of Assyrians and Babylonians to warrant a waiver of the exclusion from the religious community mandated by Deut. 23:1–2 of men whose genitals were "crushed or maimed" (Greenberg 1988:121).

Anatolia. The *galli,* devotees of the gods Cybele and Attis (see below), originally may have been members of a state third gender, attached to the temples of the theocratic city-states of Anatolia. Temples in this region had functioned as cultural and economic centers since Hittite times, with significant lands, servants, and various civic functions attached to them, and Hittite kings often served as head priests (Hansen 1971:179; van Loon 1985:16–17; Ramsay 1897:10, 101–5; Gurney 1977:1). Only a few inscriptions and artifacts, however, indicate the presence of a priesthood associated with the Anatolian goddess before the Phrygian period (eighth to sixth centuries B.C.E.).[12] The earliest evidence of Attis, the deified shepherd considered the patron of the *galli,* does not occur until the Hellenistic period (Roller 1994). Before this, "Ates" appears as a personal name in Phrygian inscriptions and seems to have become the title of a religious official. At Pessinus, the "Attis" was a priest-king who supervised a college of priests in the city's central temple.[13] The *fanatici galli* and *galli matris magnae* encountered by the Romans in their campaigns in Asia Minor in 190 and 189 B.C.E. also appear to have been fulfilling traditional roles as theocratic officials (Livy, 37.9.9, 38.18.9–10; Polybius 21.6.7, 37.4–7). The origin of *galli* castration is uncertain. The traditional view that it is a late accretion to Phrygian religion (e.g., Hepding 1903:128–29; Sanders 1972:994–96), has been challenged by Gasparro, who argues for an ancient, indigenous origin (1985:28–29).

Greece. Mainland Greeks did not institutionalize alternative gender statuses or make use of eunuchs in civic or religious institutions. Indeed, when a *mētragyrtēs* (from *mētēr*, mother + *agyrtēs*, mendicant priest), appeared in Athens around 500 B.C.E., he was stoned to death. The one use the Greeks seem to have found for eunuchs was as tutors for their sons, since presumably they would not attempt to seduce them. (Even so, relationships between students and eunuch tutors were often close. Peter Brown characterizes the influence of the Gothic eunuch Mardonius on the young future emperor Julian as decisive [1982:149].) Ionian Greeks, on the other hand, appear not to have shared this aversion to gender variance. Herodotus refers to a regular trade in good-looking, castrated youth at Sardis and Ephesus, where eunuchs were also valued for their trustworthiness (8.105). The temple of Artemis at Ephesus was administered by a eunuch priest known as the Megabyzoi (Strabo, 14.1.23; Xenophon, *Anabasis*, 5.3.6–7), and inscriptions from Caria also refer to a eunuch who held a sacred office in service of Zeus and Hekate (Hatzfeld 1920, nos. 11d, 16; Le Bas 1888, nos. 519–20, li. 19).

Egypt. An inventory of war trophies from 1300 B.C.E. listing 13,230 penises of captive Libyans indicates that castration was practiced by the Egyptian state (Greenberg 1988:121). There is no evidence that ancient Egyptian religious and bureaucratic functionaries were gender defined or eunuchs, although much later Eusebius refers to a class of effeminate priests in Alexandria "exterminated" by Constantine (*Vitae Constantinae*, 4.25).

Rome. Like Greeks, Romans looked dimly on the practice of castration (see Seneca, *De superstitione dialogus* 34). Beginning with the *lex Cornelius*, penalties were imposed on those who castrated humans (*Digesta* 68.8.3.4–5). Domitian and Nerva also adopted laws against castration in the late first century C.E. (Dio Cassius, 67.2–3, 68.4; Suetonius, *Domitian*, 7; Ammianus Marcellinus 18.4.5), which were repeated in the *Digest* (63.8.4.2). Additional penalties were enacted during the reigns of Constantine (ruled 306–37 C.E.), Leo I (457–74 C.E.), and Justinian (527–65 C.E.) (Greenberg 1988:123). By all indications, they had little effect. Laws did not deter Plautianus, praetorian prefect in 203 C.E., who castrated one hundred free Roman youth as a wedding gift to his daughter (Dio 76.14), nor traders who circumvented them by kidnapping or purchasing boys from outside the empire (Boswell 1980: 67n25). Most eunuchs were barbarians by birth and slaves or former slaves (Hopkins 1978:172).

Eunuchs first appeared in influential court positions under Claudius (10 B.C.E.–54 C.E.; Suetonius, *Claudius*, 28) and Hadrian (117–38 C.E.) (Stevenson 1995:503–5). By the early third century, they were regularly employed in private households. Ammianus Marcellinus describes hordes of them, "sallow and deformed," clearing the way for the sedan chairs of noble Roman women (14.6.17). In the late third century, Diocletian began appointing eunuchs as palace attendants and civil servants. Their role appears to have expanded from this point, especially in the eastern empire. The eunuch Eusebius served as chief executive of the empire under Constantius (337–61 C.E.). Under Arcadius (395–408 B.C.E.), Eutropius progressed from the status of catamite to grand chamberlain, the fourth highest rank in the realm (Claudian, *Against Eutropius*, 1.62–169; Hopkins 1978:175, 180). In the fifth century, offices for eunuchs multiplied until they held nearly every official post in the eastern empire (Hopkins 1978:176–77, 194–95; Greenberg 1988:123). Eunuchs were also performers and entertainers, and a significant number of boys were castrated for the purpose of prostitution (Hopkins 1978:194).

In accusing eunuchs of exercising an evil influence at the courts of several emperors in his *Rise and Fall of the Roman Empire*, Gibbon merely gave new life to a cant dating back to Ammianus Marcellinus (18.5.4; Gibbon, *Decline and Fall*, chaps. 7, 19, 32, 33). In fact, eunuchs fulfilled several indispensable functions—as intermediaries for the emperors who sought to cloak themselves in divinity and enhance their authority through social distance; as confidants and servants who lacked competing loyalties and therefore could be used to counter the power of the aristocracy; and, finally, when needed as scapegoats for social or political ills (Hopkins 1978:173; see also Ringrose 1994:97–98). All these functions are characteristic of third-gender roles in other culture areas (see Roscoe 1994, 1996). Hopkins concludes, "The political power of eunuchs in general, far from being a sign of the emperor's weakness, was, in the Byzantine Empire of the fourth and fifth centuries, a token of, and a factor in, the survival of the emperor as an effective ruler" (1978:196). Eunuchs flourished no less under soldier-emperors like Valentinian I and Theodosius the Great, than they did under weak emperors like Theodosius II.

Byzantium. Eunuchs played important roles in the Byzantine Empire and church for a thousand years. They filled imperial posts, staffed the households of the emperor and empress, served as military officers, doctors, and teachers, and occupied positions at all levels of the ecclesiastical hierarchy (Ringrose 1994). Ambitious Byzantine families sometimes had their sons castrated to take advantage of these career opportunities (Coser 1964:882; Pellat 1978:- 1088). Outside state and church institutions, eunuchs were often singers, actors, and prostitutes—as they had been since ancient times (Ringrose 1994:98, 103). As late as the twelfth century, Theophylaktos, archbishop of Ohrid, wrote a *Defense of Eunuchs* (Ringrose 1994:105).

South Asia. Early Indian law books proscribe "eunuchs" from inheriting while specifying that they be maintained by the king (*Gautama-dharmasūtra* [300–100 B.C.E.], 28.43; *Arthaśāstra* [324–300 B.C.E.], 3.5; *Vasiṣṭha-dharmasūtra* [300–100 B.C.E.], 17.52–53, 19.35; *Manusmṛti*, 9.201). Eunuchs filled key posts in Indian courts as early as the fourth century B.C.E., as Kautilya's *Arthaśāstra* and other texts show (1.12, 20; Saletore 1974:43–47, 195–99). By medieval times, as many as three to four hundred were employed to guard harem women. Their status and numbers increased under Muslim rulers, and several became famous and powerful, especially under the Khaljis of Delhi (1290– 1320 C.E.). By the time of the Mughals, an elaborate organization of eunuchs existed in most courts (*Fo-Sho-Hing-Tsan-King*, 1.5.388; Saletore 1974:47, 196–209; Sharma 1984:383–84; Artola 1975:58–59; Sethi 1970:45). Some had affairs with their masters; many were made eunuchs for sexual purposes. Their role in Indian life continued well into the nineteenth century.

Folk Third Gender

Mediterranean. The outstanding examples of a folk third-gender role in the ancient world were the priests of the gods Cybele and Attis known as the *galli*. (Priests of Dea Syria and Ma Bellona were also called *galli*.) Although *galli* may have originated as a state third gender in Anatolia, in Hellenistic times they were most often itinerant devotees, sometimes organized in collectives loosely attached to temples. These "Phrygian missionaries," as Farnell termed them, seem to have played a key role in disseminating the worship of the Anatolian goddess in the Greek world (1896:297, 300). By the sixth century B.C.E., inscriptions from Lokroi in southern Italy and artifacts from Marseilles attest to well-developed Cybele and Attis worship (Guarducci 1970; Vermaseren 1977:132). Literary references to and depictions of Attis, the patron of the *galli*, become increasingly common after the fourth century B.C.E.[14]

In 204 B.C.E., the Roman senate, responding to oracles, imported Cybele (or the black meteorite said to represent her) from Phrygia and installed her with great fanfare in a temple on the Palatine hill. Her annual festival, the April *megalensia/megalesia*, became a regular feature of the religious calendar. Initially, however, the *galli* and their patron Attis were missing from the Roman worship of Cybele, and Roman citizens were forbidden to become *galli*.[15] By the first century B.C.E., however, literary references and artifacts found at the site of the Cybele temple suggest that the popularity of Attis and the presence of *galli* were growing.[16] The senate responded by regulating the activities of begging priests (Cicero, *De Legibus*, 2.16.40). But Claudius accommodated the cult's growing appeal, moving the *megalensia* to March and officially instituting rites honoring Attis in which *galli* were prominent.

References from the first century by Ovid, Seneca, Persius, Martial, Statius, and others, indicate that *galli* had become a common sight throughout the empire. Prowling the streets and countryside to beg for alms, they performed spectacular religious rites. "Even till yesterday," wrote Saint Augustine, "they passed through the streets and alleys of Carthage, with dripping hair and painted faces, with flowing limbs and feminine walk, exacting from merchants that by which they might shamefully live" (*De civitate Dei* 7.26). Although exaggerated for comic effect, Apuleius's description of the religious performances of the *galli* is confirmed by other sources.

With their arms bared to the shoulders, hoisting enormous swords and battle-axes, they leapt about shouting and raving in a religious dance to the singing of pipes. After wandering by not a few small cottages, we arrived at some villas of landowners, and entering the first one, they immediately flew around every which way, howling cacophonously. For a long time they would hang their heads down on their necks and with quick, twisting motions whirl their hanging hair around in circles, and sometimes assail their flesh with bites. At last, with a two-edged ax that they carried, everyone cut their arms. Then, from among them, one of those pouring forth in raving pretended to be stricken with madness and affected repeated gasps from the depths of his breast, as if filled with the power of a divine spirit. (8.27–28; my translation.)

Undoubtedly the most shocking practice attributed to *galli* was that of self-castration. Details of the actual procedure are few, however. The spontaneous self-mutilation described by Lucian, for example, was probably not the usual method (*Dea Syria*, 51). As Pliny relates, the *galli* practiced emasculation "within the limits of injury" to avoid "dangerous results" (*Natural History*, 11.261, 35.165). Nor is it clear that every *gallus* necessarily underwent the operation or at what point in his career. There appears to have been an initiatory period of unknown length (Parsons 1971). The outcome, in any case, was ambiguous. "Neither is he changed into a woman, nor does he remain a man," wrote Augustine (*De civitate Dei*, 7.24). Various authors describe *galli* as a *medium genus* or a *tertium sexus*—terms that literally translate as "intermediate kind" and "third sex" (Tertullian *Ad nationes*, 1.20.4; *Scriptores historiae Augustae, Alexander Severus*, 23.7; Prudentius, *Peristephanon*, 10.1071; Sanders 1978:1080–81). Although they are sometimes described as cross-dressing, their usual outlandish garb was neither that of women nor of men.

The final public observance of the religion of Cybele and Attis in Rome occurred in 394 C.E. (Showerman 1900:311–12). Texts from late antiquity, however, continue to reveal a fascination with the figure of Attis (e.g., Nonnus, *Dionysiaca*, 20.35–41; Damascius in Photius, *Bibliotheca*, 344b–345a), while Magna Mater, the great mother of the gods, was assimilated to Mater Dei, the virgin mother of Christ (see James 1959, chap. 7).

South Asia. A cult of goddess worshipers whose roots may be as old or older than those of the *galli* flourishes in present-day Pakistan and northern India. *Hijra* (an Urdu term) are males and physically intersexed individuals who worship Bahucharā Mātā, one of the many Indian mother goddess figures. Although the cult's existence has long been known to Europeans, Serena Nanda's recent ethnography, *Neither Man nor Woman* (1990), offers the first intimate view of its members.[17]

Hijra live in collectives with recognized leaders, or gurus, which are linked, in turn, into interurban and transnational networks. Sometimes serving as temple functionaries, *hijra* appear most often in bands, each with established territories in which they enjoy acknowledged begging rights. Their primary religious role is to bless newlywed couples and newborn males by "calling down the blessings" of their goddess, fertility being foremost. Their performances share several features with those of the *galli*, including loud, rhythmic music with flutes and drums, wild dancing, and bawdy behavior. Also like the *galli*, they are credited with the ability to foretell the future and to utter fearful curses, and they earn their livelihood through institutionalized begging. Many *hijra* also engage in prostitution.

The most striking parallel between the two cults is the practice of castration, ideally performed, in both cases, in a temple with the parts buried there or under a tree (Nanda 1990:28; for the *galli* castration, see Sanders 1972; Hepding 1903:158–65, 182–201). In the case of the *hijra*, both penis and testicles are removed by an expert (called *dai ma*, or midwife), while the initiate chants the name of the mother goddess (Nanda 1990:26–29). As a result, the initiate is *nirvan*, liberated, reborn, as a *sannyasi*, an itinerant saint who embodies the strength, or *shakti*, of the goddess and is able to impart it to others in the form of blessings (Mitra 1983:25; Nanda 1990:10, 28). According to Nanda, many *hijra* postpone the operation, and some forgo it altogether, despite pressure from other cult members and severe ridicule if they are discovered in public to have a penis (1990:xxiv, 11, 118). Castration does not transform *hijra* into women, however. As Nanda's informants explain, "We are neither men nor women" (1990:15). Although *hijra* generally wear women's clothing in public, their exaggerated "femininity" and bawdy public behavior immediately give them away.[18]

Hijra are habitually described (and describe themselves) as "impotent," although they are frequently and admittedly sexually active. As one *hijra* explained to Nanda, "When we look at women, we don't have any desire for them. When we see men, we like them" (1990:16). This, and reports of the impotence of *hijra* initiates being tested by having them sleep with prostitutes, suggest that the contextual meaning of "impotence" is "absence of heterosexual desire" (Salunke 1976:20; Kirpārām 1901:506–7). Although *hijra* freely refer to their homosexual desires, the closest one gets to the representation of this in myths and tales is a kind of *negative* marking in which protagonists are portrayed as merely *lacking* heterosexual traits. Obviously, the Indian understanding of impotency is quite different from that of modern Western societies. Present distinctions of impotency, castration, asceticism, homosexuality, and congenital sexual anomalies are largely ignored in Hindu sexual taxonomies. The *Nārada Smṛti*, an Indian law book from the fourth or fifth century c.e., defines fourteen categories of "impotent men," including those "naturally impotent," men who have been castrated, those cursed by a supernatural being, those afflicted by jealousy, those who spill their seed, and those who are shy (12.11–19; see also Sweet and Zwilling 1993).[19] The most salient feature of all these conditions from the traditional Indian perspective is their non-procreativity. Individuals so affected are conceptualized as a distinct gender status, neither male nor female.

When the British entered India, *hijra* were a well-established feature of the social landscape. They enjoyed begging rights, title to lands, and other privileges granted to them by both Muslim and Hindu rulers (Preston 1987). Sanskrit literature provides evidence of alternative genders in the early first millennium B.C.E. (see Sweet and Zwilling 1993). *Hijra* themselves often cite the episode in the fourth book of the *Mahābhārata* (ca. 200 B.C.E. and 200 C.E.) as an origin myth (Salunke 1976:20): The hero Arjuna disguises himself as a eunuch and lives in a harem for a year, teaching the arts of dance (see Hiltebeitel 1980:165–66). An even older text, the *Śatapatha Brāhmaṇa* (as early as the eighth century B.C.E.) specifies the use of a "long-haired man" (*puruṣa*) in one of its rites because he is "neither man [*puṃs*] nor woman [*strī*]" (5.1.2.14; cf. *Kātyāyana Śrautasūtra*, 14.1.14, 15.5.22). In the *Ubhayā-bhisārikā* a humorous monologue play from the first century C.E., a character of the *tṛtīyā prakṛti* is described as "the pest of the public thoroughfares" and a freelance courtesan (v. 21–22). The *Kāmasūtra* (500–200 B.C.E.) includes instructions (for men) concerning sexual practices to be performed with the *tṛtīyā prakṛti* (2.9; cf. *Bhāva-prakāśana* 11–12, 19–20), while the *Nāṭya-śāstra*, a drama manual (200 B.C.E.–200 C.E.), places guidelines for portraying such persons together with those for male and female roles in a chapter on the *prakṛti*, literally, the "genders" (chap. 24).[20]

While Mediterranean and southwest Asian state and folk third genders can be clearly distinguished (and in Mesopotamia state third genders can be further subdivided according to religious and civic versions), in India these distinctions are less salient. Individuals frequently migrated between the roles of *hijra*, court eunuchs, and transvestite actors (Sinha 1967:175; Faridi 1899:22; Rose 1911:332; Ebden 1856).

Southeast Asia. Beyond India, modern ethnographic literature documents gender-variant shaman-priests throughout southeast Asia, Borneo, and Sulawesi (see S. Murray 1992:257–92). All these roles share the traits of devotion to a goddess (or female spirits), gender transgression, homosexuality, and ecstatic ritual techniques which were curative and/or promoted fertility.

Transmission

State Third-Gender Roles. Muslim conquerors encountered state third genders in Persia, the Byzantine Empire, and India. By the eighth century, eunuchs were numerous in the palaces of the caliphs, from Cordoba to Baghdad, even though they cost twice as much as other slaves. Eventually a regular trade in eunuchs developed (Pellat 1978:1088a–b). White slaves were taken to Spain and Verdun to be castrated, and a similar trade developed in Africa. Eunuchs filled roles as mediators, servants, and sometimes supervisors of the harems. Rulers made them trusted advisors and even military commanders. As Pellat notes, "it would be easy to multiply the examples" of eunuchs who gained prestige and power in Islamic societies (1978:1091b). By the tenth century, they constituted organized bodies in many Muslim courts (1978:1092a). Their use spread to Africa, Egypt, Syria, the Persian Gulf, and to Ottoman courts, and survived until the early twentieth century.

Eunuchs acquired functions within Islamic religion as well. They staffed the mosque of Jerusalem as early as 891 C.E. In 1161, Nūr al-Dīn instituted a body of ministers of the *hudjra* of the Prophet comprised of twelve Abyssinian eunuchs, a number doubled by Saladin (Pellat 1978:1088). In the period of Ibn Battūta, the servants and doorkeepers of the Mosque of the Prophet at Medina were also eunuchs, and as late as the nineteenth century a body of African eunuchs tended the Ka'ba. Under the Ottomans, the control of the *wakfs* of the holy cities and most of the mosques was assured by a chief white eunuch and/or a chief black eunuch (Pellat 1978:1092a; see also Marmon 1995).

Folk Third-Gender Roles. Religious androgyny, whether conceived as a union of opposites or the transcendence of social (profane) differences, captured the imagination of Christians no less than it had pagans before them. One need only recall the many versions of the logion attributed to Jesus himself, "When you make the male and the female one and the same, so that the male not be male nor the female female . . . then will you enter the Kingdom" (Robinson 1977:121; cf. Matt. 19.12; see also R. Murray 1975:303–4; Delcourt 1961: 75–83). Nonetheless, it was always a spiritual androgyny to be attained in the afterlife that Christians idealized, not a magical operation that could be performed in the here and now, let alone a social identity.

For early Christians, sexual desire was precisely what kept individuals locked into the performance of gender roles and the perpetuation of the secular world through biological reproduction. Transcending gender had to begin with the renunciation of sexuality. Given this prerequisite, Christian men often identified themselves with androgynous images of the deity; while Christian women, through ascetic practices, could become, in effect, spiritual men, and thereby escape certain limitations of the female role (see Delcourt 1961:84–102; Rousselle 1988:187; Castelli 1982; Anson 1974; Meeks 1974; Brown 1988; Salisbury 1991). (In this regard, the several early Christian women who cross-dressed or otherwise altered their gender status may be important for understanding patterns of female gender-crossing in the Balkans and southern Iraq described by Dickemann and Westphal-Hellbusch in this volume.)

Consequently, the relationship between Christianity and Cybele worship was more complex than one of antagonism alone, although there was plenty of that. In some areas, interesting syncreticisms of Christianity and Cybele-Attis worship developed. Montanism, the "Phrygian heresy," which arose in Anatolia in the mid-second century C.E., was fomented by two female prophets, one of whom had visions of Christ as a woman (Schepelern 1929:10–33, 53–59, 89–91, 130–59). Hippolytus, writing in the first half of the third century, described at length the cult of the Naasenes in which the worship of Attis and Jesus were thoroughly merged. He reports that its followers also participated in the mysteries of Cybele as if they were emasculated persons—that is, *galli* (*Ref.* 5.9.74–81).

In Syria, uneven conversion resulted in a long period of pagan-Christian coexistence (Drijvers 1982; see also Kaegi 1966). Although Bardesanes/Bar Dai-san (154–222 C.E.) endorsed King Abgar of Edessa's ban on castration, a measure undoubtedly aimed at the worship of Atargatis/Dea Syria, his own writings show signs of an attempt to adapt her worship to Christianity (Drijvers 1980, 77–79; Drijvers 1982, 38; Segal 1970:56). At Hieropolis the sanctuary of Dea Syria survived until 384 C.E., while at Edessa pagan shrines were not destroyed until the time of Bishop Rabbula (d. 436) (Drijvers 1982:39). Even so, at the end of the fifth century pagan spring festivals were still being observed in that city, and in 639, when the Muslim army arrived, it still had an organized pagan community (Segal 1970:108). In nearby Harran, the syncretistic cult of the Sabians/Sabaeans, in which castration and other elements of pagan religion played a role, flourished well into Islamic times (Pellat 1978:1088a, 1090b; Nöldeke 1907:151–52; see also Gündüz 1994). At the same time, it appears that many individuals in the Christian east who might have joined the cult of the mother goddess found an outlet for their religious impulses in Christian asceticism instead (see R. Murray 1982:7). In Syria the practice of religious self-castration continued without interruption, and Christian fathers found it necessary to pass canon laws against it.[21] Yet other problems were posed by the conversion of individuals who were already eunuchs, some of whom became quite prominent in church circles.

Another dimension of folk third-gender roles survived in the performers and entertainers (and often prostitutes) known as *mukhannathūn* (sg. *mukhannath*), a term defined by the ninth-century Qu'rān commentator, Bukhāri, as "men who wish to resemble women, and women who wish to resemble men" (Pellat 1992:156; Rowson 1991:672). As Rowson (1991) relates, in the first Islamic century networks of these non-masculine singers, dancers, and entertainers were prominent in Medina and Mecca. Their appearance in prophetic *hadīth* suggests that their role was well-defined in pre-Islamic Arabian society. They have been compared to the *khāwal* in Egypt described in the nineteenth century, who danced at circumcisions, weddings and births (Patai 1959:171–73; Rowson 1991:69)—much as *hijra* do in India and Pakistan and the *mustachnet*, or transvestite dancers, in southern Iraq (see Westphal-Hellbusch's chapter; Fernea 1969, 145–56).

CONCLUSION

Islam sustained patterns of status-differentiated and gender-defined homosexuality that had been part of the cultural heritage of the Oikoumene for millennia. This contrasts sharply with the history of the Christian West, where all forms of homosexuality were suppressed beginning in late antiquity. Both status- and gender-differentiated patterns were evaluated in terms of the single paradigm of sodomy. Driven underground, gender- and status-differentiated homosexuality met up, as it were, in the sexual subcultures that developed in European cities (exactly when—whether in the late nineteenth century, the early modern period, the Renaissance, or even in the middle ages—is the subject of ongoing debate). The conflation of status-based and gender-based homosexuality is what gave birth in the late nineteenth century to the "homosexual species," a category of persons defined in terms of their sexual object choice without reference to gender difference, social status, or sexual positions.

Today "homosexualization," the social forces and historical events that produce homosexual identity, is spreading throughout the world. This, together with internal forces within Islamic societies—in particular, the conjunction of Islamic fundamentalism and the emergence of modern nation-states with all their pervasive means of social regulation—make the future of traditional forms of homosexuality in the Oikoumene region uncertain for the first time in their long history.

Notes

1. While I agree with Foucault, Halperin, Winkler, and others that a concept of orientation was not part of the official vocabulary of ancient Greek sexuality, this fact on its own does not allow us to conclude that no one could or did conceptualize such a possibility in those times or that relations between males close in age never occurred. Similarly, to show that Greek youths and women were not believed to enjoy the experience of penetration is not to prove that no youths or women did enjoy such contact. (Richlin 1993 points out Halperin's inconsistencies on this point—sometimes he attributes desire to youths, sometimes he denies it.) As Winkler puts it, "Simply knowing the protocols does not tell us how people behaved" (1990:45). In the end, given the human propensity to deviate from or exceed, or simply misunderstand, formal rules and regulations, drawing overly sharp distinctions based on official beliefs becomes hairsplitting. Only the most mechanistic functionalism would lead to the conclusion that behavior and emotion were unilineally determined by what a society "believed" or did not believe—or project "societies" as entities that hold beliefs. Further, if practices vary from ideals, if significant and regular contradictions between sexual ideology and sexual practice exist, then a more complex model of causation is needed than one in which normative social forces are the only variable.

2. The distinction between "state" and "folk" third gender is based on concepts developed by Harry Hay in the 1950s. I am indebted to him for sharing his unpublished research notes.

3. A similar effeminization of boys and a slide from age-based to gender-defined homosexuality occured around 1700 in China and Japan (S. Murray 1992:146).

4. See, for example, Cicero's denunciation of Mark Antony (*Philippicae*, 2.18.44–20.77). On Cicero's use of anti-homosexual invective, see Lilja (1983:88–97, 125), MacMullen (1982:490–91), and Richlin (1992:86–104). The homosexual jokes in Plautus and other Latin authors are always directed at the male who takes the receptive role (Lilja 1983:32). Still, there appears to have been no law to apply against such men comparable to that on which Aeschines's prosecution of Timarkhos was based (Boswell 1980:77; Lilja 1983:93–94, 125). Richlin argues that in imperial times passive homosexuals could be struck from the list of citizens by the censors and lose certain civil

rights, their rights in praetorian courts could be restricted, and they could be charged with *stuprum* under the *lex Scantinia* (1993:555–71), but there is little evidence that any of these measures were used for this purpose.

5. The belief that "our people" (whatever people that is) didn't engage in homosexuality, but learned it from x (where x are aliens regarded with contempt) is very common, as is the view that if people learn of the possibility of homosexuality, they will be unable to resist engaging in it, which is the continued rationale for blocking any representations of homosexuality without condemnation in contemporary U.S. society. I do not mean to suggest that pederasty really diffused from Persia to the Arabs, although some Greek ideas about it probably did—SM.

6. See Duchesne-Guillemin (1966:149ff), Darmesteter (1880:101–2), Surieu (1967: 16). Zaehner (1961:27,171) questions any real application. Zoroastrianism was a sect, albeit an increasingly influential one before the Arab conquest of Persia, not a state religion, except briefly. Greenberg suggested that abhorrence of pederasty may have served as an ethnic marker for Parsis (contemporary Zoroastrians) in contrast to Muslims, as it did earlier for Parthians in contrast to their Macedonian conquerors (1988:188–9). Some scholars (viz., Wikander 1938; Widengren 1969:52) have argued that there were earlier Persian pederastic initiation rites, though the European interpretations of proto–Indo-European pederastic initiation has been rejected by English-language classicists, most notably Dover (1988)—SM.

7. Becoming a *kinaidos* was a condition to which all Greek males were at risk should they fail to safeguard their masculinity. This belief made gender-defined homosexuality an indispensable adjunct to age-defined homosexuality. Although Greek terminology lacked a generic category for all forms of same-sex object choice comparable to modern homosexuality, such a categorization is incipient in the perennial fear of Greek men that *paiderastia*, if pursued beyond the bounds of convention, could lead to another, deviant form of homosexuality—the gender-defined identity of the *kinaidos*.

8. Sources for the following summary of the *gala* include Hartmann 1960:129–46; Gelb 1975; Renger 1969:187–95; Krecher 1966:27–42; and Henshaw 1994:84–96.

9. Other gender-variant roles include the *sag-ur-sag, pi-li-pi-li/pilpilū, sinnišānu* and *parrū* (Civil s.v.; Henshaw 1994:284–311; Bottéro and Petschow 1975; Lambert 1992: 149–53).

10. Texts also describe ritual games on behalf of the goddess and the use of bawdy speech (Kilmer 1991; Harris 1991:273). The *galli*, too, were reported to lampoon their goddess (*Hephaestion Scholia*, 12.38.13).

11. Henshaw finds no evidence that *qedeshīm* or their female counterparts practiced "sacred prositítution," despite the common assumption that they did (1994:12, 220–22, 233, 243, 305).

12. A priest of "Kubabat" is mentioned in cuneiform records from Caesarea (Hawkins 1981:257). A few figurines appear to represent male functionaries (Naumann 1983:pl. 7:1; Roller 1988:44; van Loon 1991:34, 47, pl. XLIIb).

13. Ancient sources on Pessinus include Polybius, 31.37.4–5; Cicero, *Pro Sestio*, 56, 58, 59; Diodorus Siculus, 3.59.8; Herodian, 1.11.1–4; Pausanias, 1.4.5–6; and Strabo, 12.567 (12.5.3). See also Lenaghan 1969:130–33, 134; Vermaseren 1977:26–27, 98–99; and Graillot 1912:19, 316, 348–55.

14. For example, Theopompus, 1.740 (=*Fragmenta comicorum Graecorum*, 2.800); Hermesianax (Pausanias, 17.9–10); *Anthologia Palatina*, 6.217–20, 237; Neanthes of Cyzicus (Harpocration s.v., *Attēs*); Manetho, *Apotelesmaticorum*, 4.218–23; 5.177–80; 6[3].295–99; and Theocritus, 20.40.

15. On the Roman worship of Cybele, see Bremmer 1979; Carcopino 1941:49-171; Fishwick 1966; Graillot 1912:25-69,74-78; Hepding 1903:142-60; Sanders 1972:1001-2; Showerman 1900:46-59; G. Thomas 1984:1502-8, 1518-21; Vermaseren 1977:38-41, 96, 113-24.

16. Literary references: Catullus, 63; Lucretius, *De Rerum Natura*, 2.595ff; Varro, *Menippearum fragmenta*, 119–21, 131–32, 149–50, 364. Artifacts: Vermaseren 1977:43, 56, 114.

17. The following description of the *hijra* is based primarily on Nanda 1990. See also Penzer 1924:319–29; Shah 1961:1325–23; Sinha 1967:168–76; Sharma 1984:381–89. For historical references, see Dubois 1906:311–12; Faridi 1899:21–22; Kirpárám 1901:506–8; Saletore 1974:43–47, 93–95, 192–222. Related roles in other parts of India include the *jogappa* in southern India and Kalhapur (Bradford 1983; Enthoven [1915] 1976:app. xv), the *ali* in Tamilnadu (Hiltebeitel 1980:163), and the priests of the goddesses Chatushsrngi at Poona and Huligamma in Karnataka (Hutton 1946:142). These and similar roles throughout southeast Asia do not involve castration.

18. In current terminology, the *hijra* represent a third *sex*, based on their anatomical difference, most of whom have adopted a feminine *gender*. According to Pimpley and Sharma (1985), however, who appear to be describing practices in the Punjab, a system of gender differentiation exists within some *hijra* collectives. Less feminine *hijra* are given masculine names and perform the heavier chores, while others have female names and specialize in traditional female activities. The overall organization of the collective, these authors argue, is that of a matrilineal, matrilocal household.

19. Clement of Alexandria cites the followers of Basilides regarding "eunuchs from birth" who have a "physical aversion in relation to women" and "do well not to marry" (*Stromateis*, 3.1).

20. Other relevant Sanskrit terms include *tṛtīyā prakṛti*, or "third nature" (*Kāmasūtra*, 2.9; *Mahābhārata*, 4.59 [northern variant]; *Ubhayābhisārikā,* v. 21), *strīrūpini/strīpumān*, "woman-man," (*Kāmasūtra*, 2.9; *Mahābhārata*, 5.189.5; *Śuka-saptati* [Mathur 1971: 179–81]; Artola 1975:65) and *napuṃsaka*, "not male" (*Naṭya-śāstra*, 24.68-69; *Ayurveda* [in Sethi 1970:42]).

21. For example, the Apostolic Canons 21–24; Commands of Mar Rabbula 55 (Vööbus 1960:4); Synod of Mar Isaac 2, Synod of Mar Ezechiel 2, and Canons of Mar Aba 20 (Chabot 1902:263, 375, 558). See also Nöldeke (1907) and Sanders (1978: 1069–71).

References

Adam, Barry D. 1986. "Age, structure, and sexuality: Reflections on the anthropological evidence on homosexual relations." In *The many faces of homosexuality: Anthropological approaches to homosexual behavior*, ed. Evelyn Blackwood, 19–33. New York: Harrington Park Press.

Anson, John. 1974. "The female transvestite in early monasticism: The origin and development of a motif." *Viator* 5:1–32.

Artola, George T. 1975. "The transvestite in Sanskrit story and drama." *Annals of Oriental Research of the University of Madras* 25:57–68.

Boswell, John. 1980. *Christianity, social tolerance, and homosexuality: Gay people in western Europe from the beginning of the Christian era to the fourteenth century.* Chicago: University of Chicago Press.

———. 1990. "Concepts, experience, and sexuality." *differences* 2(1):67–87.

Bottéro, J., and H. Petschow. 1975. "Homosexualität." Vol. 4, *Reallexikon der Assyriologie und vorderasiatischen Archäologie*, ed. Dietz O. Edzard, 459–68. Berlin: Walter de Gruyter.

Bradford, Nicholas. 1983. "Transgenderism and the cult of Yellamma: Heat, sex, and sickness in south Indian ritual." *Journal of Anthropological Research* 39(3):307–22.

Bremmer, Jan. 1979. "The legend of Cybele's arrival in Rome." In *Studies in Hellenistic Religions*, ed. M. J. Vermaseren, 9–22. Leiden: Brill.

———. 1980. "An enigmatic Indo-European rite: Pederasty." *Arethusa* 13(2):279–98.

Brooks, Beatrice A. 1941. "Fertility cult functionaries in the Old Testament." *Journal of Biblical Literature* 60:227–53.

Brown, Peter. 1982. *Society and the holy in late antiquity.* Berkeley: University of California Press.

———. 1988. *The body and society: Men, women, and sexual renunciation in early Christianity.* New York: Columbia University Press.

Carcopino, Jérôme. 1941. *Aspects mystiques de la Rome païenne,* 6th ed. Paris: L'artisan du livre.

Cartledge, Paul. 1981. "The politics of Spartan pederasty." *Cambridge Philological Society Proceedings* 27:17–36.

Castelli, E. 1982. "Virginity and its meaning for women's sexuality in early Christianity." *Journal of Feminist Studies in Religion* 2(1):61–88.

Chabot, J. B., ed. 1902. *Synodicon orientale ou recueil des synodes nestoriens. Notices et extraits des manuscrits de la Bibliothèque Nationale et autres bibliothèques.* Paris: Klincksieck.

Civil, Miguel et al., eds. 1956–. *The Assyrian dictionary of the Oriental Institute of the University of Chicago.* Chicago and Glückstadt, Germany: Oriental Institute and J. J. Augustin.

Clarke, John R. 1993. "The Warren cup and the contexts for representations of male-to-male lovemaking in Augustan and early Julio-Claudian art." *Art Bulletin* 75(2): 275–94.

Cohen, Mark. 1974. *Balag-Compositions: Sumerian lamentation liturgies of the second and first millennium B.C. Sources from the Ancient Near East,* Vol. 1, fasc. 2. Malibu, CA: Undena.

Coser, Lewis A. 1964. "The political functions of eunuchism." *American Sociological Review* 29(6):880–85.

Crompton, Louis. 1994. "An army of lovers: The sacred band of Thebes." *History Today* 44(11):23–29.

Dalley, Stephanie, trans. 1991. *Myths from Mesopotamia: Creation, the flood, Gilgamesh, and others.* Oxford: Oxford University Press.

Daniel, Marc. 1991. "Arab civilization and male love." In *Gay roots: Twenty years of Gay Sunshine, an anthology of gay history, sex, politics, and culture,* ed. Winston Leyland. San Francisco: Gay Sunshine Press.

Darmesteter, James. 1880. *The Zend-Avesta.* Oxford: Clarendon Press.

Delcourt, Marie. 1961. *Hermaphrodite: Myths and rites of the bisexual figure in classical antiquity,* trans. Jennifer Nicholson. London: Studio.

Dover, Kenneth J. 1978. *Greek homosexuality.* Cambridge: Harvard University Press.

———. 1988. "Greek homosexuality and initiation." In *The Greeks and their legacy.* Vol. 2, *Collected papers: Prose literature, history, society, transmission, influence,* 115–34. Oxford: Basil Blackwell.

Drijvers, Hans J. W. 1980. *Cults and beliefs at Edessa.* Leiden: Brill.

———. 1982. "The persistence of pagan cults and practices in Christian Syria." In *East of Byzantium: Syria and Armenia in the formative period,* ed. Nina G. Garsoïan, Thomas F. Mathews, and Robert W. Thomson, 35–43. Washington, DC: Dumbarton Oaks.

Dubois, J. A. 1906. *Hindu manners, customs and ceremonies,* trans. H. K. Beauchamp. Oxford: Clarendon Press.

Duchesne-Guillemin, Jacques. 1966. *Symbols and values in Zoroastrianism.* New York: Harper and Row.

Ebden, H. 1856. "A few notes, with reference to 'the eunuchs,' to be found in the large households of the state of Rajpootana." *Indian Annals of Medical Science* 3:520–25.

Enthoven, R. E. [1915] 1976. *Folklore of the Konkan, compiled from materials collected by the late A. M. T. Jackson, Indian Civil Service.* Delhi: Cosmo.

Fantham, Elaine. 1991. *"Stuprum*: Public attitudes and penalties for sexual offences in republican Rome." *Échos du Monde Classique/Classical View* 35 (n.s. 10): 267–91.

Farber-Flügge, Gertrud. 1973. *Der Mythos Inanna und Enki unter desonderer Berücksichtigung der Liste der* m e. Rome: Biblical Institute Press.

Faridi, Fazálullah L. 1899. "The Musalmáns." In *Gujarát population: Musalmans and Parsis.* Vol. 9, pt. 2, *Gazetteer of the Bombay presidency,* ed. J. M. Campbell, 21–22. Bombay: Government Central Press.

Farnell, Lewis R. 1896. *Cults of the Greek states.* Vol. 1. Oxford: Clarendon Press.

Fernea, Elizabeth Warnock. 1969. *Guests of the sheik: An ethnography of an Iraqi village.* Garden City, NY: Anchor Books.

Fishwick, Duncan. 1966. "The *cannophori* and the march festival of Magna Mater." *Transactions and Proceedings of the American Philological Association* 97:193–202.

Foster, Benjamin. 1993. *Before the muses: An anthology of Akkadian literature.* Vol. 1. Bethesda, MD: CDL.

Gasparro, Giulia S. 1985. *Soteriology and mystic aspects in the cult of Cybele and Attis.* Vol. 103. Études Préliminaires aux Religions Orientales dans l'Empire Romain. Leiden: Brill.

Gelb, I. J. 1975. "Homo ludens in early Mesopotamia." In *Haec studia orientalia professori Assyriologia, et filologiae Semiticae in Universitate Helsingensi Armas I. Salonen, S.Q.A.: Anno 1975 sexagenario,* 43–76. Studia Orientalia 46. Amsterdam: Elsevier North-Holland.

Gleason, Maud W. 1990. "The semiotics of gender: Physiognomy and self-fashioning in the second century C.E." In *Before sexuality: The construction of erotic experience in the ancient Greek world,* ed. D. M. Halperin, J. J. Winkler, and F. I. Zeitlin, 389–415. Princeton: Princeton University Press.

Golden, Mark. 1984. "Slavery and homosexuality at Athens." *Phoenix* 38(4):309–78

Gordon, Edmund. 1959. *Sumerian proverbs: Glimpses of everyday life in ancient Mesopotamia.* Philadelphia: University Museum.

Graillot, Henri. 1912. *Le culte de Cybele, mere des dieus, a Rome at dans l'empire romain.* Vol. 107. Bibliothèque des Écoles Françaises d'Athènes et de Rome. Paris: Fontemoing.

Gray, Louis H. 1912. "Eunuch." Vol. 5, *Encyclopaedia of religion and ethics,* ed. James Hastings, 579–85. New York: Scribner's.

Grayson, A. Kirk, and Donald B. Redford, eds. 1973. *Papyrus and tablet.* Englewood Cliffs, NJ: Prentice-Hall.

Greenberg, David F. 1988. *The construction of homosexuality.* Chicago: University of Chicago Press.

Griffith, F. L., ed., 1898. *The Petrie papyri: Hieratic papyri from Kahun and Gurob.* Vol. 1. London: Bernard Quaritch.

Groneberg, B. 1986. "Die sumerisch-akkadische Inanna/Ištar: Hermaphroditos?" *Die Welt des Orients* 17:25–46.

Guarducci, M. 1970. "Cibele in un' epigrafe arcaica di Locri Epizefirī." *Klio* 52:133–38.

Gündüz, Şinasi. 1994. *The knowledge of life: The origins and early history of the Mandaeans and their relation to the Sabians of the Qur'ān and to the Harranians.* Journal of Semitic Studies Supplement 3. Oxford: Oxford University Press.

Gurney, O. R. 1977. *Some aspects of Hittite religion.* Oxford: Oxford University Press.

Halperin, David M. 1990. *One hundred years of homosexuality and other essays on Greek love.* New York: Routledge.

Hansen, Esther V. 1971. *The Attalids of Pergamon.* 2d ed. Ithaca, NY: Cornell University Press.

Harris, Rivkah. 1991. "Inanna-Ishtar as paradox and a coincidence of opposites." *History of Religions* 30(3):261–78.

Hartmann, Henrike. 1960. *Die Musik der Sumerischen Kultur.* Frankfurt am Main.

Hatzfeld, J. 1920. "Inscriptions de Lagina en Carie." *Bulletin de Correspondence Hellénique* 44:70–100.

Hawkins, J. D. 1981. "Kubaba. A. Philologisch." Vol. 6, *Reallexikon der Assyriologie und vorderasiatischen Archäologie,* ed. Dietz O. Edzard, 257–61. Berlin: Walter de Gruyter.

Henderson, Jeffrey. 1975. *The maculate muse: Obscene language in Attic comedy.* New Haven: Yale University Press.

Henshaw, Richard A. 1994. *Male and female, the cultic personnel: The Bible and the rest of the ancient Near East.* Princeton Theological Monograph Series 31. Allison Park, PA: Pickwick Publications.

Hepding, Hugo. 1903. *Attis: Seine Mythen und sein Kult.* Gieszen: J. Richersche.

Herdt, Gilbert H. 1993. *Ritualized homosexuality in Melanesia.* 2d ed. Berkeley: University of California Press.

Hiltebeitel, Alf. 1980. "Śiva, the goddess, and the disguises of the Pandavas and Draupadi." *History of Religions* 20(1/2):147–74.

Hoffner, Jr., Harry A. 1973. "Incest, sodomy and bestiality in the ancient Near East." In *Orient and occident: Essays presented to Cyrus H. Gordon on the occasion of his sixty-fifth birthday,* ed. Harry A. Hoffner, Jr., 81–90. Alter Orient und Altes Testament 22. Neukirchen-Vluyn: Neukirchener.

Hopkins, Keith. 1978. *Conquerors and slaves: Sociological studies in Roman history.* Vol. 1. Cambridge: Cambridge University Press.

———. 1980. "Brother-sister marriage in Roman Egypt." *Comparative Studies in Society and History* 22(3):303–54.

Hutton, J. H. 1946. *Caste in India: Its nature, function, and origins.* Cambridge: Cambridge University Press.

Jacobsen, Thorkild. 1976. *The treasures of darkness: A history of Mesopotamian religion.* New Haven: Yale University Press.

———. 1987. *The harps that once . . . : Sumerian poetry in translation.* New Haven: Yale University Press.

James, E. O. 1959. *The cult of the mother-goddess: An archaeological and documentary study.* London: Thames and Hudson.

Kaegi, Walter E. 1966. "The fifth-century twilight of Byzantine paganism." *Classica et Mediaevalia* 27:243–75.

Kilmer, Anne D. 1972. "The Mesopotamian concept of overpopulation." *Orientalia,* n.s. 41:160–77.

———. 1991. "An oration on Babylon." *Altorientalische Forschungen* 18(1):9–22.

Kirpárám, Bhimbhái. 1901. "Gujarát population: Hindus." Vol. 9, pt. 1, *Gazetteer of the Bombay Presidency,* ed. J. M. Campbell, 506–8. Bombay: Government Central Press.

Koehl, Robert B. 1986. "The chieftain cup and a Minoan rite of passage." *Journal of Hellenic Studies* 106:99–110.

Kramer, Samuel N. 1981a. "BM 29616: The fashioning of the gala." *Acta Sumerologica* 3:1–12.

———. 1981b. *History begins at Sumer: Thirty-nine firsts in man's recorded history.* Rev. ed. Philadelphia: University of Philadelphia Press.

Krecher, Joachim. 1966. *Sumerische Kultlyrik.* Wiesbaden: Harrassowitz.

Kroll, Wilhelm. 1921. "Kinaidos." Vol. 21, pt. 1, *Paulys Realencyclopädie der Classischen Altertumswissenschaft,* ed. Georg Wissowa, 459–62. Rev. ed. München: Alfred Druckenmüller im Artermis.

Lambert, Wilfried G. 1960. *Babylonian wisdom literature.* Oxford: Clarendon Press.

———. 1992. "Prostitution." *Xenia* 32:127–57.

Le Bas, M. Philippe. 1888. *Asie Mineure.* Pt. 5, *Voyage archéologique en Grèce et en Asie Mineure, 1842–1844,* ed. Salomon Reinach. Paris: Firmin-Didot.

Lenaghan, John O. 1969. *A commentary on Cicero's oration* De Haruspicum Responso. *Studies in Classical Literature* 5. The Hague: Mouton.

Lilja, Saara. 1983. *Homosexuality in republican and Augustan Rome, Commentationes Humanarum Litterarum* 74. Helsinki: Finnish Society of Sciences and Letters.

MacMullen, Ramsay. 1982. "Roman attitudes to Greek love." *Historia* 31(4):484–502.

Manniche, Lise. 1977. "Some aspects of ancient Egyptian sexual life." *Acta Orientalia* 38:11–23.

Marmom, Shaun. 1995. *Eunuchs and sacred boundaries in Islamic society.* Oxford: Oxford University Press.

Mathur, G. L., trans. 1971. *Erotic Indian tales from the Sanskrit classic Suksaptati.* Delhi: Hind.

Meeks, Wayne A. 1974. "The image of the androgyne: Some uses of a symbol in earliest Christianity." *History of Religions* 13(3):165–208.

Meissner, Bruno. 1907. "Homosexualität bei den Assyrern." *Assyriologische Studien IV.* Vol. 12, pt. 3, Mitteilungen der Vorderasiatischen Gesellschaft. Berlin: Peiser.

Menzel, Brigitte. 1981. *Assyrische Tempel.* Vol. 1. Rome: Biblical Institute Press.

Mez, Adam. 1937. *The renaissance of Islam.* Patna: Jubilee.

Mitra, Nirmal. 1983. "The Making of a 'Hijra.'" *Onlooker National Newsmagazine,* 28 February:14–25.

Murray, Robert. 1975. *Symbols of church and kingdom: A study in early Syriac tradition.* Cambridge: Cambridge University Press.

————. 1982. "The characteristics of the earliest Syriac Christianity." In *East of Byzantium: Syria and Armenia in the formative period,* ed. Nina G. Garsoïan, Thomas F. Mathews, and Robert W. Thomson, 3–16. Washington, DC: Dumbarton Oaks.

Murray, Stephen O. 1992. *Oceanic homosexualities.* New York: Garland.

Nanda, Serena. 1990. *Neither man nor woman: The hijra of India.* Belmont, CA: Wadsworth.

Naumann, Friederike. 1983. *Die Ikonographie der Kybele in der Phrygischen und der Griechischen Kunst.* Istanbluer Mitteilungen 28. Tubingen: Ernst Wasmuth.

Nöldeke, Th. 1907. "Die Selbstentmannung bei den Syrern." *Archiv fur Religionswissenshaft* 10(1):150–52.

O'Flaherty, Wendy D. 1980. *Women, androgynes, and other mythical beasts.* Chicago: University of Chicago Press.

Oppenheim, A. L. 1956. "The interpretation of dreams in the ancient Near East." *Transactions of the American Philosophical Society* 46:179–374.

Parsons, Peter H. 1971. "A Greek Satyricon?" *Bulletin of the Institute of Classical Studies* 18:53–68.

Patai, Raphael. 1959. *Sex and family in the Bible.* Garden City, NY: Doubleday.

Pellat, Charles, et al. 1978."Khāṣī." *Encyclopedia of Islam,* 4:1087–93. Leiden: Brill.

————. 1992. "Liwāt." In *Sexuality and eroticism among males in Moslem societies,* ed. Arno Schmitt and Jehoeda Sofer, 151–64. Binghamton, NY: Harrington Park Press.

Penzer, N. M., ed. 1924. *The ocean of story, being C. H. Tawney's translation of Somadeva's Kathā Sarit Sāgara (or Ocean of streams of story).* Vol. 3. London: Sawyer.

Pimpley, P. N., and S. K. Sharma. 1985. "Hijaras: A study of an atypical role." *Avadh Journal of Social Sciences* 2:381–89.

Preston, Laurence W. 1987. "A right to exist: Eunuchs and the state in nineteenth-century India." *Modern Asian Studies* 21(2):371–87.

Ramsay, W. M. 1897. *The cities and bishoprics of Phrygia.* Vol. 1. Oxford: Clarendon Press.

Reisman, D. D. 1973. "Iddin-Dagan's sacred marriage hymn." *Journal of Cuneiform Studies* 25:185–202.

Renger, Johannes. 1969. "Untersuchungen zum Priestertum der altbabylonischen Zeit, 2. Teil." *Zeitschrift für Assyriologie* 59 (n.f. 25):104–230.

Richlin, Amy. 1992. *The garden of Priapus: Sexuality and aggression in Roman humor.* Rev. ed. New York: Oxford University Press.

———. 1993. "Not before homosexuality: The materiality of the *cinaedus* and the Roman law against love between men." *Journal of the History of Sexuality* 3(3):523–73.

Ringrose, Kathryn M. 1994. "Living in the shadows: Eunuchs and gender in Byzantium." In *Third sex, third gender: Beyond sexual dimorphism in culture and history*, ed. Gilbert Herdt, 85–109. New York: Zone Books.

Ritter, Hellmut 1955. *Das Meer der Seele.* Leiden: Brill.

Robinson, James M., ed. 1977. *The Nag Hammadi library in English.* San Francisco: Harper and Row.

Roller, Lynn E. 1988. "Phrygian myth and cult." *Source: Notes in the History of Art* 7(3/4): 44–50.

———. 1994. "Attis on Greek votive monuments: Greek god or Phrygian?" *Hesperia* 63(2):245–62.

Römer, W. H. Ph. 1965. *Sumerische Königshymnen der Isin-Zeit.* Documenta et Monumenta Orientis Antiqui 13. Leiden: Brill.

Roscoe, Will. 1994. "How to become a berdache: Toward a unified analysis of multiple genders." In *Third sex, third gender: Beyond sexual dimorphism in culture and history*, ed. Gilbert Herdt, 329–72. New York: Zone Books.

———. 1996. "Priests of the goddess: Gender transgression in ancient religion." *History of Religions* 35(3):295–330.

Rose, H. A., comp. 1911. *A glossary of the tribes and castes of the Punjab and North-West Frontier Province.* Vol. 2. Lahore, Pakistan: Civil and Military Gazette Press.

Rousselle, Aline. 1988. *Porneia: On desire and the body in antiquity*, trans. Felicia Pheasant. New York: Blackwell.

Rowson, Everett K. 1991. "The effeminates of early Medina." *Journal of the American Oriental Society* 111(4):671–93.

Saletore, R. N. 1974. *Sex life under Indian rulers.* Delhi: Hind Pocket.

Salisbury, Joyce E. 1991. *Church fathers, independent virgins.* London: Verso.

Salonen, Erkki. 1970. *Über das Erwerbsleben im Alten Mesopotamien: Untersuchungen zu den Akkadischen Berufsnamen.* Vol. 1. Studia Orientalia 41. Helsinki. suomalaisen Kirjallisunden Kivjapainoi.

Salunke, G. R. 1976. "The cult of the hijras." *Illustrated Weekly of India*, 8 August: 16–21.

Sanders, G. M. 1972. "Gallos." Vol. 8, *Reallexikon für Antike und Christentum*, 984–1034. Bonn: Universität Bonn.

———. 1978. "Les galles et le gallat devant l'opinion chrétienne." *Hommages à Maarten J. Vermaseren*, ed. Margreet de Boer and T. A. Edridge, 1062–91. Vol. 3. Leiden: Brill.

Schepelern, Wilhelm. 1929. *Der Montanismus und die Phrygischen Kulte: Eine Religionsgeschichtliche Untersuchung.* Tübingen: Mohr [Paul Siebeck].

Segal, J. B. 1970. *Edessa: "The blessed city."* Oxford: Clarendon Press.

Sethi, Patanjali. 1970. "The hijras." *Illustrated Weekly of India*, 13 December:40–45.

Shah, A. M. 1961. "A note on the hijadās of Gujarat." *American Anthropologist* 63:1325–30.

Sharma, Satish K. 1984. "Eunuchs: Past and present." *Eastern Anthropologist* 37(4): 381–89.

Showerman, Grant. 1900. "Was Attis at Rome under the republic?" *Transactions and Proceedings of the American Philological Association* 31:46–59.

Sinha, A. P. 1967. "Procreation among the eunuchs." *Eastern Anthropologist* 20(2): 168–76.

Sjöberg, Å. W. 1975. "in-nin Šà-gur-ra: A hymn to the goddess Inanna." *Zeitschrift für Assyriologie* 65(2):161–253.

Steinkeller, Piotr. 1992. *Third-millennium legal and administrative texts in the Iraq Museum, Baghdad.* Winona Lake, IN: Eisenbrauns.

Stevenson, Walter. 1995. "The rise of eunuchs in Greco-Roman antiquity." *Journal of the History of Sexuality* 5(4):495–511.

Surieu, Robert. 1967. *Sarve naz: An essay on love and the representation of erotic themes in ancient Iran.* Geneva: Nagel.

Sutton, Jr., Robert F. 1992. "Pornography and persuasion on Attic pottery." In *Pornography and representation in Greece and Rome,* ed. Amy Richlin, 3–37. New York: Oxford University Press.

Sweet, Michael J., and Leonard Zwilling. 1993. "The first medicalization: The taxonomy and etiology of queerness in classical Indian medicine." *Journal of the History of Sexuality* 3(4):590–607.

Thomas, D. Winton. 1960. "*Kelebh* 'Dog': Its origin and some usages of it in the Old Testament." *Vetus Testamentum* 10:410–27.

Thomas, Garth. 1984. "Magna Mater and Attis." In *Religion,* ed. Wolfgang Haase, 1500–35. Vol. 17, pt. 3, *Aufstieg und Niedergang der römischen Welt.* Vol. 2, ed. Hildegrad Temporino and Wolfang Haase. Berlin and New York: Walter de Gruyter.

Tracy, Valerie A. 1976. "Roman dandies and transvestites." *Échos du Monde Classique/ Classical Views* 20:60–63.

van Loon, Maurits N. 1985. *Anatolia in the second millennium B.C.* Iconography of Religions, Section XV: Mesopotamia and the Near East, fasc. 12. Leiden: Brill.

———. 1991. *Anatolia in the earlier first millennium B.C.* Iconography of Religions, Section XV: Mesopotamia and the Near East, fasc. 13. Leiden: Brill.

Vermaseren, Maarten J. 1977. *Cybele and Attis: The myth and the cult.* London: Thames and Hudson.

Verstraete, Beert C. 1980. "Slavery and the social dynamics of male homosexual relations in ancient Rome." *Journal of Homosexuality* 5(3):227–36.

Veyne, Paul. 1985. "Homosexuality in ancient Rome." In *Western sexuality: Practice and precept in past and present times,* ed. Philippe Ariès and André Béjin, 26–35. Oxford: Basil Blackwell.

Vööbus, Arthur, ed. 1960. "Syriac and Arabic documents regarding legislation relative to Syrian asceticism." *Papers of the Estonian Theological Society in Exile* 11.

Widengren, Gro. 1969. *Der Feudalismus in alten Iran: Männerbund, Gefolgswesen, Feudalismis der iranischen Gesselschaft im Hinblick aufdie ineogermanischen Verhältnisse.* Koln: Westdeutscher Verlag.

Wikander, Stig. 1938. *Der arische Männerbund.* Lund: H. Olson.

Winkler, John J. 1990. *The constraints of desire: The anthropology of sex and gender in ancient Greece.* New York: Routledge.

Wolkstein, Diane, and Samuel N. Kramer. 1983. *Inanna: Queen of heaven and earth, her stories and hymns from Sumer.* New York: Harper and Row.

Zaehner, R. C. 1961. *The dawn and twilight of Zoroastrianism.* London: Weidenfeld and Nicolson.

CHAPTER 4

Muhammad and Male Homosexuality

Jim Wafer

The *sharī'a*, or traditional law of Islam, is based on the Qur'ān, which was revealed to the Prophet Muhammad by God, and on the *hadīth*,[1] or "traditions," which are sayings attributed to the Prophet. These texts, from which Islamic policies toward homosexuality are derived, have been generally interpreted as condemning sexual relations between persons of the same sex.

In countries where Islam is the dominant religion, equal rights for gays and lesbians are unlikely to be achieved by means of secular arguments that do not pay due respect to the sacred sources of Islamic culture. Such an approach is more likely, as Khalid Duran points out, to result in a backlash against what is perceived as an attempt to impose the values of the former colonial powers (1993:186). Duran, who is one of the few Muslim scholars to have addressed homosexuality as a human rights issue, believes that the best hope for gays and lesbians in Muslim countries is to find some form of "theological accommodation" with Islam, based on the development of a "new *sharī'a* comparatively detached from the social climate of seventh-century Arabia" and emphasizing "the ethical principles of freedom and justice enunciated by the Prophet Muhammad in Mecca" (pp. 181, 195).

In this chapter I discuss the foundation texts of Islam, as a tentative step in the direction of such a "theological accommodation." My purpose is twofold. First, I examine these texts to determine whether they are as unambiguous and severe in their condemnation of homosexuality as is often supposed. Second, I consider the symbolic organization of male-male behavior[2] that is based on these texts, and show that it bears striking resemblances to that of cultures in which all males undergo an initiation that entails participation in homosexual practices. My intention in this second phase of the argument is not to satirize Islam, but rather to suggest that the masculine culture of Islam, by giving such a central place to homosexual imagery, involves itself in some profound contradictions. For Muslim scholars to address these contradictions would be a significant step in the development of the "new *sharī'a*" that Duran mentions.

HOMOSEXUALITY AND THE FOUNDATION TEXTS OF ISLAM

Jehoeda Sofer's survey of the laws pertaining to sodomy in Muslim states (1992) shows that there is no uniform legal position in relation to sex between males, even among states that have a penal code based on the *sharī'a*. However, in general, states that have instituted *sharī'a* law regard sodomy as illegal.

There are seven references in the Qur'ān to the story of Lot and "the people of Lot," that is, the Sodomites: 7:80–84; 11:77–83; 21:74; 22:43; 26:165–75; 27:56–59; 29:27–33. The destruction of the people of Lot is thought to be explicitly associated with their sexual practices:

What! Of all creatures do ye come
unto the males,
And leave the wives your Lord created for you?
Nay but ye are forward folk. . . .
And we rained on them a rain.
And dreadful is the rain
of those who have been warned.
(26.165–75; Pickthall translation; cf. Bell 1979:30)

There is, however, only one passage in the Qur'ān that can be interpreted as prescribing a particular legal position toward sexual relations between males within the *umma* (community of believers). It is translated by Pickthall as follows:

And as for the two of you who are guilty thereof,
punish them both.
And if they repent and improve, then let them be.
Lo! Allah is Relenting, Merciful. (4.16)

Ben Nahum's translation of the first part of this verse captures the sense in which it has traditionally been understood: "If two men commit an unchastity with each other, then punish them both" (Ben Nahum 1933:88).

The mildness of this passage contrasts markedly with quranic verses where severe punishments are prescribed for other crimes. (For example, Sūra 24:2 specifies a penalty of one hundred lashes for *zinā*, or "fornication.") This mildness has provided the basis for the view that the Prophet took a lenient attitude toward sex between males. Ben Nahum, for example, says that "it is obvious that the Prophet viewed the vice with philosophic indifference. Not only is the punishment not indicated—it was probably some public reproach or insult of a slight nature—but mere penitence sufficed to escape the punishment" (1933:88).

The *hadīth* and stories of the Prophet's life provide more detail about his supposed views on the matter, but they are inconsistent, and their authenticity is difficult to ascertain. It is thus possible for different writers to interpret the Prophet's position in rather different ways. On the one hand al-Tīfāshī, for example, says that "inverts"[3] were common in the Prophet's own tribe, the Quraysh, and the Prophet is supposed to have been particularly amused by the wit of one invert called Hayth. He is also reported to have permitted inverts to be in the same room as his wives when the latter were not veiled (Khawam 1971:255).[4]

On the other hand, according to the Hanbalite[5] Ibn al-Jawzi, the Prophet is supposed to have cursed the sodomite in several *hadīth* (Bellamy 1979:37). Commentators on the traditions denounce anal intercourse in the most extravagant terms, for example, "Whenever a male mounts another male, the throne of God trembles; the angels look on in loathing and say, Lord, why do you not command the earth to punish them and the heavens to rain stones on them?" (Bellamy 1979:37).

There is also a *hadīth* which recommends the stoning of "those who practice sodomy, both the passive and the active," although apparently its practical influence was negligible (Daniel 1975–76:no. 254, 87). Bellamy maintains that all the *hadīth* and most of the *akhbār* (anecdotes about the life of the Prophet) reported by the compilers he draws on insist on the death penalty for sodomy (1979:38). However there must, in fact, have been a diversity of opinion about the Prophet's views on the matter, since sex between males was treated differently by the various legal schools, on the basis of differing interpretations of the traditional literature. All the legal schools regard sex between males as unlawful, but they differ over the severity of the punishment. The Hanafite school (see note 4) maintains that it does not merit any physical punishment, because of the *hadīth* "Muslim blood can only be spilled because of adultery,[6] apostasy, or homicide" (Daniel 1975–76:no. 254, 88). The Hanbalites, on the other hand, believe that sex between males must be punished severely. They draw on the quranic references to the rain of stones that destroyed Lot's people, on the *hadīth* about stoning mentioned above, and on later authorities. The Prophet's successor and father-in-law Abu Bakr is supposed to have had a *lūtī* ("sodomite," from the Arabic work for Lot) burned alive.[7] And Ibn 'Abbās said that "the sodomite should be thrown from the highest building in the town and then stoned" (Bell 1979:31).

When we turn from the question of sex between males to that of love or attraction between males, the picture is a little different. There are a number of indications that the Prophet was not insensitive to the attractiveness of other males. In the Qur'ān, Paradise is furnished not only with female attendants (the *houri*) but also with immortal youths who serve as cupbearers to the faithful (Sūra 56:17–18; also see Ben Nahum 1933:89). There is also the *hadīth* (existing in a number of variants) according to which the Prophet said, "I have seen my Lord in a form of the greatest beauty, as a youth with abundant hair, seated on the throne of grace, clad in a garment of gold, on his hair a golden crown, on his feet sandals" (Wilson and Weischer 1978:8; also see Ritter 1928:257; Corbin 1969:272–77). The variants mention that the youth was in a heavenly garden; that his robe was green rather than gold; that he was beardless; or that he wore his cap awry (Ritter 1928:257; Corbin 1969:272; Schimmel 1982:67–68).

There are also a number of *hadīth* in which the Prophet warns his followers against gazing at youths precisely because they are so attractive. One of these is quoted in the *Arabian nights*: "Do not gaze at beardless youths, for they have eyes more tempting than the *hūrīs*" (Cardin 1984:73). Bell quotes another *hadīth* to the same effect: "According to Anas, the Prophet said: 'Keep not company with the sons of kings, for verily souls desire them in a way they do not desire freed slave-girls'" (1979:21; cf. Bellamy 1979:37).

It seems evident that, whatever susceptibility the Prophet may have had to the charms of beautiful youths, he disapproved of giving in to this attraction. But there is no evidence that he regarded the *attraction itself* as foreign to his own nature, rather the contrary. In fact later writers, such as Ibn al-Fārid, assumed that the Prophet himself loved another man, namely, his Companion Mu'adh ibn Jabal. The Prophet is reported to have said, "O Mu'adh, truly I love thee" (Arberry 1956:53n24). Ibn al-Fārid takes this relationship as a paradigm of chaste love between males.

THE SYMBOLIC ORGANIZATION OF RELATIONS
BETWEEN MALES IN ISLAM

Romantic love between males, provided it is chaste, appears to have had an accepted place in Islamic cultures, in a way it has rarely if ever had in Judeo-Christian ones. The Arabic writers who developed the genre that has become known as "love theory," such as Ibn Dawud and Ibn Hazm (see Giffen 1971; Arberry 1953; Crompton infra), treated the love of males and the love of females according to the same theoretical framework. Even the conservative love theorists who saw it as a dangerous source of temptation took it for granted that attraction between males is natural (Bell 1979:23, 26–27).

The reason that Arab cultures have so much difficulty dealing with sex between males is that a man's masculinity is compromised by taking the passive role in sexual relations; and for an Arab male to have his masculinity doubted is "a supreme affront," according to Chebel (1988:18; also see Schmitt 1992:7). The opposite side of this coin is that the image of the active partner is colored by "the role of homosexual assault in traditional societies with frozen codes of honor" (Duran 1993:187). Because some Muslim males penetrate other males less for sexual gratification than to humiliate perceived opponents, the active role in homosexual relations is widely associated with brutal aggression (Duran 1993:187–88; also see De Martino 1992:27).

These considerations make it is easier to understand the reasons behind the Prophet's supposed prohibition of homosexual relations. They also provide an insight into the cultural background in which the initiation symbolism of Islam developed. At the time of its origin, Islam was a warrior religion, and acceptance of Islam entailed induction into its military organization. This induction parallels, in a number of ways, the sexual initiation that takes place in some other parts of the world, where the chain of cultural transmission is symbolically associated with a sexual relationship between an older male, who is already initiated, and a younger male, who is the receptive partner. This sexual symbolism of cultural transmission is clearest in some Melanesian cultures (see Layard 1942:489; Herdt 1984).

The *umma*, or Islamic community, is analogous to the body of initiates, and those outside the *umma* to the uninitiated. *Islām*, of course, means "submission," and to become a Muslim means to "submit" to the will of God, the laws of the *umma*, and the collective authority of those who are already "initiated."

In cultures where there is a male sexual initiation, the central symbol of the collective authority to which the initiate submits is the penis. However in Islam it is the sword, the holy war being a central notion in Islamic cosmogony. Sheryl Burkhalter points out that the cosmogony of the Qur'ān is "intentionally incomplete," and that man's duty is to bring about "the completion of the cosmic order, a task realized through the establishment of divine justice in the human situation" (1985:231). The holy war (*jihād*) is the means by which this divine justice is established (Guénon 1962:201). This implies that once a man has been inducted into Islam, it is his duty to bring others to submission through the holy war.

We observe here the same transition from the passive to the active role as occurs in those cultures with a sexual initiation. After a man has been made to submit in the process of initiation, he is placed in the role of making others submit. Moreover, the fact that sexual relations are forbidden between male members of the Islamic community is not inconsistent with the principles of sexual initiation in other cultures, where those who have undergone initiation are not supposed to engage in sexual relations with each other.

Orthodox Islam does not, of course, suggest that this makes sexual relations between Muslims and non-Muslims legitimate, although the great Arabic poet Abū Nuwās said that he slept with Christian, Jewish, and Zoroastrian boys because he regarded it as "the duty of every Muslim to sleep with them" (Wagner 1965:188). A number of other Muslim poets also had a predilection for boys who were not Muslims (Schimmel 1979:140). Abū Nuwās does not specify *why* he regarded this as a duty, but it seems fairly clear that it was because he was making non-Muslim boys submit to a Muslim.

The "holy war" also has a spiritual meaning in Islam. There is a famous *hadīth* according to which the Prophet, on his return from a military expedition, said, "We have returned from the little holy war to the great holy war" (Guénon 1962:198). The traditional interpretation of this *hadīth*, summed up by Guénon, is that the great holy war symbolizes "the struggle that man should carry out against the enemies that he carries within him, that is, against all the elements in him which are contrary to order and unity" (Guénon 1962:198).

In other words, the soul is conceptualized as a social world in which there are initiates, or "Muslims," and enemies, who are implicitly non-Muslims. It is the duty of the "Muslim" elements of the soul to bring the "non-Muslim" elements to submission. The symbolism of initiation in this way becomes a part of the Islamic spiritual method.

The chief enemy in this social world of the soul is the *nafs*, which is variously translated as "self," "ego," "lower nature," "animal nature," and the like. Interestingly, in Islamic spiritual writings the *nafs* is sometimes conceived of as "effeminate" (e.g., in poems of Rūmī translated by Chittick 1983:165, 167, 348), and thus equated with the catamite (pp. 56, 242, 335).

The duty of the Muslim elements of the soul is to make the *nafs* submit to the will of God. While the accounts of this process draw on the symbolism of spiritual warfare, the fact that the *nafs* is thought of as being in some ways analogous to a sexually passive male suggests, again, that there is an implicit erotic element in the symbolism of the holy war.

It would not be an exaggeration to say that in Islam the fight against sexual attraction to members of one's own sex is paradigmatic for the "great holy war" waged against the *nafs*. Because *liwāt*, or "sodomy," has an extended meaning which includes "all forms of sexual and parasexual perversion" (Bouhdiba 1985:31), when one struggles against any forbidden sexual desire one is struggling against something for which sex between males provides the model. "In Islam, male homosexuality stands for all the perversions and con- stitutes in a sense the depravity of depravities" (Bouhdibah 1985:31). So the rebellious desires of the *nafs*, against which the great holy war is directed, are summed up in the temptation to *liwāt* or "sodomy."

There is clearly a deep irony here. If we reduce the initiatory symbolism of Islam to its simplest components, it entails treating non-Muslims, or the "non-Muslim" elements of the soul, as catamites, and conquering them by means of homosexual aggression. In other words, it involves overcoming sodomy by means of sodomy.

This contradiction has profound implications at every level of Muslim cul- ture, from routine male interaction to international relations. The West is regarded as "decadent" by Muslims not just because it is becoming more accepting of homosexuality (cf. Duran 1993:186) but because, according to the initiatory symbolism of Islam, it *has* to be seen as effeminate.

It is presumably because of the deeply contradictory nature of Islamic atti- tudes toward homosexuality that contemporary Muslim cultures maintain a conspiracy of silence about the issue, falling back on "a stagnated *sharī'a* of the seventh and eighth centuries as an unchangeable holy norm in its most rigid form" (Duran 1993:195, cf. 187). It is hardly likely that the silence will be broken by criticisms coming from the West. The only real hope for change is for gay and lesbian Muslims, and their heterosexual allies, to initi- ate an indigenous discussion, within Islamic cultures, that will be more open and discerning. This is already happening to some extent, particularly in Islamic diaspora communities.[8] This may oblige Muslim scholars to attempt to resolve the contradictions inherent in current Islamic policies toward homosexuality, and to consider more carefully the Prophet's views on free- dom and justice.

Notes

This chapter is a revised version of chapter 1 of an unpublished thesis (Wafer 1986). I am grateful for the editorial advice of Stephen O. Murray and Peter Lamborn Wilson.

1. The plural of *hadīth* is *ahadīth*. However, as a stylistic accommodation to English, I have not inflected Arabic terms when they are used in the plural.

2. The paucity of relevant sources has made it impossible to cover lesbianism.

3. I have based my references to al-Tīfāshī on the complete French translation by R. R. Khawam. Khawam uses the term *invertis*, which I have translated as "inverts." Lacey translates this term as "queens" (1988:162).

4. It is not clear from the translation whether there is a difference between the Arabic term for "invert" and the term which Bellamy translates as "transvestite" (*mukhannath*) (1979:36). One "transvestite," called Mati', also used to visit the Prophet's wives freely, up to the time when he was banished from Medina. (The Prophet later allowed him to come into town on Saturdays to beg.) In any case Bellamy believes that "the mukhannath (or: transvestite) . . . is . . . not classed with the sodomites" (1979:36). Pérès, on the other hand, says that the term *mukhannath* has to do with effeminacy, and is similar to *hāwī*, which he translates as "catamite" (1953:341). Further discussion of both these terms is contained in Pellat (1983), and of *mukhannath* in Rowson (1991).

5. Hanafism and Hanbalism are both based on the Qur'ān and the *sunna* (the deeds, utterances and unspoken approval of the Prophet), but the Hanbalite school recognizes no other source, and is also hostile to speculative theology and to Sufism. It could thus be characterized as the more fundamentalist of the two schools. The Hanafites, in the absence of a precedent, are prepared to accept personal opinion (van Donzel 1994:128).

6. On the possibility of considering sodomy as a form of adultery (*zinā*), see Bousquet 1966:68, and Sofer 1992:139, 141–42. *Zinā* is actually broader than "adultery." Bouhdiba translates it as "fornication" (1985:15), and Bellamy paraphrases it as "illegal intercourse between a man and a woman" (1979:38). For a discussion of the incongruities of contemporary *zinā* legislation, see Mayer 1990:192–97.

7. Since burning is not a traditional punishment in Islam, several historians have disputed the authenticity of this story (Daniel 1975–76 [254]: 88).

8. For example, there are several Muslim contributors to Ratti (1993).

References

Arberry, Arthur J. 1953. *The ring of the dove, by Ibn Hazm (994–1064): A treatise on the art and practice of Arab love.* London: Luzac.
———. 1956. *The mystical poems of Ibn al-Farid.* Dublin: Emery Walker.
Bell, Joseph Norment. 1979. *Love theory in later Hanbalite Islam.* Albany, NY: State University of New York Press.
Bellamy, James A. 1979. "Sex and society in Islamic popular literature." In *Society and the sexes in medieval Islam*, ed. Afaf Lutfi al-Sayyid Marsot, 23–42. Malibu, CA: Undena.
Ben Nahum, Pinhas. 1933. *The Turkish art of love.* New York: Panurge Press.
Bouhdiba, Abdelwahab. 1985. *Sexuality in Islam.* London: Kegan Paul.
Bousquet, Georges-Henri. 1966. *La morale de l'Islam et son éthique sexuelle.* Paris: Maisonneuve et Larose.
Burkhalter, Sheryl L. 1985. "Completion and continuity: Cosmogony and ethics in Islam." In *Cosmogony and ethical order: New studies in comparative ethics*, ed. Robin W. Lovin and F. E. Reynolds, 225–50. Chicago: University of Chicago Press.

Cardin, Alberto. 1984. *Guerreros, chamanes y travestís: Indicios de homosexualidad entre los exóticos.* Barcelona: Tusquets.

Chebel, Malek. 1988. *L'esprit de sérail: Perversions et marginalités au Maghreb.* Paris: Lieu Commun.

Chittick, William C. 1983. *The Sufi path of love: The spiritual teachings of Rumi.* Albany, NY: State University of New York Press.

Corbin, Henry. 1969. *Creative imagination in the Sufism of Ibn 'Arabi.* Princeton: Princeton University Press.

Daniel, Marc. 1975–76. "La civilisation arabe et l'amour masculin." *Arcadie* 22–23, nos. 253:8–19; 254:83–93; 255:142–53; 257:269–74; 258:326–30; 259–60:391–95; 261:-487–92; 263:619–26; 266:117–20; 267:182–87.

De Martino, Gianni. 1992. "An Italian in Morocco." In *Sexuality and eroticism among males in Moslem societies,* ed. Arno Schmitt and Jehoeda Sofer, 25–32. Binghamton, NY: Harrington Park Press.

Duran, Khalid. 1993. "Homosexuality and Islam." In *Homosexuality and world religions,* ed. Arlene Swidler, 181–97. Valley Forge, PA: Trinity Press International.

Giffen, Lois A. 1971. *Theory of profane love among the Arabs: The development of the genre.* New York: New York University Press.

Guénon, René. [1937] 1962. *Symboles fondamentaux de la science sacrée.* Paris: Gallimard.

Herdt, Gilbert H. 1984. *Ritualized homosexuality in Melanesia.* Berkeley: University of California Press.

Khawam, René R. 1971. *Les délices des coeurs par Ahmad al-Tīfāchī (1184–1253).* Paris: Jérôme Martineau.

Lacey, Edward A. 1988. *The delight of hearts.* San Francisco: Gay Sunshine Press.

Layard, John. 1942. *Stone Men of Malekula: Vao.* Vol. 1. London: Chatto and Windus.

Mayer, Ann E. 1990. "The shari'ah: A methodology or a body of substantive rules?" In *Islamic law and jurisprudence,* ed. Nicholas Heer, 177–98. Seattle: University of Washington Press.

Pellat, Charles. 1983. "Liwāt." *Encyclopedia of Islam,* 5:776–79. Leiden: Brill.

Pérès, Henri. 1953. *La poésie andalouse en arabe classique au XIe siècle.* 2d ed. Paris: Adrien-Maisonneuve.

Pickthall, Mohammed M. n.d. *The meaning of the glorious Quran.* Karachi: Wal Uloomil Islamia.

Ratti, Rakesh. 1993. *A lotus of another color: An unfolding of the South Asian gay and lesbian experience.* Boston: Alyson.

Ritter, Hellmut. 1928. "Philologika II: Über einige Koran und Hadith betreffende Handschriften hauptsächlich Stambuler Bibliotheken." *Der Islam* 17:249–57.

Rowson, Everett K. 1991. "The effeminates of early Medina." *Journal of the American Oriental Society* 111:671–93.

Schimmel, Annemarie. 1979. "Eros—heavenly and not so heavenly—in Sufi literature and life." In *Society and the sexes in medieval Islam,* ed. Afaf Lutfi al-Sayyid Marsot, 119–42. Malibu, CA: Undena.

_____. 1982. *As through a veil: Mystical poetry in Islam.* New York: Columbia University Press.

Schmitt, Arno. 1992. "Different approaches to male-male sexuality/eroticism from Morocco to Uzbekistan." In *Sexuality and eroticism among males in Moslem societies,* ed. Arno Schmitt and Jehoeda Sofer, 1–24 . Binghamton, NY: Harrington Park Press.

Sofer, Jehoeda. 1992. Sodomy in the law of Muslim states. In *Sexuality and eroticism among males in Moslem societies,* ed. Arno Schmitt and Jehoeda Sofer, 131–149. New York: Haworth.

van Donzel, E. 1994. *Islamic desk reference: Compiled from The Encyclopaedia of Islam.* Leiden: Brill.

Wafer, James. 1986. "Sacred and profane love in Islam: Dimensions of gay religious history." M.A. thesis, Religious Studies, Indiana University, Bloomington.

Wagner, Ewald. 1965. *Abu Nuwas: Eine Studie zur arabischen Literatur der frühen Abbāsīdenzeit*. Wiesbaden: Franz Steiner.

Wilson, Peter Lamborn, and Bernd Manuel Weischer. 1978. *Heart's witness: The Sufi quatrains of Awhaduddin Kirmānī*. Tehran: Imperial Iranian Academy of Philosophy.

CHAPTER 5

Woman-Woman Love in Islamic Societies

Stephen O. Murray

Women have only recently become visible at all in Islamicist/Orientalist discourse.[1] Within most present-day Islamic states, where representation of even married heterosexual conduct is heavily censored, woman-woman sexuality remains thoroughly submerged. What follows is a brief compilation and discussion of the evidence that does exist concerning woman-woman sexual relations in Islamic societies.

Classical treatises on sexual vice discuss tribadism (*sahq*)—from a male perspective (see Rowson 1991:63 for some unilluminating examples). There is also a tradition that women "practiced the vice [of sodomy] for forty years among the tribe of Lot before the men took it up" (Bellamy 1979:37, citing the *Dhamm al-hawā* of Abū al-Faraj ibn al-Jawzī, ca. 1116–1201). Sexual relations between women within harems has been more supposed than observed. There is an occasional dramatic report, such as that concerning the 'Abbāsid Khalif Musa al-Hadi who beheaded two beautiful young women from his harem who had been caught together in flagrante delicto and decorated the detached and perfumed heads with diadems (Walther 1981:118). Similarly, in a note to a story from the *Thousand and One Nights* in which a man comes upon a beloved being kissed by her maid, Richard Burton claimed that harems "are hot-beds of Sapphism and tribadism. Every woman past her first youth has a girl who she calls 'Myrtle' (in Damascus)," and he added, "Amongst the wild Arabs [i.e., Bedouins], who ignore Socratic and Sapphic perversions, the lover is always more jealous of his beloved's girl-friends than of men rivals" (1885–88, 4:234n1).[2]

Ottaviano Boy, a Venetian envoy to the Ottoman court in Constantinople during the mid-sixteenth century, reported that for the "lustie and lascivious wenches" in the harem of Suleiman the Magnificent, "it is not lawfull for any one to bring ought in unto them, with which they may commit deeds of beastly uncleannesse; so that if they have a will to eate Cucumbers, they are sent in unto them sliced to deprive them of the meanes of playing the wantons" (whether singularly or with each other).[3]

Allen Edwardes's lurid survey of various hostile reports of other peoples' alleged customs asserts that,

isolated in enormous seraglios, females were generally given over to fanatic sapphism (sehhaukeh) employing the ancient substitutes for the appeasing phallus, the tongue, candle, banana, and artificial penis. . . . [The women were] scornfully called sehheek-ehs (rubbers, fricatrices). . . . Apart from sehhaukeh, various crude and euphemistic titles were granted female inversion, among them mejhool-el-izarbund (laxity of the trouser-string) and lisaun-fee-gubb (tongue in bush, cunnilingus). Most Arabs were of the opinion that women corrupt women more than men do; thus the prudent Arab was always more jealous of his sweetheart's lady friends than any suspected male admirers. . . . In the restricted harem, esh-sheykheh-el-bezzreh (one who teaches the art of rubbing clitoris against clitoris) taught every girl in the sapphic sciences. To solace her in long hours of desire for the male, nearly every concubine had her own private companion whom she styled merseeneh or reehauneh (myrtle) and with whom she practices all the sapphic pleasures. (1959:255)

Edwardes does not indicate where he found these terms and claims. The rhetoric surely had a quaint ring even in 1959, when it was published (with an introduction by that determined "curer" of homosexuality, Albert Ellis).

Herbert mentions an occasion in which the great Persian Safavid Shah 'Abbas rode "to hunt the Tygre, accompanied only with two hundred Women, his Wiues and Concubines, most of them were attired like couragious Amazons with Semiter, Bow and Arrowes" ([1626] 1971:98). He does not say whether those he called "Amazons" had sexual relations with women, men, or with no one, but "Amazon" seems a term for which heterosexual assumptions are particularly inapt.

Chebel takes the absence of mention of lesbian love in the *Qur'ān* as evidence of absence in "the traditions of primitive Islam" (and, presumably, Arabia at the time of Mohammed) (1995:314). Rowson argues that sex between women was entirely distinct from gender variance in medieval Arabic and Persian:[4]

Neither in al-Jurjani nor al-Raghib, nor elsewhere in the literature I have investigated, is there any suggestion that women involved in same-sex relations take on any of the nonsexual gender attributes of men; nor do we find any reference to active-passive role differentiation in lesbian relationships. There are, to be sure, occasional descriptions of women adopting masculine modes of behavior—donning male attire and swords, riding horseback, and so forth—particularly in the early (seventh and eighth) Islamic centuries, when conventions of seclusion were apparently less rigorous. Such women were sometimes admired, sometimes criticized for venturing into the public world of men; but they were never associated with any particular form of sexual irregularity [!]. Even the ghulamiyat, singing slave girls who were dressed up as boys (on occasion complete with painted mustaches) and became the rage at the caliphal court in ninth-century Baghdad, were not known for having sexual interest in or relations with other women; on the contrary, . . . they were competing with boys for the attention of men. (1991:68)

AbuKhalil reports *suhaqiyyat* as a venerable Arabic term for "self-declared lesbian" and notes that much of the poetry of the Arab Sappho, Walladah bint al-Mustakfi, "in praise of her female lover poetess Muhjah was lost because most authors refused to cite them due to their explicit sexual language" (1993:33). He goes on to assert:

There are episodes in the turath in which men tolerated lesbian love. One man was told that his wife was tusahiq (having sex with other women), and he responded: "As long as she frees me from any sexual obligation towards her, let her do what she wants." One poetess declared: "I drank wine for love of flirting/and I shifted towards lesbianism for fear of pregnancy." (p. 34)

Sharif al-Idrisi (1100–66) attributes woman-woman relations to choice rather than to the lack or infrequent availability of male sexual partners, that is, so-called "situational homosexuality":

There are also women who are more intelligent than the others. They possess many of the ways of men so that they resemble them even in their movements, the manner in which they talk, and their voice. Such women would like to be the active partner, and they would like to be superior to the man who makes this possible for them. Such a woman does not shame herself, either, if she seduces whom she desires. If she has no inclination, he cannot force her to make love. This makes it difficult for her to submit to the wishes of men and brings her to lesbian love. Most of the women with these characteristics are to be found among the educated and elegant women, the scribes, Koran readers, and female scholars. (*Kitab nuzhat al-mushtaq fi ikhtiraq al-afaq*, in Walther 1981:118)

Busbecq asserted that some Turkish men refused to let their wives go to the women's baths because of the reputation for lesbian activities (1744 [1562]:146).

More common than these glimmers of women choosing women are inter-pretations (native and alien) of women driven into each others' embraces by the lack of male sexual partners. Campbell (1949) cites an Iraqi view that harem girls kiss and make love to each other from sadness of heart. The extent to which this reflects male fantasies or female realities is impossible to distinguish. (See Figure 5.1.) As Southgate notes, "Whether coy or indifferent, male poets and writers kept silent about lesbian practices" (1984:438). Especially since women did not leave records of their behaviors or feelings, we cannot take absence of literary evidence as evidence of absence.[5] Male suppositions and fears of woman-woman sexuality within Islamic societies along with hostility toward Islamic societies from Europeans writing about harems' reputations for lesbianism make it difficult to interpret (the usually terse) statements about "Sapphic vice." Westphal-Hellbusch's discussion of South Arabian transvestite/homosexual dancers (in chapter 15) is similarly less than clear:

Women transvestites constitute a social phenomenon of much greater import. Such women, either for the whole or part of their lives, lead a male existence, giving out-ward expression to this change of role by donning male attire. They cannot, however, attain the legal status of a male and do not engage in sexual activities with members of either sex. (1956:137)

Then there is Chebel's reference to Ester Panetta's sensational report at a 1948 international congress of orientalists describing a women's milieu in Benghazi, Libya in which women "offered themselves in a lascivious delirium to demons of two sexes: incubuses, but, seemingly more often, succubuses. Moreover, their incantations to djenoun were equally offered at weddings 'where after the consummation of the marriage, the friends of the bride passed a lascivious night with a woman, usually a male-dressed courtesan'" (1988:47; my translation).

The passing comment by Feuerstein and al-Marzooq that "lesbianism is pre-sumably rare, although we have reliable evidence for its existence in [Muscat,] Oman" is not much more helpful (1978:666). Nor does it contradict Wikan's statement that "no social role involving lesbian relationships is found or accepted in Sohar." She acknowledges that it would be "silly to declare that sexual relations have never ever taken place between two [Sohari] women" (1978:474)—that is, attestation of female-female sexual behavior is insuffi-cient to establish that there is a recognized role or identity. And, although the Human Relations Area Files keyed Ingrams's (1938) mention of a Hadramaut (i.e., from southeastern Arabia, east of Aden) woman who dressed as a man

5.1 Women with dildo, seventeenth-century Mughal. Bibliothèque Nationale, Paris.

(which included wearing a dagger), under the classification "homosexuality," what Ingrams wrote did not disclose anything of the woman's sexual habits. In her chapter in this volume Dickemann discusses the lack of clarity about gender and sexuality of Balkan women socially accepted as men in both native views and external observers' attempts to analyze what appears to me to be a gender-crossing role. In discussing dervish organization, Bliss mentions "the only maids in Islam are female dervishes. One lives at 'Ain Ka'rim, near Jerusalem, known as Bint-esh-Sheikh, or the sheikh's daughter" (1912:-254). Given the centrality of childbearing to the Arab woman's role, this might be seen as a departure from their gender, although Bliss goes out of his way to note that women are "held by the fellahīn to incarnate many of the attributes of holiness which should distinguish a dervish: she does not bear arms, she suffers beatings, she serves others" (254).

The inability of Yemenis to conceive that a young African-American anthropologist accompanied by her older white lover were not daughter and mother, as Delores Walters relates, suggests acute denial or the lack of any conception of ongoing and preferential female-female sexuality. According to Walters:

In Yemen, decorum regarding sexual behavior is more crucial than the behavior itself. Since we lived in a small village shack that afforded us little privacy, our lesbian relationship was probably not a secret. As in other situations of non-conformity to sexual mores, such as adultery for example, a woman's friends and neighbors will protect the participants if the illicit relationship is carried out with discretion. On the other hand, it was possible that some people easily avoided acknowledging the reality of my lesbian partnership. (1991:45–46)

What Baraheni wrote could be generalized westward to Arab societies as well: "Female homosexuality in Iran is hushed up in such a way that no woman, in the whole of Iranian history, has been allowed to speak out for such tendencies. . . . To attest to lesbian desires would be an unforgivable crime" (1977:47–48). Note his stress on repression of any affirmation or self-representation: not that it does not exist but that it cannot be spoken of, and, especially, not written about. Although Fernea (1965), el-Messiri (1978), Nelson (1974), and Wikan (1980, 1982) have revealed an extensive women's culture in the homosocial Arab women's sphere—and shown that ethnography of women's worlds in these patriarchal societies is possible—female ethnographers have, so far, been unwilling (or constrained) to write about female-female sexuality in Arab or in other Muslim societies. Beyond the paltry references cited here, there is nothing in the way of published ethnographic literature on "lesbians" in Islamic societies to discuss at this point in time.

Notes

1. The most important of the pioneering collections are Fernea and Bezirgan (1977) and Beck and Keddie (1978), the former more experiential, the latter more analytical. See Nelson on earlier anthropological work, in which women were more visible than in the study of written texts that is characteristic of "Orientalism" as a field of study (1974). On the history of conceptions of women in Islamic societies, see Abu-Lughod (1990), Ahmed (1986, 1992). Mahlouf-Obermeyer (1992, 1995), Ong (1990), and Stowasser (1987) discuss some of the variety of current conceptions.

2. Between these two quotations, he mentions that "at Agbome, capital of Dahome, I found that a troop of women was kept for the use of the 'Amazons.'" What he published about these troops in his report of that mission (Burton 1864:ii, 73) treated them as wives of the Dahomean king and does not provide any indication of woman-woman amours among the "Amazons." Edwardes claims that in harems murder by poison or strangulation was prevalent "because of rabid lesbian rivalry and infidelity, as one girl enticed or stole another's companion" (1959:256).

3. Quoted by Barber (1973:35).

4. One exception is Jinan, the ghulamiyya for whom Abū Nuwās expressed love. As I discuss in more detail in "The will not to know," the ghulamiyyat fashion was launched by Zubayda, mother of Abū Nuwās's patron, Khalif al-Amin, to get him away from exclusively loving boys. It seems to have worked briefly on Abū Nuwās as well.

5. The absence of evidence may not have always been the case. In a paragraph in his *liwāt* entry to the *Encyclopedia of Islam* (which Schmitt chose to cut in Schmitt and Sofer 1992:155; see note 163n27), Pellat referred to "a dozen love romances with female names in their title" listed in Ibn al-Nadim's *Kitab Hind wa-bint al-Nu'man* (1983:777). There are also terms for woman-woman relations, including *sahq, sihaq,* and *musahaqah,* and, in Arabic, *tassahouq.* The root common to these terms (and to the nominalization of a person: *sahhāqu*) means grinding. "Lesbianism is *anamika* in South Asian [Hindu/Urdu], without/beyond name. . . . This is a subculture produced publicly as ghost, namelessness, passivity and silence," according to Fernando (1995:23).

References

AbuKhalil, As'ad. 1993. "A note on the study of homosexuality in the Arab/Islamic civilization." *Arab Studies Journal* 1(2):32–34,48.

Abu-Lughod, Lila. 1990. "The romance of resistance: Tracing transformations of power through Bedouin women." *American Ethnologist* 17:41–55.

Ahmed, Leila. 1986. "Women and the advent of Islam." *Signs* 11:665–91.

———. 1992. *Women and gender in Islam.* New Haven: Yale University Press.

Baraheni, Reza. 1977. *The crowned cannibals: Writings on repression in Iran.* New York: Vintage.

Barber, Noel. 1973. *The sultans.* New York: Simon and Schuster.

Beck, Lois, and Nikki Keddie. 1978. *Women in the Muslim world.* Cambridge: Harvard University Press.

Bellamy, James A. 1979. "Sex and society in Islamic popular literature." *Society and the sexes in medieval Islam,* ed. Afaf Lutfi al-Sayyid Marsot, 23–42. Malibu, CA: Undena.

Bliss, Frederick Jones. 1912. *The religions of modern Syria and Palestine.* New York: Scribner's.

Burton, Richard F. 1864. *A mission to Gelele, King of Dahome.* 2 vols. London: Tinsely Brothers.

———. 1885–88. *The book of the thousand nights and a night.* 10 vols. Benares: Kama Shastra Society. (See volume 10: 63–260.)

Busbecq, Ogier Ghilsian de. [1562] 1744. *Travels into Turkey.* London: J. Robinson.

Campbell, Charles G. 1949. *Tales from the Arab tribes*. London: Drummond.

Chebel, Malek. 1988. *L'esprit de sérail: Perversions et marginalités au Maghreb*. Paris: Lieu Commun.

———. 1995. *Encyclopédie de l'amour en Islam*. Paris: Payot.

Edwardes, Allen. 1959. *The jewel in the lotus: A historical survey of the sexual culture of the East*. New York: Julian Press.

el-Messiri, Saswan. 1978. "Self-images of traditional urban women in Cairo." In *Women in the Muslim World*, ed. L. Beck & N. Keddie, 522–40. Cambridge: Harvard University Press.

Fernando, Sonali. 1995. "Tantrik droplets." *Rungh: A South Asian Quarterly of Culture, Comment & Criticism* 3,3:23–26.

Fernea, Elizabeth Warnock. 1965. *Guests of the Sheik*. Garden City, NY: Doubleday.

Fernea, Elizabeth Warnock, and Basima Qattan Bezirgan. 1977. *Middle Eastern Muslim women speak*. Austin: University of Texas Press.

Feuerstein, G., and S. al-Marzooq. 1978. "Omani xanith." *Man* 13:665–67.

Herbert, Thomas. [1626] 1971. *A relation of some yeares travaile into Afrique, Aisa, and the Indies*. New York: Capo.

Ingrams, W. H. 1938. "The Hadramaut." *Geographical Journal* 92:289–312.

Mahlouf-Obermeyer, Carla. 1992. "Islam, women, and politics." *Population and Development Review* 18:33–57.

———. 1995. "Reproductive choice in Islam: Gender and state in Iran and Tunisia." *Radical America* 25:22–36.

Nelson, Cynthia. 1974. "Public and private politics: Women in the Middle Eastern world." *American Ethnologist* 1:551–63.

Ong, Aihwa. 1990. "State versus Islam: Malay families, women's bodies, and the body politic in Malaysia." *American Ethnologist* 17:258–76.

Pellat, Charles. 1983. "Liwāt." *Encyclopedia of Islam* 5:776–79. Leiden: Brill.

Rowson, Everett K. 1991. "The categorization of gender and sexual irregularity in medieval Arab vice lists." In *Body Guards*, ed. J. Epstein and K. Straub, 50–79. New York: Routledge.

Schmitt, Arno and Jehoeda Sofer. 1992. *Sexuality and eroticism among males in Moslem societies*. Binghamton, NY: Harrington Park Press.

Southgate, Minoo S. 1984. "Men, women, and boys: love and sex in the works of Saʿdī." *Iranian Studies* 17:413–52.

Stowasser, Barbara F. 1987. "Liberated equal or protected dependent? Contemporary religious paradigms on women's status in Islam." *Arab Studies Quarterly* 9:260–83.

Walters, Delores M. 1991. "Cast among the outcastes: Interpreting sexual orientation, racial, and gender identity in Yemen." *Society of Lesbian and Gay Anthropologists' Newsletter* 13:43–46.

Walther, Wiebke. 1981. *Woman in Islam*. Montclair, NJ: A. Schram.

Westphal-Hellbusch, Sigrid. 1956. "Transvestiten bei arabischen Stämmen." *Sociologus* 6:126–37. (Translation in this volume.)

Wikan, Unni. 1978. "The Omani xanith: A third gender role?" *Man* 13:473–75.

———. 1980. *Life among the poor in Cairo*. London: Tavistock.

———. 1982. *Behind the veil in Arabia: Women in Oman*. Baltimore: Johns Hopkins University Press.

PART II

Literary Studies

CHAPTER 6

Vision and Passion

The Symbolism of Male Love in
Islamic Mystical Literature

Jim Wafer

The mystical literature of both Islam and Christianity has used the symbolism of romantic love to represent the love of God.[1] In Christianity, however, this love is exclusively heterosexual. Either the soul is regarded as female in relation to God, as in Gregory of Nyssa's *Commentary on the Canticle of Canticles* (Daniélou and Musurillo 1961:30, 161, and passim) or the poems of Saint John of the Cross (Hardy 1987:134–36); or else the divine nature is represented in female form, symbolizing Wisdom or Gnosis, in relation to a male lover, as in the poetry of the medieval Worshippers of Love (Evola 1983:194, 200). In Christian literature it is virtually unthinkable to represent the love of God in terms of a romantic relationship between two males. It is rare enough, as C. S. Lewis points out, for it to be represented as friendship (1960:73, 81).

Islamic mysticism allows for a more complex set of possibilities. Although some Muslim mystics adopt a similar heterosexual symbolism to that of the Worshippers of Love,[2] there is a parallel tradition in which the love of God is represented using the imagery of romantic relationships between males. There are two recurrent sets of tropes in the Islamic mystical literature that draw on this imagery. I call these the "vision complex" and the "passion complex."

A key term in the development of the vision complex is *nazar*, or "gazing"—that is, looking with admiration at a beloved person. For secular writers who regarded themselves as orthodox Muslims, "gazing" at another male was the principal expression of their love, since a sexual consummation was forbidden. The mystics gave this idea a religious meaning by treating *nazar* as equivalent to the vision of God Himself (Bell 1979:144–45). The symbolism of the gaze was given added theological depth by being linked to the ancient gnostic tradition of the "heavenly twin" who is also the "witness."

Ritter (1955:470–77) discusses the development in certain Sufi groups of what he calls a "mystical ephebe-cult," based on the belief that the love of God could be practiced through contemplation of a *shahid*—that is, literally, a "witness," or something that gives evidence of God's beauty. This was "by ancient convention usually a comely and still beardless youth" (Bell 1979: 139). The theological premise of this practice is that "every beauty is derived from the universal beauty," a notion early elaborated by al-Daylami (Giffen 1971:166), and by subsequent theologians, such as Abū Hamīd al-Ghazzālī (Bell 1979:166). The Arabic writers who recommended the contemplation of beautiful beardless youths, such as al-Sulamī and al-Maqdisī (Bell 1979:23, 142), saw themselves as simply drawing logical conclusions from this apparently orthodox doctrine. This doctrine has much in common with what one writer has called "the divine imprint in manifestation" (Perry 1971:306), that is, the notion that the visible world is a reflection of a supernatural reality, and that this relationship can be perceived particularly clearly in certain phenomena that display direct evidence of their supernatural origin.

Corbin (1978:33–37) sees the Sufi contemplation of "witnesses" as being linked to the Mandaean and Manichean doctrine of the "heavenly twin." In both Mandaeism and Manicheism, every being in the physical universe has a heavenly counterpart, partner, or twin, who is its guardian and guide (a similar doctrine is encountered in parts of Africa: Brain 1976:133). This twin is also a witness, because it gives testimony of the soul's capacity to perceive the beauty of its double as theophany (Corbin 1978:36).

The passion complex is often used in the same mystical texts as the vision complex, but it is analytically distinguishable. Whereas in the vision complex the relationship between lover and beloved is mediated symbolically by the faculty of sight, in the passion complex it entails a symbolic physical interaction in which the lover is wounded or killed by his beloved. This is as close as Islam ever comes to giving a positive meaning to erotic passivity in males, although, of course, the imagery of the passion complex is sado-masochistic rather than coital. Since the killing of the lover is conventionally represented as a beheading, it is not even necessary to engage too deeply in Freudian interpretations to see this death as symbolic feminization of the lover. In fact, it would probably not be overstating the case to suggest a parallel with shamanic experiences in which the shaman makes himself passive by adopting the cultural attributes of a woman and engages in a relationship with a male spirit who is a kind of "supernatural husband" (Bogoras [1904] 1975:451–52).

If the vision complex is concerned with God's immanence, or presence in manifestation, the passion complex is concerned with God's transcendence. The human lover allows himself to be beheaded by the divine beloved because it is only thus that he can enter the mystery that is beyond human comprehension. The sado-masochistic symbolism is not accidental. Evola points out in this regard that "pain is a means by which individual consciousness experiences something that has a more or less destructive nature but, for that very reason, contains an impetus to transcendence as compared with the closed and stationary nature of the finite individual" (1983:84–85). He also notes that "many ancient divinities of love were at the same time divinities of death" (1983:83).

The present chapter shows how the vision complex and the passion complex were elaborated in Islamic mystical literature, in order to illustrate possibilities of religious symbolism based on love between males that have been almost entirely neglected in Judeo-Christian cultures.

THE DEVELOPMENT OF ISLAMIC MYSTICAL LITERATURE

The question of "the reality of love as an attribute of God and the nature of the love-relationship between God and man" (Bell 1979:46) is one that has long exercised Muslim theologians. While certain schools, such as the Ash'arites, hold that the idea of a love relationship with God must be rejected because of its implicit anthropomorphism (Bell 1979:47–48), the more general view is that love is an attribute of God, and requires reciprocation from man.

The fact that Love is an Attribute of God is confirmed implicitly by numerous quranic verses in which God is said to "love" something. The Sufis usually quote the following verse, since it shows clearly the hierarchical relationship between God's love for man and man's love for God, the latter of which derives its existence from the former: "God will bring a people whom He loves and who love Him, humble towards the believers, disdainful towards the unbelievers, men who struggle in the path of God, not fearing the reproach of any reproacher." (V 54) (Chittick 1983:195–96)

Moreover, one of the divine names is al-Wadūd (Qur'ān 11:90; 85:14), meaning "one who loves" (Bell 1979:74, 236n2; Bouhdiba 1985:124; and Schimmel 1982:16, who quotes Sūra 5:59).

For Sufism the symbolism of love is particularly important, to the extent that certain Sufis refer to themselves, in their capacity as practitioners of a spiritual method, simply as "lovers." The theme of love continues to be of central significance in Sufi works of the present day, such as recent books by Mir Valiuddin ([1968] 1972) and Muzaffer Ozak (1981).

Mystical themes began to appear in Arabic literature during the Umayyad dynasty, for example in the work of Hasan of Basra (d. 728). In this period mystical writings were principally ascetic and voluntaristic, "aiming at the complete unification of man's will with the Divine will" (Schimmel 1982:15). Love was not considered an appropriate theme for religious literature, even by writers such as Abū'l-Atahiya, who had themselves composed secular works on love before they turned their attention to religion (Schimmel 1982:14–15).

Early in the succeeding 'Abbāsid dynasty love mysticism made its appearance in the mystical school of Basra, at the same time as the spiritual practice emanating from the cities of Basra and Kūfa came to be called *Tasawwuf*, or Sufism (Giffen 1971:86, 146; Ullah 1963:149).[3] The school of Basra introduced the usage of the term *'ishq* ("eros," "passionate love," "romantic love") to apply to the relation between man and God. This term was deliberately used rather than more neutral or generic terms such as the quranic *mahabba* (Bell 1979:105; Giffen 1971:86).[4]

This development of love mysticism was contemporaneous with the early flowering of erotic secular poetry, in particular in the work of Abū Nuwās, who spent his early years in Basra, and may have been born there. Abū Nuwās had contact with the Sufis of Basra, and is reported to have undertaken a journey with them to the Sufi settlement of 'Abbādān, on the Persian Gulf (Wagner 1965:80 and note). It is an interesting and possibly significant coincidence that the *hadīth* according to which the Prophet saw God in the form of a beautiful beardless youth has been traced to 'Abbādān (Ritter 1928: 526–7; 1955:445).[5]

Ritter sees a possible connection between this *hadīth* and the "mystical ephebe-cult" that consisted of the contemplation of beautiful youths referred to as "witnesses" (1955:470–77). The Sufis who engaged in this practice based it on the theological premise that "he who meditates must meditate on form, since Essence in itself is unknowable. Through the form, the symbol, one comes to realize the Essence, which is the Oneness of Being" (Wilson 1988: 96–97).

There is a fine distinction between this notion and the heresy of *hulūl*, of which the Sufis were periodically accused. *Hulūl*, or "incarnationism," is the doctrine that "God indwells in certain bodies in this world, often in human forms and especially in the beautiful" (Bell 1979:21–2). In particular the Sufis who contemplated God's beauty in the form of "witnesses" were accused of believing that "God is incarnate in or united with the beloved" (p. 142), and of justifying on these grounds their indulgence not only in "gazing" but also in "touching" and "the act" (p. 21). They were thus thought to be guilty of a double heresy, which combined the transgressions of idolaters and sodomites: "worshipping their minions and copulating with their idols" (p. 143).

It is possible that certain mystical groups did in fact engage in practices of this kind in the context of religious exercises, and that there is a historical connection with the Sufi institution called *samā'*. According to Ritter (1955: 491–92) this term means literally "listening to music," and originally referred to gatherings which took place after religious exercises, devoted to feasting, drinking, music, dancing, and flirtation with the young males and women who sang and served refreshments.[6]

When the term was taken over by Sufism, it was given a more austere meaning. For the Sufis, *samā'* was itself a religious exercise. Drunkenness and sensuality were forbidden, but singing and dancing remained part of the proceedings, and some Sufi groups also included the contemplation of one or more beautiful youths, who was especially dressed up for the occasion. The youth was regarded as a *shahid* or "witness" of God's beauty (Ritter 1955: 470–77). In spite of the condemnation of these customs and of the theological premises underlying them by conservative theologians, the practice of gathering to contemplate the beauty of a boy or young man is one that has survived in Islamic countries "until the most recent times" (p. 500). Ritter gives an example from Albania, and of the survival of the associated theological premises in Turkey (pp. 500, 491).

These practices provided a fund of images drawn upon by mystical writers who gave them a spiritual interpretation: the musical gathering is the company of the faithful, the garden in which it takes place is Paradise, the drinking of wine is the intoxication of divine love, and the beautiful youth, who may be the cupbearer, is the Divine Beloved Himself.[7]

Whether the origins of Sufi love mysticism had any connection with actual erotic practices (a topic that has not, to my knowledge, been systematically investigated), the mere suggestion of such a connection was apparently enough to scandalize more conservative Muslims; it is no doubt for this reason that later writers felt obliged to draw clear distinctions between sacred and profane love, either condemning altogether the notion that God could be loved with *'ishq* (the position of the Hanbalites, such as Ibn al-Jawzī), or else defending the notion but attempting to reconcile it with orthodox Islamic sexual morality and conceptions of God, as for example in the work of Ibn Sīna and Abū Hamīd al-Ghazzālī (Giffen 1971:145–46; Bell 1979:166).

The writers who were particularly concerned with this distinction were primarily theologians and metaphysicians: Ibn Sīna, for example, who says that spiritual inclination is not to be a pretext for sensuality, and that the embracing and kissing of boys is only permitted if it does not lead to sexual immorality (Bannerth 1957:43). Others, such as the Hanbalites, went even further, and forbade altogether any practice, such as, for example, *nazar* or the "amorous gaze," which indicated a sensual attraction between males (Bell 1979:21–28).

This background makes it easier to understand why some of the poets who wrote on mystical love were concerned to make explicit that their erotic imagery was to be understood in a spiritual sense. This is true, for example, of Ibn 'Arabī, who was particularly influential in the development of a body of conventions for the mystical interpretation of love symbolism. Ibn 'Arabī used this technique of interpretation to justify his own love poems inspired by a learned young Persian woman in Mecca (Schimmel 1982:39–40; Wilson 1988:chap. 3, and 97–98).[8] The development of an exegetic tradition which enabled poets to give even the most worldly poem a spiritual interpretation made it possible for them to draw on the works of profane writers (such as Abū Nuwās), and still to "avoid the wrath of the orthodox" (Schimmel 1982:41).

However there were also poets whose work seems to be deliberately ambiguous, in that it is not possible to make a clear distinction between an erotic and a mystical meaning in their poetry. As Schimmel notes, "the constant oscillation between the two levels of experience often makes it next to impossible to translate or even to understand a poem correctly" (1982:68). To restrict oneself to the "heavy and usually quite tasteless theological interpretation" (Schimmel 1982:68–69) is to overlook the possibility that the poets may be trying to suggest the unreality of the distinction between eroticism and spirituality.

Sufi love poetry can be divided into various categories according to the type of love object to which the poetry is ostensibly addressed. As Ritter has pointed out, there are some poems in which only God appears as the object, and others in which a human love object is "somehow" drawn into the realm of love mysticism (1933:90). The poems addressed to God may represent Him in the form of one of His attributes, such as Love personified, or Beauty. The human object may also be of various kinds: the Prophet Muhammad, or another prophet or saint; the spiritual teacher; or some secular personage, either male or female.

These various categories are not mutually exclusive, and much of the ambiguity of this literature arises from the uncertainty over which of these love objects is being literally addressed and which metaphorically. The usual theological interpretation assumes that God is always the ultimate object of these poems, whoever the literal addressee may be. But other "intermediate" correspondences are also possible, as, for example, when the spiritual teacher represents the Prophet (Schimmel 1982:37).

The imagery used in Sufi love poetry may also draw on a number of legendary secular love relationships. These include the love of Qays (Majnūn) for Laylā, that of Zulaykhā for Joseph, that of Mahmūd for Ayāz, and that of the dervish for the prince. (See the dervish whirling in Figure 6.1.) The first two of these relationships are heterosexual, while each of the second two involves two males.[9]

Sufi writings on mystical love can be divided into two great traditions, the Arabic and the Persian.[10] Schimmel contrasts the mystical poetry in these two languages by saying that in Arabic the relation between man and God is usually "expressed in metaphors of man's longing for a beautiful maiden," while in Persian it is symbolized in the love between a man and a beautiful youth (1982:151). This overstates the case somewhat, since both types of metaphor are used in both traditions. In fact many mystics, whether writing in Arabic or Persian, use the symbolism of love between two males or between a man and a woman interchangeably in their writings.

ARABIC MYSTICAL LITERATURE

In Arabic the early mystical writers began to adapt to their own purposes genres that had previously had a secular content: "shorter love poems and wine poems and especially the art of descriptive poetry (wasf)" (Schimmel 1982: 19). Possibly the earliest mystic to use these conventions was the ninth-century Egyptian writer Dhū'l-Nūn, who was followed by numerous others (see Schimmel 1982:chap. 1; Ullah 1963:155–56). However, according to Schimmel "the only truly great mystical poetry in Arabic" was written by Mansūr al-Hallāj (d. 922) and Ibn al-Fārid (d. 1235) (1982:45). After the thirteenth century the tradition of Arabic writing on mystical love seems to have stagnated (Schimmel 1982:35, 46–48).

Hallāj was one of the most celebrated of all Sufi mystics. According to Schimmel, "with Hallāj, Sufi history and, in a certain way, Sufi poetry reached its first climax" (1982:35). He was a Baghdadi of Persian origins, who wrote in Arabic of the oneness of existence, the unity of man and God, and of the love which he regarded as being the essence of God. He was executed for reasons that were partly political, on the grounds that he was preaching a heretical pantheism. For later writers, he became emblematic of martyrdom for the love of God (Schimmel 1982:30).

6.1 Dervish, nineteenth-century Turkey. From *Mevlana Celaleddin Rumi and the Whirling Dervishes*, Istanbul: Dost, 1983.

Massignon says that Hallāj did not use any symbols from profane love, in contrast with later mystical poets (quoted in Schimmel 1982:31). Hallāj may not have used the symbolism of physical eroticism, as did some later mystics who wrote of the kisses and embraces of the Divine Beloved, and described His physical beauty; but profane love is not confined to the physical dimension. Hallāj wrote of the love of God in terms which derive from the emotional side of love between males, in some cases drawing his inspiration even from such a profane writer as Abū Nuwās (Bannerth 1957:38), whose homosexual proclivities were so legendary that they became the subject of a number of stories in the *Arabian nights* (Burton 1894,3:31–35; Christman 1989:65–71).[11] The following poem, for example, treats mystical love as a relationship between two souls, in terms which, Wagner (1965:327n5) suggested, are derived from an idea expressed by Abū Nuwās:

I am he whom I love, and he whom I love is I.
We are two spirits who live in one body.
So when you see me, you see him.
And when you see him, you see us. (Gramlich 1976:11)

The theme of this poem has obvious affinities with the gnostic idea of "twin souls," discussed above, and thus with the vision complex. The poem is a clear illustration of the immanence of the divine in the human. Hallāj also deals with the theme of the inequality of man and God, in terms which link the symbolism of love between males to the passion complex. For example, the following mystical allegory is attributed to him by the Persian mystic 'Ayn al-Qudāt al-Hamadhani (himself executed in 1131):

When does the joy of the lover reach its height? When the beloved has spread out the blood-leather for the execution and has prepared the lover to be slain. The latter is lost in admiration of the beloved's beauty and says: He is preparing to kill me, but I only admire how well his brandishing of the sword becomes him. (Ritter 1955:399)

In this allegory the lover submits to his divine beloved. However, the symbol of this submission is not sexual passivity, but death at the hands of the beloved—a theme we will see repeated throughout Islamic mystical poetry.

It is true that the imagery in Hallāj's writings is rather more chaste[12] than in the work of, say, Umar ibn al-Fārid, who not only used erotic imagery in his mystical poetry (and, like Hallāj, drew on the work of Abū Nuwās; Arberry 1956:84), but also wrote profane verse, for example a poem in popular style about a handsome butcher boy (Schimmel 1982:45). Fārid was born in Cairo in 1181–82. He achieved fame as a mystic and poet, but, although widely venerated, he was accused by certain theologians of the heresy of "incarnationism" (Ullah 1963:156; Arberry 1956:51n14). Certainly his poems employ a very anthropomorphic symbolism, drawn from the love of both males and females. Arberry interprets those mystical poems which refer to a male beloved as being actually directed to the Prophet, or to the Divine Beauty, and those which refer to a female beloved as being concerned with the "Spirit of the Prophet," or, again, with the Divine Beauty (Arberry 1956:51, 53n24, 77, 92, 124).

By way of illustration, here are some verses from the fifth poem of Ibn al-Fārid's *dīwān* as translated by Arberry:

A sword his eyelids draw against my heart, and I see the
very languor thereof doth whet its blade;
All the more sheds he suddenly our blood, picturing them
that Musawir slew among the Beni Yazdadh.
No wonder is it, that he should have taken the hairs upon
his cheeks to be the suspender-thongs of his sword, seeing
that he is ever smiting and slaying therewith. . . .
The sun's self, yea, and the graceful gazelle submit humbly
 before his face as he gazes about him, and take refuge
 and shelter in his beauty. . . . The harshness of his
 heart rivals the tempered steel.
The mole upon his cheek embraces in its conflagration what
man soever is passionately occupied with him, and scorneth
to seek deliverance.
Ice-cool are his deep-red lips, and sweet his mouth to kiss
 in the morning, yea, even before the toothpick's
 cleansing excelling the musk in fragrance and investing it
 with its own perfume.
Of his mouth and his glances cometh my intoxication; nay,
but I see a vintner in his every limb. (1956:46–47)

Arberry notes that these lines "suggest that the poet now has in mind a mortal beloved, no doubt a handsome disciple, in whom he is seeing after Sufi fashion the embodiment of the Divine Beauty" (1956:53n24).[13] From this perspective the poem draws on the symbolism of the vision complex. But it also uses the same symbolism from the passion complex as we have seen above in the work of Hallāj: the beloved wields a sword that slays his lovers.

The fact that Fārid writes of kissing the mouth of the beloved would no doubt have been more than enough to disturb the more puritanical theologians, and to make them suspect him of *shahid*-worship and *hulūl* ("incarnationism").

PERSIAN MYSTICAL LITERATURE

These particular issues become crucial in the history of Persian mystical poetry, where the number of mystics who were accused of believing that the love of God could be practiced through the contemplation of a *shahid*, or "witness," is greater than in the Arabic tradition. These mystics include Ahmad al-Ghazzālī, Fakhr al-Dīn 'Irāqī, and Awhad al-Dīn Kirmānī (see Bell 1979:142; Chittick 1983:288; Ritter 1955:473).

In the following account of the theme of male love in Persian mystical literature I will treat the writers in three groups: those who aroused the opposition of conservative theologians by their practice of *shahid-bāzī* (literally, "witness play," but having also the sense of "love of boys"; Wilson 1988:95; Chittick 1983:289); those who used the symbolism of love between males in their writing but managed to avoid gaining a reputation for heretical practices; and those who disapproved of *shahid-bāzī*, and tried to distinguish themselves from its supposed practitioners.

Mystical literature in Persian developed later than that in Arabic, around the second half of the eleventh century.[14] The divergence of opinions over *shahid-bāzī* may have had its origins early in the history of this literary tradition. Among the first mystical writers in Persian were Ansārī (d. 1089) and Hujwīrī (d. 1071). Ansārī translated works of al-Sulami, who was one of the Arabic writers who defended the contemplation of beautiful youths (Bell 1979:23, 142). Hujwīrī, on the other hand, forbade looking at youths and associating with them (Schimmel 1982:232n71).

The earliest of the great Persian mystics to be accused of *shahid-bāzī* was Ahmad al-Ghazzālī (d. 1126), younger brother of the mystical theologian Abū Hamīd al-Ghazzālī, and successor to his teaching position in Baghdad (Corbin 1964:278–83). A number of stories are reported by others[15] about his practice of the contemplation of beautiful youths. Ritter, however, asserts that there is nothing in the younger Ghazzālī's extant writings to indicate that he gave his admiration of beautiful youths a religious meaning (1955:474). His short book of aphorisms on love, the *Sawanih* (Gramlich 1976), had a particularly powerful historical influence (Ritter 1933:93).

This work, which is dedicated to "a dear friend, who is as much to me as the dearest brother, and who is intimately close to me" (Gramlich 1976:2), is about the nature of love in the abstract; for, as he says, "the difference between the objects of love is accidental, but its essence is sublime beyond all determinations" (p. 10). Ghazzālī views the rules of love as being the same whether the object of love is human or divine—in fact, he expressly denies the alternative between the two (Ritter 1955:371). However, there are occasions in the work where he refers to a particular masculine beloved, as when he writes: "Every night the image of my Turk is transformed into the characteristics of my being" (Gramlich 1976:11).

The symbolism in this verse is derived from the vision complex, the beautiful Turkish boy being a form through which God is made visible (p. 11n3). The *Sawanih* does not, in fact, contain a great deal of symbolism of this kind (see Pourjavady 1986). Yet it is for seeing the Divine Beloved in the form of beautiful boys that Ghazzālī is particularly remembered by later writers. 'Irāqī, for example, wrote two poems defending Ghazzālī for this (Arberry 1939:41–44, 61–62).

Ghazzālī was one of the mystics who was familiar with and drew on the writings of Abū Nuwās. For example, he quotes one of the most famous verses of Abū Nuwās: "Come, give me wine to drink and say 'It's wine.' And don't give me to drink in secret, when it is possible to do it in public" (Gramlich 1976:72; Wagner 1965:103).

Ghazzālī's influence can be seen in the work of his disciple 'Ayn al-Qudāt al-Hamadhānī, for example, the following passage from his *Tamhid*:

A piece of the heavenly love-play is contained in this earthly *shahid*, the lovely face. That "truth" can take the form of this beautiful form. I praise indeed the man who venerates an earthly *shahid*, for the venerators of the supernatural *shahid* are very few. But do not think that I am referring to sensual love. (Ritter 1955:478)

"The most prominent exponent" of *shahid-bāzī*, according to Schimmel (1982:233n74), was Awhad al-Dīn Kirmānī (d. 1237). There are a number of stories about how he was criticized by his contemporaries for this practice:

Being asked by Shams-i-Tabríz what he was doing, he replied, "I am contemplating the Moon in a bowl of water," meaning the Beauty of the Creator in the beauty of the creature; to which Shams-i-Tabríz replied, "Unless you are afflicted with a carbuncle on the back of your neck, why do you not look at the Moon in the sky?" Similarly Mawlānā Jalālu'd-Dīn Rūmī, being told that Awhadu'd-Dīn sought the society of the beautiful, but with purity of purpose, exclaimed, "Would that his desires had been carnal, and that he had outgrown them!" (Browne [1920] 1956:139–40; see Ritter 1955:474–76)

A more positive picture of his practice of *shahid-bāzī* emerges from the following story:

When he became excited during the *samā'*, he [Ahwaduddin] rent the shirts of the unbearded and danced with them breast to breast. While he was in Baghdad, the beautiful son of the Caliph heard of this practice and said, "He is an innovator and an unbeliever. If he acts in my presence in this way I shall kill him."

Now, when the *samā'* became heated, Awhaduddin realized by his miraculous powers the hidden intentions of the Caliph's son, and said

It's nothing for me
to balance on the
    knife's edge
to lie
beheaded beneath
    the beloved's feet.
You came to kill
an unbeliever.
But if *you*
are a fighter
for the Faith
then must *I* not be
    an infidel?

At this the Caliph's son bowed his own head upon the foot of the shaykh and became his disciple. (Wilson and Weischer 1978:4–5; the story is also recounted by Valiuddin 1972:185–86.)

Awhad al-Dīn was a disciple of Shaykh Sijāssi, whose spiritual lineage included Ahmad al-Ghazzālī. Among Awhad al-Dīn's fellow disciples was Shamsi Tabrīz, whose disapproval of Awhad al-Dīn we have already noted. Awhad al-Dīn traveled extensively, and in Damascus met and became a friend of Ibn 'Arabī, whose ideas about the created world as "the visible reflection of the unique Divine essence" had an important influence on him (Wilson and Weischer 1978:1, 5–6).

Awhad al-Dīn believed that "the (supernatural) meaning can only be perceived in earthly form" because "this world is a visible form and we are in visible forms" (Ritter 1955:474). However he carefully distinguished himself from those who do not get beyond earthly beauty: "And that beautiful face that you call *shahid*, that is not the *shahid*, but His dwelling place" (Ritter 1955:476). This position enabled him, in his poetry, to treat the love of boys as a metaphor for divine love, as in the following quatrain:

My heart
will not search
  for another house
What shame
if my heart turn away
  from love.
My eye
may wander after
  some pretty boy
he is but the Witness
of my eye
you of my heart. (Wilson and Weischer 1978:163)

As in the work of other mystics, there is an oscillation in Awhad al-Dīn's poetry between the vision complex (as in the poem just cited) and the passion complex, in which the beloved, or love, appears as the slayer of the lover. Let me quote a poem of his on this second theme:

Love's a guillotine
where a man
  must lose his head
or else
he is not shriven
  in the Church of Love.
"Well," you say,
"I'd like to love—but
  can't I keep my head?"
Keep it then—
but I fear you're not
destined for much success (Wilson and Weischer 1978:99)

The mystical practices which earned Awhad al-Dīn such suspicion were part of a system which was also taught by 'Irāqī (Wilson and Weischer 1978: 5). Fakhr al-Dīn 'Irāqī (who died in Damascus in 1289) was born at Hamadān. "When he was about seventeen years of age, a party of *qalandars*, amongst whom was a very beautiful youth, came to Hamadān, and, when they left, 'Irāqī, attracted by the beauty of the young dervish, followed them to India" (Browne [1920] 1956:125). The *qalandars* were wandering dervishes, who, given to wine and love and the "satisfaction of the heart," observed only the bare minimum of conventional religious practices, and were not interested in morality and custom, nor in the asceticism, renunciation, "stations," and miracles of the Sufis (Ritter 1955:487–91).

'Irāqī became the disciple of Shaykh Bahā al-Dīn Zakariyyā and would have been his successor, except that the other dervishes disapproved of his antinomianism. He traveled to Arabia, Syria, Egypt, and Turkey. At Qonya he wrote his most celebrated prose work, the *Lama'āt* (translated by Chittick and Wilson as *Divine Flashes* [1982]), influenced by Ibn 'Arabī. A more complete account of 'Irāqī's life, including the poem he wrote to the young *qalandar* with whom he fell in love, is in Chittick and Wilson (1982:33–66) and Wilson (1988:123–34).

According to Browne, 'Irāqī's writings are "almost entirely of a mystical and erotic character" ([1920] 1956:124). As with other Sufis, it is possible to discern in 'Irāqī's work the use of the imagery of both the vision and the passion complex. The following poem employs the imagery of vision:

It needs an eye of vision undefiled
to see His beauty in its loveliness:
the Sweetheart's beauty doth the heart behold,
not every eye may see it. Thou that criest
"A roguish heart hath trapped me," blame not me,
for I am well excused. If thou dost gaze
upon my Darling's beauty, thou wilt rend
thy hands, with heart distraught: if thou beholdest
His form and qualities, His stature tall
all flowing locks, like mine Thy [sic] heart shall be,
His prisoner—to be idolater
will be thy whole desire. What man is there
that, having eyes to see, hath not surrendered
his heart to that fair face? No vision true
was e'er by man possessed, who did not yield
his soul and heart and body unto Him.
The heart cannot withstand His loveliness:
it steals away the mind, and cheats the heart.
That slender grace, that is His beauty's charm,
ensnares the hearts of spiritual men,
and His primaeval lovers bear the mark
of servitude eternal to His love. (Arberry 1939:56–57)

Arberry's use of capital letters for the pronouns which refer to the beloved make the translation less ambiguous than one may suppose the original to have been. In Persian it would not have been clear whether the poet was addressing God or a human beloved. In any case, this poem is a clear expression of the vision complex, though it also hints at the passion complex in soul-yielding. This symbolism is taken further in another poem in which

'Irāqī uses the image of the death of the lover at the hands of his beloved or of love itself:

The lover is a victim, sacrificed
to love, cast down at the Beloved's door:
the lover, slain, yet lives, his heart throbs
though in love's furnace he is all afire. (Arberry 1939:28)

The stories told of 'Irāqī's attraction to beautiful youths are still current in Sufi circles. The episode from his biography recounted by Wilson (1988:134), concerning his falling in love with a cobbler's son in Cairo, is cited, for example, by the contemporary Sufi writer Mir Valiuddin (1972:184–85) as an example of that chaste love through which the Sufi beholds "Real Beauty in phenomenal forms" (1972:170). Valiuddin adds that "it is necessary to presume that the great Sufis, such as Shaykh Ahmad Ghazālī, Shaykh Auhad-ud-dīn Kirmānī and Shaykh Fakhrud-dīn 'Irāqī, who seemed to be indulging in beholding the beauty of sensuous forms, did really behold the Absolute Beauty of God in them and were not interested in the forms *per se*" (1972:171). It is also necessary to presume that this kind of casuistry is a convention that homoerotically inclined Sufis have employed for many centuries to give themselves some measure of protection from conservative theologians and their political allies.

The best known of the mystics who used the symbolism of love between males in their writing but managed to avoid being denounced by the guardians of orthodoxy were Rūzbihān-i Baqlī, Hāfiz, 'Attār, and Jāmī.

In the writings of Rūzbihān-i Baqlī (d. 1209), according to Schimmel, the Persian language "reaches its most sublime form" (1982:54). From an early age he experienced visions, such as dancing with God, or having his tongue sucked by the angels and the Prophet (Massignon 1953:237–39). He wrote a number of works on love theory, dealing with the relationship between earthly and heavenly love, with the creation of man in the image of God, and with *'ishq* as an attribute of God (Ritter 1933:100–106; 1955:556–57). His *Jasmine of the Worshippers of Love* (Corbin and Mo'in 1958) is a "virtual treatise" on the subject of *shahid-bāzī*, according to Wilson (1988:95). He also wrote important commentaries on the work of Hallāj (Massignon 1953: 244–47). In Rūzbihān's view, the idea of a passage from a human object of love to a divine one is a trap. Human love is indispensable, because "divine love is not a transfer of love to a divine object, but a metamorphosis of the subject of human love" (quoted in Bell 1979:224n49).

Most of what we know about Rūzbihān's love of other males comes from the work of other writers. 'Irāqī, for example, wrote a poem about the purity of Rūzbihān's love of a beardless youth who was seen kissing Rūzbihān's feet (Arberry 1939:57–58). And Ritter recounts the following story about Rūzbihān:

In a state of ecstasy the great shaykh Ruzbihan Baqlī of Shiraz said: I saw God in the form of a Turk, with a silk cap, which He wore awry. I gripped the hem of His robe and spoke: By the unity of Your being! In whatever form You appear and in whatever form You show yourself to the loving eye, I will recognize You behind it." (Ritter 1955:448)

This story, which is a fairly clear example of the vision complex, shows a connection with the *hadīth* according to which the Prophet saw God in the form of a beautiful youth, since this *hadīth* was sometimes expanded with the detail that the youth wore his cap awry (Schimmel 1982:67–68). The Turk is a conventional image of the beloved (Schimmel 1982:116, 229–30).

Rūzbihān founded his own Sufi order, the Rūzbihāniya, of which Hāfiz may have been a member, according to evidence adduced by Corbin and Mo'in (1958:57). Shams al-Dīn Hāfiz (d. 1389) was, like Rūzbihān, a native of the city of Shiraz, which is an important source of imagery in his poetry. The *Dīwān* of Hāfiz is held in such high esteem that it is used in Persia for oracular purposes; the only other book the Persians use in this way is the *Qur'ān* (Browne [1920] 1956:311). Although some of Hāfiz's contemporaries considered his verse to be impious, I have not found any indication that he practiced *shahid-bāzī*. Burton noted "that almost all the poetry of Hāfiz is addressed to youths"—a feature which is obscured by the fact that "Persian has no genders properly so called" (1894, 3:115n1). However, the occasional introduction of Arabic in the poems leaves no doubt that the beloved is masculine (Wagner 1965:309).

Browne says this of Hāfiz's poetry: "[t]hat many of the odes are to be taken in a symbolic sense few will deny; that others mean what they say, and celebrate a beauty not celestial and a wine not allegorical can hardly be questioned" ([1920] 1956:299). But in most cases the meaning is ambiguous. The interplay of eroticism and mysticism is illustrated by the following poem:

With a flagon in hand, singing a song and laughing, wine inside;
Sweating all over, hair everywhere, garment torn down the side,
That eye looking for battle and mocking lips mouthing "O no;"
Last night at midnight You came to my pillow, sat by my side.
To my ear You bent Your head and said in a sad soft whisper:
"My poor mad lover are you awake, or do you sleep?" You sighed.
If a wise man is given late at night such a drink, this is his Fate;
Unfaithful to Love he would be if he praised wine, then denied.

Go away preacher, stop ranting about us drinking leftover dregs;
Only this was given us, morning before Creation's clay was fired.
Whatever You have poured into our cup, we've swallowed it all;
Either the wine of drunkards or the elixir of Paradise, we tried.
The laughter of wine in the cup and long curling hair of the Beloved:
How many vows of repentance, like Hafiz's have they untied?
(Smith 1986:poem 44)

In this poem Hāfiz uses the cupbearer as an image of God. He pushes the eroticism of the imagery further than other mystics had done, but the poem is still fairly clearly an instance of the vision complex, that is, of the idea of God appearing in the form of a human beloved. Elsewhere Hāfiz also draws on the passion complex:

I was longing to die at Your feet, wasting like the candle. . . .
O soul, what person is so stone-hearted and weak that he
Didn't make himself the shield against arrows You let fly? (Smith 1986:poem 131)

The next mystic to be considered, Fārid al-Dīn 'Attār (d. 1220), poet of Nishapur, only infrequently writes of the beauty of God being mirrored in human form, according to Ritter (1955:501; see 364). While it is true that 'Attār does often use the symbolism of love between males, "the love of the dervishes for their princes and of the Sufis for their youths etc. is not represented as though the love of God were contained in it, rather is it the symbol and model of this love" (Ritter 1955:502). The content of 'Attār's *dīwān* has much in common with that of 'Irāqī, for example the same oscillation between the love of a boy and the desire for God. "Yet the two conceptions do not coincide as clearly as in 'Iraqi. God reveals his beauty in the world, but it is more a question of the reflection of his beauty in the whole of nature rather than in the appearance of the beautiful person" (Ritter 1955:503).

As an example of 'Attār's love symbolism, let me quote one of his many Mahmūd and Ayāz stories:

One day it is announced to Mahmūd that Ayāz has gone to the baths. The sultan hurries after him, and now sees the youth in his full beauty, on account of which "the wall of the baths was full of fire, and from the roof to the door it began to dance," and falls stunned to the ground. The slave falls at his master's feet and says: What happened to you, my shah, that your so perfect mind left you? Mahmūd answers: As long as I only saw your face, I knew nothing of your limbs; now that I see all your limbs, I have become quite wretched. My soul was already on fire with love of your face, but now a hundred new fires have ignited in me, and I don't know which of your limbs I should love more. (Ritter 1955:405)

The stories in which Mahmūd and Ayāz are represented as ideal lovers (Ritter 1955:298, 371) are based on the lives of historical personages: Mahmud is Sultan Mahmud the Great of Ghazna (d. 1030), who "established his empire all over the Iranian plateau and introduced Islam to India" (Ullah 1963:238). He was a conqueror and crusader for Islam, and also a great patron of the arts, sciences, and literature. Ayāz is referred to as both a Turkish slave and an army officer (Ritter 1955:297–98; Schimmel 1982:74). The ideal behavior of Ayāz toward his royal master is supposed to be a model for the faithful Muslim, who considers himself the slave of God. The relationship is not just one of perfect submission on the part of Ayāz, but also of mutual love (Ritter 1955:365).

The story of the baths, however, suggests that Mahmud is the lover and sees Ayāz, his beloved, in terms of the vision complex. On the other hand, 'Attār also wrote stories in which Ayāz expresses a willingness, even an eagerness, to die at the hands of Mahmud (Ritter 1955:396 and passim). In this case it is Mahmud who represents the Divine Beloved, and death at his hands is clearly an expression of the passion complex.

The last mystic I want to consider before turning to the opponents of *shahid-bāzī* is Jāmī. Nur al-Dīn Jāmī was born in the town of Jam in Khurasan, and died at Herat in 1492 (Browne [1920] 1956:507). He was a great scholar as well as a mystical poet, writing commentaries on the Qur'ān and on the work of earlier mystics, including 'Irāqī and Ibn al-Fārid. In his *Nafahāt al-Uns* ("Breaths of Fellowship"), which is a biography of Sufi saints, he defends some of the great Persian mystics against the accusation that their practice of *shahid-bāzī* was heretical. These include Ahmad al-Ghazzālī, Awhad al-Dīn Kirmānī, and 'Irāqī. Jāmī's argument is the same one we have seen used in more recent times by Mir Valiuddin: that these Sufis were concerned with contemplating absolute beauty when they regarded sensuous forms, and were not caught in the forms themselves (Ritter 1955:475).

Jāmī developed a mystical cosmogony—apparently deriving from the monistic system of Ibn 'Arabī—in which he conceptualizes the One as a *shahid*, a youth contemplating his own beauty in the differentiation of his qualities (Ritter 1955:609; see 477). Jāmī himself practiced *shahid-bāzī* (Wilson 1988: 95–96), but, like Rūzbihān, Hāfiz, and 'Attār, seems to have been able to avoid arousing the suspicion of heresy.

There is another group of mystics who were concerned to distinguish themselves from the supposed *shahid*-worshipers, among whom the outstanding figure is Rūmī. Both in his literary style and his disapproval of the contemplation of "witnesses," Rūmī followed the example of Sana'i of Ghazna (d. ca. 1131) (Schimmel 1982:52–53, 68–69). But Rūmī's spiritual mentor was Shams al-Dīn of Tabrīz (d. 1248), the wandering dervish who appears in the story about Awhad al-Dīn Kirmānī quoted above, in which he criticizes the latter for contemplating God through sensuous forms. As related above, Shams believed that God should be contemplated directly, and not through His manifestations.

Rūmī was born in Balkh (now Afghanistan), but his family settled in Anatolia (Rum), where his father taught at Qonya. Rūmī succeeded to this teaching position, and died in Qonya in 1273. We have seen above how Rūmī, like Shams-i Tabrīz, criticized Awhad al-Dīn Kirmānī for his contemplation of "witnesses." Yet Rūmī's emotional life was centered on his relationships with other males. The first and most important of these was with Shams. "The intimate relation of the two mystics aroused the wrath and jealousy of Rūmī's students and family," and Shams was eventually killed, apparently with the complicity of Rūmī's son 'Ala' al-Dīn (Schimmel 1982:85–86). It was as a result of this relationship that Rūmī began to write poetry, and in the *Dīwān of Shams-i Tabrīzi*, where Rūmī uses Shams's name as his own pen-name, Shams appears as representative of the Divine Beauty (Ritter 1955:476)—clearly an instance of the vision complex.

Rūmī's second important relationship was with the goldsmith Salah al-Dīn Zarkūb, to whom he dedicated a number of poems. If he saw Shamsi as the sun (*shams*="sun"), he saw Salah either as the moon or as a ray from the sun (Schimmel 1982:90–91). The third important friendship was with his disciple and successor, Husam al-Dīn Chalabi. Rūmī's *Mathnawi*, a "veritable encyclopedia of mystical lore" of nearly twenty-six thousand verses, was inspired by this relationship (Schimmel 1982:92–93).

In spite of the significant part played in his life by his relations with other males, Rūmī was critical of the practitioners of *shahid-bāzī*, as we have seen above in the case of Awhad al-Dīn. And according to Chittick, "to the extent that Rumi speaks of the outward physical forms of human beings as 'witnesses,' or manifestations of God's Beauty, he either makes no allusion to their gender or makes them female" (1983:289). Moreover, there are numerous negative references to sexual relations between males in Rūmī's writings. He says, for example,

The Sufi is he who seeks purity, not he who wears a garment of wool, patches it, and commits sodomy.
In the eyes of these despicable people, "Sufism" is patching and sodomy, nothing else. (Chittick 1983:190)

And he uses the "catamite" repeatedly as an image of the "effeminate ego," the *nafs* or lower self, which is contrasted with the Persian hero Rustam. He writes, for example,

Had war no blows of the sword and spears and arrows, Rustam would be no different from a catamite. (Chittick 1983:242)

and

A thousand Rustams cannot approach me—why should I be subject to the effeminate ego?
I take the bloody sword in hand—I am a martyr to love in the midst of my own blood. (Chittick 1983:348; also see 56, 165, 167, 335)

Rūmī was thus faithful to the letter of his religion, in maintaining that love relations between males should be absolutely pure. But it is worth noting that he recognized that the temptation to intimacy with males was not foreign to his own nature:

Yesterday your intoxicated dream image came with a cup in his hand.
I said: "I don't drink wine!" He said: "Don't do it then [but] it is a pity!"
I said: "I am afraid that if I drink, shame will fly out of my head,
and I may put my hand on your curls, and then you'll recede from me!" (Schimmel 1982:99)

Rūmī's use of the symbolism of love between males was not restricted to the vision complex. He also used the conventional imagery of death at the hands of love, or of the Divine Beloved, to represent the mystical experience, as in the following lines:

I had followed the way of the prayer carpet and the mosque with all sincerity and effort. I wore the marks of asceticism to increase my good works.
Love came into the mosque and said, "Oh great teacher. Rend the shackles of existence. Why are you tied to prayer carpets?
Let not your heart tremble before the blows of my sword! Do you want to travel from knowledge to vision? Then lay down your head! . . ." (Chittick 1983:3)

CONCLUSION

The elaboration of the symbolism of love between males in Islamic mystical literature presents us with a set of possibilities that have been largely ignored in the various Western discourses concerned with subjective experience—not just in the field of religion, but also in psychology (for example, the work of C. G. Jung) and sexual metaphysics (for example, the work of Julius Evola). Gay men and lesbians are starting to question the heterosexual bias of these discourses. Gay and lesbian Jungians, for instance, are revising Jungian theory to include love between men and between women as paths to individuation (Hopcke et al. 1993). The present chapter deals with material that may be useful in the ongoing task of reshaping these discourses.

This is not to say that Islam does not have its own heterosexist and patriarchal biases, the most obvious being that its official doctrines forbid sexual relationships between males and pay almost no attention at all to love between females.[16] The official doctrines are not, of course, a reliable guide to the realities of erotic conduct in Islamic cultures. Clearly, homosexual practices have always been a part of these cultures; and the elite literary discourses dealt with in this chapter may, in fact, have been partly motivated by the aspiration to mediate between Islamic ideology and the experience of love between males, in their own lives or in their social environment. However that may be, the development in Islamic mysticism of a sort of "Imaginal Yoga" (Wilson 1988:94) based on the symbolism of love between males enables us to recognize the limitations of what we might call "Western love theory," and, perhaps, to conceive of ways of going beyond those limitations.

Notes

1. This chapter is a revised version of chapter 3 of an unpublished thesis (Wafer 1986). I am grateful for the editorial advice of Stephen O. Murray and Peter Lamborn Wilson. I am also grateful to the latter for giving permission to quote from his book *Heart's Witness* and to Paul Smith for permission to quote from his translation of *The Divan of Hafiz*.

2. Arabic secular love poetry may in fact have influenced the medieval literature of courtly love (Nykl [1946] 1970).

3. Schimmel (1982:15, 18) sees the lead in the development of love mysticism as having been taken by Ja'far al-Sādiq, the sixth Imām of the Shi'a, and by his younger contemporary, the woman saint Rabi'a al-Adawiyya of Basra (d. 801).

4. One of the earliest users of *'ishq* in a mystical sense was 'Abd al-Wāhid ibn Zayd (d. 793) (Giffen 1971:86, 146). *'Ishq* was also given a mystical interpretation by Hallāj (d. 922) and his followers, who regarded it as "the very essence of God" (Massignon in Giffen 1971:146), and by later mystics, such as Ibn Sīnā (d. 1037; Giffen 1971:146) and Ghazzālī (d. 1111; Bell 1979:166).

5. Cf. Ritter 1928:257; Corbin 1969:272–77; Wilson and Weischer 1978:8; Schimmel 1982:67–68. It is also worth noting that the Prophet's guide during his ascent to Paradise in the "night journey" was a male figure, the angel Gabriel, who is thus the structural equivalent of Dante's beloved Beatrice. Some scholars have suggested that the *Divine Comedy* may have been directly influenced by the account of Muhammad's ascent in the *Mirāj Nāmeh* (Séguy 1977:19).

6. There seems to be a similarity between these gatherings and the saints' festivals of the Maghrib called *mouled*, or the Marabutist festivals called *ziyāra* of the Maghrib and the Middle East (Bouhdiba 1985:120). From 'Abd Allah's account of a *mouled* at the Siwah Oasis, it appears that sexual relations between men were a common feature of such celebrations, at least in that particular location (1917:20). Bouhdiba also mentions that *ziyāra* "turn very easily into licentiousness" (1985:120). I have not come across any

suggestion of a historical connection between these popular festivals and the institution of *samā'*, but the subject may merit further investigation. Cf. Wilson 1988:111–12.

7. A good illustration is provided in a poem of Abū Madyan translated by Dermenghem (1951:269). In this poem the Beloved and the cupbearer appear to be separate. But in a great deal of mystical poetry the cupbearer or *saki* is himself the Beloved. Chittick (1983:314) writes (in relation to the poetry of Rūmī): "The saki or cupbearer is Love or the Beloved, or the Form of the Beloved seen in the heart; sometimes it may allude to the saint, who is the outward and human form of Love. Rūmī often refers to Koranic verses which speak of the wines of Paradise and of God as 'He who gives to drink' (*saqā*, i.e., the saki). The verse he quotes most often is 'Their Lord shall give them to drink a pure draught' (LXXVI 21)."

8. Ibn 'Arabī was opposed to giving a mystical interpretation to love between men, believing this was only appropriate for the relationship between a man and a woman. However, he does refer to the legendary relationship between Mahmūd and Ayāz in his *Meccan Revelations* (Ritter 1955:480, 367).

9. Numerous legends concerning all these lovers are recounted in Ritter's (1955) study of Attār. A famous literary treatment of the relationship between the dervish and the prince is contained in Arīfī of Herāt's *The Ball and the Polo Stick* (trans. A. S. Greenshields [1932] 1980).

10. What Schimmel calls the "vernacular" traditions are beyond the scope of the present study.

11. For an English translations of Abū Nuwās's *Dīwān*, see Wormhoudt 1974, 1989; Bey 1993.

12. It is also true that Hallāj is on record as having opposed the contemplation of beautiful youths (Bell 1979:142).

13. Bell, referring only to Ibn al-Fārid's *Tā'īya*, sees his poetry as an exception the the general rule that the symbolic object of love in Arabic mystical poetry is a beautiful youth, since in that work he draws his inspiration from "feminine objects" (1979:139–40). Clearly this generalization cannot be applied to the *Dīwān*. (Another translation of poems by Ibn al-Fārid is contained in Nicholson [1921] 1976, chap. 3.)

14. However, the teachings of Hallāj had been brought to Persia earlier by Ibn-i Khafīf of Shīrāz, who was the last to visit Hallāj in prison before the latter's execution (Schimmel 1982:51).

15. For example, by 'Irāqī (Ritter 1955:473–74; Arberry 1939:41–44, 61–62; Wilson 1988:95) and by his opponent Ibn al-Jawzī (Bell 1979:2).

16. The references I have come across are mainly to legal prohibitions of *sahq* ("lesbianism"; cf. Sofer 1992:135, 140, 147n18). For an account of the role of women in Sufism, see Schimmel 1975:426–35.

References

'Abd Allah, Mahmud Mohammad. 1917. "Siwan customs." *Varia Africana* 1:6–28.

Arberry, Arthur J. 1939. *The song of lovers, by 'Iraqi*. Oxford: Islamic Research Association.

———. 1956. *The mystical poems of Ibn al-Farid*. Dublin: Emery Walker.

Bannerth, Ernst. 1957. "Der Dīwān des maghribinischen Sufi Su'aib Abū Madjan" (gest. 1197–98 n. Ch.). *Wiener Zeitschrift für die Kunde des Morgenlandes* 53:28–56, 237–66.

Bell, Joseph Norment. 1979. *Love theory in later Hanbalite Islam*. Albany, NY: State University of New York Press.

Bey, Hakim. 1993. *O tribe that loves boys: The poetry of Abu Nuwas*. Utrecht: Abu Nuwas Society.

Bogoras, Waldemar. [1904] 1975. *The Chukchee*. Vol. 7, *The Jesup North Pacific Expedition*, ed. F. Boas. Memoir of the American Museum of Natural History. Leiden: Brill. Reprint. New York: AMS Press.

Bouhdiba, Abdelwahab. 1985. *Sexuality in Islam*. London: Kegan Paul.

Brain, Robert. 1976. *Friends and lovers*. London: Hart-Davis, MacGibbon.

Browne, Edward G. [1920] 1956. *A literary history of Persia*. Vol. 3. Cambridge: Cambridge University Press.

Burton, Richard F. 1894. *The book of the thousand nights and a night*. 12 vols. London: H. S. Nichols and Co.

Chittick, William C. 1983. *The Sufi path of love: The spiritual teachings of Rumi*. Albany, NY: State University of New York Press.

Chittick, William C., and Peter Lamborn Wilson. 1982. *Fakhruddin 'Iraqi: Divine flashes*. New York: Paulist Press.

Christman, Henry M. 1989. *Gay tales and verses from the Arabian nights*. Austin: Banned Books.

Corbin, Henry. 1964. *Histoire de la philosophie islamique*. Paris: Gallimard.

———. 1969. *Creative imagination in the Sufism of Ibn 'Arabī*. Princeton: Princeton University Press.

———. 1978. *The man of light in Iranian Sufism*. Boulder, CO: Shambhala.

Corbin, Henry, and Mohammed Mo'in. 1958. *Ruzbehan Baqli Shirazi: Le jasmin des fidèles d'amour*. Tehran: Département d'Iranologie de l'Institut Franco-Iranien/Paris: Adrien-Maisonneuve.

Daniélou, Jean, and Herbert Musurillo. 1961. *From glory to glory: Texts from Gregory of Nyssa's mystical writings*. New York: Scribner.

Dermenghem, Émile. 1951. *Les plus beaux textes arabes*. Paris: La Colombe.

Evola, Julius. 1983. *The metaphysics of sex*. New York: Inner Traditions International.

Giffen, Lois A. 1971. *Theory of profane love among the Arabs: The development of the genre*. New York: New York University Press.

Gramlich, Richard. 1976. *Ahmad Ghazzali: Gedanken über die Liebe*. Mainz: Akademie der Wissenschaften und der Literatur.

Greenshields, R. S. [1932] 1980. *'Arifi, the ball and the polo stick or book of ecstasy: On the path of the mystic*. London: Octagon.

Hardy, Richard. 1987. *Search for nothing: The life of John of the Cross*. New York: Crossroad.

Hopcke, Robert H., Karin L. Carrington, and Scott Wirth. 1993. *Same-sex love and the path to wholeness*. Boston: Shambhala.

Lewis, C. S. 1960. *The four loves*. London: Geoffrey Bles.

Massignon, Louis. 1953. "La Vie et les oeuvres de Rūzbehān Baqlī." In *Studia orientalia Ioanni Pedersen dicata*. Hauniae: Einar Munksgaard.

———. 1982. *The passion of al-Hallāj: Mystic and martyr of Islam*. Princeton: Princeton University Press.

Nicholson, Reynold A. [1921] 1976. *Studies in Islamic mysticism*. Delhi: Idarah-i Adabiyat-i Delli.

Nykl, Alois R. [1946] 1970. *Hispano-Arabic poetry and its relations with the Old Provençal troubadours*. Baltimore: by subscription.

Ozak, Muzaffer. 1981. *The unveiling of love: Sufism and the remembrance of God*. New York: Inner Traditions International.

Perry, Whitall N. 1971. *A treasury of traditional wisdom*. New York: Simon and Schuster.

Pourjavady, Nasrollah. 1986. *Sawanih: Inspirations from the world of pure spirits*. London: Iran University Press.

Ritter, Hellmut. 1928. "Philologika II: Über einige Koran und Hadith betreffende Handschriften hauptsächlich Stambuler Bibliotheken." *Der Islam* 17:249–57.

———. 1933. "Philologika VII: Arabische und persische Schriften über die profane und die mystische Liebe." *Der Islam* 21:84–109.

———. 1955. *Das Meer der Seele: Mensch, Welt und Gott in den Geschichten des Fariduddin 'Attār.* Leiden: Brill.

Schimmel, Annemarie. 1975. *Mystical dimensions of Islam.* Chapel Hill: University of North Carolina Press.

———. 1982. *As through a veil: Mystical poetry in Islam.* New York: Columbia University Press.

Séguy, Marie-Rose. 1977. *The miraculous journey of Mahomet: Mirāj Nāmeh.* London: Scolar Press.

Smith, Paul. 1986. *Divan of Hafiz.* Melbourne: New Humanity Books.

Sofer, Jehoeda. 1992. "Sodomy in the law of Muslim states." In *Sexuality and eroticism among Males in Moslem societies,* ed. Arno Schmitt and Jehoeda Sofer, 131–49. Binghamton, NY: Harrington Park Press.

Ullah, Najib. 1963. *Islamic literature: An introductory history with selections.* New York: Washington Square Press.

Valiuddin, Mir. [1968] 1972. *Love of God: A Sufic approach.* Farnham, Surrey: Sufi Publishing Company.

Wafer, James. 1986. "Sacred and profane love in Islam: Dimensions of gay religious history." M.A. thesis, Religious Studies, Indiana University, Bloomington.

Wagner, Ewald. 1965. *Abū Nuwās: Eine Studie zur arabischen Literatur der frühen 'Abbāsidenzeit.* Wiesbaden: Franz Steiner.

Wilson, Peter Lamborn. 1988. *Scandal: Essays in Islamic heresy.* New York: Autonomedia.

Wilson, Peter Lamborn, and Bernd Manuel Weischer. 1978. *Heart's witness: The Sufi quatrains of Awhaduddīn Kirmānī.* Tehran: Imperial Iranian Academy of Philosophy.

Wormhoudt, Arthur. 1974. *The Diwan of Abu Nuwas al Hasan ibn Hani al Hakami, translated from the recension of Abu Bakr al Suli (d. 946 A.D.).* Oskaloosa, IA: William Penn College.

———. 1989. *Poems of male love by Al-Hasan ibn Hani Abu Nuwas.* Oskaloosa, IA: William Penn College.

CHAPTER 7

Corporealizing Medieval Persian and Turkish Tropes

Stephen O. Murray

Love lies out of the reach of dogma.
Beyond belief and faithlessness there lies the space
In whose heartland this love of ours has found its place:
It holds no room for religion and sacrilege—
That's the ground where the man of wisdom rubs his face.
Jalal al-Dīn Rūmī (translated by Halman 1983:26, 22)

The Persians were conquered by Arabs in 637. Most Persians converted to
Shi'a Islam after the fall of the (Sunni) Caliphate in the mid-thirteenth century. (Quite a few had done so before.) The famed medieval poets who wrote
in Persian or Turkish all wrote poems about desired boys. Indeed, not only
poetry but all genres were written about men, by men, and for exclusively
male audiences. Often, its pederastic content has been obscured in translation with female pronouns. As Baraheni notes, one aspect of this poetry "is
the difficulty in deciding whether the poet is addressing himself to a man or
a woman. Generally, the beloved has all the characteristics of a beautiful
male with some feminine qualities. What is explicit in Rumi, in connection
to his male lover, Shams-e Tabrizi, is implicit in the poetry of Hāfiz and Saadi,
the other two major Iranian lyrical poets" (1977:75).

Even more often, the imagery of beautiful young boys has been interpreted away as an idiom for loving/worshiping God. Schimmel wisely suggests that it is futile

to look for either a purely mystical or a purely profane interpretation of the poems of Hāfiz, Jāmī, or Irāqī—their ambiguity is intended, the oscillation between the two levels of being is consciously maintained. . . . One cannot derive a mystical system out of Persian or Turkish poetry or see in it an expression of experiences to be taken at face value. (1975:288)

She also stresses that the recurrent tropes of human (viz., young male) embodiment of Divine Love developed over time, especially after the fall of the 'Abbāsid caliphate, during the Il-khānī (Mongol) period (1265–1337) and the Tīmūr (Tartar) period (1335–1502): "The early Sufis would never have accepted a human medium for the feeling of love, but concentrated exclusively on divine love" (1975:289). As Wafer shows in the previous chapter, later Sufi writing is less clear and simple, and writers were suspected by various moralists of extolling boy-love in occasionally transparent code. In this chapter, I will argue that the beloved in at least some medieval Persian and Turkish literature is clearly a boy, since the attributes cannot be those of Allah.

In distinguishing mystical ecstasy from "lust," there is a tendency to occlude or even to deny physical aspects.[1] Especially for the Mevlevi ("whirling dervish") Sufis, the techniques for ecstasy involve physical movement, though not physical contact with others who may be whirling nearby. While I do not mean to imply that Sufi whirling is specifically homoerotic, I bring it up as a reminder that ecstasy is not wholly distinct from physical techniques. Love may also have physical manifestations. If ecstasy involves transcending one's body, disembodiment is the end, not the basis. "United in ecstasy, we shall no longer be you and I" implies initial distinctness: "two shapes, two bodies" even if (eventually) a single soul (Rūmī, translated by Halman 1983:19–20).[2]

Love for the divinely beautiful boy clearly mixed with love of the Creator in Sufi poetry from medieval Persia and Turkey. However, if the boys are only epiphenomenal, and the poetry is all "really" about Allah one would have to conclude that the Creator is more than a little coquettish: (naz), a "hunter of hearts" ('Irāqī, "aspiring to have his desire of thy mouth, O Love" in his Diwan, in Browne's translation [1920:129]). As Schimmel notes, "Beauty, though basically a static concept, has no full meaning without admiration and love, and the beloved needs the lover for his perfection" (1975:291). To a non-believer the need of a god for worshipers is thinkable, but to believers? Even more than coquettishness, the incompleteness and passive need for the love borders on blasphemy within Islamic cosmologies where will and agency are Allah's, not humans'. In asserting that the beloved is not just a passive object—"the fire of love which burns the lover burns the loved one, too" (translated in Walsh 1978:63)—the fourteenth-century Turkish poet Kadi Burhanettin seems to me to have been writing of human love. I find it hard to imagine Allah being burned by devotees' ardor, and as Wafer discusses, it is not easy to establish which is the lover and which the beloved in the poetry of Attār (d. 1220): they suggest mutuality.

It is even harder to extend the mystification of boys as instances of divinity to poems disparaging boys either for not being more complaisant (to the poet/suitor) or too complaisant (to other admirers). First, three instances from Sa'di's *Būstān* ("Orchard," ca.1257):

Though you may kiss his feet, he'll give you no regard:
Though you be dust before him, no gratitude he'll show you.
Empty your head of brains, of coins your hands
If you would set your mind on other people's children
(lines 3264–65, translated by Wickens 1974)

A certain lad some days ago my heart did steal away,
And my affection for him is such that I no longer can endure;
Yet he's not once enquired of me with pleasant disposition:
See, then, what I must make my soul to suffer for his disdainful ways? (Ibid., ll. 1953–54)

When awake, there's mischief in his cheek and beauty-spot—
And sleeping, you are fettered to the image of him. (l. 1685)

In the following two couplets from the fourteenth-century Turkish poet Necati (d. 1509), it might be possible (though to me it is implausible) to interpret the referent to a deity like the Jewish one who tested Job:

Unkindness, yes, and cruelty, are what the Beauties practice best;
But they did things to me such as no other lover ever bore. . . .
Necati, face it, there is precious little such as you can do;
We are all schooled in suffering by those fair creatures we adore. (translated by Walsh 1978:72–73)

However, it seems impossible to take the following one as only metaphorically directed to a human boy:

Of Beauties there are thousands, all as fair as Joseph, yet you'll find
That they do not show off their charms and let themselves be bidden for. (p. 72)

Similarly, if the Persian writer 'Obeyd-e Zākānī (ca. 1300–ca.1371) was writing about God in the following poem, would he have sought a cure from his
love? Or faulted God for making specious promises (to show oats and only
provide barley)?

Once again a passion has entered my head;
again my heart inclines in a certain direction.
    He is of royal birth, I am of dust;
he is a king, and I am portionless.
    One tall of stature with locks like lassoes,
an autocrat descended from Sultan Husayn:
    One with eyebrows like bows and slender waist,
one unkind, fair and deceitful.
    Such a charmer of hearts, such a graceful cypress-tree,
such a shower of oats and seller of barley!
    Without him the sun gives no light;
without him the world has no lustre.

Wherever his ruby-lip smiles,
there sugar is of no account.
Everywhere the heart holds with his vision,
pleasant speech and sweet discourse.
Thou wouldst say that I come to the house of the physician,
that perhaps I may procure a remedy for my heart.
Everyone else's complaint is of a foe,
but our complaint is of a friend.
Should the eyes of 'Obeyd not look their fill upon him,
then his eyes do not regard any other misfortune. (translated by Browne 1920:236)

The jealous complaints of the Turkish poets Fuzūlī (1494–1556), Nābī (1642–
1712), and Nedīm (1681–1730) also must be directed at fickle/promiscuous
human beloveds, not at God:

    Why do you keep strolling through the gardens with my enemy,
Lavishing your favours on him, publicly and privately?
    Is it seemly that you wreck the structure of fidelity;
When, you torment, will you keep those promises you made me?
    Time and time again you've heeded other suitors' false advice;
Draught on draught you've drained my rival's cup of joy and found it nice;
    One by one they're all forgotten, pledges made in terms precise;

When, you torment, will you keep those promises you made me? . . .
  tis I who suffer for you—others get your tenderness! . . .
  Like the Sphere you've made the arts of perfidy your wherewithal;
Once you had an honoured name but now you've gone and spoiled it all.
  Ever changing, you have made me sad while others you enthrall
When, you torment, will you keep those promises you made me? (Fuzūlī, translated
by Walsh 1978:84–85)

Fed up being nice to rivals just to see my Sweetheart near. . . .
I'm tired of wrestling rivals for a love, however dear. (Nābī, translated by Walsh
1978:106)

Saucy the way he ogles . . .
  Hundreds of thousands of languages speak in his eloquent eyes;
Thousands there are who respond to their message. (Nedīm, translated by Walsh
1978:110)

Lying, ogling, and promiscuously giving favors to rivals are not plausible
attributes of an omnipotent, omniscient God. In much other poetry I am not
convinced that the rose, a recurrent metaphor for the beloved object of the
yearning poet's phallic nightingale, is "really" God and not a boy's anus (the
tulip similarly figures as a metaphor for a vagina). In a way ecstasy is ecstasy
is ecstasy, and perhaps a rose is not a rose is not a rose—if a rose is sometimes
a metaphor for the gateway to sexual pleasure (a *zinā*) and at others is a
synecdoche for the glory of divine creation, and if contemplation of beauty is
a gateway to union with the Creator of all beauty. The metaphor, to put it
mildly, is overdetermined. Poetry in general is polysemous, and Islamic
poetry about love is especially veiled (see Schimmel 1982). A particular
instance may carry more than one of these meanings, while sexual acts are
never explicitly mentioned.

In the *Bahāristān* ("Spring garden") Jāmī (1414–92) recounted a Sufi monastery smitten by one handsome boy "who had wound the noose of desire
round the neck of the dervishes." The monastery's head (*khāneghāh*),

who was no less involved than the others, and was unable to conceal his desires, sent
for the boy and set to giving him advice: "My son," he said, "talented and charming
as you are, you must cease mingling with all and sundry as sugar mingles with milk.
Cease, therefore, trying on everyone the halter of deceit, whether he merits your
interest or not. You are a mirror in which God is reflected. It would be a pity if your
face were to light up at sight of anyone, lacking head or feet as he might be." (Surieu
1967:173)

Although the *khāneghāh* did not specify what part of a man between head and feet interested this youth, it is not hard to imagine, any more than is the "private dwelling" in the continuation of the admonition:

Do not yield up the bridle you wear in the hands of the unworthy,
Do not admit the vulgar throng into your private dwelling.
Your face is a mirror most carefully polished:
 Take care you do not rust this limpid mirror. (Ibid.)

The boy, incidentally, rejected the advice, and was bid to return, the dervishes acknowledging that "no one can lay down the law to thee, fair youth," and acquiescing that he can "grant thy company to whom thou wilt, refuse it to whom thou wilt" (p. 176). As in other literary traditions, the lover is ever captivated and willingly victimized by the beloved (also as in other literary traditions, what the beloved thinks/feels remains mysterious: only the tormented lovers write).[3] As Sa'di put it,

If you're a lover, you will learn
That only by undergoing death will you win ease from burning (*Būstān* 2032)

Night and day you're in the sea of passion and of flame
And know not, in your agitation, night from day (*Būstān* 1703)

In the *Gulistān*, he wrote of the indifference of beloved boys for those who desire them, quoting two:

"What is it to me if a moth kills itself?" (5:7)
I heard him saying when he went away:
"If the bat desires not union with the sun
The beauty of the sun will not decrease." (5:10)

and abjectly concluded:

It is easier to accustom the heart to strife,
than to turn away from seeing the beloved.
Who has his heart with a heart-ravisher
Has his beard in another's hand.
A gazelle with a halter on the neck
Is not able to walk of its own accord.
If he, without whom one cannot abide,
Becomes insolent it must be endured. . . .
I submit my heart to what he wills. (5:9)

There are Arab exemplars of similar plaints, for example, the following from two or three centuries before Sa'di:

Oh you whose waist is so slender it almost breaks,
Why is your heart not fine, too?
I gave him what he asked for
made him my master . . .
Love has put fetters on my heart
As herdsmen put fetters on a camel. (Nykl 1946:39)

The section of the *Gulistān* dealing with love and youth includes a number of metaphors for boys' beauty spoiled by sprouting facial hair. The evanescence of youth provides some bittersweet respite from particular longing. That is, as one boy rots, another blooms, though both poets and former beauties in Persia and Turkey (as in medieval Japan and ancient Greece) mourned the passing of youthful beauty. Sa'di asked one:

"What has befallen the beauty of thy face
That ants are crawling round the moon?"
He replied, smiling: "I know not what is the matter with my face.
Perhaps it wears black as mourning for my beauty." (*Gulistān* 5:10)

Sa'di quoted with some satisfaction a Baghdad friend telling him that "when one of them is yet delicate and wanted, he is insolent; but when he becomes rough and is not wanted, he is affable" (5:11). However, in the *Būstān* he faulted even a presumably adult male (since he exercised a profession) for obliviousness to the effect of his male beauty on those stricken by it:

There was in Marv a beautifully [*pari*] visaged physician,
Whose stature was a cypress in the garden of the heart:
No pain reached him of the pain of wounded hearts. (1839–40)

The latter two quotations are from a sequence of four stories in which self-immolation is presented as prerequisite to rebirth (1958–60, 1985–87, 2035–36). Giving up one's riches and reputation should be of little concern to the lover, although elsewhere (e.g., 3249–54) Sa'di condemned the unmanliness of a beardless youth and counseled flight rather than surrender of self: "Set not your heart on smooth-faced ones" (p. 354) and (drawing on the conventional imagery of the deranged lover as a nightingale or moth and the heedless beloved as a rose or a candle):

A man should not indulge his fancy with a rose
Who has a different nightingale at every dawning;

While if at every gathering he makes himself a candle,
Don't hang around him longer like a moth. . . .
See him not as heart-enchanting, like the *hur* of Paradise,
For he on the reverse side is ugly as a ghoul (3258–59, 3260).

As Southgate (1984:434) explains:

The Persian language reflects the same ambivalence toward the love of boys. The *Lughatnamah* (Encyclopedia Dictionary) defines *shahid* as (1) a man who has a beautiful face, a youth whose beard has just sprouted, and (2) the beloved, a beautiful woman or youth. Both in its literal and figurative sense the term's connotations are positive and tend to emphasize the physical beauty of the youth, not his role in the homosexual act. Social disapproval of pederasty is reflected in derogatory terms like *amrad* and *mukhannas* (catamite). *Amrad* (beardless) also means effeminate and passive (*maf'ul*, the done). The term's other definitions (stupid, crafty, cowardly, spiritless, ignoble, infamous, disgraced) also suggest social disapproval of the catamite. The catamite is the object of much more severe disapproval than the sodomite (*fa'il*, the doer). Iranian medieval writings reveal a strong stigma against the passive homosexual. The boy one loved passionately was the *shahid*, but the boy one sodomized was the *mukhannas* or *amrad*.

In the *Qabus-nama*, written in 1082, Kai Ka'us ibn Iskander, prince of Gurgan, advised his son, Gilanshah, "As between women and youths, do not confine your inclinations to either sex; thus you may find enjoyment from both kinds," adding a seasonal allocation of partners: "During the summer let your desires incline toward youths and during the winter towards women" (Levy 1951:77–78). Kai Ka'us went on to warn that "in passion there is no happiness," and that it is especially unseemly for aged princes:

If during your youth you toy with passion, there will be some excuse for you; men will regard you with indulgence and say that you are young. But strive never to have such passion when you are old. No indulgence is granted to old men, although, if you were of the ordinary run of men, the matter might be simpler. Being a prince, and old, by no means let your thoughts stray in that direction, nor let it be apparent that your affections are attached to any person. That a prince in old age should indulge in passion is a matter of grave concern. (Levy 1951:73)

And if while young he must succumb to passion, his son should be sure that the *ma'shuq* (male beloved) is worthy:

Although the object of one's affection cannot always be a Ptolemy or a Plato, he should have some endowment of good sense. Although I know, too, that not everyone can be Joseph [the ideal of male beauty] son of Jacob, yet there must be in him some pleasing quality which shall prevent men from cavilling and allow indulgence to be readily accorded you. (Levy 1951: 75–76)

Even then, the prince should remember that his favorite(s) "will not be viewed with the same eyes as your own" and that the prince's amour should never be too public a preoccupation.

Although these (and other) writers could not write directly of sex, they were not entirely aim-inhibited, sublimating sexual desire into love for the Creator of beauty (including boys, roses, and the moon). I have quoted a number of instances of irritation at beloveds for conduct that I cannot imagine attributing to Allah. I do not mean to reduce all love in this vast canon to lust. But instead of seeing the indirect language as establishing a lack of any physical longings, I would remind readers of medieval Persian and Turkish writers that physical love does not preclude feeling various other kinds of love, even during coitus, even for those who have granted their "favors." Certainly in the view of critics of Sufi practices such as the Hanbalite jurist Ibn Taymīya (1262–1328) and his most prominent student Ibn Qayyim al-Jawzīya (1292–1350) defenses of *nazar* (gazing) and *'ishq al-suwar* (passionate love of bodily forms) were at best a grave error, at worst a cover for unchastity (Bell 1979:143).

Notes

1. In the parallel instance of Arabic and Hebrew love-poetry in medieval Spain, Norman Roth notes that "it is evident that the poetry reflects very real and quite prevalent practices which were by no means limited to the circle of poets. . . . [The] poets, like poets of any culture, did not write about things which they did not experience and consider important in their lives. Perhaps just as importantly, they did not write about things which their readers could not understand and identify at once" (1989:114). See also Roth 1991, 1994; and Dermenghem 1942. On Arabic boy-love poetry, see Roth 1991, 1994; and Dermenghem 1942, and on nineteenth- and twentieth-century Urdu, see Naim 1979 and Rahman 1989.

2. Baraheni notes that "Rumi's leader, who represents God on earth, is Shams-e Tabrizi, about whose homosexual love affair with Rumi there can be little doubt" (1977:72). I would suggest that one reason Rūmī signed much of his poetry as Shams after Rūmī's family slew him is the cultural incongruity of the beloved (Shams) being the elder and spiritual superior. Generally, a *tālib* (Sufi "seeker") is supposed to love his *murshid* (teacher) before he "can reach his true love, God, who is again always referred to in the masculine" (Naim 1979:123). The more powerful older male in both instances becomes the object of a kind of agency (love) by the inferior young male, who does not just wait to be filled by God—or by the *murshid*—with greater insight than the *tālib* into God.

3. A modern exception is the novel *Kyra Kyralina* (Istrati 1926), whose narrator recalls several Turkish lovers of his youth.

References

Arberry, Arthur J. 1945. *Kings and beggars*. (Translation of part of Sa'di's [1257] *Būstān*.) London: Luzac and Co.
———. 1958. *Classical Persian literature*. London: Macmillan.
Baraheni, Reza. 1977. *The crowned cannibals: Writings on repression in Iran*. New York: Vintage.
Bell, Joseph Norment. 1979. *Love theory in later Hanbalite Islam*. Albany, NY: State University of New York Press.
Browne, Edward G. 1920. *A history of Persian literature: The Tartar dominion, 1265–1502*. New York: Cambridge University Press.
Dermenghem, Émile. 1942. "Les grandes thèmes de la poésie amoureuse chez les Arabes." *Cahiers du Sud* (août–octobre) 26–38.
Halman, Talat Sait. 1983. "Love is all: Mevlana's poetry and philosophy." In *Mevlana Celaleddin Rumi and the whirling dervishes*, 9–46. Istanbul: Dost.
Istrati, Panaït. 1926. *Kyra Kyralina*. New York: Knopf.
Levy, Reuben. 1951. *A mirror for princes: The Qabus Nama* [of Kaykavus ibn Iskandar ibn Qabus, 1082]. New York: Dutton.
Naim, C. M. 1979. "The theme of homosexual (pederastic) love in pre-modern Urdu poetry." In *Studies in Urdu gazal and prose fiction*, ed. Umar Memon, 120–42. Madison: University of Wisconsin Press.
Nykl, Alois Richard. 1946. *Hispano-Arabic poetry, and its relations with the Old Provençal troubadours*. Baltimore: J. H. Furst.
Rahman, Tariq. 1989. "Boy love in the Urdu ghazal." *Paidika* 2(1):10–27.
Rehatsek, Edward. [1888] 1965. *The Gulistan or rose garden of Sa'di* [1258]. New York: G. P. Putnam's Sons.
Roth, Norman. 1989. "The care and feeding of gazelles: Medieval Hebrew and Arabic love poetry." In *Poetics of love in the middle ages*, ed. M. Lazar and N. Lacy, 95–115. Fairfax, VA: George Mason University Press.
———. 1991. "Fawn of my delights: Boy-love in Hebrew and Arabic verse." In *Sex in the middle ages*, 157–72. New York: Garland.
———. 1994. "Boy-love in Medieval Arabic verse." *Paidika* 3(3): 12–17.
Rypka, Jan. 1968. *History of Iranian literature*. Dordrecht: Reidel.
Schimmel, Annemarie. 1975. *Mystical dimensions of Islam*. Chapel Hill: University of North Carolina Press.
———. 1982. *As through a veil: Mystical poetry in Islam*. New York: Columbia University Press.
Southgate, Minoo S. 1984. "Men, women, and boys: Love and sex in the works of Sa'di." *Iranian Studies* 17:413–52.
Surieu, Robert. 1967. *Sarve naz: An essay on love and the representation of erotic themes in ancient Iran*. Geneva: Nagel.
Walsh, John R. 1978. "Divan poetry." In *The Penguin book of Turkish verse*, ed. Nermin Menemencioglu and Fahir Iz, 59–119. Middlesex: Penguin.
Wickens, G. M. 1974. *Morals pointed and tales adorned*. (Translation of Sa'di's [1257] *Bustan*.) Toronto: University of Toronto Press.
Yarshater, Y. 1960. "The theme of drinking and the concept of the beloved in early Persian poetry." *Studia Islamica* 13:43–53.

CHAPTER 8

Male Love and Islamic Law in Arab Spain

Louis Crompton

A unique flowering of homoerotic poetry took place in Iberia after the Arab conquest in 711. The efflorescence there repeated a phenomenon of the Islamic world generally, paralleling the erotic lyrics of Iraq, Persia, Afghanistan, Mughal India, Turkey, and the North African states of Egypt, Tunis, and Morocco. The anthologies of medieval Islamic poetry, whether compiled in Baghdad, Damascus, Isfahan, Delhi, Kabul, Istanbul, Cairo, Kairouan, or Fez reveal, with astonishing consistency over a period of a millennium, the same strain of passionate homoeroticism we find in love poems from Cordoba, Seville, and Granada.

The civilization created by the Umayyad rulers of Spain, who reigned in Cordoba from 756 until 1031, vied with and even surpassed that of Christian Europe. After the death of Charlemagne in 814, Cordoba's only rival among European cities was Constantinople at the other end of the continent. The caliphs may have exceeded the contemporary Byzantine emperors in culture and probably maintained a higher standard of public administration. Their laws were no more intolerantly cruel than Christian laws: many of their Christian subjects (and certainly Spain's Jews) preferred these infidel rulers to the illiberal Visigoths. Literature, in the form of poetry, was enthusiastically cultivated, as in all Arab countries. Christian Spaniards avidly studied Arabic to perfect an elegant and expressive style and scholars from Christian Europe came to Toledo and Cordoba to study in an age when Arabic outranked Latin as the language of medical studies, astronomy, and mathematics.

To moralists beyond the Pyrenees who had no direct contact with Moorish Spain, Islam appeared a luxurious paradise tantalizingly endowed with harems, pretty slave girls, and handsome sakis. But in sexual matters, Islamic cultures in fact maintained a paradoxical ambivalence, not least with respect to homosexuality. The severity and intolerance that characterized traditional Judaism and Christianity reappear unmistakably in the laws of this third "Abrahamic" religion, many of which derive ultimately from the Hebrew scriptures. The Qur'ān, in particular, shows both Jewish and Christian influence in its interpretation of the Sodom story (7.80–81, 11.78–83, 15.51–74, 27.54–55; see chapter 4 in this volume).

In the *hadīth*, collected "traditions" or sayings attributed (rightly or wrongly) to Muhammad, which appeared in five enormous collections in the ninth century, is a decree that both the active and passive partners should be stoned, a tradition which had a definitive influence on Islamic law. The theologian Malik of Medina (d. 795), whose school of jurisprudence eventually became the dominant one in Spain and North Africa, endorsed the death penalty: so did the leader of another important school, the literalist Ibn Hanbal (d. 855) (Bosworth 1954–5:777b). Other more liberal schools of law reduced the punishment to flagellation, usually one hundred strokes. These penalties were not merely theoretical. Barbaric sentences were in fact meted out by Muhammad's immediate successors. The first caliph, Abū Bakr, a close intimate of the Prophet, had a homosexual "buried under the debris of a wall"—presumably the stones of the wall were pushed over on him. He was also reputed to have prescribed burning alive as an alternative punishment. Muhammad's son-in-law Ali, the fourth caliph (later regarded as infallible and semi-divine by Shi'ite Muslims), ordered a guilty man to be thrown headlong from the top of a minaret. Others he ordered to be stoned (Bosworth 1954–5:777a). Thus, through early judicial theory and practice, Old Testament harshness came to dominate the legal side of Islam.

When we look at other aspects of Islamic culture, however, the indices are strikingly contradictory. Popular attitudes appear much less hostile than in Christendom, and European visitors to Muslim lands were repeatedly shocked by the relaxed tolerance of Arabs, Turks, and Persians who seemed to find nothing unnatural in relations between men and boys (Greenberg 1988:178–81; Crompton 1985:111–18). One measure of this important cultural difference is a vein of ardent romanticism in medieval Arab treatises on love. For Arab writers this "emotional intoxication," as it has been called, springs not just from the love of women, as with the troubadours, but also from the love of boys and other men.

Arab enthusiasts were concerned to establish that romantic love was an experience meaningful and valuable for its own sake. But how were they to reconcile such a view with their faith? They did this did by appealing to a curious *hadīth* ascribed to Muhammad himself—"He who loves and remains chaste and conceals his secret and dies, dies a martyr" (Giffen 1971:99). The Iraqi essayist Jāhiz, who wrote extensively on the subject of love, had laid down the rule that *'ishq*—or passionate love—could exist only between a man and a woman. But Ibn Da'ud, who was born the year Jāhiz died (868), extended the possibility to love between males in his *Book of the flower*, and this view seems to have prevailed in Arab culture subsequently (Giffen 1971:86). Ibn Da'ud was a learned jurisprudent as well as a literary man: according to an account frequently mentioned in Arab writings on love, his passion for his friend Muhammad ibn Jāmī (to whom his book was dedicated) made him a "martyr of love." Another friend told their story:

I went to see [Ibn Da'ud] during the illness in which he died and I said to him, "How do you feel?" He said to me, "Love of you-know-who has brought upon me what you see!" So I said to him, "What prevents you from enjoying him, as long as you have the power to do so?" He said, "Enjoyment has two aspects: One of them is the permitted gaze and the other is the forbidden pleasure. As for the permitted gaze, it has brought upon me the condition that you see, and as for the forbidden pleasure, something my father told me has kept me from it. He said . . . "the Prophet said . . . 'He who loves passionately and conceals his secret and remains chaste and patient, God will forgive him and make him enter Paradise,'" . . . and he died that very night or perhaps it was the next day. (Giffen 1971:10–11)

Both these traditions, the punitive and the sentimental, figure in the literature of Arab Spain, and especially in the writings of its foremost theorist of love, Ibn Hazm. Ibn Hazm was born in Cordoba in 994 during the last days of the Umayyad dynasty. He died in 1064, seven years before the birth of William IX of Aquitaine, the first of the troubadours. Ibn Hazm's father had held political office under the Umayyad caliphs but Ibn Hazm was forced to flee from Cordoba in 1013 when the caliph was overthrown. Later in life he became famous—and controversial—as a theologian and the author of many books, including a notable essay on comparative religion. Sometime between 1022 and 1027, in exile at Játiva near Valencia, he wrote a treatise on love called, in the poetic style favored by Arab writers, *The Dove's Neck-Ring about Love and Lovers*.

Ibn Hazm begins his book with a conventional Muslim prayer and makes haste to justify his undertaking on religious grounds: "Love is neither disapproved by Religion, nor prohibited by the Law; for every heart is in God's hands." Love itself is an inborn disposition "which men cannot control" (1953:21–22).[1] Later he elaborates on this defense—"it is sufficient for a good Moslem to abstain from those things which Allah has forbidden, and which, if he choose to do, he will find charged to his account on the Day of Resurrection. But to admire beauty, and to be mastered by love—that is a natural thing, and comes not within the range of Divine commandment and prohibition: all hearts are in God's hands, to dispose them what way He will, and all that is required of them is that they should know and consider the difference between right and wrong, and believe firmly what is true" (Ibn Hazm 1953:76).

Ibn Hazm declares that "Many rightly-guided caliphs and orthodox imams have been lovers" (1953:22). Readers reared in the Judeo-Christian tradition will find this declaration somewhat surprising. We are used to biographers recounting the erotic entanglements of secular rulers: it is more difficult to imagine them celebrating the love affairs of saints or church fathers. Yet Ibn Hazm assures us that "of the saints and learned doctors of the faith who lived in past ages and times long ago, some there are whose love lyrics are sufficient testimony to their passion, so that they require no further notice" (1953:23).He then mentions several famous religious jurists of Medina.

Ibn Hazm's theory of love is vaguely Platonic, but though he repeats an anecdote about the Greek philosopher he does not seem to know the *Phaedrus* or the *Symposium*. He considers love "a conjunction between scattered parts of souls that have become divided in this physical universe, a union effected within the substance of the original sublime element" (1953:23). Love is most often aroused by physical beauty but this is not the whole story—harmony of characters is also important. Love is of several kinds: love based on shared religious beliefs, love of kin or of comrades, love inspired by the desire to benefit from the higher rank of the beloved, love that is purely carnal, and "passionate love, that has no other cause but that union of souls to which we have referred above" (1953:25). But the only love which lasts is the love of true passion, which has mastery of the soul: only it produces mental preoccupation, melancholia, moodiness, sighing, and the other familiar symptoms.

Though Ibn Hazm is pro-love he is not writing a simple panegyric. He does not exalt love because it leads to courage, virtue, and wisdom as the Greeks did. It may do so, but it may also produce simple derangement (1953:35). The Arab psychologist dwells on its paradoxical nature as a "delightful malady, a most desirable sickness. Whoever is free of it likes not to be immune, and whoever is struck down by it yearns not to recover" (1953:31). He emphasizes, and seems almost to relish, a masochist element in love: he tells how a suffering friend of his was displeased when Ibn Hazm expressed a hope that he might be freed from his miserable condition. At one point he tells the story of a man of rank and power who was delighted when a page boy took notice of his infatuation by slapping him (1953:90).

What does Ibn Hazm's treatise tell us about Hispano-Arabic attitudes to homosexuality? This is not a question that can be simply answered. His book is a mixture of theoretical generalizations and personal anecdotes, most of them based on his own observations. Of the anecdotes perhaps nine-tenths concern the love of men for women, especially for lovely slave girls. Yet Ibn Hazm repeatedly intermingles stories of men falling in love with other males.

This sudden, unprepared transition from one kind of experience startles us since we tend, of course, to be intensely self-conscious about such matters. Often we are left in the dark—the love poem could be about a woman or another man, so could the story, which mentions simply a lover and beloved, with no sex indicated. Where the European or American reader of today would ordinarily think that a love story is about a woman and a man unless there is some indication to the contrary, and an ancient Greek might have assumed the opposite, we are often in the dark in *The Dove's Neck-Ring*.

When Ibn Hazm comes to theorize about the experiences of lovers he is even more disorienting. Though the anecdotes in the book are far more numerous on the heterosexual side, in general descriptions of erotic phenomena he feels quite at ease using male pronouns. As an example, we may take the following passage from his second chapter, "On the Signs of Love":

The lover will direct his conversation to the beloved, even when he purports however earnestly to address another: the affectation is apparent to anyone with eyes to see. When the loved one speaks, the lover listens with rapt attention to his every word; he marvels at everything the beloved says, however extraordinary and absurd his observations may be; he believes him implicitly even when he is clearly lying; agrees with him even though he is obviously in the wrong, testifies on his behalf for all that he may be unjust, follows after him however he may proceed and whatever argument he may adopt. The lover hurries to the spot where the beloved is at the moment, endeavors to sit as near to him as possible, sidles up close to him, lays aside all occupations that might oblige him to leave his company, makes light of any matter however weighty that would demand his parting from him, is very slow to leave when he takes his leave of him. (Ibn Hazm 1953:33–34)

Presuming that Ibn Hazm means his masculine pronouns to be read inclusively, so that his observations would be applicable both to heterosexual and homosexual situations, what post-Hellenic Western writer would feel comfortable with such a convention? We may consider, for example, Andreas Capellanus. Capellanus wrote his famous essay "On love" a century and a half later at the court of Eleanor of Aquitaine's daughter, Marie de Champagne. In the opening paragraph of his second chapter Andreas states categorically the assumptions of medieval Christian Europe:

The main point to be noted about love is that it can exist only between persons of different sex. Between two males or between two females it can claim no place, for two persons of the same sex are in no way fitted to reciprocate each other's love or to practise its natural acts. Love blushes to embrace what nature denies. (Capellanus 1982:35)

Later writers on the subject of love north of the Pyrenees would overwhelmingly have agreed. What we may call Ibn Hazm's romantic bisexuality would have been incomprehensible to them. On this point of sensibility a chasm existed between Christendom and Islam.

What is likely to disconcert the modern western reader is that Ibn Hazm seems oblivious to the idea that same-sex love might be any different from the love of men and women. Just as he makes no distinction between the love for slave women and free, so he makes no distinction between the love of women and the love of youths, morally or socially. To him all love is psychologically one and the same. The Greeks also recognized both homosexual and heterosexual love as valid. Nevertheless, they differentiated between them. In the *Symposium* Phaedrus makes a point of arguing that women can love men heroically just as men can. Aristotle is keenly aware of the love of males as something distinct from the love of women. Plutarch and the pseudo-Lucian of the *Erotes* contrast the two kinds of love sharply. But Ibn Hazm moves from a story about a man's infatuation for a slave girl to a story of male love with no suggestion that the one experience differs from the other. Only in the penultimate chapter of his book when he takes up legal issues does he consider them separately.

We may glean some insight as to how Ibn Hazm and his fellow religionists viewed love between men indirectly from his anecdotes and poems. In a chapter in which he argues that lovers should keep their love secret and not divulge it even to the beloved he tells the story of a well-known poet, whom he names, who was "deeply smitten" by another man. Scolded by the man for gazing at him so intently, the poet excused himself on the grounds that he would not have done so had he not been under the impression that the man was drunk and insensible (Ibn Hazm 1953:80). Arab delicacy and discretion are amply illustrated by Ibn Hazm's tales of men who kept silent about women or men they loved. He tells of a man who carefully refrained from letting a friend know of his love for him, knowing that any openness would end their intimacy (1953:80–81). This suggests that it was not regarded as proper in polite Arab society for two men to avow their love publicly, in contrast, say, to ancient Greece, Imperial China, or Tokugawa Japan, though it was perceived as highly romantic to harbor such feelings without naming the beloved. Here is a Platonism which out-Platos Plato.

Ibn Hazm's treatise contains, as we might anticipate, a chapter on "martyrs of love." He quotes the well-known tradition: "He who loves, and controls himself, and so dies, the same is a martyr," and cites six cases of persons who died, or nearly died, of love (1953:220). Interestingly, two cases involve women who loved men, two men who loved women, and two men who loved men. The tales are intermixed, not grouped by gender. The first story is about an official of Cordoba, Ibn Quzman, who fell in love with Aslam, the brother of the prime minister—"an exceedingly handsome man." He became ill from love, but though Aslam frequently visited him he was not aware he was the cause of his friend's decline and death. When another friend explained to Aslam what had happened, Aslam rebuked him: "Why did you not let me know? . . . I would have kept myself even more closely in touch with him, and would scarcely have left his bedside; that could have done me no harm" (1953:220; but see Nykl 1946:167).

The other case involved a close personal friend of Ibn Hazm's, Ibn al-Tubni, whom he praises highly for his learning, personal qualities, and his beauty—"It might have been said that beauty itself was created in his likeness, or fashioned out of the sighs of those who looked upon him" (Ibn Hazm 1953:222). They were separated when Berber troops overran Cordoba. In exile in Valencia Ibn Hazm was saddened by the news that Ibn al-Tubni was dead. When a friend had asked Ibn al-Tubni what made him sick and emaciated he had replied:

"Yes, I will tell you. I was standing at the door of my house in Ghadir Ibn al-Shammas at the time that 'Ali ibn Hammud entered Cordoba, and his armies were pouring into the city from all directions. I saw among them a youth of such striking appearance, that I could never have believed until that moment that beauty could be so embodied in a living form. He mastered my reason, and my mind was wholly enraptured with him. I enquired after him and was told that he was So-and-so, the son of So-and-so, and that he inhabited such and such a district—a province far distant from Cordoba, and virtually inaccessible. I despaired of ever seeing him again; and by my life . . . I shall never give up loving him, until I am laid in the tomb." And so indeed it was. (Ibn Hazm 1953:225)

Both Ibn Hazm's anecdotes and his poems, from which he quotes unabashedly in *The Dove's Neck-Ring*, reveal something of his own erotic sensibility. His grand passion seems to have been an infatuation which he experienced at sixteen with a slave girl in his family household. However, he does include several poems in *The Dove's Neck-Ring* about his feelings for other men. One of these appears in his chapter on the signs of love. As a poet Ibn Hazm rarely rises above mediocrity; but his very banalities are instructive:

If he should speak, among those who sit in my company, I listen only to the words of that marvelous charmer.

Even if the Prince of the Faithful should be with me, I would not turn aside from [my love] for the former.

If I am compelled to leave him, I look back constantly, and walk [like an animal] wounded in the hoof.

My eyes remain fixed firmly upon him though my body has departed, as the drowning man looks at the shore from the fathomless sea.

If I recall my distance from him, I choke as if with water, like the man who yawns in the midst of a dust storm and the sun's noonday heat.

And if you say: "It is possible to reach the sky," I reply: "yes, and I know where the stairs may be found." (Ibn Hazm 1953:225)

When he discusses sex and morality, Ibn Hazm assures us, with naive candor, of his own purity: "I am completely guiltless, entirely sound, without reproach ... and I do swear by God by the most solemn oath that I have never taken off my underwear to have an illicit sexual intercourse" (Ibn Hazm 1931:181).[1] Yet he admits to being tempted by the beauty of men. On one occasion he dared not attend a party where he would meet a handsome man who attracted him, in order to avoid any occasion for sin (Ibn Hazm 1953:267).

In the last two chapters of his book Ibn Hazm turns to the moral, religious, and legal questions raised by love. (In Muslim culture, these are of course one.) Several of the transgressions he describes in "The Vileness of Sinning" are homosexual. In one case a man of his circle who was a noted religious scholar lost his high repute because of his open liaison with a boy. He mentions another scholar, no less renowned, and the former head of an important Muslim sect, who fell so madly in love with a Christian boy that he committed the ultimate enormity—that is, he composed a treatise in favor of the Trinity. Another man allowed "his harem to be violated, and exposed his family to dishonour, all for the sake of gratifying his amorous whim for a boy" (Ibn Hazm 1953:244). But not all Arabs were as censorious as Ibn Hazm. At a reception given by a wealthy businessman, a guest withdrew repeatedly with a relative of the host into a private chamber. When Ibn Hazm hinted at his disapproval of their misconduct—characteristically by reciting a poem—the host ignored him.

This chapter also contains Ibn Hazm's sole reference to lesbianism. "I once saw a woman," he tells us, "who had bestowed her affections in ways not pleasing to Almighty God." But her love changed to an "enmity the like of which is not engendered by hatred, or revenge, or the murder of a father, or the carrying of a mother into captivity. Such is Allah's wont with all those who practice abomination" (Ibn Hazm 1953:249). But again, Islamic references to lesbianism were apparently not always this condemnatory. At least a dozen love romances in which the lovers were women are mentioned in *The Book of Hind*, who was herself an archetypal lesbian. The ninth century produced a lost *Treatise on Lesbianism (Kitab al-Sahhakat)* (Bosworth 1954–5:777b; Foster 1958:84–85) and later Arab works on eroticism contained chapters on the subject. In this respect they are perhaps unique in premodern literature.

In Islam questions of morality were inevitably also questions of law. So Ibn Hazm's chapter on the sins of fornication, adultery, and sodomy ends with detailed discussions of various penalties prescribed by religious tradition. Among these he speaks of executions for homosexual acts. He recounts a story of Abū Bakr's burning a man alive for playing the passive role (Ibn Hazm 1953:259). The first caliph, he tells us, could be equally severe about acts which were not quite sodomy in the traditional sense; Abū Bakr struck and killed a man "who had pressed himself against a youth until he had an orgasm" (Ibn Hazm 1931:200). Ibn Hazm also notes that the jurist Malik expressed approval of an emir who beat a young man to death for allowing another man to embrace him in a similar way. But for Ibn Hazm this is excessive zeal; he thinks that the relatively lenient punishment of ten lashes might have sufficed, though he admits this is a heterodox view (Ibn Hazm 1953: 258). As to the completed act of sodomy, he cites only Malik's opinion that both parties should be stoned. Ibn Hazm pointedly declines to say whether he agrees with him or not.

In this atmosphere of harsh religious laws and overcharged romanticism, men loved, expressed their feelings openly in fervent verse, and loudly proclaimed their chastity. Perhaps some of the poetic fervor was merely literary. Perhaps some of the protestations were sincere.

Occasionally, these affairs involved famous rulers. Caliph 'Abd al-Rahman III who ruled Cordoba at its political and cultural zenith (912–61) was attracted to a young Christian hostage, was repulsed, and had him barbarously executed. The boy was canonized as Saint Pelagius, and became the martyr-hero of a narrative poem by the German nun Hrosvitha which condemned Arab lust and glorified Christian chastity (Hrosvitha 1936:129–53).

Architecture, belles lettres, and scholarship flourished in Cordoba under 'Abd al-Rahman's son al-Hakam II, who was their eager and discriminating patron. In his youth his loves seem to have been entirely homosexual. This exclusivity was a problem when he succeeded to the throne, since it was incumbent upon the new caliph to produce a male heir. The impasse was resolved by his coupling with a concubine who dressed in boy's clothes and was given the masculine name of "Jafar" (Lévi-Provençal 1950:173n4).

The love of al-Mu'tamid, emir of Seville and the outstanding Andalusian poet of his day, for the poet Ibn 'Ammar ended violently after a long friendship. Al-Mu'tamid was a passionate lover of women but also loved males. Of a cupbearer he wrote, "They named him Sword; two other swords: his eyes!/ . . . now we both are masters, both slaves!" (Ibn Hazm 1931:143). His love for Ibn 'Ammar is the most famous, and most tragic, romance in the history of al-Andalus. In 1053 al-Mu'tamid, aged thirteen, had been appointed titular governor at Silves by his father with Ibn 'Ammar, who was nine years his senior, as his vizier. A story tells how after an evening of wine and poetry his fondness led him to declare to Ibn 'Ammar, "Tonight you will sleep with me on the same pillow!" (Ibn Hazm 1931:156). In a poem he sent to al-Mu'tamid's father Ibn 'Ammar declared:

During the night of union there was wafted
To me, in his caresses, the perfume of its dawns,
My tears streamed out over the beautiful gardens
Of his cheeks to moisten its myrtles and lilies. . . . (Ibn Hazm 1931:157)

Apparently the prince's father came to disapprove of the relation with the commoner, for he exiled the poet to separate them (Daniel 1977:10). After his father's death al-Mu'tamid recalled Ibn 'Ammar and gave him great political and military power. A famous tale, which we are not required to believe, tells how, when they were sleeping together in one bed, the poet dreamed that his lover would kill him, fled the scene, and was wooed back by the king who assured him that this could never happen (Ibn Hazm 1931:156).

But later the two men quarreled bitterly. In a poem full of scurrilous abuse Ibn 'Ammar nevertheless reminded his lover of their former intimacy in terms that are startling specific:

Do you recall the days of our early youth,
When you resembled a crescent on the sky?
I would embrace your body that was fresh,
And from your lips I sipped pure water as well,

Contenting myself in loving you, short of *haram* [forbidden acts],
When you did swear that what I did was *halal* [permitted]! (Ibn Hazm 1931:160)

It is hard to understand how such tender lines found their way into a poem that is otherwise a violent assault on al-Mu'tamid's honor. Perhaps Ibn 'Ammar meant to imply that, despite his disclaimers, the youth had been his catamite. Finally, when Ibn 'Ammar fell into his hands, the ordinarily humane and generous al-Mu'tamid first pardoned him, and then, when Ibn 'Ammar boasted too triumphantly of his reprieve, fell into a rage and hacked him to death with his own hands. "Afterwards he wept, as long ago Alexander had wept for Hephestion, and gave him a sumptuous funeral" (Daniel 1977:10).

Almost any collection of Hispano-Arabic poetry yields a plethora of love poems by men to or about other males. Erotic poetry first flourished in Andalusia at Cordoba under 'Abd al-Rahman II (822–52). His grandson, 'Abdallah (888–912) penned amorous verses to a "dark-eyed fawn" (Ibn Hazm 1931:22). Ibn 'Abd Rabbihi, a freedman poet at 'Abdallah's court, wrote of another young man in a typical mood of subjection—

I gave him what he asked for, made him my master . . .
Love has put fetters on my heart
As a herdsman puts fetters on a camel. (Ibn Hazm 1931:39)

Ramadi, the most foremost poet in Cordoba in the tenth century, was enamored of a young Christian to the point of making the sign of the cross when he drank wine. When his turbulent political career landed him in prison he fell in love with a black slave. Again we see the submissiveness of the lover and the conscious reversal of social roles: "I looked into his eyes, and became drunken. . . . I am his slave, he is the lord" (Ibn Hazm 1931:59). Latin poets in Augustan Rome had likewise addressed love poems to slave boys; but the extreme self-abasement of these Andalusians is closer to the chivalric romanticism of medieval France.

After the fall of the Umayyads at Cordoba Arabic Spain was fatally weakened. It disintegrated under the "Kings of the Taifas" (i.e., "parties" or "factions") into more than twenty petty states. But despite this political disarray the eleventh century was a golden age of Arabic poetry in the Iberian peninsula, and poetry continued to pour forth in the Almoravid period (1090–1145) and under the Almohad rulers (1145–1223). Homoerotic verse proliferated with the rest. Ibn al-Farra' taught the Qur'ān and poetry at Almería about 1220. "He liked beautiful boys and did not shun addressing aesthetic compliments to them in his class." When a favored student asked him to complete a poem with the line "What a beauteous fawn I see!" the facile teacher quipped:

If your roses can't be culled,
If your white teeth can't be kissed,
What's the use my saying then:
"What a beauteous fawn I see!" (Ibn Hazm 1931:257)

Andalusian poets wrote much poetry in the classical language and rhythms that had been traditional in Arabic since pre-Islamic times. They also invented two new stanza forms, the *muwashshah* and the *zajal*. At first disdained as an illegitimate experiment unfit for serious anthologies, the *muwashshah* eventually gained popularity throughout the Arab world. Its fame was spread by an Egyptian literary scholar, Ibn Sana al-Mulk (d. 1211), who collected examples in his *House of embroidery* (*Dar al-Tiraz*). He praised the Andalusian *muwashshah* as a new poetic form of high merit, and traced its origin to ninth-century Spain. There is some dispute as to how many of the love poems in his collection are addressed to males. One scholar has asserted that all are, which would make the collection a kind of Arabic counterpart to Book 12 of the *Greek anthology* (Roth 1982:27n29). (However, since the imagery in poems about boys is almost identical with those about women, the descriptions rarely provide a clue to gender—with one exception, playful references to the blossoming beard.) Another specialist, less certain as to the gender of the adored, notes that it was sometimes the convention in Arabic verse to use masculine pronouns in love poems to women, as more discreetly proper; nevertheless, she identifies a significant number of the poems as male oriented (Compton 1976:67). As an example we may take a *muwashshah* by Ibn 'Ubda, a poet writing about 1100 at the court of al-Mut'asim of Almería:

I loved a new moon, incomparable in its beauty. The eyes and long lovely neck of the gazelle are modeled after it.
He swaggered in his beauty, which desires no increase, a full moon shining in perfect proportion.
Elegance adorned him and his figure was slender
He is a full moon that triumphs with sheer magic. The down on his cheek is curved over jasmine.
A lily was placed beside a well-guarded rose whenever he came into view. . . .
(Compton 1976:18)

The most acclaimed lyricist of this brilliant era, Ibn Quzman (ca. 1080–1160), has been called one of the greatest of medieval poets.

An irreverent Bohemian of the cut of François Villon, he composed racy, colloquial *zajals*, far removed in style from the canons of classical Arabic verse. Tall, blond, and blue-eyed, Ibn Quzman led a licentious life resembling that of Haroun al-Rashid's boon companion in Baghdad, the poet Abū Nuwās, who was also unabashedly explicit about his homosexuality. In short, terse lines and elliptical stanzas that are almost untranslatable, he celebrates "wine, adultery and sodomy" (Ibn Hazm 1931:268). Like the troubadours of Provence he complains of the hauteur and disdain of his lovers, who are often male, but laughs at the refined conventions of idealistic love: "What do you say about a beloved, when he and you, without anyone else, are alone, and the house door is locked?" (Ibn Hazm 1931:283, and passim) Poverty-stricken, he ended his days not on the gallows but as an imam teaching in a mosque.

The philosopher Ibn Bajja, better known to Latin Europe as Avempace, was in every respect a more respectable figure. It was he who introduced Aristotelianism to Spain and paved the way for Averroes. Ibn Bajja, we are told by the anthologist Al-Fath ibn Haqan, wrote memorial verses on the death of "a black slave with whom he was infatuated . . . who died at Barcelona, much to his grief" (Ibn Hazm 1931:252). Al-Fath was at daggers drawn with Ibn Bajja, but his anthology, *Necklaces of pure gold*, compiled about 1120 is an important source of Andalusian poetry. His sobriquet "Ibn Haqan" has been taken to imply that he was a passive homosexual. (Ibn Hazm 1931:226).

Several other anthologies by native Andalusians appeared in the twelfth and thirteenth centuries. Perhaps the most important is the collection by Ibn Sa'id which appeared in 1243 under the title *The Pennants of the Champions*. Its fame in our day has been enhanced by a translation into Spanish by the scholar Emilio García Gómez which has in turn inspired English versions of many of the poems. A selection of these poems, translated by the poet-scholar A. J. Arberry has been published in his *Moorish Poetry*. (Ibn Sa'id 1953) The cautious Briton seems to have eschewed poems whose sexual details were explicit, but his book nevertheless reveals an astonishingly broad range of homoerotic poems intermixed with other lyrics (Roth 1982:28n34–35). Ibn Sa'id, who was born at Alcalá la Real near Granada, arranged his anthology according to the poets' birthplaces and occupations. Verse in praise of boys appears from Seville, Lisbon, Cordoba, Toledo, Granada, Alcalá, Murcia, Valencia, and Saragossa, authored by kings, ministers of state, scholars, men of letters and civil servants, as well as professional poets.

From the beginning of the thirteenth century Arab power ebbed in Spain, until it surrendered its last outpost, Granada, in 1492. To the end its poets hymned the love of boys, as in the case of Yusuf III, who reigned in the Alhambra from 1408 to 1417, and composed this *muwashshah*:

O you who have aimed at my heart with the dart of a piercing glance:
Meet one who's dying, whose eye is shedding fast-flowing tears!
Who will claim justice from an alluring fawn
Slender of body as is the fresh, green bough,
Who has insisted on distance and shunning? . . .
He has seduced me with the spell of his eyelids
Had it been allowed—yet he shuns me ever—
I'd have won my desires by undoing his sash. (Monroe 1974:372)

As the Christian advance continued, many Arab families of note emigrated to Morocco or Tunis. Among them was the clan of Ibn Khaldun (1332–1406), the great Arab historian, whose *Muqaddimah* (or "Introduction" to his work) has been called the first significant work on the philosophical foundations of history. Ibn Khaldun looked back to Arabic Spain and its culture with appreciative admiration and reflected its attitudes to homosexuality with all their contradictions. Thus the *Muqaddimah* condemns male love as a non-procreative threat to population, approves the judgment of Malik that homosexuals should be stoned, and at the same time rounds off its fifteen hundred pages with an extensive anthology of Spanish and Moorish poetry, freely sprinkled with ardent homoerotic verse (Ibn Khaldun 1967, 2:295–96; 3:344–71, and passim).

How are we to explain this legal-lyrical schizophrenia, where a potent religion and a vibrant secular culture seem so at odds? The religious prohibition derived its force from the Arabs' claim to be the descendants of Abraham's son Ishmael, and Muhammad's view of Abraham's nephew Lot as a prophet who condemned men who favored men. This racial-religious affiliation ensured that Islam would share the prejudices of Judaism and Christianity. One might have even expected the general cultural stance to be, if anything, more hostile, since homosexuality seems to have been comparatively little known among the Bedouins of Arabia in pre-Islamic times. It has frequently been suggested that Arab attitudes to sex underwent a change as they conquered more advanced and sophisticated empires, especially Sassanian Persia. Culturally, the conquest of Persia did for the Arabs what the conquest of Greece did for Rome—it introduced a rather primitive tribal society to a markedly more advanced and luxurious one. Unfortunately, though we know boy-love flourished spectacularly in Islamic Persia, inspiring a very substantial literature, we know little about Persian mores before the Arab conquest. One thing the conquest did indubitably effect, however: it provided an ample supply of young male slaves.

A crucially important difference between Islam and Christianity was their relation to slavery: Islam freely granted men sexual access to their slaves, Christianity did not. Fiercely condemnatory of adultery with other men's wives, Muhammad nevertheless made an exception in the case of married women who were purchased or captured and enslaved. Unlike Christianity, which for its first three hundred years lacked political or military power, Islam from the start had enormous military success, conquering nation after nation. In this triumphal atmosphere few moralists were prepared to challenge the victors' prerogatives, which included sexual rights to women, married or unmarried, belonging to men defeated in battle. To these all- powerful rulers, riding the crest of a wave of military good fortune, it must have seemed eminently reasonable that attractive young male captives should also be regarded as legitimate bedmates. Some authorities seem to have sanctioned such intercourse (Greenberg 1988:177).

The parallel with Rome is clear. But this is not the whole story, for though a significant number of love affairs with male slaves are recorded (and poetry on this theme abounds), we note that in the circles of Ibn Da'ud, Ibn Hazm, and various royal courts, men repeatedly fall in love with friends, acquaintances, and sometimes strangers of equal rank with themselves. Here we have a pattern akin to the ancient Greeks. However, the emphasis in such affairs is not on mentorship, as in Sparta and Athens, but on feeling itself, which is regarded as especially privileged, and allowable under the guise of a quasi-religious Platonism.

It was the "love-martyr" *hadīth* that conferred an exalted status on love in Islam. It opened the door and provided religious sanction to a fervent romanticism, which later crossed the Pyrenees and found its way into medieval Provence. The startling thing (from a Christian point of view) is that this Islamic glorification of love was gender-blind. Linked with a theoretically perfect chastity it could escape moral condemnation. In the literature of Sufi mysticism, rapturous love poems ostensibly addressed to male lovers became a common way of symbolizing union with the divine. So Islam paradoxically forbade, allowed, and exploited homoerotic desire, providing striking similarities with Judaism and Christianity in the sphere of law, yet fostered a radically different literary, social, and affective atmosphere.

By combining the menacing legalism of the Judeo-Christian world with a remarkable expressive freedom in their poetry, the Arabs of Spain created a situation in which a formal disapproval of homosexual acts was balanced by a popular acceptance of bisexual amorousness. The result was to create a status for the male homosexual lover somewhat akin to that of the romantic devotee of women in the medieval West. Homosexuality was officially decried, but the man who admitted to such feelings might still be respected and admired; he was not in Islamic culture regarded as a pariah, a moral monster, or a threat to the safety of the state.

Note

1. Arberry's translation is generally the better, but occasionally obfuscates sexual details. Where this is the case, I have used Nykl's.

References

Bashir-ud-Din Mahmud Ahmad, trans. 1988. *The Holy Qur'ān*, 5 vols. Tilford, UK: Islam International Publications.

Bosworth, C. E., ed. 1954–. *Encyclopaedia of Islam*. Rev. ed. 6 vols. Leiden: Brill.

Capellanus, Andreas. 1982. *Andreas Capellanus on love*, trans. P. G. Walsh. London: Duckworth.

Compton, Linda F. 1976. *Andalusian lyric poetry and old Spanish love songs: The muwashshaḥ and its* kharja. New York: New York University Press.

Crompton, Louis. 1985. *Byron and Greek love*. Berkeley: University of California Press.

Daniel, Marc. 1977. "Arab civilization and male love." *Gay Sunshine* 21:1–11, 27.

Foster, Jeannette. 1958. *Sex variant women in literature*. London: F. Muller.

Giffen, Lois A. 1971. *Theory of profane love among the Arabs: The development of the genre*. New York: New York University Press.

Greenberg, David F. 1988. *The construction of homosexuality*. Chicago: University of Chicago Press.

Hrosvitha. 1936. *The non-dramatic works: Text, translation, and commentary*, trans. M. G. Wiegand. St. Louis: St. Louis University.

Ibn Hazm. 1931. *A book containing the Risala known as the Dove's neck-ring about love and lovers*, trans. A. R. Nykl. Paris: Paul Geuthner.

———. 1953. *The ring of the dove: A treatise on the art and practice of Arab love*, trans. Alois J. Arberry. London: Luzac.

Ibn Khaldun. 1967. *The Muqaddimah: An introduction to history*, trans. Franz Rosenthal. Princeton: Princeton University Press.

Ibn Sa'id, comp. 1953. *Moorish poetry: A translation of "The pennants," an anthology compiled in 1243*, trans. A. J. Arberry. Cambridge: Cambridge University Press.

Lane, Erskine. 1975. *In praise of boys: Moorish poems from Al-Andalus*. San Francisco: Gay Sunshine Press.

Lévi-Provençal, Evariste. 1950. *Histoire de l'Espagne musulmane*. Vol. 2. Paris: G. P. Maisonneuve.

Monroe, James T. 1974. *Hispano-Arabic poetry: A student anthology*. Berkeley: University of California Press.

Nykl, Alois R. 1946. *Hispano-Arabic poetry and its relations with the old Provençal troubadors*. Baltimore: J. H. Furst.

Roth, Norman. 1982. "'Deal gently with the young man': Love of boys in medieval Hebrew poetry of Spain." *Speculum* 57:20–51.

PART III

Historical Studies

CHAPTER 9

Male Homosexuality, Inheritance Rules, and the Status of Women in Medieval Egypt

The Case of the Mamlūks

Stephen O. Murray

"To one dark feature we can but distantly allude," Sir William Muir, a Victorian Orientalist, wrote in 1896 (p. 217).[1] Typical of the discussion of homosexuality by Western historians, that distant allusion is all there is in a long volume. Sixty-six years later, mention is more explicit, but no lengthier: "They were addicted to homosexuality" (Moorhead 1962:72).

The mamlūk military elite, purchased anew in each generation from the steppes of Eurasia, ruled Egypt and Syria from 1249,[2] when they defeated an invading army of Crusaders led by Saint Louis, until they were defeated by the mass army of Napoleon in 1799. Their unusual social system suggests a relationship between the acceptance of homosexuality, the relatively high status of women, and the lack of inheritance; although amidst the details of battles and palace intrigues in histories of the period, there is practically nothing about the everyday life even of the rulers.

Whatever the actual status of women within the orbit of Islam,[3] it is certain that women's competence and independent enterprise were much greater in the Kipchak steppes than in the heartland of Islam. When Malik [i.e., King] al-Salih Ayoub, who had bought the first thousand boys in the steppes, died on the eve of the decisive battle with (Saint) Louis IX, Ayoub's wife, Shajar al-durr, herself a former slave, kept secret his demise and issued commands in his name for a period of several weeks. When the truth was finally discovered, the mamlūk warriors proclaimed her Queen of Egypt. Apparently there were no objections to a woman ruler who had proved her ability in battle, but the mamlūk warriors were but recent converts to Islam. The "spiritual leader," the 'Abbāsid Khalif Mu'tasim, wrote to them, "The Prophet said, 'Unhappy is the nation governed by a woman.' If you have no men, I shall send you one." Shajar al-durr was, therefore, forced to marry her chief *amīr* (general), Aibek, who was then proclaimed sultan. She nevertheless continued to run the country's administration (Glubb 1973; Khowaiter 1978).

Neither the wealth nor the status of mamlūk was heritable. Upon the death of a warrior, his property, house, goods, wife, and slaves were sold for the benefit of the Treasury.[4] Thus, the common motivation in most social systems of passing on wealth and position to one's children was blocked for the mamlūks. Their children (*awlād al-nās*: children of [the best] people) bore Muslim names distinct from the Turkic names of the mamlūks, and spoke Arabic rather than the Turkic languages of their fathers. The children, along with all others who were born and raised Muslim, were proscribed from becoming soldiers, riding horses, or even from dressing like their mamlūk fathers; the elite of the next generation was always recruited afresh from Eurasia and removed far from natal families (Poliak 1939; Mayer 1952). "Like all slaves, they were genealogical isolates. . . . Deracination was the very essence" of the institution, and the caliphs who imported mamlūks believed that "natally alienated persons, having no basis of existence in their new societies except their masters, were likely to be totally loyal to him" (Patterson 1982:309). However, the hopes for loyalty were structurally unsound: "Behind the trust and loyalty between the ruler and these slaves lies a complex, adversary relationship; the more he trusts them, the more power they acquire; the greater their independent power grows, the less loyal they become" (Pipes 1978:35; quoted in Patterson 1982:314). Nonetheless, status hangups (about "honor") and the degree of family aggrandizing expected from the local populace made aliens a preferable source of servants and officials (Ayalon 1975a:49; Patterson 1982:310–11). At least the mamlūk was

cut off from all his former ties: his environment, his religion, his race, his tribe, and—what is particularly important—his family. . . . He got a new family instead of that which he had lost. This was a family which was not based on blood relations, but on the relations of slavery and patronship. The patron who had bought the Mamlūk became his father; and his comrades in servitude in the school, whom he—in most cases—never knew before, and who quite often belonged to other races and other tribes, became his. (Ayalon 1980:327–28)

Separation from relatives removed temptations of nepotism and dangers of divided loyalties. Transplantation decisively removed the mamlūks far from their natal families,[5] both geographically and culturally (especially in religion). The rigorously meritocratic mamlūk system was also designed to cut them off from their descendants:

> The Mamlūk could belong to the upper class only during his lifetime. He could not transfer either his belonging to the upper class or the rank which had acquired within the class to his offspring. The Mamlūk was a "life peer," and Mamlūk society was a one-generation nobility . . . of people whose parents were (usually) anonymous and whose offspring became (mostly) anonymous, a nobility which came from obscurity, and passed into obscurity. The sons were ejected from the upper class and were assimilated in the civilian population, although not immediately. . . . The grandsons, with but a few exceptions, did not enjoy any military privileges. (Ayalon 1980:328)

Eunuchs (*khasī*), who were also taken from outside Dar al-Islam, were more decisively blocked from accumulating wealth or honor for their children. Even more than mamlūks, eunuchs in Islamic societies are the ideal type of a one-generation nobility (Ayalon 1980:338, 1979b). In buying boys from the peripheries, both those who had been or were slated for castration and those who were going to be trained to be cavalrymen, amirs, and sultans were ensuring that the natal family of the eunuch and mamlūks would not be around to be enriched. Whatever goods (including land) the eunuchs and mamlūks accumulated could not be passed on to their sons (the eunuchs not having any). Castration was not viewed as conducive to military prowess, so was unsuitable (indeed, probably, unthinkable) for those chosen for military service. Among the many duties of eunuchs "was the supervision and education of the young Mamlūks in the military schools. . . . They formed a barrier between those youngsters and adult Mamlūks," sometimes being penetrated in their stead—at least that is how I interpret the footnote to this passage: "The eunuchs themselves were a constant object of pederasty" (Ayalon 1979b:72n9). The sultan's mamlūk novices (*kuttābī*) were not herded together into a single one of the twelve barracks in the Cairo citadel, although each barracks seems to have had a special section for novices. Novices of lesser officials also were housed with the mamlūk garrison. Developing an identification with a unit (*buyūt*, house) seems to have been judged more important than protecting the cadets from their elders. Within the units, nonetheless, there existed some identification with and special feeling for one's cohort (*khushdāshiyya*) as well as for one's patron (*ustādh*). Kinship idioms were used: the patron was called "father" (*wālid*), the mamlūk "sons" (*awlād*) called each other "brothers" (*ikhwa; sg. akh*), sometimes distinguishing "older brothers" (*aghawat; sg. agha*) from "younger brothers" (*iniyyāt; sg. ini*) and *tā'ifa* was used in the sense of "family" (as well as "faction") for mamlūks. Even other mamlūks were regarded as outsiders (*gharīb*) who could not become part of such families (Ayalon 1991:318; 1980:328; 1987b:207).

Recurrently, attempts were made to pass on the sultanate itself through primogeniture, but time after time the throne was usurped by the strongest amīr.[6] A more successful attempt by lesser mamlūks to guarantee a place for descendants was to endow a pious foundation (*waqf*, generally mosques, libraries, or schools) to be administered by heirs, who could not directly receive any patrimony.[7]

The mamlūks were a caste apart with no motivation to mix with the Arab populations they were bought to protect. Their appearance was distinctive. In addition to their light skin, Browne observes that "the Mamlūks suffer not the beard to grow till they be emancipated, and hold some office, as Cashef, &c" and described their dress in Cairo circa 1792:

Mamlūks constantly appear in the military dress, and are commonly armed with a pair of pistols, a sabre, and a dagger. They wear a peculiar cap of a greenish hue, around which is wreathed a turban. The rest of their dress resembles that of other Mohammedan citizens, and is restricted to no particular colour : but another singularity is their large drawers of thick Venetian cloth, of a crimson colour, to which are attached their slippers of red leather. On horseback they add to their arms a pair of large horse-pistols, and the *Dubbūs* or battle-axe. In battle many of them wear an open helmet, and the ancient ring armour of interwoven links of steel, worn under part of their dress, and thus concealed. These are dear. . . . Some of them are made at Constantinople, others in Persia. Their horses are of the finest Arabian breeds. (1806:54–55)

For the most part the mamlūks who attained puberty in their homelands[8] despised the Arab language that they did not encounter until they were adolescents, were illiterate,[9] and spoke their Turkic native languages. They also lived apart from the existing cities in their own colonies (including the Cairo citadel with its barracks for the Royal Mamlūks, *al-mamālik al-sultāniyya*) and only rarely intermarried with local notables' daughters.[10] Besides the obvious wish to keep troops from forming social relationships with the governed, residential segregation may have been partly an attempt to preserve expensive investments from other dangers. As Ayalon notes,

The toughness which the Mamlūk acquired in his country of origin helped him very much in carrying out his military tasks. However, it did not make him in any way immune to diseases and epidemics in many of the Muslim lands, to which he had been transferred, certainly not in Egypt and Syria. He was much more vulnerable to them than the local inhabitants. Epidemics would kill off very high proportions of the Mamlūks, especially the newcomers among them. (1980:338–39)[11]

Along with many special prerogatives (notably their own courts of law), the mamlūks were distinguished from the rest of the population by being forbidden divorce.[12] Still more astonishingly, their wives received a fixed salary from the state, just as did the warriors themselves. These two customs greatly enhanced the autonomy of women among the mamlūks (Ayalon 1968), although they may, perhaps, also have discouraged some from marriage.[13]

The mode of homosexuality to which the mamlūks purportedly were "addicted" was pederasty, with boys, recruited from the wilderness, who were undergoing military training (furūsīya) in the mounted use of sword, lance, and bow, rather than with boys raised in civilized Egypt (Glubb 1973). Although Ayalon (1956:66) notes that the main function of a corps of eunuchs was "keeping Mamlūk adults away from Mamlūk boys at the military schools," it does not seem to have occurred to any of the military historians who have written about the mamlūks that sexual attraction might have played some part in selecting which boys to buy. At least one early-nineteenth-century traveler to Mesopotamia (Iraq), who was quite unimpressed with the beauty of a wanton dancing boy he saw, remarked that most of the upwards of fifty Georgian and Circassian mamlūk bodyguards of the pasha of Mousul were "extremely handsome, and all of them young and superbly dressed" (Buckingham 1827:21; cf. 167). Similarly, an earlier (pre-Napoleonic) traveler, W. G. Browne remarked that the mamlūks "are in general distinguished by the grace and beauty of their persons" (1806:54).

In addition to the general pederasty with mamlūk cadets, several amirs and sultans showed marked favoritism for some of their courtiers.[14] The most interesting case is that of the young Sultan al-Nāsir Muhammed born Kalāwūn, who scandalized his society in 1497–98 by the "unnatural" interest he showed in the (black) Sudanese slaves ('abīd) who bore firearms, and for their leader, Farajallah, in particular.[15] Nāsir attempted to raise the status of the modern weapons that only a few years later would be turned on the traditional, brave, sword-wielding mamlūk cavalry with devastating results by the Ottomans. This attempt to modernize/deskill the technology of warfare was motivated in part by the malik's taste for the black men whose proficiency with firearms confirmed in mamlūk minds the unworthiness of such weaponry for a skilled elite. Mamlūk cavalrymen literally looked down from their horses on foot soldiers, and this military elite successfully resisted the raising of mass armies of infantrymen. Mamlūks were somewhat more willing to accept artillery, because

artillery is the province of specialized technicians, whose numbers form only a small part of the fighting force, requiring little change in the structure of the army.

The arquebus, on the other hand, is a personal and mass weapon and its intro-duction affects a large number of troops. Hence its large-scale adoption was bound to involve far-reaching changes in the organisation and methods of warfare. To equip a soldier with an arquebus meant taking away his bow, and, what was to the Mamlūk more distasteful, depriving him of his horse, thereby reducing him to the humiliating status of a foot soldier . . . [whereas] horsemanship and all it stood for were the pivot around which the whole way of life of the Mamlūk upper class revolved and from which it derived its courtly pride and feeling of superiority. (Ayalon 1956:61) [16]

Homophobic historians (beginning with al-Makrīzī) are, thus, presented the dilemma that the sultan who tried to modernize the army—in precisely the way they recognize was necessary for continued military success—was a youth of "unstable character" much given to "debauchery" and that his "debauchery" was inextricably tied together with his motivation for the modernization that might have maintained mamlūk military superiority. "Less than twenty years before their own overthrow by firearms, nobody except a lightminded youth could seriously envisage the adoption of firearms as the chief weapons of the [mamlūk] Sultanate," is how Ayalon (1975b:36) puts it, perhaps overhastily accepting the horsemen's view of Nāsir as "frivo-lous" and "foolish."

When the (white) slaves revolted and slew Farajallah and about fifty other black slaves, the mamlūks told Nāsir, "We disapprove of these acts [of favor for the black firearm users]. If you wish to persist in these tastes, you had bet-ter ride by night and go away with your black slaves to faroff places!" (Lewis 1971: 75–76; Ayalon 1956:69–70 includes two slightly variant accounts). The sultan agreed to desist, and when the mamlūks began the sixteenth century with one of their traditional thirteenth century cavalry charges against the Ottoman infantry of Selim I, they met their first defeat, scandalized that Muslims would shoot other Muslims. The mamlūks regarded the Ottomans who defeated them as unchivalrous, immoral, and far inferior in the tradi-tional arts of war.[17]

Concerned more with the external Safavid threat from Persia than with internal rebellion, and short of personnel to defend and administer the vast territories he had conquered (see the discussion of motives in Ayalon 1987a), Selim largely left mamlūks in charge of Egypt and Syria. Immediately upon his death, the mamlūks in Syria rebelled and were crushed once and for all. The Egyptian mamlūks did not join the Syrian ones, and Selim's son Sulei-man continued to use them although he dispatched his Grand Vizier (and brother-in-law) Mustapha Pasha as viceroy after the death of the loyal mamlūk viceroy Khayrbak in 1522. The cavalry charge remained the main (only?) mamlūk tactic—whether against Mongols, Ottomans, or French armies of Saint Louis or Napoléon. The last charge resulted in mamlūks being mowed down by fusillades from Napoléon's army. Seventeen ninety-eight rifles proved even more deadly than the 1517 models that had first revealed the obsolescence of the mamlūk cavalry (Ayalon 1956; 1975a; 1979a,b; 1987a). The French triumph and ensuing occupation

undermined the basis of Mamlūk legitimacy and the raison d'être for the continued importation of Mamlūk slaves, for Mamlūks had failed to defend Islam against a Christian rival power. More importantly, determined French pursuit of the Mamlūks drained their forces and paved the way for their final liquidation by Muhammed 'Ali who assumed power in 1805. (Hatem 1986:264)

Lest it be supposed that the fall of the mamlūks had anything to do with homosexuality, it should be emphasized that the victors were no less pederastic than the mamlūks (as will be seen in the following chapter).

CONCLUSION

The mamlūks exemplify a social system not built on family aggrandizement and patrimony. Without inheritance, with a very slim likelihood of living to a peaceful old age, and with wives paid directly by the state, the usual motivations for building families were lacking.[18] If, as Hocquenghem (1978:136) writes, "The great fear of homosexuality is that the succession of generations on which civilization is based may stop," the mamlūk case shows that both a military tradition and an advanced artistic culture can be transmitted with no bonds of blood. The guardians of high Arabic civilization against barbarians (whether Mongols or Crusaders), each new, unrelated generation of recruits to the elite was noted for its appreciation and patronage of the arts. Although recruited from their rude surroundings not for their aestheticism or refined tastes but for their horsemanship and prowess with sword and bow, the mamlūks built the mosques, palaces, and tombs that are the glory of Cairo, and "delighted in the delicate refinement which art could afford their home life, were lavish in their endowment of pious foundations, magnificent in their mosques and palaces and fastidious in the smallest details of dress, furniture and court etiquette" (Lane-Poole 1898:97; see Lapidus 1967; Mayer 1956; Wiet 1964, 1966).

With all the ardor of converts, they were fierce (not to mention successful) defenders of Islam against both Christian Crusaders from the northwest and

Mongols from the northeast, the very regions from which they derived (see Ayalon 1972, 1980).[19] In Ayalon's summary,

> Mamlūkdom lasted in Islam about 1000 years, although as a decisive power it existed for a considerably shorter period. . . . [The] institution does not have a real parallel outside Muslim civilization. . . . Mamlūkdom is an institution which developed exclusively within Islam, and it has no parallel worthy of its name outside its boundaries. The acquisition of slaves for the purpose of using them as soldiers is not, indeed, limited to Islam alone; but nowhere outside Muslim civilization was there ever created a military slave institution which had been planned so methodically; which had been created for such a grand purpose; which succeeded in accumulating such an immense power, and in registering such astounding achievements; and which enjoyed such a long span of life, as in Islam. (1980:322–33)

Appendix: Lesbian Mamlūk fantasies

Hatem (1986:259, relying on Ayalon 1979a:284–86) claims,

> Lesbian women in Mamlūk harems behaved like Mamlūks, riding pedigreed horses, hunting, and playing *furusiya* (chivalrous) games. They are also said to have indulged in debauchery and wine drinking and to have accumulated enormous wealth and land with the full cooperation of the sultan, which impoverished and corrupted both the sultanate and the military aristocracy.

It is not clear to me how such behavior, or the "debaucheries" of Muhammad 'Ali's daughter Nazli (Marsot 1984:95), "challenged one of the basic political assumptions of heterosexuality and of the Mamlūk system of rigid sexual segregation" or "interfered with the prevalent practice of male traffic in women." Reports of cross-gender behavior, especially in sex-segregated settings, are not adequate bases for concluding that the women involved were exclusively homosexual, still less that they were not "trafficked in."

For a later period Hatem tries to incorporate consideration of homosexuality and the solidarity of oppressed women, seemingly unaware that the form of homosexuality was age-stratified (pederastic) rather than egalitarian/androphilic. Aside from the total lack of evidence she adduces for homosexual relationships being egalitarian in mamlūk Egypt at any point in time, or anyone having shown any interest in defusing stratification, Hatem's (1986: 260–61) interpretation that "the function of homosexuality in the Mamlūk system seems to have been a defensive response to the Mamlūk political system that produced endemic violence among men. Homosexuality represented an effort to cement male solidarity within and across class lines" typifies an altogether too-common vagueness about agency (whose effort?) and consciousness. Reaching even further, Hatem claims that male homosexuality "was designed to increase male control over" women (p. 265).

It seems to me that Hatem projects her vision of homosexuality as inherently egalitarian across time and space to eighteenth- and nineteenth-century Egypt, among women as among men. Although comradely/egalitarian/gay homosexuality may challenge and subvert the patterns of domination in a society, both gender-crossing and age-stratified homosexuality may reinforce gendered structures of dominance and hierarchy.

Notes

1. An earlier version of this chapter was presented at the 1983 annual meetings of the Pacific Sociological Association in Portland, Oregon, in a session organized by Wayne Wooden. His encouragement and that of Wayne Dynes and David Greenberg are gratefully acknowledged, as are the patient editorial labors of Will Roscoe.

2. Ayalon (1980:325) dates the beginnings of the institution much earlier: "As early as the first half of the ninth century A.D., in the reign of Caliph al-Mu'tasim, the first large-scale recruitment of Mamlūks in the service of the 'Abbāsids takes place." The word mamlūk means "owned thing," but "its practical meaning is 'white slave'" (Ayalon 1980:324).

3. Research based on observations of women's lives (and, especially, forms of resistance to male domination) rather than on men's ideal norms has significantly altered the picture. For example, see el-Messiri (1978), Ginat (1982), Nelson (1974), and Wikan (1980, 1982).

4. By the eighteenth and nineteenth centuries, mamlūks could transfer property to their wives, who were not sold as slaves (Hatem 1986:260), and to their sons (Ayalon 1960, 2:158, 3:288–90). Whether mamlūks remained slaves after successfully completing their training, when they took on responsibilities as warriors and tax collectors, is controversial. Volney (1787) consistently wrote of mamlūk as freedmen (*affranchis*). Ménage (1966), Repp (1968), and Glubb (1973) argue that mamlūks remained slaves. Ayalon (1987b:206; 1980:327; 1988b:248; and elsewhere) considers that most, but not all, were manumitted (also see Papoulia 1963:4–10). Because mamlūks' children were raised Muslim, they could not be sold as slaves (Ayalon 1986:4–6; 1980:329).

5. This was decreasingly the case during the rule of Circassian mamlūk sultans, that is, after 1382. "The immigration of relatives reached particularly large proportions from the middle of the fifteenth century onward" (Ayalon 1949:144) and training became more perfunctory: "The period of study was considerably curtailed as compared with the early Mamlūk period, and a large proportion of adults—relatives of the Circassian *amīrs*—were admitted to the Mamlūk corps without passing through the school at all. This practice was completely at variance with the principles underlying the system of military servitude" (p. 145). Without significant external enemies, the mamlūks of the Circassian era relaxed the rigors of the whole system, not just of training but of impersonally meritocratic standards for promotion. The Kepchak mamlūk era before that was much closer to the ideal type of genealogical isolates (as was the Ottoman system through the reign of Suleiman the Magnificent, as discussed in the next chapter). Mamlūk intrigues increased after the incorporation of Egypt as a province of the

Ottoman Empire. After 1671 local mamlūk houses (*buyūt,* sg. *bayt,* which included mamlūk sons) usurped the power and retained the revenues of the ostensible Ottoman "governors," who, de facto, were more ambassadors to the mamlūks than their governors (see Ayalon 1960, 1987a; Cezzar 1962; Holt 1961; Shaw 1962). In answering an inquiry from the treasurer of the French Republic of Egypt, Huseyn Efendī said that if a man died leaving no children, his wife should receive one-fourth of his estate and that the rest belonged to the public treasury (Beyt ul-Māl), which throughout the eighteenth century had meant to the mamlūk beys ([1801] 1964:67, see 143–44).

6. See Glubb (1973), Ayalon (1987b:210). "A magnate would usurp the throne, which on his death would pass to his son. Within a few years at most, the latter would be deposed by another usurper. . . . But the sultanate was not a prize open to all comers: the usurpers emerged from specific circles, namely the military households of previous sultans. The two principal nurseries of sultans were the households of Barkūk and of Kā'it Bay, each of which produced five rulers" (Holt 1991:323–24).

7. Ayalon (1968:327) discusses the fourteenth-century eyewitness accounts and explanations of Ibn Khaldun (specifically, *al-Ta'rīf* 279).

8. This was the point at which steppe fathers gave their sons a bow and arrows and expelled them to fend for themselves, or sold them (Ayalon 1986:2–4). As Ayalon (1988b:248) noted, such a large-scale traffic could not have occurred without willing cooperation in the slaves' places of origin, and that this included the parents of those sold to become mamlūks.

9. However, "If they have a disposition for learning they are taught the use of letters; and some of them are excellent scribes; but the greater part can neither write nor read, a striking example of which deficiency is observable in Murad Bey himself" (Browne 1806:54).

10. Mamlūks' wives and concubines were mostly slaves from the same natal region (i.e., the steppes of southwestern central Asia and, after the depopulation resulting from extensive removal of the fittest of the Kipchak young (male and female), Georgian (*al-Jurjī*) and Circassian (*al-Jarkasī*) ones.

11. The most devastating epidemic, the bubonic plague of 1348–49 was followed by severe epidemics at the rate of one every seven years during the last century of the mamlūk sultanate (Ayalon 1946:68; see also Browne 1806:76; Holt 1991:324). Non-mamlūks were also struck down (albeit not so large a proportion of the cadet *kuttābiyya*), so less wealth was produced and the tax revenue needed to purchase replacement mamlūks also diminished.

12. This is out of keeping with general Islamic doctrine, but, then, so was converting *dhimmi* a "people of the word," as the Christian youth bought to be mamlūks were. *Dhimmi* were generally accorded freedom of worship by the holy law of the *Saria* (Patterson 1982:312). See Ayalon (1980:338n15; 1986:6) on the vagueness of who was a Muslim in the border regions, and Piloti ([1420] 1958:34, 54) on mamlūk cadets' being "reduced to the perfect love of Mohammedan faith" before their serious military training commenced.

13. Circa 1394 in Damascus, Ibn Sasrā writes of mamlūks spending all their money on drink and prostitutes, even selling their horses and arms, and quotes Ahmad ibn Hanbal's despairing counsel: "If you feel no shame, do as you wish" (1963:212). In general, the "mamlūk birthrate was extremely low" (Ayalon 1960:157). Writing of his observations in Egypt before Napoléon invaded, Browne (1806:56) notes that mamlūks "seldom marry till they acquire some office. . . . It is worthy of remark that though the Mamlūks in general be strong and personable men, yet the few who marry very seldom have children. As the son even of a Bey is not honoured with any particular consideration, the women perhaps procure abortions. However this be, of eighteen Beys, whose history I particularly knew, only two had any children living" (in 1792).

14. Christian boys were also sold by their parents and transported by Christian merchants to Egypt to serve as prostitutes, horrifying William of Adam among others. See Daniel (1975:224) on it being more politic in Christendom in the eleventh and twelfth centuries to criticize the trade in boys than other kinds of trading with the enemy (of the Crusades). Boys raised Christian (and to a less extent, those raised Jewish) were taught to be antagonistic to Islam, so non-monotheists were preferred as mamlūk candidates (Ayalon 1986:4–6). Most of these were transported to Egypt by Frankish vessels, even when the mamlūks were fighting European crusaders (Ayalon 1988b:254).

15. Nāsir was also inclined to favor *halka* units (in which the children of mamlūks served), which also threatened the centrality of the mamlūk troops (Ayalon 1979c:765).

16. Also see Ayalon (1975b:37–39), including the outraged statements of the defeated mamlūk commander Amir Kurt Bay to the Ottoman conqueror Selim I about mamlūk superiority as horsemen and condemnation of shooting firearms at Muslims. In addition to a distaste for firearms, the increasing reluctance of any of the Royal Mamlūks to be garrisoned outside Cairo reduced their effectiveness in securing the borders of the sultanate or in quelling rebellions within it (Ayalon 1991:319). Since Royal Mamlūks refused to be stationed in Syria, *halka* regiments were much more important there (Ayalon 1979d:99; 1987a). "For most of the mamlūks the air and water [of Syria] were different and a great number became ill and some died. . . . Damascus swallowed them," as the chronicler Ibn Sasrā ([ca.1398] 1963:212) put it. For a late-eighteenth-century description of the mamlūk's Cairo Citadel (built by Yūsuf Salāh el-Dīn—Saladin—in the late twelfthth century) see Cezzār ([1785] 1962:20–22).

17. See Ayalon (1956:86–97) for a précis of Ibn Zunbul's history of the Ottoman occupation of Egypt, *Fath misr.*

18. See Ayalon (1987b) on why mamlūks kept other mamlūks from passing on what they accumulated to their sons.

19. Some Mongol children (stolen by their ostensible subjects who also sold their own children) were sold as mamlūks, according to al-'Umarī (1927:72,11.16–17).

References

al-'Umarī, Ibn Fadl Allah. [c. 1343] 1927. *Masalik el absar fi mamalik el amsar.* Paris: P. Geuthner. (French translation.)

Ayalon, David. 1946. "The plague and its effects upon the Mamlūk army." *Journal of the Royal Asiatic Society* 66:67–73. (Reprinted in Ayalon 1977.)

———. 1949. "The Circassians in the Mamlūk Kingdom." *Journal of the American Oriental Society* 69:135–47. (Reprinted in Ayalon 1977.)

———. 1956. *Gunpowder and firearms in the Mamlūk Kingdom.* London: Valentine and Mitchell.

———. 1960. "Studies in al-Jabartī I: Notes on the transformation of Mamlūk society in Egypt under the Ottomans." *Journal of Economic and Social History of the Orient* 2:148–74, 3:275–325. (Reprinted in Ayalon 1977.)

———. 1968. "The Muslim city and the Mamlūk military aristocracy." *Proceedings of the Israel Academy of Sciences and Humanities* 2:311–29. (Reprinted in Ayalon 1977.)

———. 1972. "The position of the *Yasa* in the Mamlūk Sultanate." *Studia Islamica* 36:113–58. (Reprinted in Ayalon 1988a.)

———. 1975a. "Preliminary remarks on the mamlūk military institution in Islam." In *War, technology and society in the Middle East,* ed. V. Parry and M. Yapp, 44–58. Oxford: Oxford University Press.

———. 1975b. "The impact of firearms on the Muslim world." *Princeton Middle East Papers* 20: 32–43. (Reprinted in Ayalon 1994.)

———. 1977. *Studies on the Mamlūks of Egypt.* London: Variorum Reprints.

———. 1979a. *The Mamlūk military society.* London: Variorum Reprints.

———. 1979b. "On the eunuchs in Islam." *Jerusalem Studies in Arabic and Islam* 1:67–124. (Reprinted in Ayalon 1988.)

———. 1979c. "Awlād al-nās." *Encyclopedia of Islam* 1:765. Leiden: Brill.

———. 1980[1950]. "Mamlūkiyat." *Jerusalem Studies in Arabic and Islam* 2:321–49. (Reprinted in Ayalon 1988a.)

———. 1986. "The Mamlūk novice: On his youthfulness and on his original religion." *Revue des études islamiques* 56:1–8. (Reprinted in Ayalon 1994.)

———. 1987a. "The end of the Mamlūk Sultanate." *Studia Islamica* 65:124–48. (Reprinted in Ayalon 1994.)

———. 1987b. "Mamlūk military aristocracy: A non-hereditary nobility." *Jerusalem Studies in Arabic and Islam* 10:205–10. (Reprinted in Ayalon 1994.)

———. 1988a. *Outsiders in the lands of Islam: Mamlūks, Mongols, and eunuchs.* London: Variorum Reprints.

———. 1988b. "Islam versus Christian Europe: The case of the Holy Land." In *Pillars of smoke and fire,* ed. M. Sharon, 247–56. Johannesburg: Southern Book.

———. 1991. "Mamlūk." *Encyclopedia of Islam* 6:314–21. Leiden: Brill. (Expanded in Ayalon 1994.)

———. 1994. *Islam and the abode of war: Military slaves and Islamic adversaries.* London: Variorum Reprints.

Browne, W. G. 1806. *Travels in Africa, Egypt and Syria from the year 1792 to 1798.* London: T. Cadell and W. Davies.

Buckingham, James Silk. 1827. *Travels in Mesopotamia.* London: Henry Colburn.

Cezzar Pasa, Ahmet [Djazzar, Ahmad Pasha]. [1785] 1962. *Ottoman Egypt in the eighteenth century: The Nizamname-i misr* (with introduction and extensive notes by Stanford J. Shaw). Harvard Middle Eastern Monograph 7.

Daniel, Norman. 1975. *The Arabs and mediaeval Europe.* London: Longman.

el-Messiri, Saswan. 1978. "Self-images of traditional urban women in Cairo." In *Women in the Muslim world.* ed. Lois Beck and Nikki Keddie, 522–40. Cambridge: Harvard University Press.

Ginat. Joseph. 1982. *Women in Muslim rural society.* New Brunswick, NJ: Transaction Books.

Glubb, John B. 1973. *Soldiers of fortune.* Toronto: Hodder and Stoughton.

Hatem, Mervat. 1986. "The politics of sexuality and gender in segregated patriarchal systems: The case of 18th and 19th century Egypt." *Feminist Studies* 12:251–74.

Hocquenghm, Guy. 1978. *Homosexual desire.* London: Allison and Busby.

Holt, P. M. 1961. "The beylicate in Ottoman Egypt during the seventeenth century." *Bulletin of the School of Oriental and African Studies* 24:214–48.

———. 1975. "The position and power of the Mamlūke sultan." *Bulletin of the School of Oriental and African Studies* 38:237–49.

———. 1991. "Mamlūks." *Encyclopedia of Islam* 6:321–31. Leiden: Brill.

Huseyn, Efendī. [1801] 1964. *Ottoman Egypt in the age of the French Revolution* (with a substantial introduction and extensive notes by Stanford J. Shaw). Harvard Middle Eastern Monograph 11.

Ibn Sasrā, Muhammad ibn Muhammad. [ca. 1398] 1963. *A chronicle of Damascus, 1389–1397.* Berkeley: University of California Press.

Ibn Taghrī Birdī, Abu al-Mahasin Yusuf. [1470] 1963. *History of Egypt, 1382–1469.* Berkeley: University of California Press.

Ibn Iyas. [ca. 1522] 1921. *An account of the Ottoman conquest of Egypt in the year A.H. 922 (A.D. 1516). Translated from the third volume of the Arabic chronicle of Muhammad ibn*

Ahmed ibn Iyas, an eyewitness of the scenes he describes. London: Royal Asiatic Society. Reprinted Westport, CT: Hyperion Press, 1981.

———. 1945. *Histoire des mamlouks circassiens*. Cairo: L'Institut français d'archeologie orientale textes et traductions d'auteurs orientaux 6.

Khowaiter, Abdul-Aziz. 1978. *Barbars I*. London: Green Mountain.

Lane-Poole, Stanley. 1989. *Cairo*. London: J. S. Virtue.

Lapidus, Ira M. 1967. *Muslim cities in the later middle ages*. Cambridge: Harvard University Press.

Lewis, Bernard. 1971. *Race and color in Islam*. New York: Harper and Row.

Makrīzī, Ahmad ibn 'Ali. [ca. 1400] 1980. *A history of the Ayyubid sultans of Egypt*. Boston: Twayne Publishers.

Marsot, Afaf Lutfi al-Sayyid. 1984. *Egypt in the reign of Muhammed Ali*. New York: Cambridge University Press.

Mayer, Leo Ary. 1952. *Mamlūk costume*. Geneva: A. Kundig.

———. 1956. *Islamic architects and their works*. Geneva: A. Kundig.

Ménage, V. L. 1966. "Some notes on the devshirme." *Bulletin of the School of Oriental and African Studies* 29:64–78.

Moorhead, Alan. 1962. *The blue Nile*. New York: Harper and Row.

Muir, William. 1896. *The Mamlūk or slave dynasty of Egypt*. London: Smith, Elder.

Nelson, Cynthia. 1974. "Public and private politics: Women in the Middle Eastern world." *American Ethnologist* 1:551–63.

Papoulia, Basilike D. 1963. *Ursprung and Wesen der "Knabenlese" in osmanischen Reich*. Munich: Oldenbourg.

Patterson, Orlando. 1982. *Slavery and social death*. Cambridge: Harvard University Press.

Piloti, Emmanuel. [1420] 1958. *Sur le passage en Terre Sainte*. Pris: Béatrice-Nauwelaerts.

Pipes, Daniel. 1978. "From Mawla to Mamlūk: The origins of Islamic military slavery." Ph.D. dissertation, Hafvard University.

Poliak, Abraham N. 1939. *Feudalism in Egypt, Syria, Palestine and Lebanon, 1250–1900*. London: Royal Asiatic Society. Reprinted, Philadelphia: Porcupine Press. 1977.

Popper, William. 1955–57. *Egypt and Syria under the Circassian sultans, 1382–1468*. 2 vols. Berkeley: University of California Press.

Quatremere, Étienne Marc. 1808. *Recherches critiques et historiques sur la langue et la litterature de l'Egypte*. Paris: Imprimerie Imperiale.

Rabie, Hassanein. 1972. *The financial system of Egypt A.H. 564–741 A.D. 1169–1341*. New York: Oxford University Press.

Repp, R. C. 1968. "Some further notes on the *devshirme*." *Bulletin of the School of Oriental and African Studies* 31:137–39.

Shaw, Stanford J. 1962. *The financial and administrative organization and development of Ottoman Egypt, 1517–1798*. Princeton: Princeton University Press.

Volney, Constantin-François. 1787. *Travels through Syria and Egypt, in the years 1783, 1784, and 1785*. London: G. G. J. and J. Robinson.

Wiet, Gaston. 1964. *Cairo: City of art and commerce*. Norman, OK: University of Oklahoma Press.

———. 1966. *The mosques of Cairo*. Paris: Hachette.

Wikan, Unni. 1980. *Life among the poor in Cairo*. London: Tavistock.

———. 1982. *Behind the veil in Arabia: Women in Oman*. Baltimore: Johns Hopkins University Press.

CHAPTER 10

Homosexuality among Slave Elites in Ottoman Turkey

Stephen O. Murray.

In the Ottoman Empire,[1] as in the mamlūk regimes eventually subdued by and incorporated within it, the ruling elite consisted of "slaves"[2] (*kullar*, sg. *kul*) who had been born outside Dar al-Islam (i.e., in Dar al-Harb), acquired mostly at ages 10 to 12 (but in some cases ranging from ages 8 to 20), then trained to defend and administer the empire. The*ajemi-oghlan*, foreign-born youths, were early separated from parents, homeland, and the Christian faith. The exclusion of those born Muslim, including the sons of the ruling elite, was consciously designed to prevent the concentration of inherited fortunes and the concomitant feudal growth in power of rich families.

Free of family obligations, carefully selected foreign-born slaves were bound only to the sultan (or vizier or bey) who raised them.[3] Originally, boys were captured as spoils of war or purchased. As the empire grew, beginning on a large-scale basis with Sultan Murād II around 1438, a head tax (*devshirme* from the verb *devshir*, "to collect") was imposed on one in forty boys for the sultan's military and other uses.[4] Reports of frequency vary from collection once every five years to annually. It seems likely that the collection became more frequent over time between the end of the fourteenth and the beginning of the seventeenth centuries. Before it lapsed, the *devshirme* was extended from European to Asian provinces during the 16th century. Reports of age vary from as low as eight to as high as twenty, though the basis for the calculations was one from every forty of those still living who had been baptized fourteen to eighteen years before.[5] According to V. J. Parry:

The actual road that a recruit might follow would depend, in large degree, on his possession or lack of high intellectual and physical qualities. Of the recruits the best endowed went into the palace schools, there to be instructed in the Muslim faith and in the arts of war, statecraft and administration. After long years of training, and in the prime of their young manhood, the most gifted among them would be sent out as governors (*sanjak-begi*) of provinces. Some of them might rise in the course of time to the rank of governor-general (*beglerbegi*) over a number of sanjaks and then, if fortune favoured them, to the status of vizier, with a seat in the Diwan, that is, the Council of State which controlled the great affairs of the empire. The most exalted office—the grand vizierate—would now be within their reach. Few, however, amongst the recruits chosen for education in the palace schools attained to high eminence. Service in the subordinate offices of the court and of the central administration or in the mounted regiments of the [sultan's] household was the lot which awaited most of these more favoured recruits (Parry 1976:103–4)

They were selected for their "bodily perfection, muscular strength, and intellectual ability, so far as it could be judged without long testing" (Lybyer 1913: 74, relying on Ricaut's late-seventeenth-century report [1971:11–12, 46]; and on Postel 1560). The very choicest—"all handsome boys, physically perfect, and of marked intellectual promise" (Lybyer 1913:74)—were taken into the palaces of the sultans as *iç oghlanlari* (pages). According to Barnette Miller:

Upon their arrival in Constantinople the tribute children, who had been collected by the palace gatekeepers, were brought before a board of expert examiners presided over by the chief white eunuch in his capacity as director-in-chief of the system of palace education, a procedure that was applied also to purchased slaves and prisoners of war. By a kind of test which in its shrewdness seems curiously to anticipate the modern intelligence test, and by an examination of physical points similar to those applied at a horse, dog, or cattle show, the youths were separated into two classes. The *sine qua non* of the sultan's service being physical beauty and bodily perfection, the most promising in every respect were set aside for palace service. . . . The remainder, who were distinguished chiefly by reason of their physical strength and dexterity, were assigned to the Janizary corps. The comeliest and cleverest, "those, in whom, besides the accomplishment of the Body, they discover also a noble Genius, fit for a high Education, and such as may render them capable of Serving their Prince, sometime or other," were designated as student pages (*ich-oghlanlar*). The remainder, who were classified as novices or apprentices (*ajemi-oghlanlar*), were put through a stiff course in manual training. . . . From a group set apart for student pages, the cream was for a third time skimmed for the Palace School of the Grand Seraglio. (1941: 81–82, quoting Baudier 1624:110)

According to Postel (1560:17), when presented before the sultan, they were clothed in silk and cloth of gold and silver thread.[6] As the Hapsburg ambassador to Suleiman the Magnificent between the years 1554–62, Ogier Busbecq ([1633] 1968:262) noted, "The Turks rejoice greatly when they find an exceptional man, as though they had acquired a precious object, and they spare no labor or effort in cultivating him." Lybyer (1913) in the major "Western" reccomendation of the system did not consider that criteria such as bodily perfection might have an attraction sexual as well as aesthetic or functional in the Ottoman Empire, where, he was forced to acknowledge, "the vice which takes its name from Sodom was very prevalent among the Ottomans, especially among those in high positions" (p. 74). He also recognized that intellectual ability could not be as readily assessed as bodily perfections, and noticed that the imperial harem was a parallel institution to the school of pages, writing that "the harem might be considered a training-school of slave wives" (p. 79). Nonetheless, Lybyer (1913:71) pressed a view of the Ottoman Empire as entirely meritocratic, even as improving upon Plato's scheme for *The Republic*. It is not surprising, however, that a Harvard scholar of the Progressive Era was likely to stress meritocracy and not wish to think about homosexual nepotism in a system he was invidiously comparing to the corruption rife in the United States. [7]

Drake (1966), Miller (1941:78–79), and Hidden (1916) all stressed that parents groomed their sons for sexual service to the rulers and, when successful, sold them. According to Richard Davey, the Muslim Georgians and especially the Muslim Kurds sent male slaves despite the religious ban on enslaving Muslims (1897:247n), and according to Miller, "The Georgians and Circassians, whose physical types were especially admired by the Turks, found the slave trade with Constantinople so profitable that they maintained slave farms to meet the demand. They not only regularly captured children for the purpose of selling them in the Turkish slave markets, but even reared their own children with this end in view" (1941:78).

Upon the Ottoman conquest of Bosnia and mass conversion to Islam in 1463, the Bosnians "requested that their children should nevertheless be eligible for the devshirme" (Ménage 1960:211). Most of the Bosnian slave boys (called *Potur oghullari*, defined as "boys who are circumcized but not Turkish-speaking") appear to have gone into Palace service, rather than through military training.

Although, in addition to conscription and purchase, many thousands of youths (Christian and Muslim) were stolen each year, slaveries do not nessarily depend on "naked violence" (to borrow a term from Patterson 1982:309, who underestimates the importance of parental consent, indeed of their initiatives, in supplying mamlūks, janissaries, and eunuchs).

FROM BEAUTY TO SEXUALITY

Because a sultan could not enjoy "association on terms of intimate friendship with those who are high officials of state," he was "practically forced by combination of principles and circumstances to spend his leisure hours with boys, eunuchs and women" (Lybyer 1913: 122). Moreover,

The visible court and retinue of the monarch was wholly ungraced by the presence of the fair sex; all great ceremonies and cavalcades were participated in by men alone. . . . Before the middle of the reign of Suleiman [Sülaymān Khān, "the Magnificent," who ruled 1520–66], no woman resided in the entire vast palace where the sultan spent most of his time. (1913:121)

The fact that the boys, organized in groups of ten, "were watched carefully by eunuchs, both day and night" (Lybyer 1913:33) "to see or overhear if there be any wanton or lewd behavior or discourse amongst them" (Ricaut 1971:27)—another parallel to the harem—indicates that homosexuality among *iç oghlans* was a concern, whether to promote/ensure bureaucratic rationality as Greenberg contends or to secure a monopoly for the master (whether he was the sultan or one of his pashas (1988:439). According to the early European observer Paul Ricaut, pages "studied Persian Novellaries [that] endues them with a kind of Platonick love to each other." Since "the restraint and strictures of Discipline makes them strangers to women; for want of converse with them, they burn in lust one towards another." They were also desired by others:

This passion is not only among the young men to each other, but persons of eminent degree in the seraglio become involved, watching out for their favourites, courting them with presents and services. . . . They call it a passion very laudable and virtuous, and a step to that perfect love of God, whereof mankind is only capable, proceeding by way of love and admiration of his image estamped on the [young, male] creature. This is the colour of virtue they paint over the deformity of their depraved inclinations; but in reality, this love of theirs is nothing but libidinous flames each to other, with which they burn so violently, that banishment and death have not been examples sufficient to deter them from demonstrations of such like addresses [to the sultan's pages] (Ricaut 1676:33).

TWO STATUS HIERARCHIES
AND ATTENUATED BUREAUCRATIC IMPERSONALITY

Greenberg and Bystryn plausibly argue that "a juvenile male can be dominated by older men in a patriarchal society without incurring a stigma because the subordination of the young is a 'natural' (and, for any individual, temporary) feature of a patriarchal social structure" (1982:518). To have so served a sultan might not be stigmatizing in itself. However, it is a past that a high-placed Ottoman official was not eager to publicize, because it too easily armed the already resentful and subordinated faithful with taunts (similar to those which reminded Julius Caesar of his youth under the royal weight of Nicomedes of Bythinia).[8] Being sodomized might have improved one's position within the Ottoman hierarchy, but not one's prestige among the faithful. Precisely because they lacked the honor of those born to Islam, they could be in intimate service (sexual and other kinds) to a sultan (see Patterson 1982:310–11). Generally, they were paid salaries rather than granted land, another attempt to keep them from becoming potentially independent feudal powers like the *sipahis* (Parry 1976:104).[9]

There are many reports that sodomy was rife in the Ottoman Empire,[10] but none I have encountered suggests that being inseminated increased one's masculinity as it did until recently in Melanesian militaristic societies.[11] Youthful homosexual receptivity did not bar one from the responsibilities and fruits of high office. Thus, while the services of Rüstem, a Croatian-born page, to Sülayman Khan were exclusively sexual, his predecessor, Ibrahim, was raised to the office of *sadr-i azam* (grand vizier) in quite unbureaucratic fashion, enjoyed favor, power, and, apparently, also Sülayman, for decades beyond his adolescent blossom.[12] "Favorite boys grew up to marry their masters' daughters, to take over management of businesses, properties, etc. The Sultan's favorite boys often grew up to be generals, governors, and high court officials" (Drake 1966:19)—and also themselves major slave-owners (Papoulia 1963:7). At the time of his death Rüstem, for instance, owned seventeen hundred slaves (Babinger 1978:87).[13]

Despite the amassing of riches by some slaves, in the Turkish stratification of honor, even the richest and most powerful slave was "socially dead." For instance, Ibrahim, "the second most powerful man in the most powerful empire of the time" could not testify in a trial (Patterson 1982:313, following Repp 1968:138–39). Especially in patriarchal cultures, genealogical isolates, whose status neither derives from nor can be transmitted through familial lines, rank lower than the poorest freeborn man.

The janissaries—the usual Western designation for the Ottoman army, derived from *yenīcherī*[14] which meant "new troops," (also known as Sipahis of the Porte)—were the sultan's infidel-born six mounted regiments, about fifty thousand men, constituting about a quarter of the army. Like court officials, the janissaries enjoyed more tangible consolations beyond the realm of honor—in which they were all equally nonentities.[15]

Equality in lack of honor/status is not sufficient reason to consider the Ottoman slave elite a rational bureaucracy. I agree with Greenberg that "advancement was generally based on seniority and merit rather than birth," and that this is a significant step away from "feudalism" (1988:439). Nonetheless, I do not believe that the advancement of a sultan's (past or present) sexual favorite posed no "organizational problem." Nepotism is not the only kind of departure from universalism, common though it has been across space and time. Precisely *within the state structure,* homosexual favoritism could stimulate resentment among those passed over. That, "with the exception of state functionaries, the Turkish population was not bureaucratized and not trained for future employment in the bureaucracy," as Greenberg argues, is true, but irrelevant (1988:439; see Mumcu 1963:71). It was precisely within the realm of the exception—"in the state structure" among "state functionaries," to use Greenberg's locutions—that there was a bureaucratic/ patrimonial tension, not just in the training academies.

Once one discounts the typical European rhetoric about "infamy," Eton's surmise seems plausible: chastity was imposed on early "janizaries," but, over time, and with their greater power (and weaker sultans), "the corps itself was bastardized and rendered contemptible by the introduction of the vilest of the people; men occupied in the lowest employments, and even tainted with the most infamous crimes, who would have been formerly expelled from the service with the greatest indignation" ([1798] 1973:29). The difficulty in extirpating same-sex sexual relations from Islamic military academies was evidenced in the assassination in 1941 of General Shahab after he had attempted to accomplish such a feat in the Persian academy (Suratgar 1951: 54). The difficulty was greatest within military-training academies, but existed throughout the Ottoman system of government among officials far away from their families (often enough, from any wives and children, as well as from parents and siblings).

Francis Osborne was one northern savant and comparativist historian who recognized distinct advantages in deploying over vast spaces an army of unmarried men, noting that for the janissaries, "quite unshackled from the magnetical force of an affection to wife and children, by use made natural (which chains Christians like fond Apes to their own doors) every place is fancied their proper sphere. . . . Neither doth the want of Wives raise such cries are made by the Relicts and Children of slain souldiers" (1656:253).[16]

That is, not only could they be dispatched anywhere, but there was no one to mourn them after they were slain, or to press their commanders not to put them in harm's way.

THE INITIAL SUCCESS BUT GRADUAL EROSION OF ONE-GENERATIONAL ELITE SYSTEMS

By short-circuiting the succession of generations and the accumulation of riches, prerogatives, and honors by powerful slaves (or former slaves), the Ottoman system effectively blocked transgenerational accumulation of official positions (and of the riches accumulated by those occupying those positions). The Ottoman system of taking youths from the peripheries of the empire was more effective in keeping its administrators from enriching their natal families than was the Chinese bureaucratic system, in which officials were dispatched (at the start of their careers at least) far from their place of origin, but eventually tended to return to the capital. Employing eunuchs in high office, as both Chinese emperors and Ottoman sultans did (see Ayalon 1979), totally blocked the enrichment of descendants. But unless considerable distance was put between the eunuch and his natal family, eunuchs promoted family interests.[17] Even more in the case of foreign-born eunuchs than in that of foreign-born but reproductively intact "slaves," the native population could invidiously compare its honor to the lack of honor of the un-men. Along with their monopoly on honor, as Parry notes, "to the Muslim-born subjects of the sultan was reserved exclusive control of the Muslim religious, legal and educational institutions of the empire" (1976:103).

For a time, the system of staffing administration and army with aliens was successful in preventing hereditary power from accumulating outside the control of the sultanate (especially insofar as they did not marry and/or procreate). Dersivh/Baktashi asceticism as well as pederastic preferences may have been involved in this demographic phenomenon. However, as among the mamlūks, the one-generation elite system did not prevent collective action against the sultans on behalf of group interests. The *yenīcherī* intrigued, meddled in successions, refused to go too far afield (thus saving Persia and Vienna from conquest), rioted, and increasingly extorted sultans in the same way the mamlūks had and continued to do, especially in the revolt of 1703 (Lybyer 1913: 91–97; Barber 1973:125–35). Moreover, as Hourani observes, "in spite of the attempt by the sultan to keep his professional army apart from the local population, in course of time they began to mingle. By the end of the seventeenth century janissaries were pursuing crafts and trades, and membership of the corps became a kind of property, conferring a right to privileges and pensions, which could be handed to sons, or be bought by members of the civil population" (Hourani 1991:237).

This process proceeded at different rates and to different extents in different provinces, with Tunis already particularly notable for both in the late sixteenth century in contrast to Algiers where control from Constantinople remained more effective (Hourani 1991:229–30). Although I have absolutely no evidence for it, I would hypothesize that over time the masculinity of those conscripted in the Ottoman *devshirme* declined in importance and that the ratio of soldiers to "sextoys" among the Christian boys decreased.[18] The latter part of this surmise at least would seem to be testable in Turkish archives, although complicated by the variety of attributes sought among those not selected for military service.[19]

The Ottoman case probably provides another example of gradual effeminization of age-stratified homosexuality (as in Tokugawa Japan). More obviously, it demonstrates the difficulty of building and maintaining a body of functionaries who will rule impersonally. The isolation of mamlūks and *yenīcherī* from their natal families and from the general population in the empires they governed and defended fostered same-sex emotional and sexual relations rather than eliminating any relationships of the foreign-born mamlūk or *yenīcherī* other than with the sultan who owned them. As both the mamlūk and *yenīcherī* cases show, even when elites are genealogically isolated, they can still manage to disrupt bureaucratic rationality (and/or other kinds of authority) by advancing favorites (friends as well as sexual partners) and by acting collectively. That is, the family is not the only impediment to impersonal order. Moreover, the history of increasing loosening of the principle of recruiting the governing elite anew also suggests that a social system without any accumulation of official status (and riches concomitant to high office) is very difficult to maintain. Men find ways to ensure the prosperity of their sons (or, in their absence, sexual favorites), even when and where their own positions cannot be inherited.

Notes

Many years ago, David Greenberg called my attention to both Lybyer (1913) and Creasy (1877), whose florid style I have sampled herein. Ulku Bates and Wayne Dynes have corrected at least some of my mistakes with Turkish words. Wayne Dynes, David Greenberg, and Will Roscoe made helpful comments on earlier drafts.

1. Othman/Osman, for whom the dynasty was named, acceded to the throne of a small state around Sögüt in northwestern Anatolia around 1281 and ruled until about 1326. The dynasty was overthrown by "the young Turks" led by Mustapha Kemal (Atatürk), founder and first president of the Turkish Republic, who abolished the caliphate in 1924. In the long durée with its vast expansion in size and slow contraction, the apogee was the reign of Suleiman (Sülayman) the Magnificent between 1520 and 1566. The particular focus of this chapter, the institution of a foreign elite troop without local ties, began devolving almost immediately thereafter with an increasing focus on firearms and the recruitment of Turkish soldiers as *kulkardasi*, "brothers of the *kul*" (Inalcik 1973:48; Parry 1976:122), and also sons of *kul* (Ménage 1966:66). On the preceding flux in the region, see Vryonis (1971). This was a major difference from Egypt and Syria, where during the mamluk era "every Royal Mamlūk, on finishing his early training at military school and becoming a fully trained soldier, legally had the same right to become Sultan as any other Royal Mamlūk. . . . the Ottoman Sultan was a free and hereditary ruler" (Ayalon 1956:99). Since they bordered Europeans who used firearms and had elite units of archers, not just cavalry like the mamlūks, the Ottomans were fairly quick to incorporate firearms, in contrast to the unstinting mamlūk resistance to such degradingly mass weapons.

2. Papoulia argues that graduation from training schools was a sort of manumission, so that thereafter those who served the sultan were clients (*mawla*) rather than slaves (1963:4–10). Ayalon asserts that "the Ottoman slave was never manumitted until his very death," in contrast to mamlūks (1956:99). On their distinctive legal status, see Mumcu (1963). Mélange discusses the status of a sultan's *kul* being greater than that of other subjects (1966:66).

3. The Ottoman sultanate, unlike mamlūk positions, was hereditary within the Osman line. Until 1617, when the principle of primogeniture was established, Christian-born troops and administrators exerted an influence on which son succeeded to the throne (and legally executed his brothers; Busbecq 1968:30; Hammer 1827:98). "The sultan's palace provided a model for the residence of viziers and statesmen in the capital and of governors in the provinces." Indeed the minimum size of their retinues was prescribed (Babinger 1978:87).

4. This is the most widely accepted—but still controversial—dating: see Babinger (1978:6, 85, 438), Cahen (1970), Papoulia (1963), Parry (1976:159). The earliest certain attestation is a 1395 sermon of Isidore Glabas (Vryonis 1956). Vryonis suggests that what is kown about the Seljuk slave institution in pre-Ottoman Anatolia indicates "(a) That the Ottoman system was directly inspired by that of the Seljuks of Rum. (b) There is great probability that the levying of Christian children from amongst the subject populations of the Muslim rulers was practiced in Anatolia between the eleventh and thirteenth centuries" (1964:150).

5. Ménage (1960) discusses the difficulties of dating the origins or end of the institution, or the ages of those subject to *devshirme*: five is from Zinkeisen (1840–63, 3:216), annual from Lybyer (1913:51). That it was ad hoc rather than on a fixed schedule is a strong possibility. Ménage (1966:77n51) discusses the possibility that *devshirme* first was practiced in Rūmeli (1966:77n51).

6. Ricaut, Lybyer's most trusted source, reported that clothing and diet of *iç-oghlans* were simple, but there is no contradiction in accepting his reports of quotidian simplicity and Postel's of imperial splendor of dress when taken into the imperial presence (Ricaut [1668] 1971:49).

7. See Hofstader 1956 on the Progressives. Lybyer's endorsement was reaffirmed by Miller, who, however, noted (based on Angiolello) that Muhammad the Conqueror, the founder of the Palace School (*Enderun*) scandalized his own son (Bayazid II) by commissioning lascivious pictures (1941:42). More elaborate and conventionally moralistic rhetoric about the horrors of Turkish taste is exemplified by Creasy:

They [specifically, Bajazet and his general Ali Pasha in the late 14th century] introduced [sic] among the Ottoman grandees (and the loathsome habit soon spread far and wide) the open and notorious practice of those unutterable deeds of vice and crime, which the natural judgment of mankind in every age and every race has branded as the most horrible of all offences against God and man. . . . The pen recoils from this detestable subject; and it is indeed one of the shameful peculiarities of such vice that its very enormity secures to a great extent its oblivion. But it is the stern duty of History not to flinch from the facts, which prove how fearful a curse the Ottoman power was to the lands which it overran during the period of its ascendancy. It became Turkish practice to procure by treaty, by purchase, by force, or by fraud, bands of the fairest children of the conquered Christians, who were placed in the palaces of the Sultan, his viziers, and his pachas, under the title of pages, but too often really to serve as the helpless materials of abomination. (1877:34)

After a quatrain of Milton, Creasy concluded with an unflinching judgment that "pity must be blended with the loathing with which we regard the dishonest splendours of these involuntary apostates; but as unmixed as inexpressible is our abhorrence of the authors of their guilt and shame" (1877:35).

8. They whose ancestors had shed their blood for the father were, in the lands which their fathers had conquered, denied admittance to the class which not only filled most of the offices of army and state but enjoyed high privileges. Sons of the conquered inhabitants, infidel-born, might alone become nobles, paid by the state rather than contributing to its expenses, not subject to the judges trained from boyhood in the Sacred Law; while their own Moslem sons were rigidly excluded from the honored class, were obliged to bear a part in the burdens of state with small hope of sharing its glory, and were expected to take their chances before the same courts to which Christians and Jews were brought for civil and criminal cases. (Lybyer 1913:117)

That the system was working smoothly, defending them, and securing the riches of empire without shedding their own blood in conquering or securing it may well not have occurred to Turks, but Lybyer was using his own standards, not reporting theirs.

9. As Parry notes, "The sultan had at his command a warrior class far more numerous than the armed forces of the imperial household and distinct from them in status [and origin]—the 'feudal' horsemen known as sipahis and located in most, but not all, of the provinces of the empire. These horsemen came to war at the call of the sultan and, in reward for their fulfillment of this obligation, held fiefs adequate to maintain them as efficient soldiers" (1976:104).

10. Lybyer assessed the reliability of various travelers (1913:304–22). See Blount (1636:14), Creasy (1877:34–35, 85–86), Eton (1973 [1798]:29), Inalcik (1973:74–75), Pitts (1731:26). The Genoese Jacopo de Promontorio (ca. 1475) attributed the low birthrate of native Turks (specifically in Anatolia and Rūmelia) to the "infinite lechery of various slaves and young boys to whom they give themselves" (quoted in Babinger 1978:450). Having more than one son was rare, he wrote.

11. Drake concludes that "Turkish evidence suggests that the boys loved most tenderly grew into the most virile men, those used most brutally became effeminates" quoting a "classical" Turkish saying: "Fear makes a boy into a woman, love makes him into a man" (1966:24–25). However, even this perhaps less-than-disinterested claim does not provide any basis for interpreting boy-insemination (in itself) as masculinizing them.

12. Ibrahim progressed from Grand Falconer and Master of the Pages to First Officer of the Royal Bedchamber, governor of a province, Vizier, and Grand Vizier, the highest position in the structure of offices.

> They ate their meals together, went boating, and in times of war shared a tent —or even the same bed. . . . When each August the Sultan moved his court (and harem) to the more bracing climate of Adrianople [now Edirne], he and Ibrahim spent days together engaged in falconry. . . and in their splendid tents each evening Ibrahim was always ready with his music, or at hand if the Sultan felt the urge to write a poem. . . . At times the two men even wore each other's clothes. . . . The Ottoman court was scandalised. To them it was totally unsuitable for the world's greatest emperor to show such favour to a slave. (Barber 1973:36–37, 47)

Ibrahim was strangled in 1536.

13. At least three became Grand Vizier: Rüstem and Ibrahim during Sülayman I's reign and Kara Mustafa during that of Mahomet IV a century later (Barber 1973:103).

14. The Arabic form *yenīshāriyye* was twisted in colloquial usage (in Egypt) to the plural *inkishāriyye* and the singular *inkishārī* (Shaw 1964:91).

15. Two of the six regiments included "men born Muslim, but born outside the confines of the Ottoman empire," hence also lacking local relatives, "the other four regiments being composed of recruits drawn in general from the palace schools" (Parry 1976:104, 158). Although there are claims that *yenicheri* existed earlier, the argument of Ménage (1966:72–76; also see Palmer 1953) that they were "new" some time between 1361 and 1365, early in the reign of Murād I, is compelling.

16. I interpret "made natural" to indicate that Osborne did not believe domesticity is natural for men, but may become habituated. He did not get into the question of what is "natural" sexual conduct for those not "chained to their own doors."

17. The same has been true of "princes" of the Catholic church. Church property was guarded from individual expropriation for the benefit of heirs by forbidding the clergy to marry (i.e., enforcing celibacy with or without chastity), but church officials throughout history have advanced the political and economic interests of their natal families, especially those of their siblings' children.

18. This conjecture is based less on hostile European discourse about janissary degeneracy than on what seems to me a tendency for the beauty of the boys involved in age-stratified homosexuality increasingly to be valued over military attributes as a rising mercantile bourgeoisie shares with the military elite in the cultivation/consumption of pretty boys , for example, in feudal Japan (see Murray 1992).

19. The Palace school produced artists and scholars as well as soldiers and administrators, and craftsmen working for the sultan created some of the finest and most original works of Ottoman civilization. The Palace was the principal creative source in Ottoman culture. The great architect Sinan (1490?–1588), for example, came originally as a *devsirme* boy from Kayseri. . . . Most poets and writers had some connection with the Palace. Bāyezīd II's account books show that about twenty poets regularly benefitted from the sultan's largesse. Historiography received similar encouragement. (Inalcik 1973:88)

Cultivation of the arts is not incompatible with homosexuality, by any means.

References

Ayalon, David. 1956. *Gunpowder and firearms in the Mamlūk kingdom.* London: Valentine & Mitchell.

————. 1979. "On the eunuchs in Islam." *Jerusalem Studies in Arabic and Islam* 1:67–124.

Babinger, Franz C. H. 1978. *Mehmed the Conqueror and his time*. Princeton: Princeton University Press. (Passing mention of boys sought or used is on pp. 96, 212, 334, 427, and on 475 a rivalry between Sultan Mehmed and Vizier Ahmed for a page in the seraglio is mentioned.)

Barber, Noel. 1973. *The sultans*. New York: Simon and Schuster.

Baudier, Michel. 1624. *Histoire générale du sérrail, e de la cour du Grand Seigneur, Empereur des Turcs*. Paris: C. Cramoisy.

Blount, Henry. 1636. *A voyage into the Levant*. London: Andrew Crooke.

Busbecq, Ogier Ghiselin de. [1633] 1968. *Augverii Gislenii Busbeqvii Omnia quæ extant* (*The Turkish letters*). Oxford: Clarendon Press.

Cahen, Claude. 1970. Note sur l'esclave musulman et la devshirme ottoman à propos de travaux récents. *Journal of the Economic and Social History of the Orient* 13:211–18.

Creasy, Edward S. 1877. *History of the Ottoman Turks*. London: Bentley.

Davey, Richard. 1897. *The sultan and his subjects*. London: Chapman and Hall.

Drake, Jonathan (pseud. Parker Rossman). 1966. "'Le vice' in Turkey." *International Journal of Greek Love* 1:13–27.

Eton, William. [1798] 1973. *A survey of the Turkish empire*. Westnead: Gregg.

Greenberg, David F. 1988. *The construction of homosexuality*. Chicago: University of Chicago Press.

Greenberg, David F., and Marcia H. Bystryn. 1982. "Christian intolerance of homosexuality." *American Journal of Sociology* 87:515–48.

————. 1984. "Capitalism, bureaucracy and male homosexuality." *Contemporary Crises* 8:33–56.

Hammer, Joseph von. 1827. *Geschichte des osmanischen Reiches*. Pest: Harleben.

Hidden, Alexander. 1916. *The Ottoman dynasty*. New York: privately printed.

Hofstader, Richard. 1956. *The progressive era*. New York: Vintage.

Hourani, Albert. 1991. *A history of the Arab peoples*. Cambridge: Harvard University Press.

Inalcik, Halil. 1973. *The Ottoman Empire: The classical age*. London: Wiedenfeld and Nicolson.

Lybyer, Albert H. 1913. *The government of the Ottoman Empire in the time of Suleiman the Magnificent*. Cambridge: Harvard University Press.

Ménage, V. L. 1960. Devshirme. *Encyclopedia of Islam* 2:210–13. Leiden: Brill.

————. 1966. "Some notes on the devshirme." *Bulletin of the School of Oriental and African Studies* 29:64–78.

Miller, Barnette. 1941. *The palace school of Muhammad the Conqueror*. Cambridge: Harvard University Press.

Mumcu, Halil. 1963. *Osmanli Devletinde Siyaseten Katl*. Ankara: Ajans-Türk Matbaasi.

Murray, Stephen O. 1992. Effeminization of beloved boys in demilitarized Tokugawa Japan. In *Oceanic Homosexualities*, 131–46. New York: Garland.

Näcke, Paul 1906. "Die homosexualität im Konstantinopel." *Archiv fur Kriminal-Anthropologie and Kriminalistik* 26:106–8.

Osborne, Francis. 1656. *Political reflections upon the government of the Turks.* . . . London: Printed by J. G. for Richard Royston, and sold by Thomas Robinson.

Palmer, J. A. B. 1953. The origins of the Janissaries. *Bulletin of the John Rylands Library* 35:448–81.

Papoulia, Basilike D. 1963. *Ursprung und Wesen der 'Knabenlese' in osmanischen Reich*. Munich: Oldenbourg.

Parry, V. J. 1976. *A history of the Ottoman empire to 1730*. New York: Cambridge University Press.

Patterson, Orlando. 1982. *Slavery and social death*. Cambridge: Harvard University Press.

Pitts, Joseph. [1704] 1731. *A true and faithful account of the religion and manners of the Mohammetans*. 3rd ed. London: Osborn, Longman and Hett.

Postel, Guillaume. 1560. *De la republique des Turcs*. Poitiers: E. de Marnef.

Repp, R. C. 1968. "Some further notes on the *devshirme*." *Bulletin of the School of Oriental and African Studies* 31:137–39.

Ricaut, Paul. [1668] 1971. *The history of the present state of the Ottoman empire*. New York: Arno Press.

Shaw, Stanford J. 1964. Introduction and notes to *Ottoman Egypt in the age of the French Revolution,* by Efendī Hyseyn. Harvard Middle Eastern Monograph 11.

Suratgar, Olive Hepburn. 1951. *I sing in the wilderness: An intimate account of Persia and the Persians*. London: E. Stanford.

Vryonis, Speros, Jr. 1956. "Isidore Glabas and the Turkish devshirme." *Speculum* 31: 433–43.

———. 1964. Review of *Papoulia* (1963). *Balkan Studies* 5:145–53.

———. 1971. *The decline of medieval Hellenism in Asia Minor and the process of Islamization from the eleventh through the fifteenth centuries*. Berkeley: University of California Press.

Zinkeisen, Johann Wilhelm. 1840–63. *Geschichte des osmanischen Reiches in Europa*. 7 vols. Hamburg: F. Perthes.

CHAPTER 11

Male Homosexuality in Ottoman Albania

Stephen O. Murray

As Edward Gibbon long ago remarked, although Albania is only fifty miles from the heel of the Italian boot, the country and its people are all but unknown.[1] The following passage from William Plomer's biography of Ali Pasha distills nineteenth-century romantic writings about the Skipetar "national character":

Perhaps of Scythian origin, they called themselves Skipetars, and spoke a mixed language with a Slavonic basis. . . . Half shepherds and half warriors, devoted to their native mountains and inheriting heroic traits from the remote past . . . they delighted to regard themselves as Palikars, or braves. . . . They were much given to homosexual practices, and were quite uninhibited about them. Parallels to this can easily be found amongst other races in various ages, living a formalized or stylized military life, keeping women in subjection or at least in the background, and having before them as an image of perfection the young warrior: one thinks of the ancient Greeks, the Germans, the Zulus at the height of their power, the Japanese as described by Saikaku. No question of degeneracy is involved, the Skipetars being a race noted for health and physical perfection and living a strenuous life in a rugged country with a pretty severe climate. Nor can hopeless moral turpitude be ascribed to them, whatever Christianity may say, for they were celebrated not merely for their bravery, their love of liberty and their devotion to their native mountains and villages, but for their faithfulness and gratitude to friends and benefactors, and their general liveliness of

187

feeling. . . . It was customary for young men who were closely attached to each other to swear eternal vows, and that this was not simply a matter of mere sentimentality of sensuality, or both, is shown by the fact that the contract was regarded as sacred and proved more durable than marriage often is with us, or friends either, for it is said that no instance was ever known of its violation. (1936:21–29)

Early in the twentieth century, an unnamed German linguist familiar with Albania (whom I would guess to be the distinguished Balkanologist Gustav Ludwig Weigand [1860–?]) wrote Paul Näcke (1851–1913) that among the Greek Orthodox Tosks of south Albania:

male love is deeply inracinated, as everyone knows from Hahn [1853]. I have made inquiries among persons familiar with the country, Germans, Russians, and likewise natives, and all confirmed Hahn's statements point for point. For handsome boys and youths these Shquipètars cherish a truly enthusiastic love. The passion and mutual jealousy are so intense that even today they kill one another for the sake of a boy. Many instances of this kind were reported to me. In particular this love is supposed to flourish among the Moslems . . . [and] even the Christians pay homage to this *amor masculus*. It is further true that pacts of brotherhood, when they occur among Christians, are blessed by the *papas* in church, both partners receiving the eucharist. Otherwise with the Turks. My innkeeper in Ohrid had concluded a pact of blood brotherhood with an Albanian Moslem (Geg). Each pricked the other in the finger and sucked out a drop of blood. Now each has to protect the other to the death, and that for the Christian host is an important guarantee. (Näcke [1907] 1965:40)

After noting that oral intercourse was in vogue with the (notoriously sensual and rape-prone) Turks, Näcke's correspondent explains that the Albanians practice intercrural intercourse. Although sexual practices are "enveloped in profound silence," Näcke and his correspondent do not think that this means that male-male love and pacts of brotherhood in Albania were "platonic." Bremmer (1980:289) culled *büthar*, literally butt-fucker, and *madzüpi* for the practice of pederasty from Krauss's (1911) Albanian sexual lexicon.

Johann von Hahn reported in 1853 (pp. 166–68) that "young men between 16 and 24 love boys from 12 to 17. A Geg [Albanian Muslim] marries at the age of 24 or 25, and then he usually, but not always gives up boy-love," and quoted a native explaining that

The sight of a beautiful youth awakens astonishment in the lover, and opens the door of his heart to the delight which the contemplation of this loveliness affords. Love takes possession of him so completely that all his thought and feeling goes out in it. If he finds himself in the presence of the beloved, he rests absorbed in gazing on him. Absent, he thinks of nought but him. If the beloved unexpectedly appears, he falls into confusion, changes color, turns alternately pale and red. His heart beats faster and impedes his breathing. He has eyes and ears only for the beloved. (in Ellis 1920: 10; Crompton 1985:134–35)

Weigand assured Erich Bethe, who sought to argue that pederasty had originally diffused from the area, that the relationships were "really sexual, although tempered by idealism" and that "while most prevalent among the Moslems, they are also found among the Christians, and receive the blessing of the priest in church" (1907:475, quoted by Ellis 1920:10; Crompton 1985:135).

François Pouqueville (1770–1838), Napoleon's unhappy consul to Ali Pasha's court in Yanina, agreed that the notion of "sin" was absent in his primly appalled contrast of Albanian to Roman Catholic morality:

It seems as if a passion disowned by the first laws of our nature is one of the ordinary concomitants of barbarism. The Albanian is no less dissolute in this respect than the other inhabitants of modern Greece, without seeming to have any idea of the enormity of the crime; especially since, far from seeing it discredited, he finds it rewarded by the chief to whom he is subjected. The wandering lives led by these people, their days passed chiefly amid camps, perhaps encourage this revolting passion. It is general among all classes. (Pouqueville 1813:405, quoted by Crompton 1985:134–35)

The major difference between this report and others is that Pouqueville related acceptance of pederasty to the freedom rather than to the seclusion/subjugation of women. The next sentence of his text is: "The women are not shut up under lock and bars, but in the mountains may be seen walking about perfectly free and unveiled."

The chief to whom Pouqueville referred was Ali Pasha (1741–1822), the Ottoman vizier of Albania and father of Veli, the vizier of most of Greece (see Figure 11.1). Although possessing a harem of five or six hundred women, another French observer, the Baron de Vaudoncourt (1772–1845), wrote that Ali "is almost exclusively given up to the Socratic pleasures, and for this purpose keeps a seraglio of youths, from whom he selects his confidants, and even his principal officers" (quoted by Plomer 1936:79; Crompton 1985:135).

After mentioning Ali's Greek "ganymedes, the youthful pageboys in their crimson petticoats and silver sashes, their locks falling over their shoulders as they strutted about the serais naked of limb," Christowe contemptuously recounts

The one Greek that Ali Pasha trusted and loved was Athanassi Vaya, who was wont to say that if anyone should prove to be more faithful to his master than he, he should kill him on the spot. In this Epiran Greek the classic beauty of his race had reincarnated itself into a living model. . . . He alone of the galaxy of lieutenants, adjutants,

11.1 Ali Pasha in a boat on Lake Butrinto, drawn in 1819 by Louis Dupré. From Louis Dupré's *Voyage à Athènes*, Paris, 1825.

ministers, attendants, and servitors of all kinds was permitted to sit in the presence of Ali Pasha. He was unapproachable to the Greeks, and with characteristic selfishness and possessiveness, he was jealous of all who came into close contact with his friend, the Pasha. Of all except Yussuf-Araps [Ali's half-brother]. These two darlings of the Pasha were strangely fond of each other, neither of them being jealous of the other's favor with the master.

Athnassi consistently showed no interest in women, . . . his fidelity to his friend Ali was as enduring as his youth. He often lay like a faithful dog at the foot of the couch on which Ali took his afternoon naps. (1941:77–78)

Christowe goes on to contrast "effeminate pawing and caressing" with the "manly, sturdy, and distant" comportment with Yussuf-Araps (1941:78). Later in his biography, he described the dance of a circle of more than forty "ganymedes" staged by Ali for Frederick North, the ardently philhellenic fifth Earl of Guilford. Although it was "limited in its variety of movement, nevertheless it was full of tantalizing turns and postures, calculated to exhibit the contours of the body to the best advantage" (Christowe 1941:327).

George Gordon Lord Byron (1788–1824) and his Cambridge friend and traveling companion John Cam Hobhouse (1786–1869) visited Ali's court in the autumn of 1809. Hobhouse wrote that Albanian soldiers live

independent of the other sex, whom they never mention, nor seem to miss in their usual concerns or amusements. The same habit is productive of a system, which is carried by them to an extent of which no nation, perhaps, either modern or ancient, unless we reluctantly except the Thebans can furnish a similar instance. Not even the Gothic Taifali (I refer you to Gibbon for their depraved institution) could be quoted against this assertion, and you should have sufficient proof of its truth were I not aware of the propriety of the maxim approved, or probably invented by the great Latin historian [Tacitus in *Germania*, 12], "Scelera ostendi oporteat (dum puniuntur) flagitia abscondi" (crimes should be blazoned abroad by the retribution, but abomination should remain hidden"). (1813:130)

As Crompton explains (1985:135), these remarks were "meant only to inform the informed" with allusions to the Theban band and to the ancient Rumanian Taifali, whose military reputation the eighteenth-century historian considered

disgraced and polluted by the public infamy of their domestic manners. Every youth, on his entrance into the world, was united in ties of honourable friendship, and brutal love, to some warrior of the tribe; nor could he hope to be released from this unnatural connexion, till he had proved his manhood by slaying in single combat, some huge bear, or a wild boar of the forest. (quoted in Crompton 1985:136)

11.2 Man and boy in a boat on Lake Jannina, drawn in 1819 by Louis Dupré. From Louis Dupré's *Voyage à Athènes*, Paris, 1825.

The "lion of Yanina" was interested in cultivating English allies, and struck by the beautiful, beardless twenty-one-year-old Byron, who wrote to his mother that Ali told him

he was certain I was a man of birth because I had small ears, curling hair, and little white hands, and expressed himself pleased with my appearance and garb. He told me to consider him as a father whilst I was in Turkey, and said he looked on me as his son. Indeed he treated me like a child, sending me almonds and sugared sherbert, fruit and sweetmeats, 20 times a day. He begged me to visit him often, and at night when he was more at leisure. (12 November 1809, quoted by Crompton 1985:138)

The next year, in the original version of Canto II of *Childe Harold*, Byron wrote of Ali's pederasty:

For boyish minions of unhallowed love
The shameless torch of wild desire is lit,
Caressed, preferred even to women's self above,
Whose forms for Nature's gentler errors fit
All frailties mote excuse save that which they commit. (quoted in Crompton 1985: 139; see Figure 11.2)

Byron himself was an admirer of younger male beauty, and more interested in Ali's grandsons than in the vizier. (Byron and Hobhouse had called upon Mukhtar's son Hussein and Veli's son Mehmet in Yanina before they went on to meet Ali further north in Tebeleni.) In a postscript to the letter quoted above, Byron wrote that "they are totally unlike our lads, have painted complexions like rouged dowagers, large black eyes and features perfectly regular. They are the prettiest little animals I ever saw" (Crompton 1985:138). A decade later, when Louis Dupré drew them, they were still pretty, though not nearly as soft as they might look (see Figure 11.3).

Plomer reports that Ali's son Veli, vizier of Morea (southwestern Greece) emulated his father's appetites for money and for boys:

The inhabitants of Morea were continually presenting petitions and complaints against his government. They said that he was ruining them by his monstrous extortions and was altogether behaving exactly like his father; that no parents felt safe about their children, for whenever Veli heard of any beautiful boys or girls he had them seized at once and shut up in his palace to serve his pleasures. (1936:162; see Dupre's drawing of one of his pages, Figure 11.4)

Stowe portrays Veli as a fop:

11.3 Veli's sons, Ismail and Mehmet drawn in 1819 by Louis Dupré. From Louis Dupré's *Voyage à Athènes*, Paris, 1825.

11.4 One of Veli's pages, drawn in 1819 by Louis Dupré. From Louis Dupré's *Voyage à Athènes*, Paris, 1825.

Though personable and of military carriage, Veli Pasha was an utter disappointment to his father as a warrior. He was refined both in manner and appearances; his features were regular and pleasant; he had his father's winsome smile; and always before guests and visitors he was politeness itself. These traits and accomplishments had won for him the reputation of being the finest gentle man in the Turkish Empire. And yet in gluttony and sensuality he could match, if not surpass, both his father and his elder brother [Mukhtar]. . . .

He lived like a European prince, with a coteries of dandies about him including [his father's favorite] Athnassi Vaya's brother Luca Vay, who had studied medicine in Vienna and Leipzig at Ali Pasha's expense. . . . His chief duty was to translate for his patient the best pornographic literature in the European languages. . . . Yet in his public life Veli Pasha was decorous and restrained. His Government of Thessaly was mild compared to the heavy oppression employed in his father's other provinces. . . . The Vizier [Ali Pasha] had nothing but contempt for his second son, the dandy of the Greeks, with his veneer of European culture. (1941:199)

Veli and his son Mehmet were murdered at the Sultan's orders in 1821, and the following year Ali fell in defending the Castro fortress against Turkish forces sent to depose him.

Toward the end, Ali was funding Greek independence fighters against the Ottomans. Albania did not achieve independence until 1912, was annexed by Italy in 1939, and was ruled by the most hardcore Stalinist/Maoist communist regime in Europe from 1945 to 1989. Whitaker notes a traditional "permissive attitude to male homosexuality, particularly when shepherds were away from feminine company in the hills," and found

among my informants a common expectation that young married men would engage in such relationships, having, as one informant put it, "just learned what his penis is for." The subject of homosexual unions does not arouse among the Albanian mountaineers feelings of either shame or amusement in the same way that they do among other ethnic groups. There is instead a pragmatic assumption that the male is entitled to frequent orgasms, however these might be procured. (1981:149)

Notes

1. I am, obviously, indebted to William Plomer's and Louis Crompton's research on Byron and Ali Pasha. I am also grateful to Mildred Dickemann for calling my attention to Whitaker (1981), and to Wayne Dynes for supplying me a copy of Näcke (1965) and for referring me to two Ali Pasha biographies.

References

Bethe, Erich. 1907. "Die Dorische Knabenliebe: Ihre Ethik und Ihre Idee." *Rheinisches Museum für Philologie* 62:438–75.

Bremmer, Jan. 1980. "An enigmatic Indo-European rite: Pæderasty." *Arethusa* 13:279–98.

Byron, (James Gordon) Lord. 1973. *Letters and journals*, ed. Leslie Marchand, Vol. 1. Cambridge: Harvard University Press.

Christowe, Stoyan. 1941. *The Lion of Yanina: A narrative based on the life of Ali Pasha, despot of Epirus.* New York: Modern Age Books.

Crompton, Louis. 1985. *Byron and Greek love.* Berkeley: University of California Press.

Ellis, Havelock. 1920. *Sexual inversion.* Philadelphia: F. A. Davis.

Hahn, Johann Georg von. 1853. *Albanesische Studien.* Jena: Mauke.

Hobhouse, John Cam. 1813. *A journey through Albania, and other provinces of Turkey in Europ and Asia, to Constantinople, during the years 1809–1810.* London: J. Cawthorn.

Krauss, F. R. 1911. "Erotisch-skatologisches Glossar der Albanesen." *Anthropophyteia* 8: 35–39.

Näcke, Paul. 1907. "Über Homosexualität in Albanien." *Jahrbuch für sexuellle Zwischenstufen* 9:325–37. Translated as "On homosexuality in Albania." *International Journal of Greek Love* 1 (1965):39–47.

Plomer, William. 1936. *Ali, the lion.* London: Jonathan Cape.

Pouqueville, François C. H. L. [1805] 1813. *Travels in the Morea, Albania, and other parts of the Ottoman Empire.* London: Henry Colburn.

Vaudoncourt, Guillaume. 1816. *Memoirs on the Ionian islands. . . .* London: Baldwin, Cradock, and Joy.

Whitaker, Ian. 1981. "'A sack for carrying things': The traditional role of women in northern Albanian society." *Anthropological Quarterly* 54:146–56.

CHAPTER 12

The Balkan Sworn Virgin
A Cross-Gendered Female Role

Mildred Dickemann

The "sworn virgin" of the montane Balkans, strangely neglected by anthropology, is a theoretically important gender role, as these cross-dressed, cross-gendered females are the only known institutionalized female-to-male role and identity transformations in modern Europe, paralleling those known from native North America (Blackwood 1984; Lang 1990).[1] Indeed, Scandinavianist Carol Clover (1986) has proposed that they represent a surviving example of cross-gendered female roles widespread in pre-Christian Europe, as evidenced by sagas, folklore, and early Christian accounts. In fact, their former presence in now urbanized Dalmatia and Bosnia is attested by epic folksongs (Filipovic 1982:59–69).

Our knowledge of the sworn virgin (such is the standard appellation in English) is fragmentary, based on brief accounts by travelers, missionaries, geographers, and anthropologists. Two of the most valuable sources are Edith Durham's accounts of her Albanian travels in the early twentieth century (especially *High Albania*, first published in 1909) and René Grémaux's recent articles (1989, 1994) both based on published sources, including those in Balkan languages, and his own Yugoslavian fieldwork in the 1980s. Durham reported meeting eight sworn virgins in northern Albania, and gives brief accounts of her encounters with four; she met "several" others in the south. Grémaux has located references to a hundred and twenty instances, met two surviving sworn virgins, and interviewed relatives and acquaintances of others now deceased. He provides four short life histories, several pages in length. These accounts reveal not only a formal, socially defined role and identity for females transformed into social men, but significant individual variation in enactments of that identity and role. However, this description must be provisional, and some aspects of identity and behavior will probably never be known.

The sworn virgin role has been reported since the 1850s from Albania, Macedonia, and southern Serbia, especially Montenegro and Kosovo, primarily in mountain regions where a mixed pastoral-agricultural economy supported patrilineal nested lineages engaging in continual feuding. The lineages had defined but contested territories, elaborate oral legal codes, rigid sex segregation in association and activities, and a markedly lower status for women than for men. The assumption of masculine identity by a female generally required swearing to lifelong celibacy before a group of lineage elders. Violation of this oath, or later pregnancy of the "virgin," was said to be punished by stoning or being burned alive, though there are no recorded cases of such punishments in my sources.

Two standard rationales are given for the allocation or assumption of this role: one is the need of a patrilineal family group for a surrogate son, no sons having been born or all having died in childhood; the other is the desire of a young woman of marriageable age to escape an arranged marriage with an undesirable groom. As I elaborate elsewhere (Dickemann, n.d.), I believe these canonical rationales gloss over the complexity of the motivations and the agency of several actors, including the individual concerned.

Surrogate sons were important for the patrilineal inheritance of family holdings, but sources do not explain what value one additional generation would have, since the surrogate son bears no offspring, and holdings without direct heirs reverted in any case to the nearest male relative. Indeed, in southeast Albania, according to Durham, sworn virgins did not inherit at all, but were supported by male kin, or found employment with the Church (1910:-460; 1928:195). Five of Durham's eight north Albanian sworn virgins and three of Grémaux's four life history subjects were such surrogate sons. This too-pat rationale probably reflects an oversimple folk classification. In some cases, for example, not one but several daughters assumed a masculine identity and in others, the later birth of a brother did not end the sworn virgin's masculine role (Durham [1909] 1987:85, 81; Grémaux 1994:254). The absence of brothers must have been one of many collaborating conditions which provided both the opportunity and the justification for such a gender change.

Most sources ignore the role of mothers in allocating a daughter to this role: a widow without sons to support her was forced to return to her natal family, remain as a servant in the family of her deceased husband, or be remarried—in some areas, to a male relative of her deceased husband. All these fates involved greatly diminished status. With a son or surrogate son, she could live out her life in the marital household of her adulthood, receiving support from the person to whom she generally had the strongest affectional ties. Yet only Grémaux records an actual testimony: "'Because if you get married I'll be left alone, but if you stay with me, I'll have a son.' On hearing these words Djurdja [the daughter] threw down her embroidery" and became a man (1989:164; 1994:270–72).

Even more significantly, few accounts reveal the motivation of the individual herself in becoming a surrogate son. Thus, one girl became a sworn virgin in order not to be separated from her father (Nopcsa 1910:12–13); another transferred her inheritance to the household of a blood sister, also a sworn virgin, where they lived and worked together for the rest of their lives (Filipovic 1982:42; Grémaux 1989:164). Durham met one who "had dressed as a boy, she said, ever since she was quite a child because she had wanted to, and her father had let her. Of matrimony she was very derisive . . ." (Durham [1909] 1987:81). One of Grémaux's subjects insisted that she "was not incited by my parents' wish but because *I* wanted it that way, I started to dress and behave like a boy. As far as I remember I have always felt myself more like a male than a female" (Grémaux 1989:157; 1994:263, 265). While these accounts of cross-gender self-identification may involve some retrospective reconstruction, they cannot be dismissed out of hand.

No doubt some women assumed the sworn virgin role to avoid a specific unwanted marriage: Durham recounts such cases ([1909] 1987:85, 173). The abrogation of the marriage contract, which often involved child betrothal and early down payment of partial brideprice, was a serious offense leading to blood feuding between the two families. It could be avoided if the woman assumed sworn virgin status (apparently on the sour grapes principle). But some sworn virgins, it seems, preferred the cross-gendered role because the married life of women in general was abhorrent. One told Grémaux that "the only good thing about marriage is having children" (1989:159; 1994: 267). The classic patrilineal treatment of women, secluded if possible and always strictly sex-segregated, their premarital virginity and marital fidelity enforced through the death penalty, their betrothal as children and marriage by sale without their consent, their heavy and constant physical labor and continual childbearing and rearing, the deference demanded of them by all men and especially by their fathers and husbands, enforced by frequent beatings, while the men lounged, smoked, drank and gossiped, plotting and singing of feuds, all undoubtedly motivated some women to prefer a masculine life.[2]

Surprisingly, religion played little part in the construction or distribution of this role. In the mountain regions, men of a single household might be of different religions, conversions being motivated by personal advantage, and marriages across religious lines were not unknown. The sworn virgin's oath was witnessed by twelve elders of the local religion, whether Muslim, Eastern Orthodox, or Roman Catholic. However, in the clans of southeast Albania, more exposed to urban lowland society, sworn virgins generally did not wear men's clothes, did not inherit the family estate, and were supported by male relatives. Here the custom resembled a Christian celibate role: some became priests' servants, or worked as lay sisters in the few nunneries, and some even became nuns. Political economy seems to have more to do with the occurrence and nature of the role than religious boundaries.

Generally the sworn virgin identity was lifelong, but Grémaux (1989:162–63; 1994:270) records a case in which it was abandoned for heterosexual marriage and childbearing, while Durham ([1909] 1987:57) reports the case of a marriage refuser who, after swearing virginity and serving for many years as a priest's servant, eloped at the age of forty with a Muslim man.

Were these individuals fully cross-gendered, that is, masculine insofar as possible, or an intermediate gender with attributes of both majority genders? This is a matter of degree as well as semantics. It is striking, however, in contrast to many Native American cross-gendered individuals of both sexes, how completely most sworn virgins filled the masculine gender definition. In the highlands, most assumed masculine dress, carried a gun (a mark of masculine adulthood), engaged in the masculine farming activities of plowing and mowing, while some enjoyed hunting and participated in feuding and the recent guerrilla wars. They were accepted in all-male governing councils (though there is some variation in the degree of active participation), acted as household heads when fathers were deceased, sold off their sisters as a brother should, and sometimes attained high rank as lineage leaders and as commanders of all-male bands of bandits or guerrilla fighters. Many expressed the misogynist stereotypes and contempt for women characteristic of their male peers.

These individuals were generally known by the community in which they lived to be cross-gendered, as is indicated by the existence of many special terms for them in the languages of the region: Albanian *verginesha* (virgin or unmarried woman); Montenegrin *harambasha* (woman-man); Southern Serbian *mushkobane* (manly woman), *tombelije* or *tobelije* (from Turkish, one who forswears betrothal), *ostajnica* (one who stays [in the paternal household]), *zena covjek* (woman-man). There are several other terms in the literature that occur with less frequency than these. (Serbo-Croatian, with local variants, is spoken in the region except in Kosovo and Albania, where Albanian, which is not mutually intelligible with Serbo-Croatian, is spoken.) In some cases, the assumption of masculine dress was not complete, or the individual abjured guns and feuding. Yet, in some of Grémaux's cases, the sworn virgin so completely manifested masculine voice and comportment that outsiders and even younger members of the extended family were deceived as to their sex. *That is, sworn virgins are socially men, not treated as some intermediate or third sex or gender.*

Grémaux is the only source I have found who records the self-reference of the sworn virgin, in these two languages characterized by obligatory gender designation. Three of his four main subjects referred to themselves with masculine forms, one with feminine ones. At least one retained the feminine name given at birth, while others adopted masculine names or forms of the given name. Likewise, acquaintances and relatives were not uniform in form of address or pronouns of reference. Some sworn virgins received masculine funerals while others were denied that privilege (Grémaux 1989 and 1994).

Not surprisingly, it is only Grémaux's recent work that addresses the sexuality of these individuals. Though some travelers' accounts suggest that they occasionally engaged in heterosexual sex, Grémaux could find no certain cases. A sworn virgin met by Carleton Coon in the 1920s spent the night with his horsedriver (Coon 1950). The punishment of death for pregnancy would seem to have counseled restraint. No doubt there were exceptions, but the sources overall suggest to me and to Grémaux that heterosexual sex was extremely uncommon. Likewise with same-sex relations: there are a few cases of sworn virgins who as blood sisters lived together, but the degree of intimacy is unknown. Two of Grémaux's four instances expressed a sexual attraction to women but apparently without any actual sexual contacts. However, he found two cases in which long-term sexual liaisons were acknowledged by neighbors; in one of these, the two partners are now termed "lesbians" (1994:273). One Serbo-Croatian source reports marriages with women achieved by deception. But it appears that sexual activity of any kind was not within the "central tendency" of this role/identity.

While some individual accounts reveal women unhappy in their identities, the majority seemed proud of their masculine status, while relatives and friends generally express pride as well, though the joking that generally accompanies a statistically unusual gender role occurs. However, Grémaux makes clear that the pejoration of a traditional gender role and its assimilation to the stigmatized modern "homosexual" identity, a process we see occurring in places as distant as Thailand and East Africa, are occurring in the Balkans as well.

Nevertheless, it is too early to conclude that the institutionalized cross-gender role is a thing of the past. Grémaux (1994:242) has only met briefly with two living individuals, while Kaser's (1994) "expeditions" found none living. But Antonia Young, who continues fieldwork, has met five, and claims further that there was renewed acknowledgment of the role in the 1950s, as a reaction against the Communist government (which had outlawed it and much other traditional behavior). She states that there could be a few hundred living in northern Albania, and notes, correctly I believe, that the current increase in feuding consequent on the collapse of the Communist regime may well encourage new manifestations of a phenomenon which is fundamentally rooted in tribal patrilineal life (personal communication, January 28, 1995).

Notes

1. My thanks to Deborah Amory, Allan Bray, Jason Cromwell, Eugene Hammel, Stephen Murray, Will Roscoe, and Antonia Young for discussion and assistance with sources and terminology. All errors are my own.
2. See accounts in Durham 1928, 1987; Boehm 1984; Hasluck 1954; Kaser 1994; Whitaker 1968, 1976, 1981.

References

Blackwood, Evelyn. 1984. "Sexuality and gender in certain Native American tribes: The case of cross-gender females." *Signs* 10:27–42.
Boehm, Christopher. 1984. *Blood revenge: The anthropology of feuding in Montenegro and other tribal societies.* Lawrence, KS: University Press of Kansas.
Clover, Carol J. 1986. "Maiden warriors and other sons." *Journal of English and German Philology* 85:35–49.
Coon, Carleton. 1950. *The mountains of giants: A racial and cultural study of the north Albanian mountain Ghegs.* Papers of the Peabody Museum of American Archaeology and Ethnology 23(3).
Dickemann, Mildred. n.d. "Gender crossing and gender mixing: Balkan sworn virgins and Western women travelers." Unpublished ms.
Durham, Mary Edith. 1910. "High Albania and its customs in 1908." *Journal of the Royal Anthropological Institute* 40:453–72.
———. 1928. *Some tribal origins, laws, and customs of the Balkans.* London: Allen & Unwin.
———. [1909] 1987. *High Albania.* Boston: Beacon. Reprint. London: Edwin Arnold.
Filipovic, Milenko S. 1982. *Among the people: Selected writings of Milenko S. Filipovic.* Papers in Slavic Philology 3. Ann Arbor, MI: University of Michigan, Department of Slavic Languages and Literature.
Grémaux, René. 1989. "Mannish women of the Balkan mountains: Preliminary notes on the 'sworn virgins' in male disguise, with special reference to their sexuality and gender-identity." In *From Sappho to De Sade: Moments in the history of sexuality*, ed. Jan Bremmer, 143–72. London: Routledge.

————. 1994. "Woman becomes man in the Balkans." In *Third sex, third gender: Beyond sexual dimorphism in culture and history,* ed. Gilbert Herdt, 241–81. New York: Zone Books.

Hasluck, Margaret. 1954. *The unwritten law in Albania.* Cambridge: Cambridge University Press.

Kaser, Karl. 1994. "Die Mannfrau in den patriarchalen Gesellschaften des Balkans und der Mythos vom Matriarchat." *Zeitschrift für feministische Geschichtswissenschaft* 4.

Lang, Sabine. 1990. *Männer als Frauen-Frauen als Männer: Geschlechtsrollenwechsel bei den Indianern Nordamerikas.* Hamburg: Wayasbah Verlag.

Nopcsa, Franz. 1910. *Aus Sala und Klementi: Albanische Wanderungen. Zur Kunde der Balkanhalbinsel.* Sarajevo: Daniel A. Kajon.

Whitaker, Ian. 1968. "Tribal structure and national politics in Albania, 1910–1950." In *History and social anthropology,* ed. I. M. Lewis, 253–93. London: Tavistock.

————. 1976. "Familial roles in the extended patrilineal kin-group in northern Albania." In *Mediterranean family structures,* ed. Joseph Peristiany, 195–203. Cambridge: Cambridge University Press.

————. 1981. "'A sack for carrying things': The traditional role of women in northern Albanian society." *Anthropological Quarterly* 54:146–56.

CHAPTER 13

Some Nineteenth-Century Reports of Islamic Homosexualities

Stephen O. Murray

DEBAUCHERY AND PURITY OF BOY-LOVE IN IRAQ

For James Silk Buckingham, who journeyed through Mesopotamia in the summer of 1817, passing the ruins of Nineveh along the Tigris River on his way to Baghdad, recording the "unspeakable" lifeways of the debauched Orient was a "duty." Beyond its standard litany of the "indescribable" and the "infamous," the following passage is interesting for the way it reveals how such attitudes were reflected back by "natives," who were aware of the Christian European denigration of Islamic acceptance of "depravity," and therefore denied that anything sexual was going on. It opens with Buckingham's description of Hebheb, where the appearance of the people, their town, and the Arabic spoken remind him of Egypt:

This was the first place at which, during all my travels in Mohammedan countries, which had now been considerable, I had ever seen boys publicly exhibited and set apart for purposes of depravity not to be named. I had, indeed, heard of public establishments for such infamous practices at Constantinople, but I had always doubted the fact. I saw here, however, with my own eyes one of these youths avowedly devoted to a purpose not to be described, and from the very thought of which the mind revolts with horror. This youth was by no means remarkable for beauty of person, and was even dirtily and meanly dressed. His costume was that of an Arab, with a peculiar kind of silk handkerchief, called *keffeeah*, hanging down about the neck, and thrown over the head. He wore, however, all the silver ornaments peculiar to females; and from his travelling *khoordj* he exhibited to the persons in the coffee-house a much richer dress of muslin and gold stuffs, in which he arrayed himself on certain occasions. The boy was about ten years of age, impudent, forward, and revoltingly fond and fawning in his demeanour.

He hung about the persons of those who were seated in the coffee-house, sitting on their knees and singing indescribable songs; but no one, as far as I could learn, avowed any nearer approach. There were many of the party, indeed, who insisted that the practice had no existence in Turkey; but that the object for which boys of this description was exhibited was merely to sing, to dance, and to excite pleasurable ideas; and that for this purpose they were taught alluring ways, and furnished with splendid dresses. Others, however, more frankly admitted that the vice was not merely imaginary, and common notoriety would seem to confirm this view of the case.

This youth was under the care of an elder and a younger man, who travelled with him, and shared the profits of his exhibition and his use. As neither the state of morals nor manners in any country can be accurately judged of without facts of this nature being stated, as well as those of a more honourable kind, I have felt it my duty, as an observer of human nature to record, in the least objectionable manner in which I can convey the description so as to be intelligible, this mark of profligacy, to which the classical scholar will readily remember parallels in ancient manners, but which among the moderns has been thought by many to be nowhere openly tolerated. (1827:166–68)

In *Travels in Assyria, Media, and Persia*, published three years later, Buckingham did not try to deny that physical sex was involved in relations with public boys. He noted that "the Jelabs or public boys of Turkey and Persia are as much despised and shunned in those countries, as abandoned women are with us, or even more so" (1830:166). In contrast to carnal relations with dancing boy "prostitutes," however, Buckingham described at considerable length "platonic" love for respectable boys. That is, he again mitigated Muslim interest in boys as not really sexual. Juxtaposed to the infamous use of *jelabs* noted above, Buckingham wrote that "the youths who are the avowed favourites or beloved of particular individuals are as much respected and thought as honourably of, as any virtuous girl, whose amiable qualities should have procured her an honourable lover" (pp. 166–67).

As they were leaving Baghdad, Ismael, the Afghani ring-engraver who decided to guide Buckingham,[1] had an emotional encounter with "an elderly Christian merchant, whose name was Eleeas, and the parting between these was like that of father and a son separating never again to meet. Tears flowed fast from the eyes of both; and then I learned that this venerable old man was that father of Ismael's love" (pp. 140–41). Some way into the journey Buckingham was astonished to learn that the beloved was "the son, not the daughter, of his friend Elias who held so powerful a hold on his heart!" (p. 159). After a lengthy digression on the purity of ancient Greek boy-love (ending with the Theban Band!), Buckingham reported that he

took the greatest pains to ascertain, by a severe and minute investigation, how far it might be possible to doubt of the purity of the passion by which this Affghan Dervish was possessed, and whether it deserved to be classed with that described as prevailing among the ancient Greeks; and the result fully satisfied me that both were the same. Ismael was, however, surprised beyond measure, when I assured him that such feeling was not known at all among the people of Europe [!].

"But how?" said he: "Has Nature then constituted you of different materials from other men? Can you behold a youth, lovely as the moon, chaste, innocent, playful, generous, kind, amiable,—in short, containing all the perfections of innocent boy-hood, which like the most delicate odour of the rose, exists only in the bud, and becomes a coarser and less lovely kind when blown into maturity—can you look on a being, so fit for Heaven as this is, and not involuntarily love it?" I agreed with him that a sort of admiration or affection might be the result, but I at the same time strove to mark the distinction between an esteem founded on the admiration of such rare qualities and anything like a regard for the person. I did not succeed, however, in convincing him; for to his mind, no such distinction seemed to exist; and he contended, that if it were possible for a man to be enamoured of very thing that is fair, and lovely, and good and beautiful, in a female form, without a reference to the enjoyment of the person, which feeling may most unquestionably exist, so the same sentiment might be excited towards similar charms united in a youth of the other sex, without reference to any impure desires; and that, in short, in such a case, the lover would feel as much repugnance at the intrusion of any unchaste thought, as would the admirer of a virtuous girl at the exhibition of any indelicacy, or the presence of any thing, indeed, which could give offence to the strictest propriety in their mutual intercourse.

The Dervish added a striking instance of the force of these attachments, and the sympathy which was felt in the sorrows to which they led, by the following fact from his own history. The place of his residence, and of his usual labour, was near the bridge of the Tigris, at the gate of the Mosque of the Vizier. While he sat here, about five or six years since, surrounded by several of his friends, who came often to enjoy his conversation and beguile the tedium of his work, he observed, passing among the crowd, a young and beautiful Turkish boy, whose eyes met his, as if by destiny, and they remained fixedly gazing on each other for some time. The boy, after "blushing like the first hue of a summer morning," passed on, frequently turning back to look on the person who had regarded him so ardently. The Dervish felt his heart "revolve within him," for such was his expression, and a cold sweat came across his brow. He hung his head upon his [en]graving-tool in dejection, and excused himself to those about him, by saying he felt suddenly ill. Shortly afterwards, the boy returned, and after walking to and fro several times, drawing nearer and nearer, as if under the influence of some attracting charm, he came up to his observer and said, "Is it really true, then, that you love me?"

"This," said Ismael, "was a dagger in my heart; I could make no reply." The friends who were near him, and now saw all explained, asked him if there had been any previous acquaintance existing between them. He assured them that they had never seen each other before.

"Then," they replied, "such an event must be from God."

The boy continued to remain for a while with this party, told with great frankness the name and rank of his parents, as well as the place of his residence, and promised to repeat his visit on the following day. He did this regularly for several months in succession, sitting for hours by the Dervish, and either singing to him, or asking him interesting questions, to beguile his labours, until, as Ismael expressed himself, "though they were still two bodies, they became one soul."

The youth at length fell sick and was confined to his bed, during which time his lover, Ismael, discontinued entirely his usual occupations, and abandoned himself completely to the care of his beloved. He watched the changes of his disease with more than the anxiety of a parent, and never quitted his bed-side, night or day. Death at length separated them; but even when this stroke came, the Dervish could not be prevailed on to quit the corpse. He constantly visited the grave that contained the remains of all he held dear on earth, and, planting myrtles and flowers there, after the manner of the East, bedewed them daily with his tears.

His friends sympathized powerfully in his distress, which, he said, "continued to feed his grief," until he pined away to absolute illness, and was near following the fate of him whom he deplored. . . .

From all this [including an "Ode to Love" in Pashto], added to many other examples of similar kind, related as happening between persons who had often been pointed out to me in Arabia and Persia, I could no longer doubt the existence in the East of an affection for male youths, of as pure and honourable a kind as that which is felt in Europe for those of the other sex. The most eminent scholars have contended for the purity of a similar passion, which not only prevailed, but was publicly countenanced and praised in Greece; and if the passion there could be a chaste one, it might be admitted to be equally possible here. [Cornelius] De Pauw [1792] ascribes it in that country to the superior beauty of the males to the females, which is hardly likely to have been the sole cause; but, even admitting the admiration of personal beauty to have entered largely into the sources of this singular direction of feeling, it would be as unjust to suppose that this necessarily implied impurity of desire, as to contend that no one could admire a lovely countenance and a beautiful form in the other sex, and still be inspired with sentiments of the most pure and honourable nature toward the object of his admiration. (1830:159–64)

The most interesting element in this lengthy discourse is the friendship between Elias and the admirer of his son, Ismael. There is no reason to doubt Buckingham's report. In what follows, it is difficult to guess what Ismael said.

The purity of admiration for beautiful boys has certainly been maintained by many dervishes over the course of many centuries. Buckingham's review of then-current understandings of ancient Greek pederasty and his contrast (in sections not reproduced here) of unaccomplished, secluded Muslim women with the accomplished and unfettered women he claimed were characteristic of Christian Europe make one wonder whether he put words in Ismael's mouth. Whether or not he did, he managed to record a romantic tale of boy-love publishable in the England of 1830 along with the only line of justification that could have been accepted there and then (see Crompton 1985). Decidedly uncritical about his own culture, Buckingham was nonetheless more willing than most Europeans to exculpate boy-love, though, like many subsequent alien observers, he produced an explanation that maintained the Christian European view of its own superiority. For many, the focus on boys was discrediting. For Buckingham, this was only the result of another inferiority of Muslim societies (the seclusion and lack of educational opportunities for women—in a rather exaggerated contrast!).

As is so often the case, Buckingham's accounts of the culture of the Other reveals more about himself and his own cultural presuppositions than about Ismael's or what Ismael tried to explain to him. Some accurate recording of what he said would be helpful, but portable tape recorders were a long ways in the future, alas.

Uzbeki Dancing Boys and Their Patrons

The following passage is excerpted from the first volume of Eugene Schuyler's *Turkistan: Notes of a journey in Russian Turkistan, Kokand, Bukhara and Kuldja*. Schuyler was U.S. consul in Moscow, then in St. Petersburg before his travels in central Asia in 1867. No admirer of Islamic rule, he was expelled from Constantinople/Istanbul the same year as his books on his travels in Turkistan and on Ottoman atrocities in Bulgaria were published. He traveled in central Asia with the help and scrutiny of the Russian forces who had only recently incorporated the area (five years before in the case of Samarkand). The Soviet suppression of Uzbeki dancing boys in the twentieth century and the survival of the role among Uzbekis in Afghanistan is related by Ingeborg Baldauf (1988).

In Central Asia Mohammedan prudery prohibits the public dancing of women; but as the desire of being amused and of witnessing a graceful spectacle is the same all the world over, here boys and youths specially trained take the place of the dancing-girls of other countries. The moral tone of the society of Central Asia is scarcely improved by the change.

These *batchas*, or dancing-boys, are a recognized institution throughout the whole of the settled portions of Central Asia, though they are most in vogue in Bukhara, and the neighboring Samarkand. Batchas are as much respected as the greatest singers and *artistes* are with us. Every movement they make is followed and applauded, and I have never seen such breathless interest as they excite, for the whole crowd seems to devour them with their eyes, while their hands beat time to every step. If a batcha condescends to offer a man a bowl of tea, the recipient rises to take it with a profound obeisance, and returns the empty bowl in the say way, addressing him only as *"Taxi,"* "your Majesty," or *"kulluk,"* "I am your slave." Even when a batcha passes through the bazaar all who know him rise to salute him with hands upon their hearts, and the exclamation of "Kulluk!" and should he deign to stop and rest in any shop it is thought a great honor.

In all large towns batchas are very numerous, for it is as much the custom for a Bokhariot gentleman to keep one as it was in the Middle Ages for each knight to have his squire. In fact no establishment of a man of rank or position would be complete without one; and men of small means club together to keep one among them, to amuse them in their hours of rest and recreation. They usually set him up in a tea-shop, and if the boy is pretty his stall will be full of customers all day long. Those batchas, however, who dance in public are fewer in number, and are now to some extent under [Russian] police restrictions. In Kitab there were only about a dozen, in other towns even less, and the same dancers sometimes go from place to place. They live either with their parents or with the entrepreneur, who takes care of them and always accompanies them. He dresses them for the different dances, wraps them up when they have finished, and looks after them as well as any duenna.

At the hour appointed for the *bazem*, the boys begin to come in twos and threes, accompanied by their guardians, and after giving their hands to their host take their places on one edge of the carpet, sitting in the Asiatic respectful way upon the soles of their feet. Bowls of tea and trays of fruit and sweets are set before them. The musicians meanwhile tune their tambourines, or rather increase their resonance, by holding them over a pan of glowing coals. When the boys have devoured enough grapes and melons the dancing begins. This is very difficult to describe. With flowing robe of bright-colored variegated silk, loose trousers, and bare feet, and two long tresses of hair streaming from under their embroidered skull-cap, the batcha begins to throw himself into graceful attitudes, merely keeping time with his feet and hands to the beating of the tambourines and the weird monotonous song of the leader. Soon his movements become wilder, and the spectators all clap their hands in measure; he circles madly about, throwing out his arms, and after turning several somersaults kneels facing the musicians. After a moment's pause he begins to sing in reply to the leader, playing his arms in graceful movement over his head. Soon he rises, and, with body trembling all over, slowly waltzes about the edge of the carpet, and with still wilder and wilder motions again kneels and bows to us. A thrill and murmur of delight runs through the audience, an extra robe is thrown over him, and a bowl of tea handed to him as he takes his seat. This first dance is called *katta-uin* (the great play), in contradistinction to the special dances. The natives seem most pleased with those dances where the batcha is dressed as a girl, with long braids of false hair and tinkling anklets and bracelets. Usually but one or two in a troop can dance the women's dance, and the female attire once donned is retained for the remainder of the feast, and the batcha is much besought to sit here and there among the spectators to receive their caresses. Each dance has its special name—Afghani, Shirazi, Kashgari—according to the country where it is national or of the story it is supposed to represent; but all are much alike, differing in rapidity, or in the amount of posture and gesture. The younger boys usually perform those dances which have more of a gymnastic character, with many somersaults and hand-springs; while the elder and taller ones devote themselves more to posturing, slow movements, and amatory and lascivious gestures. The dance which pleased me most, and which I saw for the first time in Karshi, was the *Kabuli,* a sort of gymnastic game, where two boys armed each with two wands strike them constantly in alternate cadence, while performing complicated figures, twists, and somersaults. In general but one boy dances at a time, and rarely more than two together, these being usually independent of each other.

The dances, so far as I was able to judge, were by no means indecent, though they were often very lascivious. One of the most frequent gestures was that of seizing the breast in the hand and then pretending to throw it to the spectators, similar to our way of throwing kisses. In some dances the batcha goes about with a bowl of tea, and choosing one of the spectators, offers the tea to him with entreating gestures, sinks to the floor, singing constantly a stanza of praise and compliment. The favored man hands back the bowl with thanks, but the boy slips from his proffered embrace, or shyly submits to be kissed, and is off to another. If the spectator is generous he will drop some silver coins into the empty bowl, and if he is a great lover of this amusement he will take a golden *tilla* in his lips, and the batcha will put up his lips to receive it, when a kiss may perhaps be snatched.

The songs sung during the dances are always about love and are frequently responsive between the batcha and the musicians. These will serve as specimens:—

"Tchuyandy, my soul! what has become of thee? Why didst thou not come?" "An ill-natured father kept me; but I was in love with thee, and could not endure separation.'

"Tchuyandy, my soul! why didst thou delay, if thou were sad?" "Nightingale! I am sad! As passionately as thou lovest the rose, so loudly sing, that my loved one may awake. Let me die in the embrace of my dear one, for I envy no one. I know that thou hast many lovers; but what affair of mine is that? The rose would not wither if the nightingale did not win it; and man would not perish did not death come."[2]

The batchas practice their profession from a very early age until sometimes so late as twenty or twenty-five, or at all events until it is impossible to conceal their beards. The life which they have led hardly fits them for independent existence thereafter. So long as they are young and pretty they have their own way in everything; every command is obeyed by their adorers, every purse is at their disposition, and they fall into a life of caprice, extravagance, and dissipation. Rarely do they lay up any money, and more rarely still are they able to profit by it afterwards. Frequently a batcha is set up as a keeper of a tea-house by his admirers, where he will always have a good *clientèle*, and sometimes he is started as a small merchant. Occasionally one succeeds, and becomes a prosperous man, though the remembrance of his past life will frequently place the then odious affix, batcha, to his name. I have known one or two men, now rich and respected citizens, who began life in this way. In the old days it was much easier, for a handsome dancer might easily become *Kushbegi*, or Grand Vizier. More often a batcha takes to smoking opium or drinking *kukhnar* [a liqueur made from poppies from which the seeds have been removed], and soon dies of dissipation.

The Islamic Part of Burton's "Sotadic Zone"

The pioneer comparative study of homosexuality is Captain Sir Richard F. Burton's (1821–90) "Terminal Essay," which concludes his ten-volume "plain and literal translation of the Arabian nights."[3] Based on his wide travel and considerable philological scholarship, it was first privately published in 1886.

By his own account, Burton's inquiries on male-male love in what he called "the sotadic zone" began in 1845, sparked by the curiosity of Sir Charles Napier, who had conquered and annexed the Sind (i.e., the Indus valley, now in southern Pakistan). According to Burton,

It was reported to him that Karáchi, a townlet of some two thousand souls and distant not more than a mile from camp, supported no less than three lupanars or bordel[lo]s, in which not women but boys and eunuches, the former demanding nearly a double price, lay for hire. Being the only British officer who could speak Sindhi, I was asked indirectly to make enquiries and to report upon the subject.[4]

Burton's report led to his summary dismissal by Napier's successor. Nonetheless, his inquiries into the two types of homosexuality represented by the boys and the eunuchs he discovered in Karachi continued. Although Geoffrey Gorer has been credited with first recognizing the existence of these types, Burton wrote of them over a half a century earlier as *stages*, with sacralized gender-defined homosexuality being the second stage (with specific reference to the *galli* of the Cybele cult), although John Addington Symonds accused him of lumping "the complicated psychology of Urnings" (constitutionally non-masculine homosexuals) and pederasty (in Burton [1930] 1977: 103). Since Burton's discussion was organized geographically rather than typologically, it can easily be misread as wobbling between the age- and gender-defined homosexuality he had differentiated.

Moreover, it is difficult to know what distinctive "blending of the masculine and feminine temperaments" or what aspect of climate he saw as the cause of homosexuality. Burton held that the "sotadic zone" which he bounded with northern latitudes 30° and 43° (only in the eastern hemisphere; in the western hemisphere the "zone" ranged from Peru to Alaska) was "geographical and climatic, not racial." The covert geographical specification seems to be "south of Christendom" (in the Old World), which is to say more cultural than climatic. Burton's frequent forays into comparative religion bolster this interpretation of his zone. As will be apparent in the quotations that follow, Burton must not have considered climate sufficient cause, since he speculates about the diffusion of the complexes (age- and gender-defined homosexuality) from place to place (including Cairo to Paris after Napoleon's conquest of Egypt). The "Terminal Essay" does not attempt to explain gender-defined homosexuality.

Before launching his geographical survey, Burton reminds his readers that pederasty is not sheer carnality:

We must not forget that the love of boys has its noble and sentimental side. The Platonists and the pupils of the Academy, followed by the Sufis or Moslem Gnostics, held such affection, pure as ardent, to be the *beau idéa*; which united in man's soul the creature with the Creator. Professing to regard youths as the most cleanly and beautiful objects in this phenomenal world, they declared that by loving and extolling the *chef-d'oeuvre*, corporeal and intellectual, of the Demiurgus, disinterestedly and without any admixture of carnal sensuality, they are paying the most fervent adoration to the Causa causans. They add that such affection, passing as it does the love of women, is far less selfish than fondness for and admiration of the other sex, which, however innocent always suggest sexuality; and the Easterners add that the devotion of the moth to the taper is purer and more fervent than the Bulbul's love of the Rose.

From these recurrent Persian metaphors of, respectively, love for boy and for woman, the "Terminal Essay" goes on to review Greek and Roman literature, crediting the Roman Empire with a somewhat dubious diffusion of age-defined homosexuality:

Roman civilization carried pederasty also[5] to Northern Africa, where it took firm root, while the negro and negroid races to the South ignore the erotic perversion,[6] except where imported by foreigners into such kingdoms as Bornu and Haussa. In old Mauritania, now Morocco, the Moors proper [in contrast to the Berbers] are notable sodomites; Moslems, even of saintly houses, are permitted openly to keep catamites, nor do their disciples think worse of their sanctity for such license: in one case the English wife failed to banish from the home "that horrid boy."

After a discussion of the Qur'ān and speculations about the possible historical destruction of the "cities of the Plain," Burton resumes the tour:

As in Morocco, so the Vice prevails throughout the old regencies of Algiers, Tunis and Tripoli and all the cities of the South Mediterranean seaboard, whilst it is unknown to the Nubians, the Berbers and the wilder tribes dwelling inland [see no 3]. Proceeding Eastward we reach Egypt, that classical region of all abominations which, marvellous to relate, flourished in closest contact with men leading the purest of lives, models of moderation and morality, of religion and virtue. Amongst the ancient Copts the Vice was part and portion of the Ritual and was represented by two male partridges alternately copulating (Interp. in Priapi Carm. xvii). The evil would have gained strength by the invasion of Cambuses (B.C. 524), whose armies, after the victory over Psammentius, settled in the Nile Valley, and held it, despite sundry revolts, for some hundred and ninety years. During these six generations the Iranians left their mark upon lower Egypt and especially, as the late Rogers Bey proved, upon the Fayyum the most ancient Delta of the Nile. Nor would the evil be diminished by the Hellenes, who, under Alexander the Great, "liberator and savior of Egypt" (B.C. 332), extinguished the native dynasties: the love of the Macedonian for Bagoas the Eunuch being a matter of history.

From that time and under the rule of the Ptolemies the morality gradually decayed; the Canopic orgies extended into private life and the debauchery of the men was equalled only by the depravity of the women. Neither Christianity nor Al-Islam could effect a change for the better; and social morality seems to have been at its worst during the past century when Sonnini travelled (A.C. 1717).[7] The French officer, who is thoroughly trustworthy, draws the darkest picture of the widely-spread criminality especially of the bestiality and the sodomy (chapt. xv) which formed the "delight of the Egyptians." During the Napoleonic conquest Jaubert in his letter to General Bruis (p. 19) says "Les Arabes et les Mamelouks ont traité quelquest-uns des nos prisonniers comme Socarate traitat, diton, Alcibiade. Il fallait périr ou y passer."

Old Anglo-Egyptians still chuckle over the tale of [Khedive] Sa'id Pasha [1822–63, ruler of Egypt from 1854 to 1863] and M. de Ruyessenaer, the high-dried and highly respectable Consul-General for the Netherlands, who was solemnly advised to make the experiment, active and passive, before offering his opinion on the subject. In the present age extensive intercourse with Europeans has produced not a reformation but a certain reticence among the upper classes: they are as vicious as ever, but they do not care for displaying their vices to the eyes of mocking strangers.

Syria and Palestine, another ancient focus of abominations, borrowed from Egypt and exaggerated the worship of Androgynic and hermaphroditic deities.

After discussing Isis, possible Phoenician transmission of "androgynic worship" to Greece, and Hebrew temple prostitutes ("houses of sodomites that were by the house of the Lord"—II Kings 23:7) from the time of Rehoboam (975 B.C.) to Josiah (641 B.C.), Burton continues with Syria:

Syria has not forgotten her old "praxis." At Damascus I found some noteworthy cases among the religious of the great Amawi Mosque. As for the Druses we have

Bur[c]khardt's authority [(1822) 1983:202] "unnatural propensities are very common amongst them."

The Sotadic Zone covers the whole of Asia Minor and Mesopotamia, now occupied by the "unspeakable Turk," a race of born pederasts. . . . The Vice, of course, prevails more in the cities and towns of Asiatic Turkey than in the villages; yet even these are infected; while the nomad Turcomans contrast badly in this point with the Gypsies, those Badawin of India. The Kurd population is of Iranian origin, which means that the evil is deeply rooted: I have noted in the Arabian Nights that the great and glorious Saladin was a habitual pederast. The Armenians, as their national character is, will prostitute themselves for gain but prefer women to boys: Georgia supplied Turkey with catamites while Circassia sent concubines. In Mesopotamia the barbarous invader has almost obliterated the ancient civilization which is antedated only by the Nilotic: the mysteries of old Babylon nowhere survive save in certain obscure tribes like the Mandæns, the Devil-worshippers and the Alí-iláhi.

Entering Persia we find the reverse of Armenia; and, despite Herodotus, I believe that Iran borrowed her pathological love from the peoples of the Tigris Euphrates Valley and not from the then insignificant Greeks. But whatever may be its origin, the corruption is now bred in the bone. It begins in boyhood and many Persians account for it by paternal severity. Youths arrived at puberty find none of the facilities with which Europe supplied fornication. Onanism [*Genesis* 38:2–11] is to a certain extent discouraged by circumcisions, and meddling with the father's slave-girls and concubines would be risking cruel punishment if not death. Hence they use each other by turns, a "puerile practice" known as Alish-Takish the Latine facere vicibus or Mutuum facere. Temperament, media, and atavism recommend the custom to the general; and after marrying and begetting heirs, Paterfamilias returns to the Ganymede. Hence all the odes of Hafiz are addressed to youths. . . . Chardin [1691] tells us that houses of male prostitution were common in Persia whilst those of women were unknown: the same is the case in the present day and the boys are prepared with extreme care by diet, baths, depilation, unguents and a host of artists in cosmetics.

The Vice is looked upon at most as a peccadillo and its mention crops up in every jest-book. When the Isfahan man mocked Shaykh Sa'adi, by comparing the bald pates of Shirazian elders to the bottom of a lotá, a brass cup with a wide-necked opening used in the Hammam, the witty poet turned its aperture upward and thereto likened the well-abused podex of an Isfahani youth. Another favourite piece of Shirazian "chaff" is to declare that when an Isfahan father would set up his son in business he provides him with a pound of rice, meaning that he can sell the result as compost for the kitchen-garden, and with the price buy another meal; hence the saying Khakhi-i-pái káhú=the soil at the lettuce-root. The Ifhadanis retort with the name of a station or halting place between the two cities where, under pretence of making travellers stow away their riding-gear, many a Shirázi had been raped: hence "Zín o takaltú tú bi-bar"=carry within saddle and saddle-cloth!

A favourite Persian punishment for strangers caught in the Harem of Gymnæceum is to strip and throw them and expose them to the embraces of the grooms and negro-slaves. I once asked a Shirazi how penetration was possible if the patient resisted with all the force of the sphincter muscle: he smiled and said, "Ah, we Persians know a trick to get over that; we apply a sharpened tent-peg to the crupper-bone (*os coccygis*) and knock till he opens." A well-known missionary to the East during the last generation was subjected to this gross insult by one of the Persian Prince-governors, whom he had infuriated by his conversion-mania: in his memoirs he alludes to it by mentioning his "dishonoured person"; but English readers cannot comprehend the full significance of the confession.

About the same time Shaykh Nasr, Governor of Bushire, a man famed for facetious black-guardism, used to invite European youngsters serving in the Bombay Marine and ply them with liquor till they were insensible. Next morning the middies mostly complained that the champagne had caused a curious irritation and soreness in la *parte-poste*. . . .

The cities of Afghanistan and Sind are thoroughly saturated with Persian vice, and the people sing

> Kadrikus Aughán dánad, kadrikunrá Kábul:
> The worth of c____ the Afghan knows: Cabul prefers the other *chose!*

The Afghans are commercial travellers on a large scale and each caravan is accompanied by a number of boys and lads almost in woman's attire with *kohl*'d eyes and rouged cheeks, long tresses and henna'd fingers and toes, riding luxuriously in Kajaáwas or camel-panniers: they are called Kúch-i safari, or travelling wives, and the husbands trudge patiently by their sides.[8] In Afghanistan also a frantic debauchery broke out amongst the women when they found *incubi* who were not pederasts; and the scandal was not the most insignificant cause of the general rising at Cabul (Nov. 1841).

Resuming our way Eastward we find the Sikhs and the Moslems of the Panjab much addicted to the Vice, although the Himalayan tribes to the north and those lying south, the Rájputs and Marathás ignore it. The same may be said of the Kashmirians who add another Kappa to the triad Kakista, Kappadocians, Kretans, and Kilicians: the proverb says

> Agar kaht-i-mardum uftad, az ín sih jins kam gírí:
> Eki Afghán, dovvum Sindí,[9] siyuum badjins-i-Kashmírí:
> Though of men there be famine yet shun these three—
> Afghan, Sindi and rascally Kashmírí.

Louis D[e]ville describes the infamies of [Punjabi] Lahore and Lakhnau where he found men [*hijra*] dressed as women, with flowing locks under crowns of flowers, imitating the feminine walk and gestures, voices and fashion of speech, and ogling their admirers will all the coquetry of *bayadères* [prostitutes]. Victor Jacquemont's *Journal de Voyage* [(1834) 1936] describes the pederasty of Ranjít Singh, the "Lion of the Panjáb," and his pathic Guláb Singh whom the English inflicted upon Cashmir by way of paying for his treason.[10] Yet the Hindus, I repeat, hold pederasty in abhorrence and are as much scandalized by being called Gánd-márá (anus-beater) or Gándá (anuser) as Englishmen would be. . . .

Of Turkistan we know little, but what we know confirms my statement. Mr. Schuyler in his Turkistan (i 132 [see previous section in this chapter]) offers an illustration of a "Batchah" (Pers. bachcheh=catamite), "or singing-boy surrounded by his admirers."[11] Of the Tartars Master Purchas laconically says (1617:419), "They are addicted to Sodomie or Buggerie."

It is possible to read Burton's survey as a condescending British notice of wayward (vicious, pathological, etc.) "Orientals" or as a covert attempt (under the conventional rhetoric of disparagement) to establish that pederasty was widespread. Conventional Christian readers (if Burton had any!) could take satisfaction in recognition of "the Vice." The "Terminal Essay" could reinforce their sense of superiority to Muslims who did not see the seriousness of such a sin. Other readers who thought the British and other northern Christian condemnation of homosexuality excessive could find saner views elsewhere: at most a pecadillo in some places and positively valued in others. Even had he wanted to do so, Burton could not have published (even privately and ostensibly in India) a defense of pederasty.

My own view is that speaking about the unspeakable—that which was not spoken of among Christians—aimed to subvert convention and to open consideration of variability in attitudes about male-male sexuality. Since hardly any of the tales spun out across a thousand and one nights and ten large volumes touch on the topic, no explanation was needed. That is, making sense of the *Arabian nights* does *not* require a survey of homosexuality around the world. In that they appear to be merely a pretext to write about something he wanted to write about, it does not make sense for Burton to have written only to affirm conventional Victorian contempt. I would not go so far as to infer any personal self-justification from this relativizing. No one knows the extent to which Burton was a participant in pederasty in the time he spent in Islamic societies. It is possible that he only made inquiries and had no personal interest in legitimating male-male sexual relations and relationships.

The "Terminal Essay" draws extremely little on Burton's own very extensive ethnographic fieldwork. It is primarily a survey of texts—an ethnological investigation by someone who could have claimed considerable ethnographic authority. Although I think that Burton made the basic distinction between age-stratified and gender-stratified homosexualities, the geographical ordering of his survey muddies the typological distinction. As important as this essay was to comparative (homo-)sexology, I do not think that anyone credits the explanation he provided for the cultural differences (i.e., between Victorian England and "the sotadic zone").[12] Even knowing that geographical determinism was a credible, indeed widespread, viewpoint in the second half of the nineteenth century, it is hard to take seriously a zone that expands to encompass the entire "New World" (in addition to the northward contortions east of Bengal to exclude Southeast Asia and to reach Japan). No single climate characterizes the supposed "sotadic zone," and, as I have already suggested, "non-Christian" seems to be the real category.[13]

Burton was more interested in and respectful of Islamic and Hindu beliefs and cultures than were his contemporaries. (Edward Westermarck was Burton's obvious heir in spending time in Islamic society, comparing religions, and taking a special interest in Islamic homosexualities.) I believe that he sought to humanize "the heathen" and "the Oriental" caricatured by his compatriots, not to reinforce English smugness and xenophobia. Although employed by the English government in more than one of his many foreign endeavors, he became an admirer and even an advocate for the literature of "the East." He considered frankness about sexuality (not just homosexuality) admirable and he did not seek to titillate English readers with representations of "Oriental vice" to which he expected them to feel themselves superior. "Sexual heretic," Brian Reade's appellation, may be too strong, but Burton was at least a "relativist" rather than an "agent of colonialism" and promoter of the superiority of English culture.

WESTERMARCK'S NOTES ON PEDERASTY IN MOROCCO

The Finnish-British anthropologist Edward Westermarck (1862–1939) spent seven years in Morocco on twenty-one visits between 1898 and the publication in 1926 of his two-volume *Ritual and Belief in Morocco*.[14] Never married, Westermarck was accompanied on all his journeys in Morocco by his friend Shereef Sīdi 'Absslam al-Baqqāli. Westermarck's references to homosexuality are brief, but offer a rare glimpse into homosexual roles and practices in North Africa in the early twentieth century.

In his earlier two-volume tome, *The Origins and Development of Moral Ideas* (1906–8), Westermarck devotes a long chapter to the consideration of "Homosexual Love" cross-culturally (chap. 43; 2:456–89). His Moroccan book does not provide any overview of male-male sexual relations there.[15] His passing comments indicate an acceptance of sexual intercourse with boys but denigration of adult male sexual receptivity:

Sexual intercourse with a saintly person is considered beneficial. Supernatural benefits are expected even from homosexual intercourse with a person possessed of *baraka*.[16] I know of an instance in which a young man, who has been regarded as a saint on account of the miracles he performed, traced his holiness to the fact that he had been the favourite of a shereef; and it is a common belief among the Arabic-speaking mountaineers of Northern Morocco that a boy cannot learn the Koran well unless a scribe commits pederasty with him. So also an apprentice is supposed to learn his trade by having intercourse with his master. (1926:198)

According to Westermarck, positive valuation of male sexual receptivity was limited to non-commercial adolescence. He reported the Anrja belief that "a person who drinks alcohol, a boy who prostitutes himself, and a grown-up man who practises passive pederasty, will always, both in this world and the next, wash his face with the urine of Jewish *jnun* [more commonly spelled *jinn*, a spirit living underground]" (1926:272). Boy prostitutes were called *z-zāmel* or *m-mefsūd*; sexually receptive men *l-hāssas*.[17] However, calling someone a boy prostitute in Morocco, Westermarck explained, "is not considered so terrible as it would be in Europe" (1926:486).[18] In ritualized exchanges of insults, a *z-zāmel* was a counter either to a *tᵛrābi s-soq* ("one who has grown up in the market place, that is who feels shame before nobody") or a *tᵛrābi l-gūrna* ("one who has grown up in a cow pen").

Under what he called "homeopathic influences," Westermarck recorded a quaint folkloristic rationale for homosexual relations with boys:

If you intend to set out on a journey, and on getting up in the morning find your slippers or one of them turned upside down, you should not start on that day as it is a bad omen (Hiāina). Such a slipper may also mean that its owner's mind is absent (Aglu); but if the owner is a boy it may have a different meaning, prognosticating that somebody will commit pederasty with him (Tangier). A boy takes hold of another boy's slipper and throws it into the air, saying *Dir mā 'mel mūlak*, "Do what your master has done"; and if it falls down with the sole turned upwards, the boy is said to be a zāmel, and is treated accordingly (Andjrā). An intimate relation is considered to exist between a person and his slippers; to sit on somebody's slippers is the same as to sit on his face (Tangier, Ait Wāryāger) or "his heart" (Aglu). (1926:597)

Notes

1. Buckingham quotes Ismael as telling him that "from the moment that I saw you and heard your voice, I felt that your soul contained what I had all my life been searching for in vain, and that it was my destiny to follow you wherever you might go" (1830:141). Given that Ismael had traveled and studied a great deal before this, the statement is even more extravagant than it might seem.

2. The nightingale and the rose are recurrent metaphors for wooer and wooed, although the rose is usually a female beloved (in contrast to the candle drawing a moth). [Editors' note]

3. All quotations without page references are from section 4D. There is very little mention of the larger work (*The Arabian nights*) to which the essay is appended.

According to Burton,

> The pederasty of the Arabian Nights may briefly be distributed into three categories. The first is the funny form, as the unseemly practical joke of masterful Queen Budúr (vol. iii,300–306) and the not less hardy jest of the slave-princess Zumurrud (vol. iv, 226). The second is in the grimmest and most earnest phase of the perversion, for instance where Abu Nowas debauches the three youths (vol. iv, 64–69); whilst in the third form it is wisely and learnedly discussed, to be severely blamed by the Shaykhah or Reverend Woman (vol. v.154).

The references are to the original (1885–86) edition. The eighteen thousand-word section on "the sotadic zone" was reprinted separately around 1930 and was also included in Reade (1971:158–93).

4. Burton relates that after being certified as a translator of several languages he

> was thrown so entirely amongst the people as to depend upon them for society. . . . The first difficulty was to pass for an Oriental, and this was as necessary as it was difficult. . . . After trying several characters, the easiest to be assumed was, I found, that of a half Arab, half Iranian. . . . Mirza Abdullah of Bushire . . . a Bazzaz, a vendor of fine linen, calicoes, and muslins . . . [who] came as a rich man, stayed with dignity, and departed exacting all the honours. ([1852]1924:18–19).

5. The preceding example was Celtic. Given a reference to the phenomenon from Aristotle, it is hard to imagine how Romans introduced the practice to them. Burton derives Roman pederasty from the Etruscans rather than the Greeks: "Pederastia had in Greece its noble and ideal side: Rome, however, borrowed her malpractices, like her religion and polity, from those ultra-material Etruscans and debauched with a brazen face."

6. The information available to Burton was mostly from the African coasts. For a survey of age- and gender-defined homosexualities in the interior of Africa see Murray (1990, 1995).

7. Charles Sigisbert Sonnini (1751–1812) traveled to Egypt in 1777. Sonnini wrote that "the passion contrary to nature . . . is generally diffused over Egypt; the rich and the poor are equally infected with it; contrary to the effect it produces in colder countries, that of being exclusive, it is there [i.e., in Egypt] associated with the love of women" (1799, 1:251–52; translated by Wayne Dynes).

8. An interesting continuity across time and technologies has been reported by Dupree: besides "young dancing boys who dress like women and wear make-up," he wrote that "truck drivers sometimes carry young lovers with them on long trips" (1978: 198).

9. For "Sindi" Roebuck (*Oriental Proverbs* Part i:99) has Kunby (Kumboh), a Panjābi peasant and others vary the saying ad libitum. (Burton's note)

10. Foster (1978:95) translated the section of the Larousse encyclopedia entry on "Pédérastie" from which these two sentences obviously derive, and corrected Burton's "Daville" to "Deville."

11. The part of the text to which Burton refers is reprinted in this volume. Although they were more dancers than singers, contrary to Foster (1978:97), they did both.

12. Burton did not attempt to explain differences in organization or acceptance of male-male sexual relations within the "sotadic zone."

13. Nonetheless, on the historicist principle that it is necessary to try to recover how someone in the past could have believed what seems ludicrous and absurd, a study of Victorian-era geographical determinism might recover how the "sotadic zone" made sense then and there. Dialectically, I have been stimulated by Hollister's (1993) unhistoricist and very unsympathetic reading of Burton.

14. On his life and career see Westermarck 1929; Fletcher 1971; Stroup 1982; Stacking 1995:151–63.

15. Maxwell reviews a number of early twentieth-century French sources (1983: 286–89). Remlinger (1913) provides a vivid view of French colonial medical officers attempting to ban urban prostitution (male and female). Crapanzano wrote that "although homosexuality is perhaps not as common in Morocco as in Turkey, it is by no means uncommon. There is considerable scorn for the adult male who plays the passive role. Adolescent boys who play the passive role are teased and expected when they are older to assume the active role" (1973:52).

16. In the first volume (35–261; and also in Westermarck 1915) he describes *baraka* as "a mysterious wonder-working force which is looked upon as a blessing from God, a 'blessed virtue.' It may be conveniently translated into English by the word 'holiness'" (p. 35).

17. Westermarck listed these terms among Fez invectives (1926:483). All three continue to be attested in Morocco.

18 Maxwell went further, asserting that at the time of the French occupation of Morocco, "European and Moroccan attitudes differed widely in all matters pertaining to sex, and perhaps most of all as regards the two questions of homosexuality and prostitution. To be a prostitute was in no way a dishonourable occupation or one to be ashamed of. As in other aspects of life, it was simply the will of Allah. . . . Having made it clear that prostitution was a respected, even an envied profession, I should go on to say that it owed its sudden (and I admit spectacular) growth in Marrakesh entirely to the influence of the French Protectorate" (1983:289). He added that taxes on prostitution "had always and in every town been an important source of revenue; and it had been customary for a Sultan to pay his troops entirely from this tax; in this way, some wit remarked, the soldiers had their fun and got their money back " (p. 289).

References

Baldauf, Ingeborg. 1988. *Die Knabenliebe in Mittelasien: Bacabozlik*. Berlin: Das Arabische Buch. Partially translated as "Bacabozlik." *Paidika* 2, 2 (1990):12–31.

Buckingham, James Silk. 1827. *Travels in Mesopotamia*. London: Henry Colburn.

———. 1830. *Travels in Assyria, Media, and Persia*. London: Henry Colburn.

Burckhardt, John Lewis. [1822] 1983. *Travels in Syria and the Holy Land*. London: J. Murray. Reprint. New York: AMS Press.

Burton, Richard Francis. [1852] 1924. "Early days in Sind." In *Selected papers on anthropology, travel & exploration*, ed. N. M. Penzer, 13–22. London: A. M. Philpot.

———. 1885–86. *A plain and literal translation of the Arabian Nights*. 10 vols. Printed by the Kama Shastra Society for private subscribers of the Burton Club only. Facsimile edition. Denver: Press of the Carson-Harper Co., 1899–1901. Reprinted in 7 vols., New York: Limited Editions Club, 1934.

———. [1930] 1977. *The sotadic zone*. New York: Panurge. Reprint. Boston: Longwood.

Chardin, John. 1691. *The travels of Sir John Chardin into Persia and the East-Indies, through the Black Sea, and the country of Colchis: Containing the author's voyage from Paris to Ispahan*. London: Christopher Bateman.

Crapanzano, Vincent. 1973. *The Hamadsha*. Berkeley: University of California Press.

Crompton, Louis. 1985. *Byron and Greek love*. Berkeley: University of California Press.

Dupree, Louis. 1978. *Afghanistan*. Princeton: Princeton University Press.

Fletcher, Ronald. 1971. Vol. 2, *The making of sociology*. London.

Jacquemont, Victor. 1833. *Correspondance de V. Jacquemont, avec sa famille et plusieurs de ses amis, pendant son voyage dans l'Inde, 1828–1832*. Paris: Garnier Frères.

————. [1834] 1936. *Letters from India: Describing a journey in the British dominions of India, Tibet, Lahore, and Cashmere during the years 1828, 1829, 1830, 1831, 1832.* London: E. Churton. Reprint. London: Macmillan.

Maxwell, Gavin. 1983. *The lords of the Atlas.* London: Century.

Murray, Stephen O. 1990. "Africa, sub-Saharan." In *Encyclopedia of homosexuality*, ed. Wayne Dynes, 22–24. New York: Garland.

————. 1995. "African homosexualities." Unpublished ms.

Pauw, Cornelius de. 1792. *The history of the Spartans or Lacedemonians: Translated from Les recherches philosophiques sur les grecs.* London: Farago.

Purchas, Samuel. 1617. *Pvrchas his pilgrimage, or relations of the world and the religions observed in all ages and places discouered, from the creation vnto this present.* 3d ed. London: Printed by W. Stansby for H. Fetherstone.

Remlinger, Pierre. 1913. *Annales d'Hygiene Publique et de Medecine Legale* 19:97–105.

Schuyler, Eugene. 1877. *Turkistan: Notes of a journey in Russian Turkistan, Khokand, Bukhara, and Kuldja.* New York: F. A. Praeger.

Sonnini, Charles Sigisbert. 1799. *Voyage dans la haute et basse Egypte, fait par ordre de l'ancien gouvernement.* Paris: F. Buisson. Translated as *Travels in Upper and Lower Egypt. Undertaken by order of the old government of France.* London: J. Stockdale, 1799.

Stocking, George W. 1995. *After Tylor: British social anthropology, 1888–1951.* Madison: University at Wisconsin Press.

Stroup, Timothy. 1982. "Edward Westermarck: Essays on his life and work." *Acta Philosophica Fennica* 34. Helsinki.

Westermarck, Edward A. 1900. "The nature of the Arab *ginn*, illustrated by the present beliefs of the people of Morocco." *Journal of the Anthropological Institute of Great Britain and Ireland* 29:252–69 .

————. 1906–8. *The origins and development of moral ideas.* 2 vols. London: Macmillan.

————. 1915. "The Moorish conception of holiness." *Finska Vetenskaps-Societens Forhandlingar* 58:85–97.

————. 1926. *Ritual and belief in Morocco.* London: Macmillan.

————. 1929. *Memories of my life.* London: Macmillan.

Biobibliographic Works on Burton

Brodie, Fawn McKay. 1967. *The devil drives: A life of Sir Richard Burton.* New York: Norton.

Burne, Glenn S. 1985. *Richard F. Burton.* Boston: Twayne.

Casada, James A. 1990. *Sir Richard F. Burton: A biobibliographical study.* London: Mansell.

Farwell, Byron. 1963. *Burton.* London: Longman.

Foster, Stephen W. 1978. "The annotated Burton." In *The gay academic*, ed. Louie Crew, 92–103. Palm Springs, CA: ETC.

Hastings, Michael. 1978. *Sir Richard Burton: A biography.* London: Hodder & Stoughton.

Hollister, John. 1993. "Beyond the sotadic zone: Colonization and sexuality in Burton's 'Terminal Essay.'" Paper presented at the annual meeting of the Society for the Study of Social Problems in Miami, Florida.

McLynn, F. J. 1990. *Burton: Snow upon the desert.* London: John Murray.

Reade, Brian. 1971. *Sexual heretics.* New York: Coward-McCann.

Rice, Edward. 1990. *Captain Sir Richard Francis Burton.* New York: Scribner's.

Spink & Son. 1976. *Catalogue of valuable books, manuscripts & autograph letters of Sir Richard Francis Burton, 1821–1890.* London: Spink & Son.

CHAPTER 14

Gender-Defined Homosexual Roles in Sub-Saharan African Islamic Cultures

Stephen O. Murray

Arab traders (allied with coastal African tribes against enemies from the interior) carried Islam down both the eastern and the western coasts of Africa. The conventional wisdom used to be that possession cults in which women played leading roles were residues of pre-Islamic traditional religions, "little traditions" persisting in the shadow of the quranic "great tradition." In recent years, anthropologists have focused on the extent to which Islam is a "folk religion" rather than a "religion of the book."[1] They have also suggested that rather than fading away under increasing Islamic hegemony, possession cults seem especially to flourish in cultures that are officially Islamic, so that perhaps they are reactions to Islam rather than pre-Islamic residues (Lewis 1966).

As in the more extensively discussed Afro-Brazilian religions,[2] West African possession cults provide a niche for effeminate and/or homosexual men in the predominantly female leadership. This chapter will discuss one instance from the Hausa (the dominant group in Nigeria), a Sudanic analog, and also a role in the semi-Arab Kenyan coast city of Mombasa that seems to be one of secular transvestitic male prostitution.

A Hausa Cosmological Niche

In his study of the Hausa possession cults, Fremont Besmer discusses in detail a possession cult among the (generally) Islamic Hausa that is strikingly similar to New World possession cults of West African descent. Until recently the Hausa cult was "generally regarded as the displaced religious tradition of the pre-Islamic Hausa" (Greenberg 1941; Lewis 1966:324).[3] As in Haitian *vou-dou(n)*, the metaphor for those possessed by spirits is horses "ridden" by the spirit. Homosexual transvestites in the Hausa *bori* cult are called 'Yan Daudu, son of Daudu.

Daudu is a praise name for any Galadima (a ranked title), but specifically refers to the *bori* spirit Dan Galadima (literally, son of Galadima; the Prince) who is said to be "a handsome young man, popular with women, a spend-thrift, and a gambler." Informants were unable to provide a reason why male homosexuals should be identified with his name (Besmer 1983:30n4).

Linguist Joseph Greenberg notes that "the group of Hausa spirits known as 'Yan Dawa, 'children of the forest' have their counterpart in the Dahomey *aziza*, the Bambara *kokolo*,[4] and the Yoruba divinity Arnoi" (1941:56). Accord-ing to Besmer, 'Yan Daudu are not possessed by Dan Galadima and are not possessed by other spirits when he is present (1983:18). Rather, they make and sell "luxury snacks"—that is, more expensive, more prestigious food such as fried chicken (Pittin 1983:297).[5] 'Yan Daudu also operate as intermediaries between female prostitutes and prospective clients. "Women provide the bulk of membership for the cult and are stereotyped as prostitutes" (Besmer 1983:18; cf. Smith 1954:64, Hill 1967:233). Pittin reports:

The economic enterprises of the 'Yan Daudu are centered on three related activities: procuring, cooking, and prostitution. Procuring, the mobilisation of women for illicit sexual purposes, clearly demands close ties between the procurer and the women. The dan daudu [sg.], in his combination of male and female roles, can and does medi-ate between men and women in this context. . . . (1983:296)

Living among women in the strangers' quarters of Hausa towns provides "a cover for men seeking homosexual services. The dan daudu and his sexual partners can carry out their assignations with greater discretion than would be possible if the yan daudu lived together, or on their own outside the gidan mata," where visitors would be marked as seeking sex with she-males (Pittin 1983:296–97).

In patriarchal Hausa society, the *bori* cult provides a niche for various sorts of low-status persons: "Women in general and prostitutes in particular. . . . Jurally-deprived categories of men, including both deviants (homosexuals) and despised or lowly-ranked categories (butchers, night-soil workers, poor farmers, and musicians) constitute the central group of possessed or partici-pating males" plus "an element of psychologically disturbed individuals which cuts across social distinctions" (Pittin 1983:19).

Besmer's account leaves problematic how Hausa individuals come to be defined by themselves or by others as homosexual or transvestitic.[6] In the terms of labeling theory, joining the *bori* cult is "secondary deviance."

One whose status identity is somewhat ambiguous, arising from some personal characteristic, specific social condition, or regularly recurring condition associated with the life cycle can seek either to have his social identity changed or his social status regularized and defined through participation in bori rituals. Marked by "abnormality" and accepted as a candidate for membership in the cult through an identification of *iskoki* as the cause of the problem, a person's behavior becomes explainable, and simultaneously earns a degree of acceptability, after the completion of the *bori* initiation. Symbolic transformation from a suffering outsider—outside both the society and the cult—to one whose status includes the description horse of the gods is achieved. (1983:122–3)

Although the *bori* cult provides a niche with an alternative (to the larger society's) prestige hierarchy, the cult itself remains marginal. Besmer notes:

Status ambiguity is not completely eliminated through involvement in the *bori* cult. While an initiated individual achieves a specific, formal status within the cult since possession is institutionalized, it is not possible for him to escape the general social assessment of his behavior as deviant. (1983:21)

Nonetheless, there are at least indications of "tertiary deviance," which is to say rejection of the stigma of the cult and its adepts (1983:18),[7] although Besmer did not attempt to discover the degree to which adepts accept the devaluation of their "kinds of people" in the dominant Islamic Hausa culture.

A SUDANESE CULT

Among the riverine tribes of Muslim northern Sudan, Constantinides (1977:63) mentions male participation in a similar healing cult called *zar* or *zaar* that is mostly the domain of women (in a society with a marked sexual division of labor and sexual segregation).[8] "Some men are regular participants at cult rituals, and a few become cult group leaders. Of this male minority some are overt homosexuals, while others may initially have symptoms, such as bleeding from the anus or penis, which tend symbolically to classify them with women." Although "men who attend zaar rituals regularly are suspected by both men and women of being homosexual," there is also suspicion that some men may "dishonourably [be] gaining access to women by feigning illness"(Constantinides 1977:63).

Bashas and Their Mashoga in Mombasa

Among Swahili-speakers on the Kenya coast, Shepherd reports, "In Mombasa, both male and female homosexuality is relatively common among Muslims; involving perhaps one in twenty-five adults" (1978a:133). Later (with no data nor discussion of the basis for either the earlier estimate or its revision) she raised the estimated rate to one in ten (1987:240). In her first report, male homosexuality was confined to prostitution:

Mombasa's *washoga* are passive male homosexuals offering their persons for money. They advertise themselves in bright tight *male* attire in public places, usually, but may, when mingling with women at weddings, don women's *leso* cloths, make-up and jasmine posies. *Washoga* have all the liberties of men and are also welcome in *many*[9] contexts otherwise exclusive to women. (Shepherd 1978a: 133; emphasis added)

Shepherd asserted that "though there are long-lasting relationships between homosexuals in Mombasa, most homosexual acts are fleeting, paid for in cash" (1978b: 644). In a more recent analysis, she explains:

The Swahili [word] for a male homosexual is *shoga*, a word also used between women to mean "friend." Homosexual relations in Mombasa are almost without exception between a younger, poorer partner and an older, richer one, whether their connection is for a brief act of prostitution or a more lengthy relationship. In the former case, there are fixed rates of payment, and in the latter, presents and perhaps full financial support for a while. But financial considerations are always involved and it is generally only the person who is paid who is called *shoga*. The older partner may have been a *shoga* himself in his youth, but is very likely to be successfully married to a woman as well as maintaining an interest in boys. Only if he is not married and has an apparently exclusive interest in homosexual contacts will he perhaps still be referred to as a *shoga*. The paid partner usually takes the passive role during intercourse, but I think it is true to say that his inferiority derives from the fact that he is paid to provide what is asked for, rather than for the [sexual] role he adopts. . . . The paying partner is usually known as the *basha*—the Pasha, the local term for the king in packs of playing cards. (1987:250)

Shepherd's main thesis throughout is that rank is more important than gender in Mombasa and in the Mombasan conception of homosexuality (1978a, 1987). She stresses the primacy of wealth to sexual behavior in the passage just quoted, but it is followed by a discussion of a folk view which recognizes which boys will engage in homosexuality on the basis not just of relative wealth but also of effeminacy (i.e., "prettiness"):

People say that they can predict who will be a homosexual, even with boys as young as 5 or 6 years old at times. They seem to base their prediction upon prettiness and family circumstances; boys reared in all-female households by a divorced mother and several sisters are likely to become homosexuals, they say, and the prediction is self-fulfilling since these are the boys whom men are certain to approach. "If he's not a homosexual yet, he will be," say women of teenage boys from such households. (Shepherd 1987:250–51)

To me, this suggests that more than economics is involved, even if it is primary in differentiating the *basha* and the *shoga*.

Although Shepherd (1978a,b) strenuously objects to Wikan's (1977) suggestion of a "transsexual" or "third gender" conception in Oman,[10] she acknowledges some gender variance in dress among the Mombasan *shoga* and asserts that *shoga* "tend to employ the gait and voice which are the international signals of homosexuality." These seem to be imitated from other homosexuals, not from women, and the modesty and quietness of ideal Swahili womanhood are "quite absent in homosexual behaviour" (Shepherd 1987:259–60).[11]

Wilson earlier reported that in Lamu, a Swahili town north of Mombasa, boys dressed as women, performed a striptease and then paired off with older men from the audience (1957:1; Shepherd 1987:269n9). The first Swahili-English dictionary included *hānithi* (clearly cognate to what Wikan romanized as *xanith* and I romanize as *khanith*) for "catamite," as well as *mumémke* (*mume*=man, *mke*=woman) (Krapf 1882:891).[12]

In the homosexual life history of a Kikukuyu, Kamau recalls seeing young men in Mombasa who

have a big flowered sheet tied around their waist. They wear nothing under the sheet but they have a t-shirt on top and that thing underneath. That's how they excite, how they get men doing very, very weird things. There are places on the coast where these things are really alive, it's happening, the gay life is very active and is more accepted by the Arab community [than among interior groups such as the Kikuyu]. (Murray, forthcoming)

Clearly there are men not dressed like other men who are available for receptive homosexual intercourse on the Kenyan coast. Shepherd argues convincingly that *shoga* are not classified as "women," the "second sex." There is no evidence in any of Shepherd's publications, however, which bear on whether *shoga* departures from the expectations of masculine deportment, dress, and financial independence are considered a *third* sex or gender.[13]

Notes

1. For an excellent African example, see Holy 1991.

2. See Landes 1940, 1946; Carneiro 1981; Fry 1982, 1995; Wafer 1991 on Brazilian cults; Murray (1987:92–100) on Haitian ones.

3. It is notable that Besmer writes about an urban cult, especially in contrast to (mistaken) claims that *voudou(n)* in the New World is confined to the countryside. Also see Smith (1954). Lewis (1966:317; 1986:35) noted that the *bori* cult had spread northward into Tunisia, Syria, Egypt, and even to Mecca.

4. Torday and Joyce noted "sterile" *mokobo*, and mentioned castrated *tongo* (1905: 420, 424).

5. As in many other cultures, men doing "women's work" use more prestigious raw materials and/or serve more elite customers/patrons. I believe this reflects some residual male status rather than indicating that men do "women's work" better than women.

6. Moses Meyer asserts that the "'Yan Daudu are not the same as homosexuals. There is a distinct homosexual identity in Nigeria that is different from the 'Yan Daudu. They overlap socially because both communities practice same-sex sex" (1993, personal communication).

7. "Primary deviance" is behavior proscribed by norms or laws, "secondary deviance" is being labeled or self-labeled as the kind of person who breaks the law and/or violates norms. Within "secondary deviance," the "deviant" accepts the rightness of the norms s/he breaks. "Tertiary deviance" involves challenging the wrongness of the "deviant" deeds and asserting the validity of being the kind of person who breaks an invalid norm. For application to homosexuality, see Murray 1996:45–52. More generally, see Kitsuse 1962, 1980.

8. See Messing's (1959:327) discussion of the preponderance of women in what Cerulli (1923:2) contended was a marginalized residue of the ancient Cushitic religion displaced by Christianity and Islam (with their patriarchal leaders).

9. In a subsequent communiqué, Shepherd noted the atypicality of weddings and reported that "when the mood is less playful—at a prayer-time, for instance, or at a funeral—the *shoga* must attend with men or not attend at all" (1978b:664). Shepherd reiterated that "weddings are light-hearted occasions" and that *washoga* gather with men on other occasions, concluding, "It would be quite wrong to suggest that homosexuals ought always to be in the company of women in situations where there is formal segregation" (1987:253).

10. Shepherd (1978b) closed by making the *shoga* (and, by Shepherd's ready extrapolation, the Omani *khanith*) age- rather than gender-defined homosexuality. Wikan justly labeled the departure from Shepherd's vehement emphasis on poverty (class-conditioned homosexual prostitution) "startling" (1978:669). Shepherd's stress that "many passive homosexuals, far from viewing their activity as joyless, are brought to orgasm by it" (1978b:664) does not fit well with her explanation of dire economic necessity (besides reducing "sexual pleasure" to ejaculation, as Carrier 1980 objected).

11. Roscoe cautions against a widespread failure in writing about what Whitam calls "transvestitic homosexuals" to distinguish female behavior from the stereotyping and exaggerations of flamboyant male performances of "femininity" (Roscoe 1988:28).

12. Madan spelled it *hanisi*, which he glossed as "effeminate" (1902:92). Sacleux attested *kaumu lut'i* for "sodomite" ([1891] 1949:95). The usual etymology for *lûtî* in Arabic is "Lot's people" (see the discussion above in chapter 2). Madan added *watu wa Sodom* (men of Sodom) (1902:376).

13. As noted in chapter 16 in this volume, Wikan (1977) vacillated between an "intermediate" gender and a distinct "third sex" in Sohar, Oman (not an African soci-

ety, but long involved in trade with and domination of both Zanzibar and Mombasa). On Zanzibar, Haberlandt reported that "homosexuals of both sex are called *mke-si-mume* (woman, not man) in Swahili" (1899:670).

References

Besmer, Fremont E. 1983. *Horses, musicians, and gods: The Hausa possession trance.* S. Hadley, MA: Bergin and Garvey.

Carneiro, Edison. 1981. *Religiões Negra: Notas de etnografia religiosa.* Rio de Janeiro: Civilização Brasileira.

Carrier, Joseph M. 1980. "The Omani *xanith* controversy." *Man* 15:541–42.

Cerulli, Enrico. 1923. "Note sul movimento musulamano della Somalia." *Rivista Studias Orientales* 10:1–36.

Constantinides, Pamela. 1977. "'Ill at ease and sick at heart': Symbolic behaviour in a Sudanese healing cult." In *Symbols and sentiments*, ed. I. M. Lewis, 61–84. San Francisco: Academic Press.

Fry, Peter. 1982. *Para Inglês ver.* Rio de Janeiro: Zahar Editores.

———. 1995. "Male homosexuality and Afro-Brazilian possession cults." In *Latin American male homosexualities*, by Stephen O. Murray, 193–220. Albuquerque: University of New Mexico Press.

Greenberg, Joseph H. 1941. "Some aspects of Negro-Mohammedan culture contact among the Hausa." *American Anthropologist* 43:51–61.

Haberlandt, Michael. 1899. "Conträre Sexualerscheinungen bei der Negerbevölkerung Sansibars." *Zeitschrift für Ethnologie* 31:668–70.

Hill, Polly. 1967. *Rural Hausa.* New York: Cambridge University Press.

Holy, Ladislav. 1991. *Religion and custom in a Muslim society: The Berti of Sudan.* New York: Cambridge University Press.

Kitsuse, John I. 1962. "Societal reactions to deviant behavior." *Social Problems* 9:247–56.

———. 1980. "Coming out all over: Deviants and the politics of social problems." *Social Problems* 28:1–13.

Krapf, Johann Ludwig. 1882. *A dictionary of the Suaheli language.* London: Trübner & Co.

Landes, Ruth. 1940. "A cult matriarchate and male homosexuality." *Journal of Abnormal and Social Psychology* 35:386–97.

———. 1946. *City of women.* New York: Macmillan.

Lewis, Ioan M. 1966. "Spirit possession and deprivation cults." *Man* 1:307–29.

———. 1986. *Religion in context: Cults and charisma.* New York: Cambridge University Press.

Madan, Arthur Cornwallis. 1902. *English-Swahili dictionary.* Oxford: Clarendon Press.

Messing, Simon D. 1959. "Group therapy and social status in the Zar cult of Ethiopia." In *Culture and mental illness*, ed. Marvin K. Opler, 319–32. New York: Macmillan.

Murray, Stephen O. 1987. "A note on Haitian (in?)tolerance of male homosexuality." In *Male homosexuality in Central and South America*, 92–100. New York: Gay Academic Union.

———. 1996. *American gay.* Chicago: University of Chicago Press.

——— Forthcoming. "Kamau, a 26-year-old Kikuyu." In *African Homosexualities.*

Pittin, Christin. 1983. "Houses of women: A focus on alternative life-styles in Katsina City." In *Female and male in West Africa,* ed. C. Oppong, 291–302. London: Allen and Unwin.

Roscoe, Will. 1988. "Making history: The challenge of gay and lesbian studies." *Journal of Homosexuality* 15:1–40.

Sacleux, Charles. [1891] 1949. *Dictionnaire Français-Swahili*. Paris: Institut d'ethnologie.

Shepherd, Gill. 1978a. "Transsexualism in Oman?" *Man* 13:133–34.

———. 1978b. "Oman *xanith*." *Man* 13:663–65.

———. 1987. "Rank, gender and homosexuality: Mombasa as a key to understanding sexual options." In *The cultural construction of sexuality,* ed. Pat Caplan, 240–70. London: Tavistock.

Smith, Mary F. 1954. *Baba of Karo: A woman of the Muslim Hausa*. London: Faber & Faber.

Torday, Emil, and Thomas Athol Joyce. 1905. "Notes on the ethnography of the Ba-Mbala." *Journal of the Anthropological Institute of Great Britain and Ireland* 35:398–426.

Wafer, Jim. 1991. *The taste of blood: Spirit possession in Brazilian Candomblé*. Philadelphia: University of Pennsylvania Press.

Wikan, Unni. 1977. "Man becomes woman: Transsexualism in Oman as a key to gender roles." *Man* 13:304–19.

———. 1978. "The Omani *xanith*." *Man* 14:667–71.

Wilson, Godfrey M. 1957. "Male prostitution and homosexuals." Appendix to *Mombasa Social Survey*. Nairobi: Government Printer.

PART IV

Anthropological Studies

>—✹—<

CHAPTER 15

Institutionalized Gender-Crossing in Southern Iraq

Sigrid Westphal-Hellbusch

(translated by Bradley Rose)

During our study of the Ma'dan clans of the lower Euphrates-Tigris[1] we were able to establish rather close contact with a female poet of local fame. She led her life as a *mustergil*, that is, a woman in men's clothing. The phenomenon of transvestites has been reported, for instance, among South and North American tribes, but for the Arabic world it has met with little notice.[2] As our poet is not an isolated case—she maintained that in her own clan alone approximately fifty women lived as men—the question as to the basis for this phenomenon merits attention.

Not treated in this chapter are those frequent cases in which women at present take up a male occupation merely out of economic necessity. Thus, for example, the following was reported to us: A native doctor had to treat a young laborer whose sex proved to be, after examination, female. The laborer, whom one assessed from appearance and conduct to be a lad, stated that he was the only child of his parents and had to support them. They were poor and had to earn their money through work. Because of the higher wages available, he worked as a laborer, but was not fundamentally against marrying. There are bound to be more cases of this kind, although one cannot count them among actual *mustergil*. Even so, they should not be thought of as wholly irrelevant to the known facts concerning women living as men.

233

There are also isolated cases of men who lead a "female" life, namely as dancers and singers. These men are mostly known as *mustachnet*. They do not lead a feminine life in any real sense but have made a "non-masculine" application of their skills—singing and dancing—and wear female clothing in the practice of their calling. The *mustachnet* do not stand in opposition to the prevailing social order as the *mustergil* do. A root cause of these occurrences no doubt should be sought in homosexuality, which is widely distributed throughout the Orient. Strict customs generally hinder close contact with the other sex until marriage is consummated. The sexual urge searches for substitute objects among the same sex or, more rarely, with animals. Homosexual relations die away after marriage, although even then much of these men's conduct is still reminiscent of their former homosexual life. They embrace friends, walk about with their arms around one another or holding hands, sit in close proximity to one another, sleep in each other's lap, and so on. With the *mustachnet*, however, we are always dealing with isolated cases without particular cultural relevance. In contrast, the much higher number of *mustergil* cannot be attributed to sexual motivations but rather is a function of the overall social order.

As for men who also wear female clothing in daily life and lead a female life nobody ever mentioned anything to us. To be sure, we ourselves observed one such case, apparently rare, although we were unable to study it more closely. The case in question was a man, at that time approximately forty years old, who was taken in as an orphan by an unrelated family and had been brought up without being adopted into the family. He still lives today [i.e., mid-1950s] with this family, wears women's clothes and does work as ordered by the head of the household. He appears to be moderately feeble-minded, never asserts himself nor expresses his views, and avoids looking at people who engage him in conversation. The family dealt with him affably. Neither the family nor the neighbors would tell us anything about him; one gets the impression that he himself and those around him are a little embarrassed by his existence.

A general description of the social situation of the settled clans of southern Iraq will help us better understand our particular case.

Our poet descends from one of the richest sheik families of lower Iraq, which has acquired a name, not always praiseworthy, as "rice sheiks." Without entering into the history and the economic situation of this region, the relevant social order—which makes the desire of many women to change this system understandable—will be described. It must be emphasized that the social order under discussion applies mainly to the "Arabic" clans and in a strict sense only to those tribes inhabiting the same region as the Ma'dan.

The social order of the Arabic clans in southern Iraq is extremely patriar-chal. It has taken over the legal system of Islam or, as the case may be, intro-duced it in this region. According to Islamic law, the woman has no say in family matters or public life. Once a marriage contract is settled by full pay-ment of the brideprice, the girl's family has little influence over the fate of the daughter. One of our informants expressed himself regarding the prevail-ing marriage laws as follows: "It is not good if two men marry each other's sisters. One such man once saw that his sister was weeping because she had been beaten by her husband. What was he to do then? To the brother-in-law he could say nothing, so he went home and beat his own wife, who was after all the sister of his brother-in-law, in order to retaliate. Thus, there is always trouble when families exchange sisters." Regardless of whatever might take place, the prescribed role for the woman, according to law, is totally passive.

The husband or his family—who are usually in agreement, if the declara-tion is from "the man"—have all power of disposition over inherited or acquired possessions. The determinations that restrict the right of disposition are in accord with Islamic legal precepts and are taken for granted.

The inheritance of possessions from the ground and earth and of assets, be they money, house, or livestock descend through the male line. The wife is an outsider in her husband's family, and because of the bounty she expects—through the death of the father or on the occasion of her wedding—they make her economically dependent. Her standing is measured according to the number of children she brings into the world and raises—the more sons among them, the higher her status. The wife's functions are limited to the sphere of the family: the rearing of children, meal preparation, getting mate-rial for fires, getting water, selling milk, helping with the work in the fields or other male occupations fill up the day, and not seldom does she work until late in the night or begin her workday well before dawn. For all her trouble and work she receives little recognition from her husband. "The best wife is one who works the most." As reported also by many other peoples, the fact that the husband has the legal right of corporal punishment over his wife is not exaggerated; this right holds in the frontiers and is fostered by the per-sonalities of both marriage partners. There are those of the opinion that there are also "henpecked husbands." Nevertheless the matter of legal corporal punishment must be noted in regard to the phenomenon of the *mustergil*.

To the man alone belongs the right to lead a "public" life. He seeks recre-ation and stimulation in gatherings with other men. In larger settlements he visits the coffeehouses (in villages, the meeting houses), where he drinks cof-fee and tea, and smokes the waterpipe and, of late, cigarettes, and has unend-ing conversations. In these gatherings he cuts himself off from his wife and appears to lead a meaningful life compared with hers. The "better" the wife, the more time the husband has for these recreational pursuits. As in all cultures, the men here too feel that they are "higher" than the excluded ones—in this case, the women—and they endorse this state of affairs polemically in resounding speeches. Certainly this portrayal applies only to daily life. The meeting houses also have a really important function in clan life regarding special events. The owner of a house, the sheik of a clan, the leader of a clan or a village—also make known in that assembly declarations of war, vendetta, or joint projects of every kind; and there they are discussed and brought to conclusion.

During childhood, the girl comes to know the feeling of being excluded and the inferiority bound up with it. Her later experiences incessantly confirm this. The boy may reach his tenth year without any particular duties. Mostly, he spends his time playing. The girl, on the other hand, must help her mother as soon as possible: keeping an eye on the younger siblings, hauling them around with her, getting water and fire-material, working in the fields, and so on. If guests come, the boy sits nearby; the girl can see and hear what goes on only furtively. If the men have a debate over money, feuds, or planned undertakings, the boy sits listening, and if he is somewhat older he takes part; the girl is just an onlooker in family matters or is entirely excluded if the men have their own assembly place.

Of the exciting discussions about hunting expeditions, war campaigns, retaliation against wrongs suffered, reports on events in the wider world, the girl hears, if at all, only second- or third-hand—to every girl with some ambition the life of the boy must seem enviable. So long as the girl is not married, she can "equal the man" through alternative activities and challenge him directly. She can refuse to do disagreeable work for him or she can make herself scarce; she can withdraw to the pasturing of the herd and there behave "like a boy." But upon marriage she comes into a situation in which the difference between female and male roles is a fact of life she can no longer evade.

The marriage age for girls is normally fifteen, for men about eighteen. First marriages often take place earlier in life, seldom later. The father's-brother's-son has first claim to a marriageable girl but does not always exercise this right, although he still has an important voice in any marriage arrangements. Marrying a girl from among one's own kin is preferred, so that upon divorce all possessions stay in the family. On the other hand, if a man marries an outside girl, he is unsure where he stands during the marriage; it is widely assumed that an outside girl seeks to cause trouble for her husband through marital fights in which she obviously finds support from her own family. One never feels wholly connected to an outside girl and also expects her not to have sincere attachment to her husband's family.

If the marriage of the young pair is forbidden by the parents, the young people can only in rare cases succeed with respect to their possibly wasted wish for a marriage partner. Thus girls and lads meet without being able to form a reasonable assessment of one another. Because of the law of virginity, marriage is generally the first time that close contact is established with the other sex. These preconditions do not favor happy marriages, and, indeed, at least 50 percent of all marriages are unsatisfactory for both parties. However, while the men can remove themselves from this state of affairs through divorce, or are able to lighten the burden by taking a second, third, and fourth wife, Islamic law virtually binds the wife inseparably to her husband, although in isolated cases the wife, too, can be successful in divorce.

In her own marriage, the wife witnesses most clearly the privileges of leading a male lifestyle. She fully and totally takes care of the physical well-being of her husband; but in all matters of daily life, family affairs, and household management, she has influence only as long as she holds her own vis-à-vis him. The rapid sequence of births prematurely exhausts the wife. The husband, avoids the household turmoil, seeking recreation and rest in the coffee-house or the meeting house. Thus it is not surprising that the wives become nagging, embittered, unobliging, and ugly inside and out—calm, affable wives are an infrequent exception.

Into this picture fits the fact that many *mustergil* declare their decision to lead a manly life after their first menstruation, shortly after which marriage is expected. This decision is generally accepted without opposition by the community. The young girl, if she has not already begun to live like a boy, henceforth dresses as a man, sits together with the men in the meeting house, takes an active part in her own life, and procures weapons for herself to take part in hunts and war campaigns. There are bound to be cases in which only after the death of a "man" did it come to light that a *mustergil* had been living unrecognized among the men, which is easy to explain, as such things generally were not mentioned. If the family moves and the parents, as usual, remain silent about their daughter living as a man, a *mustergil* can remain undetected until death.

The acknowledgment of a *mustergil* as a man refers exclusively to her manner of life. She can never quite gain the status of a man, since no real estate can be bequeathed by her and any potential wealth she acquires is governed by the rules of inheritance for women, which differ from those for men.

Certainly it does happen that a *mustergil*, after some years of manly living, decides to marry. Among girls who in childhood already dressed and went about as boys, this decision can be made at the onset of menstruation, when the discrepancy between biological being and outward appearance makes itself obviously apparent. For a *mustergil* in later life, a love affair most proba-

bly underlies the decision. How such marriages turn out later we have, unfortunately, not been able to investigate. A *mustergil* marrying by her own
choice, must completely break with her past; none of her former relationships in the men's world survive, and, should her marriage take an unhappy
course, she cannot return to her former manly life, for she is now, like other
wives, bound to the marriage. On the other hand, a wife can take up a manly
life after the death of her husband. Such cases arise if a wife is willing to
struggle alone with her children and to accept a man's responsibilities along
with a woman's. For men's work she would then adopt male clothing, obtain
weapons for her protection, and thus be tolerated in the men's world, especially if she proves to be self-reliant and gains the respect of her neighbors.

Our poet, then, is an exception in this regard since she comes from a very
rich sheik family and the role of a rich female sheik is far more pleasant than
that of a poor farming woman. Physical labor is not expected of her; rather
the grievance of all well-to-do Iraqi women is the emptiness of their lives.
Our poet's decision to live as a man apparently has two causes: First, she is
moderately deformed and very small, which was surely a major hindrance to
marriage, although she does not speak about it; and second, she hates her
father because of certain personal experiences; on this she speaks and produces poetry at every opportunity.

Her life's purpose is to strive not only to live like a man but also to be
legally classified as a man. In a long battle with the authorities she succeeded
in having her family land signed over to her—not only in usufruct but given
to her outright. It is a source of great satisfaction to her that the land legally
belongs to her; she is a man. The battle with the authorities, meaning the
simultaneous battle against the claims of her own family, has reinforced her
grumbling. She spends most of her time in the magistrate's office fighting to
resolve the disputes that upset her, which are connected with her landowner-
ship. Her behavior is no doubt based on a series of personal experiences with
father-family-authorities, in which she has the same experiences in ever-
widening frameworks: If it comes to do or die, one may be abandoned by all,
but one can still battle successfully for "justice."

Her culture, however, also has a strong idea of what a father should be like.
This father she finds in Allah. In Him she receives a hearing for her complaints: He helps her in this life and in the next world will rectify injustices
suffered here. She is an actively religious person and has irrevocably decided
to deny her family any part of her inheritance after her death by donating
her land and possessions to a high religious official who will then do good
deeds for the poor in her name.

These actions partly clarify her outward appearance. She wears male under-
and outer-clothing, but female tresses and female kerchief. She retains these

outward marks distinguishing her sex because she prays to Allah every day and has to do so as a woman or else her prayers would be of no consequence. The government has forbidden the carrying of weapons in any urban districts, but in her village she carries a rifle and revolver and can shoot well with them. She has yet to kill a person. With respect to her declared age, she is reticent; she has not freed herself from the general desire of women in her milieu to be young and thereby considered desirable. After rather more discussion, she disclosed her age to be forty, which, to judge by her outward appearance, is incorrect.

At first she tells her life history in fragments, but she later completes it with the help of her poems and at the prodding of her erstwhile listeners. Her father married twice, as her mother also did. She is the only child her parents had together, but through her father she has five half brothers; through her mother, a half brother and a half sister. Her father's mother raised her; she was hardly ever in the houses of her parents. But her mother and a sister of her mother's sometimes looked after her; though from presents to her mother the aunt could have enriched herself, she received few presents. All her brothers were very rich; however, none of them ever helped her out. With the half brothers by her father she broke off all relationships as a child; with the siblings by her mother she maintained a relationship, though, not living in their city, she seldom saw them.

Already as a child she wanted to live as a boy and the family had nothing against it; on the contrary: "A family is proud of a girl who wants to live like a boy." She was already carrying weapons then and went on hunts, and this lifestyle she maintained. She would never marry and was never "intimate" with a man. When she was about twenty years old (in 1937–38), her mother was murdered by the family of her second husband. The son, whom she had had by her second husband, stood so high in the father's regard, although he was the youngest, that his older half brothers feared for their inheritance. They hesitated to murder the brother because thereby they would have shed their own blood; his mother, however, was an outsider in the family, so she was shot dead by order of the brothers. That was bound to bring the father to his senses and remind him that he had older sons and should devote himself to them again. However, this desired outcome failed to materialize, and to the despair of our poet, her mother's murder remained unavenged. The pretext used was that the murderer was unknown, which in fact was not true.

The murder was supposed to have been avenged by the family of the first husband, but as both husbands were sheiks from different clans, the vendetta could easily have led to a clan feud, and that would have meant, in turn, the intervention of the government. Besides, in the long run, the murder happened to a woman whom her first husband had willingly divorced. Thus he had no desire for such possible complications and let it rest by saying that the murderer was not known to him and revenge would not be possible. For that, the daughter never forgave him: ridiculing and insulting poems about the first husband and his family make up a large part of her poetry. For a long time she hoped it would incite him to action, but finally had to give up this hope when, in due course, the murderer himself was murdered, but not by the family of the first husband. Still, when she speaks of the murder of her mother, her feelings are strong and unchanged. She despises the family of the first husband deeply.

Through the unavenged murder, her resentment against the brothers suddenly turned to hate. This hatred received new nourishment when the father turned her and her grandmother out of the village she had lived in until then, in order to bring both of them securely under his supervision in one of his permanent houses. There the girl found less freedom than in village life, felt unhappy, and believed that, if she left, her brothers would seize the land she believed belonged to her in usufruct according to inheritance rules. Many farming families would then move off her land and no one would be able to prevent them from leaving.

As a result, she resolved to pursue her claim. Women of the sheik families can have land allocated by the government for their own cultivation; after their death it falls back to the general family possessions. However, she wanted to own her land outright. For that she had to go to the authorities in Basra. Until 1945 she would have to pay tenure-fees to the government for her land; then title would be legally signed over to her. Fifty to sixty rice-growing families—practically a village—live on her land. She does not cultivate rice herself. In the village she erected a meeting house like a male sheik, but she retains no bodyguards. For her own protection she possesses rifle and revolver and can handle them well. In her meeting house she has coffee distributed every morning to the men of the village, just as the rich sheiks do—though she herself is not at all rich—and thereby gains high regard for herself at a disproportionately high cost.

Only at harvesttime does she go to the village to manage and inspect the harvest—that is, to see to it that she is not defrauded of her share. The usual payment ratio of a farmer to his landlord amounts to 50 percent or, in the event that the seedlings have to be provided by the owner of the estate, even 75 percent. The landlord then pays 3 to 5 percent of the harvest as tax to the government. This tax payment is a constant source of irritation to our poet, since the government assessment is always higher than her own; moreover, she suffers from the notion that the government would like to cheat her. Thus, it allegedly once demanded duplicate payment for taxes she had already paid, and caused her much annoyance and trouble by asking her to trace the original payment. Even then, the government did not acknowledge the wrong done her, but, lacking a receipt for her payments, insisted that she had paid only half. Except at harvesttime, she had to live in the city in order to obtain justice from the authorities. To this end she rented a house in the city.

Her hatred of her father, brothers, and men in general did not dissuade her from being like a man; indeed, she wanted to be more like a man. She learned to read and write and began to make poetry. Among rural females, she was the only woman known to us who could write (later, among the sheik women, we once met a woman who could read). Creating poetry was a tradition in her family; both her fathers were famous local poets and her half brother by her mother earned fame outside his own region as a poet. He not only produces poetry but is also a good judge of Arabic poetry. She did not achieve his success with her poetry, however, something she passes over in silence. On the other hand, she ceaselessly talks about her success in being more like "the men." Thus she repeatedly complained: "I gave and gave (i.e., poetry), more than any man, but still one was not satisfied with it and always wanted more from me (i.e., taxes)."

Her poems have two main themes: (1) complaints about her own hard fate and the difficulties of life in general, and (2) calls to fight against the murderer of her mother, invectives against the band to which the murderer belonged, and ridicule of her own band in cowardly leaving the vendetta unfinished. As she herself said, she should have been a celebrated choral singer because of her dirge. It presents a singer an opportunity to use incidents in the personal life of a dead person to comment on past events and to incite the men to present deeds. Unfortunately we could not record such a dirge since no death occurred, and a theoretical recollection or contriving of a dirge did not seem to be possible.

The following very free translations of three poems are to illustrate their contents only.

1. Farewell, the love of my soul is lost,
Which Zeine promised to look after.
I love the village of Arraiye, the house.
By force they compelled me to live in Nahadhiye.

This poem comes from the time when she and her grandmother were compelled to leave the village Arraiye, in which they had lived happily. Zeine is a male relative who had promised to see to it that she could remain in the village.

2. Whose name is hidden between *kaf* and *nun*
Whenever I kiss it, I smell *mim-sin-kaf.*
My friends, which *mim-älif-kaf.*
Sin is for me not at hand.

Kaf, nun, mim, sin, älif are letters of the alphabet. The one whose name is hidden between *kaf* and *nun* is Allah. Whenever she brings His name to her lips a wonderful aroma encircles her (*misk* = musk). Of friends she has none (*mim-älif-kaf* = *maku*, there are none). She cannot even obtain poison (*sin-mim* = *simm*, poison) in order to come to her one friend, Allah. On this the poet gives the following information: When she was rich she had many friends, but when the times changed, she lost them and no one helped her. She was so poor then that she did not even have poison with which to put an end to her life.

3. I am the woman who sings *hosses* to the men, and all women must be like me
    today,
My father, I am my brother. They rush at the enemy.
Naked and without clothing they go against the rifles.
If you think I lie, ask my family; am I a liar?

This poem was occasioned by of a fight between her and another clan. *Hosses* are the fighting songs of the men. A solo speaker gives a short address, which ends in a line that is then repeated by the men in chorus. A stamp dance is performed to it, and rifles are raised in the air and fired off, until ever new addresses and dances bring the men to the state of excitement required for the success of the war campaign. A good *hoss*-speaker can inspire people to heroic deeds. Thus, our poet also demands that all women follow her example and rouse their men to bold deeds. The women may not take part in the war dance itself and in general cannot be solo speakers either. Our poet, as a *mustergil*, enjoys this prerogative, which explains the line: My father, I am my brother. The description of how her clan members advance naked against the rifles of the enemy could perhaps be understood as exaggeration; thus she calls on her own family as witnesses that she has never lied.

The poems reproduced here show how strongly the contents are bound up with her personal life. However, during the recording, her recitations frequently met with spontaneous applause from the participating audience. Only the specialist could properly appreciate the effectiveness of her oral expressions.

It should be mentioned that the poet brought to us at the close of our stay a document in high Arabic, in which she sang a praise-song to the government in an effort to improve the position of women. This we were to officially read out in Germany. Time and again she asked after the position of women in Germany and showed a great desire to leave her homeland to settle down for the rest of her life in a country where the women "are identical to the men." She often asked me if I might not also like to be a man, and as I cautiously replied that it was "unnecessary" for me, she remarked on the relationship between me and my husband. She threatened to shoot him dead should he not be good to me, and was once quite agitated when I expressed the view that he could speak better Arabic than I. "If that's true then I'll dash myself against the earth," she cried out. It was the first time that she did not threaten him but rather was angry that I was less able than he.

This line of speech, which points to the subject of women's status and operates in terms of female rights, developed even further during our meetings. The threats to shoot both of us, or my husband, the constant comment that she possessed a revolver, which in her eyes appeared as a rifle, diminished and finally stopped altogether. In delivering her document she did not say, as in the early days, "Whoever dares to say anything against it will be shot," but, rather, "Whoever says anything against it, I will answer him with a poem." It would be interesting to examine at a later time this spontaneously formed outlook on women's rights.

Notes

Originally published as "Transvestiten bei Arabischen Stämmen" ("Transvestites: Institutionalized possibilities of challenging customary women's and men's roles in Southern Iraq"), *Sociologus*, n.f. 6, 1 (1956), Berlin. Reprinted by permission of Verlag Duncker & Humboldt ©1956.

    1. Cf. my travel report in vol. 1, Jhrg. VI of *Sociologus*.

    2. Cf. primarily Hermann Baumann, *Das doppelte Geschlecht*. Berlin: D. Reimer, 1955.

CHAPTER 16

The Sohari *Khanith*

Stephen O. Murray

Halfway through her first fieldwork in the town of Sohar on the northeastern coast of Oman, in the summer of 1974, the Norwegian anthropologist Unni Wikan was astonished one day when one of her women friends stopped and talked freely with a man. Equally surprising was the man's costume: he was wearing a pink tunic. Wikan's friend explained that this gaudily dressed man was a *xanith* (*khanith* is a more conventional romanization of the Arabic term and will be used here except in direct quotations). In the course of a twenty-minute walk through town, she pointed out four more. Her friend "explained that all male servants (slaves apart) are *xanith*, that all *xanith* are homosexual prostitutes." Wikan estimated that 2 percent ("about sixty" of three thousand) of adult Sohari men are *khanith* (1977:305; 1982:169).[1]

Wikan then realized that a man who had earlier startled and puzzled her by penetrating a bride's seclusion chamber and seeing her unveiled before a wedding, and who later ate with the women at the wedding meal, was also a *khanith*. "Women bare their faces freely" to *khanith* (1977:307). Neither Wikan nor her critics presented any evidence (from Sohar or anywhere else) that "the natives" consider that there are three sexes (male, female, *khanith*), or three genders (man, woman, *khanith*). The existence and application to people of a word (*khanith*) establishes that there is a role, but not that this is a sex, gender, or sexual role. In appearance, the *khanith* is neither male nor female:

[The *khanith*] is not allowed to wear the mask, or other female clothing. His clothes are intermediate between male and female: he wears the ankle-length tunic of the male, but with the tight waist of the female dress. Male clothing is white, females wear patterned cloth in bright colours, and xaniths wear unpatterned coloured clothes. Men cut their hair short, women wear theirs long, the xaniths medium long. Men comb their hair backward away from the face, women comb theirs diagonally forward from a central parting, [*khaniths*] comb theirs diagonally forward from a side parting, and they oil it heavily in the style of women. Both men and women cover their head, xaniths go bare-headed. Perfume is used by both sexes, especially at festive occasions and during intercourse. The xanith is generally heavily perfumed, and uses much make-up to draw attention to himself. This is also achieved by his affected swaying gait, emphasized by the close-fitting garments. His sweet falsetto voice and facial expressions and movements also closely mimic those of women. If xaniths wore female clothes I doubt that it would in many instances be possible to see that they are, anatomically speaking, male not female. (Wikan 1977:307; I have followed her practice in 1982:172, substituting "xanith" where the original had "transsexual").

The *khanith* is also intermediate in mobility: moving freely (like men) during the day, secluded (like women) at night. Moreover, their occupations (domestic servants and prostitutes) are ones unacceptable for either proper men or proper women (1977:307; 1982:173).[2] Doing housework is considered "women's work," but Sohari Arab women do not do housework for employers. Although gender variance most struck Wikan, "homosexual prostitute" is the native characterization Wikan quoted, and, in her original article, she wrote that homosexual relations are "the essence" of Omani *khanith* behavior (Wikan 1977:310).[3]

Just across the Arabian Sea, much closer to Sohar than Mombasa, are *hijra*.[4] The *hijra* have also been classified by a feminist anthropologist as a "third gender role," though desire for sex with men was consistently specified as the motivation for becoming *hijra* in the statements Nanda reported (1990).[5] From 1784 until 1958 the southwestern Pakistan port of Gwadar belonged to the family of the Sultan of Oman, who still has a palace in Karachi. Oman's major trade was traditionally with the Sind. Temporary Pakistani workers and long-established Baluchis live in Oman.[6] Ethnic/cultural/linguistic differences continue to be marked in Sohar (see Barth 1983). I do not at all mean to argue that there is a single Pakistani-Omani culture, only that important contacts of long duration may have produced some convergence of cultural conceptions of *hijra* and *khanith*.

Wikan argues that I overly foreground "homosexual prostitute," and emphasizes that "prostitute" does not have the ugly connotations in Oman that it has in northern (European and American) Protestant societies (personal communication, February 1, 1994).[7] "*Several* aspects of xanith behaviour and identity *converge* in people's characterization of it. One prominent one is that xanith sing at weddings.[8] But this is not taken up by my Western colleagues much more interested in prostitution than singing at weddings."

Legally, *khanith* are men. That is, they are able to represent themselves in legal proceedings, whereas, in contrast, "women are jurally minors and must be represented" by an adult male (1977:308; 1982:174). The *khanith* are "referred to in the masculine grammatical gender." The first-person plural in Arabic, which they use to refer to themselves, does not specify gender (Wikan 1994). Wikan reports that *khanith* "speak of themselves with emphasis and pride as 'women,'" but also that "when in old age a xanith loses his attraction and stops his trade, he is assimilated to the old-man (*agoz*) category" (1982:168, 176).

Khanith "are not allowed to dress in women's clothes"; indeed, they are punished by imprisonment and flogging if they cross-dress (1977:309; 1982: 175).[9] Perhaps most interestingly of all, a *khanith* may marry a woman. So long as consummation of the marriage is publicly verified, the groom will be respected as a man (and thereby will lose the prerogative of easy familiarity with women). This seems to me to indicate that sexuality, not gender, is the most salient part of the *khanith* role in the Sohari view.

Despite Wikan's (1978b:668) assertion that her "purpose was to provide a relatively thick description of the khanith," there is little in the way of description of specific *khanith* (or former *khanith*) and none of their own accounts of motivation/causation, concerns, or desires. The only assertion that is explicitly marked as coming directly from a *khanith* challenges the *non-khanith* view that *khanith* cannot attain erection (1977:318n8; 1982:177–78n6; cf. Roscoe 1991:122). Whether *khanith* identify themselves as women (or, for that matter, whether *khanith* identify themselves as *khanith*) and whether they "derive fetishistic pleasure from female clothing" are the defining features for the etic distinction of transsexual and transvestite from homosexual that Wikan insisted upon (1978b:669).

If Wikan's article, rebuttals, and book chapter are the "conceptualisation of xanith identity by the xanith himself" (1978a:474; 1978b:668), it is entirely mediated by the author (in a way quite different from her representation of Sohari male and female honor—which has direct native testimony). In her 1982 book, *Behind the Veil in Arabia: Women in Oman* she included a photograph of a *khanith* (1982:171; reproduced here, Figure 16.1). Presumably, she spoke to him and to other *khanith* and did not derive her analysis entirely from what her women friends said, but as is all too often the case in anthropological discourse, she (and, even more so, her critics) makes categorical

16.1 *Khanith* (photo by Unni Wikan, ca. 1976).

statements with no indication of their warrant. "In culture C people P do X and Y and are conceived as Z" is how ethnography continues to be written—with ever more interpretation and less data either about behavior or about native conceptions.

I have already quoted Wikan's report of her friend's assertion that all servants are *khanith* and all *khanith* are female prostitutes. Her article tells the reader nothing about verifying this. It does not specify how many of the sixty Sohari *khanith* were available for sexual rent or, of those, how many had regular patrons, or how many servants identified themselves as *khanith* (or were so-labeled by others), or whether they considered themselves men or women or a third category.[10] A little of the formal elicitation Wikan finds dehumanizing (1992; also see 1982:299–303) might have resolved such questions as, "Is a *khanith* a kind of man?" and "Is a *khanith* a kind of woman?" in the views of *khanith* and *non-khanith*. Even if, as Wikan thinks likely, they had answered both questions in the affirmative, there would be a clearer picture of Soharis' conceptions.

There does not seem to be a lexicalized or a covert role category "ex-*khanith*." Nor are there any indications of a role of connoisseur/frequenter of *khanith*.[11] As in other cultures with an institutionalized transvestitic homosexual role (e.g., the North American *berdache,* the eastern Siberian shamans, and the Polynesian *māhū*), those who sexually use the *khanith* do not seem to be marked or differentiated from men in general (Wikan 1977:314; 1982:182).

UNEDIFYING POLEMICS

It is difficult to understand why so heated a discussion followed publication of Wikan's initial 1977 report. What I see as the vulnerabilities of Wikan's article—the lack of attention to other literature on gender-stratified homosexuality in Arab societies and the low ratio of empirical evidence to categorical assertions—were not the focus of attacks. Indeed, her critics made assertions as categorical as hers, not only about places to which they had been, but also about Sohar, without even the "I was there and am writing about what I saw" authority upon which so much anthropology relies.

The first two critics (Shepherd 1978a; Brain 1978) threw together, respectively, assertions about homosexual prostitution in Mombasa (a city on the Kenyan coast with historical connections to Zanzibar and to the sultanate of Oman) and a grab-bag of theories about age-stratified, gender-defined, and egalitarian homosexualities.[12] To Brain, Wikan replied that sexual behavior, gender presentation, and institutionalization need to be clearly specified before combinations of them (and possibly others) can be compared meaningfully (1978a). She rejected Shepherd's extrapolation from Mombasa concerning male prostitution being determined by economic need: *khanith* "are in stable, well paid jobs and the Sohari view is that it is some form of lust or desire that drives them to sexual activity," and do not regard *khanith* as inferior.[13]

In the next round Shepherd inferred that *khanith* are of lowly status, mostly of slave descent (1978b); Feuerstein and al-Marzooq that they are non-Arab (1978). Shepherd referred to information obtained from an unspecified number of "ex-Zanzibari Omanis in London refer[ring] to Muscat" (1978b:664), and Feuerstein and al-Marzooq added some incidental observations in Mutrah (1978:665). Such data cannot refute Wikan's claims, however, because in her original article she limited her meaning of "Omani" to "a culture area stretching from Kaborah (some miles north of Muscat) to the northern boundary of the Sultanate of Oman. When I refer to Oman, this should be understood as coastline, whereas Omani is a shorthand abbreviation for the numerically predominant Arab population of this coastline" (Wikan 1977:352).

Feuerstein and al-Marzooq (1978) called attention to the ethnic heterogeneity of Oman, contending that "the population of Sohar town is predominantly non-Arab (Persian and Baluchis)." Having insisted on the necessity of specifying who is what, they nonetheless neglected to mention what kind of "native from 'the Gulf'" the second author is, or what kind(s) of "Omani expatriates" are "well-known for their custom of contractual marriage between men" living in Kuwait, or about what kind of "Omanis" they "have reliable evidence" of "lesbianism."

Shorter fieldwork (seven months in contrast to ten) in a different place at a different time makes it difficult to know what explains the divergences in categorical assertions about "Omani transsexuals."[14] I agree with Feuerstein and al-Marzooq that Wikan (1977) vacillates between representing a dichotomous gender system (with "reciprocals") and a third-gender role, that the "structural concept 'role'" is inadequate to explain or predict situational dynamics, and that "we need to know more about recruitment into, and participation in, the transsexualist subculture, as also about the public interaction between transsexuals and members of the dominant culture" (1978:667; see also Carrier 1980). It seems to me that their criticism of Wikan's failure to recognize "the simultaneous existence of private homosexual ties based on friendship" does not go far enough (Feuerstein and al-Marzooq 1978:666). For keeping rapacious men off women—in Wikan's view, one of the functions of the *khanith* in a society preoccupied with restricting women's sexual behavior[15]—the typicality and frequency of *non-khanith* male homosexuality is also important. So is homosexual rape and whatever pederasty exists in Sohar. I do not know whether Feuerstein and al-Marzooq's claim of institutionalization (quasi-marriage among Omani emigrants) has any defensible basis, but I do know that Wikan's original contrast of Sohari *khanith* with the pattern of homosexuality elsewhere in Islamic cultures is quite defective. She referred to two qualities of general Islamic male homosexuality that "make it fundamentally different from that practiced in Oman: 1) It is part of a deep friendship or love relationship between two men . . . ; 2) Both parties play both the active and the passive sexual role—either simultaneously [!] or through time" (Wikan 1977:310).

Neither of these is the case in what has been reported of other Islamic cultures (see chapter 2 in this volume). Although pederastic relationships have been idealized in literature written by adults, rape (often gang rape) and promiscuity are more common in practice. Assuming that by "simultaneously" Wikan means within the same encounter, not literally at the exact same time (in anal sex, which is the preferred form), there may be some sexual versatility, though this is uncommon in what has been written about homosexual behavior in Islamic societies. It is not at all the case that all boys graduate to the role of insertor or that all insertors are former insertees. Boys growing up and then fucking the same men who fucked them as youths are surely very rare.[16]

Wikan's rejection of an age dimension for *khanith* would be bolstered by some data on the relative rates of passage into and out of the role (1978b: 667).[17] Some *khanith* marry and cease being *khanith,* and some married men "relapse" into being *khanith.*[18] Perhaps some married men take up the *khanith* role without having played it before marriage, too? Wikan does not mention the much-attested Arab view that the pleasures of being fucked are addictive and uncontrollable once awakened, although she does note that lust accounts for both female and male prostitution in the native view (Wikan 1978a:474). Desire, and indeed *khanith* motivation—beyond rejecting the need for money proposed as the sole motive by Shepherd—is very peripheral to her structural analysis of the *khanith* role and what she interpreted as its functions.[19]

Besides reiterating that the population of Sohar is predominantly Arab (1978b:670—between half and two-thirds according to Barth 1983:38), Wikan asserts that "*Xanith* are found in all major ethnic groups (Arab, Baluch, and Ajam), all social classes, and both among freemen and ex-slaves" (1978b: 669).[20] She does not offer any estimates (or hypotheses) of relative frequency regarding age. She concludes by expressing her feeling that "the confusion and regretfully, obfuscation engendered by the discussion that has followed my original article has in part been caused by thoughtless readiness to employ blanket terms—particularly 'homosexual' but also 'lowly status', 'inferiors' etc.—even where sharper concepts exist and more adequate descriptions have been provided" (Wikan 1978b:670–71). Carrier (1980:542) adds to this list of reifications and essences one that Wikan remained notably reluctant to give up, "transsexual."[21] "Prostitute," "servant," and "Arab" are other candidates. As Wikan writes, more documentation of real cases—and their distribution— in their social and cultural context is needed to understand the meaning of the role to those who play it, as well as the place of such a role in a culture such as Arab Sohar. The melange of assertions made about various places in the world other than Sohar by those writing to *Man* clarified nothing.

THE PRIMACY OF SEXUALITY IN THE NATIVE VIEW

According to her acknowledgments, Wikan wrote *Behind the veil in Arabia* between 1976 and 1978 (1982:xi). Although citing her replies to critics of her 1977 article, she did not cite any of them nor did she mention any of their criticisms. Still unwilling to let go of the Western clinical conception "trans-sexual,"[22] she simply replaced it with "*khanith*" in statements about people and role expectations in Sohar repeated from her 1977 article. In addition to including the photograph reproduced here,[23] Wikan added a native state-ment concerning the genesis of *khanith*:

The folk understanding of why some young boys turn into *khaniths* is deceptively simple. Men say that when young boys at puberty start being curious and exploring sexual matters, they may "come to do that thing" together, and then the boy "who lies underneath" may discover that he likes it. If so, he "comes to want it," and, as the Soharis say, "An egg that is once broken can never be put back together," "Water that has been spilt can not be put back again." Thus the homosexual activity of the *xanith* is seen by others as a compulsion: degrading to the person, but springing from his inner nature. Although it is performed for payment of money, its cause is emphati-cally not seen as economic. (1982:172–73)

This is the only statement I have found about the *khanith* role in any of Wikan's writings that is credited to a (non-*khanith*) male perspective. She did not say what kind of man or how many men say this. It is certainly consis-tent with the very widespread (circum-Mediterranean and beyond) belief that the pleasures of being penetrated are addictive. I discuss this belief and a number of terms for those so addicted in chapter 2. Fredrik Barth also re-ferred to the adage that once an egg is broken it cannot be put back together and quoted a Sohari man that *khanith* are happy being the way they are: "that is what they want" (1983:79). Confirmation that Wikan's final view makes sexuality the defining feature of *khanith* is provided in her husband's book on Sohar, published a year later. He writes, "In the case of gender, identity is initially ascribed by anatomical criteria, but Wikan (1977; 1978a,b; 1982) shows convincingly that its key expression, and thereby ultimate ascriptive criterion is found in the sexual act rather than sexual organs in Sohar" (Barth 1983:78).

At the risk of over-interpreting Wikan's "Men say," I would suggest that perhaps sexual behavior is more salient a feature of the *khanith* role for men than for women, and that gender markers may be somewhat more salient for women—even though it was a woman who explained *khanith* as homosexual prostitutes to Wikan, and both women and men expect a simple relationship between sex, gender, and sexual propriety—insofar as these distinctions are salient in Sohar.[24] On the last dimension, *khanith* are classified with "fallen women," but instead of taking this as evidence that they are "a kind of woman," it seems more likely that a man or a woman can be virtuous and that a man or a woman can be improper (i.e., "fallen from grace"). Pending more data from Sohar, it seems to me that the *khanith* is an instance of gender-stratified homosexuality, but that we do not know if Soharis consider there to be three genders. From the evidence Wikan presented, my hypothesis is that the answer to "Is a *khanith* a kind of woman?" would be negative, and "Is a *khanith* a kind of man?" would be yes—a less than fully realized man, perhaps even a "failed man," but still a kind of man.

Notes

1. While arguing that the *khanith* is a third gender role rather than an intermediate gender role or a male role viewed with contempt, Will Roscoe has with some success pressed me to reduce the opacity of this attempt to sort through what is known of this gender-defined homosexual role from Unni Wikan's writings and the hostile reception accorded her 1977 article. I am also grateful for the explanations of historical trade patterns across the Indian Ocean and the Arabian Sea by Deb Amory and Badruddin Khan, for the generous and patient comments of Unni Wikan, and for her permission to reproduce her photograph of a *khanith*. When he read this chapter, David Greenberg pointed out to me that Eickelman earlier interpreted Wikan's evidence as showing a "variety of role patterns, but not the existence of three genders" in the Sohari view (1981:143).

2. There are female prostitutes, although Wikan (1978b:670) rejects Feuerstein and al-Marzooq's surmise that they are "foreigners working in the country" (1978:666). On the lack of public challenge to respectability in Arab societies, see Wikan (1984), as well as the example of the female prostitute in Wikan (1977:312).

3. Wikan (personal communication, February 1, 1994) clarifies that she "did not use the word 'essence' in the sense that it has got in current anthropology," and that she did not mean to imply that there are not other essential aspects of the role. She reminded me that the binary logic of alien analysts' categorization is not a native concern. In this particular instance, for Soharis, the *khanith* need not be z or not-z (with z being various alien categories), but may be both.

4. The word is Urdu and is also used by Hindi-speakers. It has recently been attested in southern Arabia [Yemen] by Albergoni and Bédoucha (1991). The role is called *khusra* in Punjabi. Shepherd's (1978a,b) extrapolation from Mombasa to Sohar are discussed below in chapter 14.

5. See Roscoe (1991:121) concerning homosexual prostitution by *hijras* and the confusion of absence of heterosexual desire with impotence in Nanda (1990) and her predecessors, including Carstairs (1957), Shah (1961), Sinha (1967)—work that Wikan could have drawn upon for comparison in preference to that on Western "transsexuals." Kumar notes that various South Asians apply the term *hijra* to hermaphrodites, transsexuals, transvestites, and homosexuals (1993:86). Apparently relying on Nanda rather than direct observation or recollection, he privileges enactment of exaggerated stereotypes of women, writing of them as "serving as a surrogate and playing the role of a woman both in the sexual act and in visual appearance" (1993:89).

6. On the longstanding and intensive Indian influences on Oman see Wilkinson (1987:63–66).

7. This is also true in other societies such as China and Taiwan in which daughters become prostitutes for the greater good of their natal families.

8. This accepted role at one of the central celebrations of heterosexuality parallels that of the South Asian *hijra*.

9. Greenberg apparently extrapolated a British officer's report of cross-dressed Omani from Muscat in mid-nineteenth-century Zanzibar to twentieth-century Sohar (1988:179). Paragraph 33 of General Christopher Rigby's 1860 "Report on the Zanzibar Dominion," which asserted that "since the death of the late Imam [Syud Said] numbers of sodomites have come from Muscat, and these degraded wretches openly walk about dressed in female attire, with veils on their faces" (in his daughter's collection: Russell 1970:342; there is also reference to Arabs in Zanzibar considering *liwāt* "a mere peccadillo" by Burton 1872:380). The passage from Rigby's report cannot support either an assumption that cross-dressing was accepted in Muscat or that those Rigby mentioned were termed *khanith*.

10. In addition to the unfairness of faulting Wikan for being an anthropologist (since making unsubstantiated categorical statements is what anthropologists do, especially when producing analyses of a role rather than of the occupants of the role), this is unfair in that Wikan reported that some *khanith* hire sexual partners: "The young and pretty *xanith* receives substantial gifts and payments from his paramours whereas the old and unattractive *xanith*, according to Sohari, 'will pay the men to do it to them'" (1978a:474).

11. There is also no indication of pederastic role terms, but without elicitation one cannot take absence of evidence as evidence of absence. Wikan represents herself as having stumbled on the *khanith* role. Hanging out with reticent women is unlikely to lead to stumbling on pederasty. Her fieldwork was not focused on the varieties of homosexual behavior—or even roles—but on the lives of women, so, even had she been inclined to be more inquisitive, she may well not have gotten any data on this.

12. For example, it is hard to take the vague statement, "one of the authors' observation of Islamic society in Aden, where homosexual relationships between males were a standardized mode of behaviour eliciting few or any negative sanctions" (Ashworth and Walker 1972:153), as warranting that "transsexuals were certainly observed by men in Aden [Yemen]," as Brain (1978:323) did.

13. Indeed, Wikan (1978a:474) rejects the "gradated hierarchy" that is Shepherd's view of society (Sohari or all societies?), although she had written that "homosexual prostitution is shameful" and that female prostitution is "immensely wrong and sinful" (Wikan 1977:312–13). At the same time, she stresses that "it is up to every person to

behave as correctly as possible ... rather than to demand such things of others" (1977:311; also see Wikan 1984).

14. Wikan wrote that she devoted two months in 1975–76 to collecting data on the *khanith* (1977:306), whereas the subject was incidental to whatever Feuerstein and al-Marzooq were doing in Mutrah.

15. In *Corydon*, his 1911 apologia for pederasty (not least his own in North Africa), André Gide suggested that sexual relations between males was a preferable alternative to female prostitution.

16. I do not understand how the *khanith* "does not seek sexual release for himself. Indeed, till he has proved otherwise (most?) people doubt he is capable of having an erection" can be taken to support the second point (i.e., posited role reciprocity). To find out whether *khanith* (or those being penetrated elsewhere in Islamic societies) enjoy receptive intercourse and/or whether they get erections requires asking them (not their partners, still less women).

17. "The *xanith* career in Sohar is *not* coterminous with 'the years of youth and beauty' [Shepherd's assumption]. Some *xanith* reach old age without ever trying to marry, some do, but relapse later in life—and not because of poverty" (Wikan 1978b:667).

18. This is not so fluid as "shift[ing] back and forth," which is Eickelman's characterization (1981:143).

19. On the general lack of data on desire, see Herdt (1991:494–97); Herdt and Stoller (1990).

20. Readers are left to guess whether the number of *khanith* in each ethnic group is proportional to the number of *non-khanith* in the population of Sohar. Barth (1983) focused on the heterogeneity of Sohar, and continues to grapple with modeling multi-ethnic civilizations with multiple cosmologies (1993).

21. Obviously from my substitution of *khanith* for *transsexual* in this review of the controversy, I would too. Although she began by specifying *transsexual* as "a socially acknowledged role pattern whereby a person acts and is classified" (1977:304), even in her original article she mixed with this the American clinical sense of *transsexual*, as the self-identification as a woman by a male who seeks "reassignment" of sex, citing Benjamin (1966) and Stoller (1968, 1971). Over the course of the polemics, it seems to me that she mostly abandoned her own definition of "transsexual" and increasingly appealed to the authority of Western psychiatrists such as Robert Stoller and John Money. She regretfully wondered if it would not have been better to stick to the native term, *khanith*, but persisted in *transsexual* (Wikan 1978b:670).

22. A communication of unspecified date from John Money supports using the native term (*khanith*), but on the suspect grounds that Omanis are like nineteenth-century Americans not yet having recognized transsexualism (Wikan 1982:172). In her passing allusion to literature on transvestitism in various cultures, she substituted the Mesakin of Nuba for the Lango of Uganda listed in her article (cf. Wikan 1982:171, repeating 1977:339).

23. Wikan has contrasted *khanith* dress to that of both men and women: "*xanith*s characteristically expose their lower arm in public." Half the upper arm, as well, is bare in the picture of a *khanith* that she published (1982:173; Fig. 16.1 herein).

24. Recent literature takes too much for granted the universal applicability of these distinctions from the elite discourse of Western feminism (Murray 1994).

References

Albergoni, Gianni, and Geneviève Bédoucha. 1991. "Hiérarchie, médiation et tribalisme en Arabie du Sud: La *hijra* yéménite." *L'Homme* 31(2):7–36.

Ashworth, A. E., and A. M. Walker. 1972. "Social structure and homosexuality." *British Journal of Sociology* 23:146–58.

Barth, Fredrik. 1983. *Sohar: Culture and society in an Omani town.* Baltimore: Johns Hopkins University Press.

———. 1993. *Balinese worlds.* Chicago: University of Chicago Press.

Benjamin, Harry. 1966. *The transsexual phenomenon.* New York: Julian.

Brain, Robert. 1978. "Transsexualism in Oman?" *Man* 13:322–23.

Burton, Richard F. 1872. *Zanzibar.* London: Tinsley Brothers.

Carrier, Joseph M. 1980. "The Omani *xanith* controversy." *Man* 15:541–42.

Carstairs, George M. 1957. *The twice born.* London: Hogarth.

Eickelman, Dale F. 1981. *The Middle East: An anthropological approach.* Englewood Cliffs, NJ: Prentice-Hall.

Feuerstein, G. and S. al-Marzooq. 1978. "Omani *xanith.*" *Man* 13:665–67.

Greenberg, David F. 1988. *The construction of homosexuality.* Chicago: University of Chicago Press.

Herdt, Gilbert H. 1991. "Representations of homosexuality." *Journal of the History of Sexuality* 1:481–504.

Herdt, Gilbert H., and Robert J. Stoller. 1990. *Intimate communications.* New York: Columbia University Press.

Kumar, Arvind. 1993. "*Hijras*: Challenging gender dichotomies." In *A lotus of another color,* ed. Rakesh Ratti, 85–91. Boston: Alyson.

Murray, Stephen O. 1994. "Subordinating native cosmologies to the empire of gender." *Current Anthropology* 35:59–61.

Murray, Stephen O., and Keelung Hong. 1994. *Taiwanese cultural, Taiwanese society.* Lanham, MD: University Press of America.

Nanda, Serena. 1990. *Neither man nor woman: The hijras of India.* Belmont, CA: Wadsworth.

Roscoe, Will. 1991. Review of *Neither man nor woman* by Serena Nanda. *Journal of Homosexuality* 21(3):117–25.

Russell, Mrs. C. E. B. 1970. *General Rigby, Zanzibar, and the slave trade.* New York: Negro Universities Press.

Shah, A. M. 1961. "A note on the hijadas of Gujerat." *American Anthropologist* 61:-1325–30.

Shepherd, Gill. 1978a. "Transsexualism in Oman?" *Man* 13:133–34.

———. 1978b. "Omani *xanith.*" *Man* 13:663–65.

Sinha, A.P. 1967. "Procreation among the eunuchs." *Eastern Anthropologist* 20:168–76.

Stoller, Robert J. 1968. *Sex and gender.* London: Hogarth.

———. 1971. "The term 'transvestism.'" *Archives of General Psychiatry* 24:230–37.

Wikan, Unni. 1977. "Man becomes woman: Transsexualism in Oman as a key to gender roles." *Man* 12:304–19.

———. 1978a. "The Omani *xanith*: A third gender role?" *Man* 14:473–75.

———. 1978b. "The Omani *xanith.*" *Man* 13:667–71.

———. 1982. *Behind the veil in Arabia: Women in Oman.* Baltimore: Johns Hopkins University Press.

———. 1984. "Shame and honour: A contestable pair." *Man* 19:635–52.

———. 1992. "Beyond the words." *American Ethnologist* 19:460–82.

Wilkinson, John C. 1987. *The Imamate tradition in Oman.* New York: Cambridge University Press.

CHAPTER 17

Male Actresses in Islamic Parts of Indonesia and the Southern Philippines

Stephen O. Murray

Although gender and sexuality may be distinguished analytically, they are far from being independent from each other. Indeed, outside the elite realm of academic gender discoursing, sexuality and gender generally are expected to coincide (see Murray 1994, 1995). That is, effeminate males are widely supposed to be sexually receptive, masculine persons to be insertive.

Across Indonesia, traveling troupes of entertainers provide an occupational niche for men attracted to men and for men who act women's roles. Among the Makassarese of southern Sulawesi, at least through the 1940s, there were *masri* dancers aged nine to twelve, who dressed somewhat like women.[1] They covered part of their face with a long white shawl, like a veil. The main purpose of the dance they performed before audiences consisting mostly of married men, according to Chabot, was "sexual incitement, emanating from the combination of verse, rhythm and the young boys half-dressed as women" (1950:156). The men in the audiences showed their approval by slipping often large amounts of money into the necks of the young boys. In 1928 when Chabot observed it, the dance enjoyed great popularity, which continued after World War II (van der Kroef 1954:263).

On the much-longer-Islamicized island of Java, Wilken mentions boys taking girls' roles in some dance troupes in the late nineteenth century:

Sometimes the *bedaja* and *serimpi* are replaced by boys, who then are dressed as girls and also belong to the nobility. It has been rumored that they serve as concubines of prominent men, and, therefore, other boys of this kind who do not serve as dancing girls are also called *bedaja*. So little evil is seen in pederasty that no secret is made of it. (1893:118; Human Relations Area File translation)

Nearly a century later, in 1972–73 fieldwork, Weiss observed that

a form of institutionalized homosexuality occurs in the Ponorogo area. . . . The practice of keeping young boys (on the part of either individuals or service organizations) was once and still is a prestigious pattern. Formerly, men who kept boys could often get married, not because they preferred sexual relations with women, but apparently because they felt compelled to realize the Javanese ideal of marriage and procreation. Some even continued to keep boys after they were married. (1977:529–30)[2]

In contemporary rural Java, performing troupes continue to need a pretty young boy for *rayag* performances. The parents of Javanese *gemblakan* (sg. *gemblak*) trade their sons for gifts and money from the dance troupe in which their son performs women's roles (for a year or two). Offstage, a group of unmarried young men pass the boy around for intercrural intercourse (Williams 1990).[3] Displaying the resources to keep a *gemblak* and to dress him expensively is still today a source of prestige for men. Despite the increasing commercialization of the *gemblak* role, parents are both honored and enriched by having a son spend several years as a *gemblak*. As with other effeminate performers in the Philippines and Tahiti, traditional Aleutian male concubines, or eunuchs and catamites in the Roman and Ottoman Empires, some are socialized into the role by parents seeking a chance to profit from attractive sons. Moreover, a successful *rayag* troupe brings prestige to the village, and no *rayag* can be successful without a star *gemblak*, so the status of the village as well as the prosperity of the family reinforce treating the *gemblak* well.

The boy outgrows his stage role and also his desirability as a sexual partner. If he marries and bears children, like the Omani *khanith* or Moroccan boys who cease being sexually receptive, the former *gemblak* is treated like other male villagers. He is not reminded of the glory or of the sexual aspects of his earlier vocation.

The transvestite performers of the modern *ludruk* on Java are often homosexual, according to Geertz (1960:291). Hatley provides a sketch of the artform's history:

Ludruk originated as a simple entertainment routine featuring a clown and a transvestite singer. Later it developed into a full dramatic form, but the clown and the transvestite remain the dominant figures. Each *Ludruk* performance is a collection of "pre-fabricated" parts: the opening *ngremo* (a traditional East Javanese dance); a prologue consisting of songs and comic skits performed by clowns; a melodrama in which the female parts are played by transvestites. Songs and dances by female impersonators are inserted between acts. . . . Both actors and audience regard *Ludruk,* which depicts scenes from everyday life [in marked contrast to the traditional *wayang* shadow puppet theater] and encourage them to be "modern," as an art form "of the people." And it has frequently been used to influence popular thinking. During the colonial period and the revolution, *Ludruk* became a vehicle of anti-Dutch propaganda and national-istic ideas and since independence it has been used by various political groups to promote their viewpoint. (1971:94)

James Peacock mentions one *ludruk* manager "who encouraged homosexual liaisons among members of his troupe in order to hold the troupe together; at least such liaisons increased the chances that if you get one actor to show for a performance, you would get his lover as well" (1968:35). In his analysis of Surabaya communist *ludruk* in the mid-1960s, Peacock contends that "the transvestite is regarded by Javanese as the most illicit element" (1968:203). If it was "illicit" to the Javanese "masses" (and not just their self-anointed leaders and to the foreign anthropologist whose distaste is apparent in Peacock's locutions such as "some manner of homosexual relations" and "sexual escape from adult responsibilities"), transvestite singers and actors were certainly not covert. The transvestite Peacock calls the "sucking whore" talked out loud about his promiscuous and homosexual nature with "blatant oral and pseudo-genital imagery." Male actresses accentuated their gender-crossing by clearing their throats in a gruff bass. According to Peacock, "spectators never tire of discussing the fact that the transvestite singer is really a man, although he looks like a woman. Emphasis of the fact that the singer's facade covers a male body almost seems to enhance the spectator's attraction to the character" (1968:35n1; also reported by Geertz 1960:291).

Javanese also enjoy male impersonators outside the theater. Some told Peacock that they dreamed of the singers and told many stories of (usually aristocratic) spectators becoming so infatuated that they abandoned their wives and children to move in with the female impersonator (1968:35). That "perhaps males can let their erotic fantasies run wilder regarding the transvestite precisely because, along with sexy imagery, she displays 'separate from beholder and nature' symbolism that reassures males that she neither offers full sexual consummation to them nor demands full sexual output from them; they can just sit back and appreciate her as a 'beautiful' *objet d'art"* does not fit very well with the sexual availability of some performers (Ibid.).

Despite pressure from communist managers during the early 1960s to confine feminine performance to the time they were on stage (by forcing them to
cut off their long hair "the only gross male body-part that can be made more
womanly by natural process," and attempting to discourage homosexuality),
ludruk transvestites have "traditionally shown more than professional interest
in playing feminine roles. Almost all are markedly effeminate offstage. They
wear women's clothes at home" (Peacock 1968:207). Many tailor women's
clothes, and "some become 'wives' of men, living lives not unlike that of the
Plains Indian berdache. Many endure parents' discomfort and strangers'
taunts to keep the role 'woman.' Most whom I interviewed have taken feminine roles since childhood" (ibid.).

After the bloody extirpation of communists in 1965–66, the Islamic military regime adapted the *ludruk* to its own propaganda purposes. According
to Hatley, "Now all troupes have an official government sponsor and many
are associated with the military" (1971:94). Hatley described a panel of army
officers judging which performers deserved promotion (1971:99). He questioned whether they could be credible proponents of new ways and ideas.
Although transvestites increase *ludruk's* popular appeal, "It is difficult to
know how the illicit sexual appeal of the female impersonators affects their
role as spokesmen for government propaganda in the songs they sing
between the acts of the melodrama—the audience may become too involved
in watching the singer to listen carefully to his message. And it is equally difficult to know the effect on this 'modern' message of its association with a
figure dressed in traditional clothes, symbolizing the traditional ideal of
beauty and status" (pp. 100–101).

Perhaps the solution is that the transvestite is not "illicit." As Peacock
notes,

The Javanese case is complicated: "Pure" Javanese tradition does not condemn homosexuality and regards a very wide range of behavior, from he-man to rather (in our
terms) "effeminate," as properly masculine. Therefore, Javanese who condemn the
transvestite are probably doing so from the standpoint of Javanese masculinity influenced by Islam, but the transvestite legitimizes himself in terms of "pure" (non-
Islamicized) Javanese ideals. (1968:204)

Further north, in the Islamicized southern Philippine islands, there are also
roles in entertainment for gender-variant men. Among the Tausug of the Sulu
archipelago (northeast of Borneo), Kiefer (1967, 1968) described a professional
niche for "sensitive men" (*bantut*). Professional musician (*mangangalang*) is a

Tausug role providing "opportunities for temporary sex-role reversal in an expressive situation, female-like voice and mannerism, expressive bodily movements," especially in *pagsindil,* a popular performance of stylized courtship repartee in which the *bantut* takes the female role (1967:108). This niche for gender variance does not seem to extend to acceptance of a sexual component, because Kiefer asserts that in Tausug cosmology, "'overt sodomy' produces a heat *(pasuh)* which engenders drought and [thereby] endangers Tausug society" (1972:36). He does not mention sex in connection with ritualized friendship, but notes that "it is shameful *(spiug)* to discuss particulars of one's sexual activities in front of a third person" (1972:36), presumably including ethnographers. Kiefer does not attempt to assess whether such dangerous behavior as "overt sodomy" (in contrast to public cross-gender performances) actually occurred, apparently assuming that statements of norms are adequate accounts of behavior.

Nimmo asserts that few, if any, of the major communities of the Sulu archipelago are without male homosexuals—some transvestite, others not. Some islands are known locally for their large numbers of homosexuals, whereas others are known for having few. A group of male transvestites, well-known throughout southern Sulu as the *dahling-dahling* dancers, are professional entertainers who travel among the islands, singing and dancing at major celebrations and ceremonies (1978:94).[4]

In sum, on the northeastern edge of the Islamicized world, gender-mixed homosexual roles are more obvious than pederasty. Nevertheless, those who take on these roles in Indonesian and Filipino cultures often start young. A combination of youth and prettiness is preferred by the conventionally masculine men who enjoy them onstage and off. It is difficult not to infer that there was homosexuality with effeminate youths on these islands before Islam reached them. As chapters 2 and 13 show, effeminate boy entertainers have long been appreciated and courted by adult male Muslims in Egypt and across the southern, Islamic parts of mainland Asia. Those in organized troupes are able to take on other less prominent jobs within the company once their allure has faded. Some reject sexual receptivity as adults; such men are less likely to continue in the entertainment business with its uncertain income and low social status. Those who want to continue sexual receptivity (and also those who want to take the insertive role with young males) are more likely to stay in it.

Notes

1. Traditional Makassarese society included a prestigious gender-mixing shamanistic role (*bisu*). Largely dependent on a court disrupted by Dutch conquest, the role had declined by the 1920s. According to van der Kroef, "Homosexuals called *kawe* . . . have remained, seeking to satisfy their needs and playing their profession in markets and busy city quarters" (1954:261; see Murray 1992:257–61; Nootenboom 1948:245–55).

2. Weiss presented a paper at the 1974 American Anthropological Association meetings in Mexico City on kept boys in *gemblakan* troupes, but I have been unable to obtain a copy.

3. Williams adds that the *gemblak* may on occasion be fellated, that they generally marry women later, and that members of the troupe do not have sexual relations with other members except for the *gemblak*.

4. Cf. Nanda 1990 on the *hijra* of South Asia. In addition to noting these transvestite performers Nimmo focuses on exogamy between (Islamic and non-Islamic) ethnic groups for homosexual relations (1978:94).

References

Chabot, H. Thomas. 1950. *Verwantschap, Stand en Sexe in Zuid-Celeben*. Groningen: J. B. Wolters. Translated as *Kinship, status and sex in the South Celebes*. New Haven: Human Relation Area Files, 1960.

Geertz, Clifford. 1960. *The religion of Java*. New York: Free Press.

Hatley, Barbara. 1971. "*Wayang* and *ludruk:* Polarities in Java." *Drama Review* 15:88–101.

Kiefer, Thomas M. 1967. "A note on cross-sex identification among musicians." *Ethnomusicology* 12:107–9.

_____. 1968. "Institutionalized friendship and warfare among the Tausug of Jolo." *Ethnology* 7:225–44.

_____. 1972. *The Tausug*. New York: Holt.

Murray, Stephen O. 1992. *Oceanic homosexualities*. New York: Garland.

_____. 1994. "Subordinating native cosmologies to the empire of gender." *Current Anthropology* 35:59–61.

_____. 1995. *Latin American male homosexualities*. Albuquerque: University of New Mexico Press.

Nanda, Serena. 1990. *Neither man nor woman: The hijra of India*. Belmont, CA: Wadsworth.

Nimmo, H. Arlo. 1978. "The relativity of sexual deviance: A Sulu example." *Papers in Anthropology* 19:91–97.

Nootenboom, C. 1948. "Aantekeningen over de Boeginezan en Makassaren." *Indonesie* 2:245–55.

Peacock, James L. 1968, *Rites of modernization: Symbolic aspects of Indonesian proletarian drama*. Chicago: University of Chicago Press.

van der Kroef, Justus M. 1954. "Transvestism and the religious hermaphrodite in Indonesia." *University of Manila Journal of East Asiatic Studies* 3:257–65.

Weiss, Jerome. 1977. "Folk psychology of the Javanese of Ponorgo." Ph.D. dissertation, Yale University.

Wilken, G. A. 1893. *Handleiding voor de Vergelij Kende Volkenukunde van Nederlandsch-Indies*. Leiden: Brill.

Williams, Walter L. 1990. "Homosexuality as a means of promoting village unity in Ponorogo, East Java." Paper presented at the American Anthropological Association meetings, New Orleans.

CHAPTER 18

Two Baluchi *Buggas,* a Sindhi *Zenana,* and the Status of *Hijras* in Contemporary Pakistan

Nauman Naqvi and Hasan Mujtaba

Lal Bux alias Mumtaz resists emasculation, aspires to lead a normal life (with wife and progeny) and performs as a *hijra* primarily because of economic constraints. Lean and tall, with a long stride, high cheekbones, deep voice, and a muscular physique, Lal Bux is a handsome masculine specimen. But Bux/Mumtaz's hair is long and curly. "I don't do anything to it," he says, "It is naturally like this: Baluchi hair." Mumtaz invariably refers to himself in the masculine gender, although his gestures range from the archetypally masculine to the quintessentially feminine. Every once in a while there are moments when Bux/Mumtaz is neither man nor woman but that peculiar mix of both that yet is uniquely neither, a *hijra.* "A *hijra* is something other than masculine or feminine, and the true face of the *hijra* appears best when she is angry," Mumtaz says.

"I was born at Shadapur" (in the Sanghar district of Pakistan; Baluchistan is split between southern Afghanistan, southeastern Iran, and southwestern Pakistan), he reveals. "My parents died when I was two years old and my *khala* [maternal aunt] raised me. I used to play with girls and I loved dolls, so my *khala* would say I would become a *'bugga'* [Baluchi equivalent of *hijra*] when I grew up."

"Of course, I didn't know what a *bugga* was at that age. It was only because of what my *khala* said that I became aware of them. But I have been instinctively attracted to *hijras* for as long as I can remember. A friend of mine, Rasool Bux, who was as feminine as them, would watch the *hijras* sing and dance in the Syeds' house. Rasool Bux first introduced me to the *hijras* of Baghdadi. Among them were Shaantal and Chandni. These *hijras* showered me with love."

Despite his association with them, however, and despite the fact that he became Chandni's *chela* (disciple and foster child), Mumtaz was not prepared to be emasculated. "I did not get myself castrated despite constant pressure from other *hijras*. You see, these gurus get their protégés castrated for their own personal interests. Once the *chela* is castrated, he is bound to the guru for life and that means he has to give his guru the lion's share of his income. I am like other males, and I have sexual desires like them." But his preference is for male sexual partners.

Mumtaz is a good dancer and has showbiz aspirations. Mumtaz's neighbors who have seen him grow up and watched his metamorphosis into a *hijra* relate their own version of how it happened. "Lal Bux used to be a very good boy," says a video shop owner. "But there was a man who would constantly be with him and take him everywhere he went. He claimed he wanted to reform Lal Bux, to take out the feminine kinks in his personality. But the truth was that he was interested in using Lal Bux to satisfy his own sexual perversions. He was the one who ruined Lal Bux, who can't make love to a woman now, and smokes heroin."

Mumtaz acknowledges that he uses heroin, but maintains it is not a habit. "I do it every now and then, but not like I used to. When I'm with friends and they offer it to me, I take it, but not regularly."

Mumtaz's own attitude about being a *hijra* is ambivalent. He claims that he hasn't had intimate relations with anyone for the past fifteen months, although his neighbors say otherwise. Lal Bux's bashfulness about his sexuality arises from the negative image that homosexuality, especially passive homosexuality, has in the tribal, patriarchal culture of Baluchistan.

Mumtaz, who is the sole breadwinner of his family, makes most of his money from his performances as a *hijra*. He says that it takes him four hours to make-up and dress before each performance, prior to which he spends two hours bathing. He claims that "most of our earnings are spent on make-up and clothes." The rest is spent on the upkeep of his *khala* and her children. "The only reason that I can't abandon this life is because I have to provide for my aunt. I am a poor man and there is nothing else I can do. Sometimes I get angry with her and tell her that it is because of her that I became a *hijra* in the first place, and now it is because of her that I have to continue doing it. I have lots of regrets about the way I have lived my life.

But I still nurture the hope that someday I will get married, have children, and continue my line."

Rasool Bux alias Farzana was born in a Baluchi household in Lyari (a Karachi suburb). He was the eldest son, with all the expectations and responsibilities the position entailed. At the age of ten, Rasool Bux disappeared. "We looked everywhere," his mother recalls. "No one knew where he was." After many days, one of the *hijras* in the neighborhood, who until then had been part of the conspiracy of silence, spoke. He told Rasool Bux's parents that their son was living with a *hijra* in Sanghar as his *chela*.

Rasool Bux's parents went to Sanghar to get their son back. They found him and managed to secure his release from his guru, but against Rasool Bux's will. At a bus stop in Hyderabad on their way back, he escaped. Even at that tender age, Rasool Bux had recognized his *ruh*, his spirit: he knew that he was a *hijra*. From then on he lived as Farzana among kindred spirits, other *hijras*.

Farzana did not return to her parents' home until, more than twenty years later, her father died. "His father just could not accept him," his mother recounts. Farzana's loving mother, however, would go and live in the *hijra* community in Sanghar, sometimes for weeks.

Black as night and portly, with her tight curly hair done up in a chignon, Farzana cuts a maternal figure. She conducts herself with dignity. Nowhere in her demeanor is there any indication that Farzana considers herself to be inferior or to be a member of a marginalized group. Farzana equates being a *hijra* with spiritual asceticism. Indeed, the deliberate emasculation that many *hijras* undergo is said to kill the *nafs*, which in Sufism (a powerful current among *hijras*) is considered the baser part of humans, often identified with desire, of which the most powerful manifestation is sexual desire. The word *nafs* also refers to the male genitalia. So emasculation, which is often but not exclusively the rite of passage for *hijras,* is an act of spiritual devotion and sacrifice. It is a very intense and dangerous one: the life of the devotee is at risk.

Farzana has not been emasculated. "He is still physically intact," says his mother with a burst of laughter. Farzana says her devotion to God is indicated by her sexual abstinence and by the way she earns her living. "I have a special relationship with God because I make my living by uttering His name. All I do is give God's blessings to people: may God give you a son, may God give you a long life." Like many other *hijras,* Farzana frequents various shrines in Pakistan, and looks forward to performing Haj when she can afford it.

Farzana scorns *zenanas*: "There is a world of difference between *hijras* and *zenanas*. Some *zenanas* even have families, wives and children. We are certainly not the same. *Zenanas* are in just for the *dhanda* (business). The so-called *hijras* at Zinda Pir are examples."

The *zenanas* themselves do not always claim that they are *hijras*. Says Sunny, who is avowedly a *zenana*, "I am not a *hijra*. Only my *ruh* is that of a woman. I started realizing I was different from other people at the age of six-teen. It was as if flames were rising in my heart. My father used to get angry with me. 'Why do you walk like this and where do you go?' he used to ask me. He once put me in chains. Then I fell in love with a man, but he is now a *pardesi* (a lover who has gone away, perhaps to foreign lands). I lived with him for several months in his house in Sargodha. But his brother and I couldn't get along. Even though I really loved my *pardesi*, we broke up, and I haven't seen him for two years."

Sunny markets his wares in Karachi's Empress Market, hanging out with other *zenanas* in cafés and other public places. He lives with his family and does tailoring at home, but makes extra cash by prostituting himself—with-out the knowledge of his parents, of course. Sunny says that a lot of men pre-fer *hijras* to women. "They like the *hijra* gestures, which are very different from those of normal women."

Many stories are told of marriages with *hijras*. One young man from Bagh-dadi says that in days gone by, *hijras* would marry men who had donkey carts, because they were prized possessions then. "Sometimes men would marry *hijras* because the *hijras* would give them all their earnings and they could then buy a donkey cart. But there was another reason, too, for marry-ing *hijras*. People in those days were a lot stronger, worked a lot harder, and consequently had proportionately greater sexual appetites. A normal woman could not possibly satisfy them the way a *hijra* could. These days, however, young men marry *hijras* because marriages with women are too expensive."

A *hijra*'s position in society is somewhat ambiguous. Formerly, they were an integral part of society and the state: they would be placed in the harems of the emperors to serve the needs of the emperors' wives and concubines, and to protect them. They thus served an important function in the affairs of the court, like eunuchs elsewhere.

Things are quite different now, however. In the days of Ayub Khan (during the early 1960s), *hijra* activities were banned. In response, *hijras* from all the various communities got together and staged a sit-in in front of Ayub's house, complaining to his mother about her son's decision, and reminding her that they had sung a *lori* (a lullaby for infants) for Ayub when he was born. The ban was revoked.

The next *hijra* encounter with the state was during the Pakistan National Assembly movement against Zulfikar Ali Bhutto's government in 1977. *Hijras* participated in a PNA protest march. Direct *hijra* involvement in Pakistani politics, however, began in the 1990 elections, when a *hijra,* Mohammed Aslam, was put up as a candidate by the people of Abbottabad. Coming as it did after the collapse of the Benazir Bhutto government, the political message that seemed to come across was "The men have tried and failed, the women have tried and failed, maybe *hijras* will do the job better!"

Because the state recognized only two sexes, male and female, it has a dilemma when dealing with *hijras.* Bureaucrats are, therefore, unsure how to deal with *hijras.* Many *hijras* complain that they have a great deal of difficulty obtaining ID cards, and say that they are continually harassed by the police, as well.

CHAPTER 19

The Other Side of Midnight

Pakistani Male Prostitutes

Hasan Mujtaba

If you are a man alone driving a car or riding a bike in the Clifton, Defense, Tariq Road, Bahadurabad, and KDA-building areas, or around the Quaid-e-Azam's Mazaar in the evening, chances are you will be flagged down by a teenage boy ostensibly hitching a ride. If you oblige him, the young man will direct a barrage of questions at you: What do you do? Where do you live? Do you stay alone? etc. Similarly, if you are walking around the busy Saddar area or Tariq Road alone after dusk, a good-looking youth will ask for a match, the time, or an address and try to continue with a conversation. If you respond, he may ask you to share a cup of tea or a cold drink with him in one of the sidewalk cafés. Emboldened by an affirmative answer, he will reach the bottom line: Where do you want to talk me? and How much *kharcha paani* (money) are you offering? If you agree to the transaction, within a few minutes he will be accompanying you to your residence or some obscure hotel.

Male prostitution is by no means a recent phenomenon. The famous British explorer Sir Richard Burton, who visited the Sindh long before the British conquest, found a brothel of boy prostitutes in Karachi soon after he anchored there. The business has continued to flourish since then. Today, certain areas in the bigger cities of Pakistan have become virtual red-light districts for gay sex. Clients for male prostitutes come from every class, community, age group, and profession.

Upper- and middle-class homosexuals cruise around in their cars on the lookout for male prostitutes who frequent select pickup points such as video game shops, small restaurants, and cold-drink spots. In busy areas like Gulshan-e Iqbal, Sabzi Mandi, Kharadar, Lea Market, Landhi, Malir, and Lyari, less well-heeled homosexuals look for less expensive partners in a somewhat different fashion. "You can buy a boy sometimes for a whole night for the price of a meal or a ride on your motorbike," says one gay man. Clients in these areas comprise mainly bus drivers and conductors, night watchmen and laborers from upcountry, army and policemen, low-income government officials, or small-time Memon businessmen and those who come to the city for business trips and sometimes get lonely on longer stints. (Following General Zia's clampdown on the flesh trade in the early 1980s, *faujis* [soldiers] on martial law duty were the main clients of male prostitutes and visitors to their brothels.)

Male prostitutes today ply their business in almost every city and major town in Pakistan. In dark alleys, at crowded bus stops, at shopping centers, in cinemas, hotel lobbies, parks, and railway stations, in hospital and school compounds, and sometimes even in the elevators of public buildings, boys and young men stalk customers. They operate with thorough professionalism and a sharp eye for zeroing in on potential clients. From initial eye contact to cutting a deal takes barely five to ten minutes.

Many prostitutes prefer to operate from hotel rooms rather than to accompany clients to their residence where they run the risk of being assaulted or robbed. "One is totally at the customer's mercy at his place and he can do anything he wants to us," says a male prostitute working in Saddar (although "sexual deviance or sadism happens only rarely," he says).

Farrukh, who is eighteen years old, tall, and handsome enough to be a member of a pop group, operates from a famous shopping mall on Tariq Road. He prefers to "conduct business" in the backseats of his clients' cars rather than going to their houses, because "it's safer and quicker." If all goes well, he can take one customer an hour during his business hours between 6:00 and 9:30 P.M. After that, he is usually with a local policeman with whose "support" he has plied his trade for the last four years.

As a class-eight student fond of video games Farrukh frequented a shop in the neighborhood. Owner Shafiq 'Bhai' was always very friendly and gave him tokens on credit. Farrukh's debt rose to seventy rupees. "Our father was very strict and abusive and hardly gave five rupees a day as pocket money," Farrukh recalls. One day Shafiq Bhai took Farrukh to a bachelor friend's apartment. "Once we were there, he tried to pull off my pants. When I protested, he threatened to tell my father about the money I had borrowed from him.

So I submitted to Shafiq Bhai's demands. After he had had his way with me, Shafiq Bhai gave me a hundred-rupee note," he recalls. "The first experience was kind of weird and painful, but within less than half an hour I had earned a hundred rupees—twenty times my daily pocket money. After that I could play all the video games I wanted free of charge and I'd get bonus money from Shafiq Bhai and his bachelor friends in exchange for favors granted."

Farrukh's relationship with Shafiq Bhai did not last very long. The latter also kept several other boys for the same purpose. Once Farrukh was apprehended by a group of drunken policemen late at night. They beat him until he told them his name, address, and profession. "Then they took me to their quarters and gang-raped me. Following that they demanded that I 'work' for them or they would throw me behind bars and tell my father."

It was this fear of his father that turned Farrukh into a full-time prostitute. Now this son of an alcoholic contractor from Abyssinia Lines sports a gold chain around his neck, buys expensive gifts for his girlfriend—his own sexual preference—and owns a motorbike. On average he makes five-to-six hundred rupees for three to four hours' work an evening. Out of this, two hundred rupees go to the police as *bhatta* [a bribe]. Sometimes, he says, he works with the police to blackmail unsuspecting clients. Routinely, the policemen also present him as a "favor" to their homosexual seniors. Police officials also often smuggle boys into various jails across the country to service select inmates.

A large number of the full-time male prostitutes operating in Karachi are runaways. But there are also many part-time prostitutes—ranging from school-boys to salesmen to workers in hotels and garages—who prostitute themselves on the side for extra money, clothes, and gifts, or for other favors such as jobs, a role in a TV play or film. A restaurant owner told me that he could never forget the shock of catching a waiter having sex with a class-seven student who explained that he needed money for textbooks.

Male prostitutes in Pakistan usually range from fifteen to twenty-five years of age. A few are in their early thirties and some are as young as thirteen. Prostitution is a short career: generally the older you grow the less you are worth, although one successful pimp maintains that he has men in their early thirties working for him and earns at least six thousand rupees a month from them.

Like their clients, male prostitutes vary in ethnic origin, belonging to all the four provinces, as well as Afghanistan, Iran, and the Far East. Large numbers of Iranian and Afghan refugee youths entered prostitution in Quetta, Peshawar, and Karachi in the wake of upheavals in Iran and Afghanistan.

Some prostitutes are educated boys and young men—undergraduates and sometimes even graduates. Most, however, had little or no education. Prostitution earns them between five and seven thousand rupees a month. Those whose clients are foreign tourists and marines staying in five-star hotels manage to make a lot more. Many of the boys who prostitute themselves do so to supplement their families' earnings. Some even manage to save enough money to go abroad in search of a job.

The lowest stratum of prostitutes are those from poor families catering to men from similar low-income groups. These boys, in fact, function as "wives" of poor men who cannot afford to get married. Such men include waiters at fleabag hotels, semi-impotent elderly men, drug addicts, night watchmen, coolies, petty criminals such as pickpockets, and occasionally even beggars. A watchman from the northwest who often employs the services of male prostitutes explains: "My problem is simple. I can't afford a callgirl or a female prostitute. I can get boys for free, or for Rs. 15 to 20." Abdul, a cinema gatekeeper reveals, "All I have to do to get a boy is to let him into the cinema free of charge."

A Pathan male prostitute explains the cash distribution as follows: "My pimp charges about Rs. 150 from each of my clients for hardly half an hour of my time. Of this, Rs. 70 go into the hotel owner's pockets, 30 to the police in the area, and 30 to the pimp who pays me barely Rs. 20. I manage to earn between Rs. 200 and 250 a day only by taking on ten or more customers." Another boy explains that it is difficult to be independent because "pimps and the hotel owners harass us a great deal and the police are with them, so we don't dare mess with them."

Indeed, a lot of boys are frequently picked up by policemen who use them without payment. In Karachi and Hyderabad many pimps and male prostitutes act as informers for the police and the CIA. Extortion and blackmail by plainclothes police (or those pretending to be police) occurs in virtually every area where male prostitution exists. The pimps of male prostitutes are themselves mostly former male prostitutes, drug addicts, *malshis* (masseurs), some of whom also pimp for female prostitutes.

The busy Saddar area in Karachi is one of the city's key pickup points for male prostitutes. "At one time at least four hotels in Saddar used to serve as brothels for male prostitutes," one source recalls. Even now, every night, the sidewalks from United Bakery to Hotel Greenland in Saddar become a prostitution gallery. Many *malshis* operating on sidewalks or available on request through hotel staff are also often gay prostitutes. Empress Market and its surroundings are said to have been hot spots for the business even in pre-Partition days, "but it reached its present level of notoriety when people from upcountry started settling here," says an old Karachiite. "These migrants would have to live away from their wives for months, sometimes years, and found celibacy unbearable. Male prostitutes fill their need for a sexual outlet. In fact, many of the companions they choose are boys from their own area who have come to Karachi in search of jobs."

Adjacent to and underneath the overhead bridge in the Empress Market in Karachi is a thriving prostitution bazaar, teeming with male prostitutes and their clients from morning to late at night. "No boy, even if he's clearly straight, can stand around here without being propositioned," says a school-boy. "We are often stopped when we pass through here and harassed by all sorts of sleazy-looking characters." A number of school- and college-going boys are lured into the trade in this manner. "For just one or two sessions a week, I earn between Rs. 800 and 1,200 and sometimes even Rs. 1,500 a month," one reported.

Assaulting and then photographing boys in the nude is a common way of trapping them. Roshan, a sixteen-year-old boy from Larkana was kidnapped and sexually assaulted at gunpoint by a group of criminals a couple of years ago. The gangsters who raped him also took photographs of him in the nude. "They warned me not to squeal on them as they had my pictures," he says. "After that, they could have me whenever they wanted. They would some-times give me money and told me that I could even ask their friends for money in return for sexual favors."

Many male prostitutes have a history of being sexually abused at an early stage in their lives. In fact, every ninth or tenth boy in school or at local *madrassahs* or even at work, is sexually molested. He never reports this to his parents out of fear that they will blame him rather than the perpetrator, says a sociologist who worked with abused children.

Shahzada Kabir, twenty-three, is an unusual case. Scion of a nawab family of a former princely state and once a Petaro cadet, he left home after a prop-erty dispute with stepbrothers following his father's death a few years ago. He recalls spending many nights in public parks before entering the prostitution business. Today he charges two thousand rupees a night to foreign sailors and tourists, summers in the northern areas, and winters in Lahore or Karachi.

Male prostitutes of Shahzada Kabir's class are exceptional. Male prostitutes generally come from the lower-middle class. Many are forced into prostitu-tion because of poverty, although domestic compulsions also contribute to boys becoming prostitutes. One such case is that of Hamid, nineteen. His background is middle class, and he has a homosexual father. "My father ruined his business by squandering his money on a long line of male prosti-tutes, many of whom were closer to my age than to my father's, and who, subsequently, became my friends," recalls Hamid. "I had sexual relations with these friends of my father's and they would pay me for my services."

There is also another category of male prostitutes: second-generation ones.

The police recently unearthed a brothel of male prostitutes in a hotel near Larkana railway station. The brothel was being run by a police official. Young boys from the surrounding areas of Larkana and the interior of Sindh worked under pseudonyms, usually names of Pakistani and Indian film actresses. "Just as many gays in the U.S. wear rings in their ears, the trademark of the male prostitutes of Larkana is ornate henna patterns on their left palms," says one worldly-wise homosexual.

The world of male prostitutes and their clients is like a secret society with an entire underground culture since those involved cannot come out of the closet because of the social and religious barriers. Like "fallen women," homosexuals are condemned and ostracized.

Having run away from his home in the Punjab a couple of years ago because of the constant beating he was subjected to, sixteen-year-old Arshad says, "I smoke to attract clients, because the general perception is that if I can smoke despite my youth, I will be game for other vices as well."

Murad, a twenty-two-year-old male prostitute obsessed with becoming a TV actor, says, "I don't derive any sexual pleasure from my business. The charm is the easy money—which I spend on good food, good clothes—and in the fact that I can help my parents monetarily. I also spend the money I earn on cosmetics, cigarettes, an occasional drink or on visiting prostitutes on Napier Road and Siroghat in Hyderabad." The son of a peon in a government department, Murad was led into prostitution by repeated sexual abuse. His first sexual encounter with a man occurred when he was a thirteen-year-old student in grade seven. One day his teacher asked him to come to the house where he lived alone. "When I arrived he asked me to close the door and without further ado started to kiss me. He then stripped off my clothes, handed me a fifty-rupee note and, despite my protestations, assaulted me sexually," he says. It was not a one-off encounter. Murad was frequently invited back to his teacher's place. "I had begun to enjoy it: both the unfamiliar but pleasurable sensations and the money"—and rocketing from being last in the class to second due to the teacher's favoritism. "I was really happy as I took my report home, but my happiness was short-lived. Seeing my report, my brother immediately realized what was going on and beat me mercilessly." Murad confessed everything, which led to his parents pulling him out of school and apprenticing him at a motorcycle mechanic's workshop. "The motorcycle mechanic did the same thing to me as my teacher," he says. Nonetheless, Murad continued working there until he met and became sexually involved with a customer who "dressed really well: a heavy gold chain around his neck, jeans and leather jacket, riding a reconditioned Honda 175 bike. He looked like a film hero from an English film," Murad recalls. He told Murad: "You can also live the way I do if you follow my advice." Murad decided to accept the offer and his friend took him to Tariq Road where he bought him several pairs of trendy clothes and shoes. "The next evening he took me to a room in a posh hotel and introduced me to a trader. The trader gave my friend some big currency notes, after which my friend left." Murad received three hundred rupees from what his friend received.

Murad subsequently parted ways with his pimp and began to operate on his own. He says he is much in demand and has a well-off clientele, including foreign tourists. He has also introduced some boys from his area into the business and acts as their pimp. "The police leave me alone because I have good relations with some of their bosses in the city," he claims.

Murad maintains a dual life, since he is still living with his parents. "In my community I pretend to be straight, but I leave home every evening to conduct business."

Many full-time male prostitutes say they were thrown out of their homes when their parents learned about their source of income. "My brother caught me with one of my clients," says seventeen-year-old Shakil, a prostitute who operates from the PIDC-building area. "Then he had me thrown out of the house, despite my mother's protestations."

Others maintain that their families turn a blind eye to their profession because they are dependent on their income from the trade. At least ten male prostitutes hailing from poor families in southern Punjab and the North-West Frontier Province reveal that they supported their families, sending them monthly money orders.

Generally, families of male prostitutes are blissfully ignorant of their profession, because the boys take great care to avoid discovery. "We don't usually get caught, because we try to work far away from home and avoid telling our clients our real names or addresses," says Amjad who operates in Gulshan-e Iqbal.

In Pakistan bringing in boys arouses less attention than women. Thus, a group of bachelors sharing an apartment in a middle-class neighborhood bring boys to the apartment every weekend. Nobody has objected or even cottoned on. "Formerly, this apartment was rented out to a bachelor who would bring women over. The neighbors raised such a furor he was thrown out," relates Wasim, a member of the group. Now, two members of the group not only bring male prostitutes in from outside, but also have relations with some of the boys in the neighborhood.

Interviews with forty-nine male prostitutes and their clients in Karachi and Hyderabad ranging in age from fourteen to forty years and with diverse professional backgrounds (from a mullah to a university teacher, journalist, a TV producer, and even a peasant) reveal that very few of them take seriously the threat of AIDS or other sexually transmitted diseases. The general response of most of the educated ones was: "We don't care. Life and death are in the hands of God. AIDS is a problem of the West and that is why they are raising such a hue and cry about it."

Murad views AIDS as a disease of "foreign people. Two of my foreign customers use condoms, but I don't." As for his sexual practices, Murad maintains: "Many customers want me to do things to them that they have seen in porno films. But I do not oblige. After all, we are Muslims and Pakistanis."

Most prostitutes have never even heard of AIDS. One naively asked, "Have you ever heard of anyone dying of AIDS in Sindh or even in Pakistan?" Asked if they practice safe sex, the typical response was: "Are you joking?" Of the forty-nine homosexual prostitutes and their clients interviewed, only three said that they used condoms.

There is only one young man among Karachi's urban community who not only publicly confesses to being gay, but also works among groups of homosexuals and male prostitutes in the city, distributing condoms and literature on homosexuality and AIDS which he has had translated from English into Urdu. The effectiveness of one lone crusader against a tide of ignorance remains anybody's guess.

Notes

The real names of interviewees have been withheld by request. This and the previous chapter are slightly abridged and reordered versions of 1994 articles from *Newsline*, an English-language Pakistan newsmagazine, adapted with the authors' kind permission.

CHAPTER 20

Not-So-Gay Life in Pakistan in the 1980s and 1990s

Badruddin Khan

When I told a Pakistani friend who lives in Pakistan that I planned to write about gay life in Karachi, he was shocked, disbelieving, and very uncomfortable. As a gay man of Pakistani origin now living in Toronto (though I spend a month or more per year in my homeland), I could understand his discomfort. The subject is taboo. This fact also underlies my use of a pseudonym to allow this to be published.[1]

The *Spartacus* guide is not very encouraging on the subject of gay life in Pakistan or in Karachi, its largest city. Its outdated listings include big city Western-style hotels and words of caution. Indeed, a well-traveled and reasonably sophisticated gay traveler is likely to be approached for sex if he appears interested. Almost certainly, money will be involved, and the watchword is extreme caution.

The more interesting questions are: What is the nature of the "gay" experience in Pakistan? How do "gay" Pakistanis relate to their sexual orientation? What is the social context, if any, for companionship? Is there any coherent "political" context within which gays identify themselves, and is there a basis for a "gay" identity?

There is no "gay life" in Karachi, in the Western sense of the word: no bars, no newspapers, and few instances of lovers living together. Just as predictably, sex between men occurs often, and "friendships" develop that are just as committed and emotional as among gay lovers in New York. The deep differences, however, rise from tradition, history, the environment, and the culture and its expectations.

THE CITY OF KARACHI

Karachi is a large city of over eight million. As with the country, it is predominantly Muslim. Unlike other cities in Pakistan, however, it is extremely heterogeneous. At the airport, the immediate striking difference the visitor will observe in comparison to most other countries is the rich variety of dress. Ethnic groups include Sindhis, Punjabis, Pathans, and Baluchis, as well as the "Mohajir" group that collectively includes several additional ethnic groups. While it is nominally in the Sindh province, most of Karachi's residents are immigrants from other parts of the country and from India (before the partition that created Pakistan in 1947), and speak regional languages in addition to Urdu, the national language.

Regional traditions extend beyond language; among Pathans, for example, sex between men and boys is common and accepted as a necessary release in the absence of women. Sir Richard Burton, famed researcher of things sexual, references an ancient Pathan proverb in his introduction to the *Kama Sutra*, an ancient Hindu treatise that describes more than a hundred positions for lovemaking, and includes a discussion of the role of masseurs: "Women for breeding, boys for pleasure, but melons for sheer delight." Since before the days of Alexander the Great, the peoples of this region have been recognized as pragmatists who practiced war with ferocity and love with great dedication.

SOCIAL STRUCTURE

Pakistani society is based on very fundamentalist communal precepts, and the central institution is the biological family. The purpose of life, and its meaning, are rooted in loyalty to family, procreation, protecting the family's honor and stature, and caring for its children and property. While these values are common to most societies, in Pakistan they are the clear and unswerving raison d'être for life itself, and supersede individual desires and differences when there is conflict.

This results in lifestyles and social values that are not conducive to a gay identity. Children live with their parents until they get married. It is virtually unheard of for an unmarried son to live in the same city as his biological family and apart from it. Single men and women may live with their parents (even without economic need) through middle age and beyond. Even separate households function as social satellites, linked inexorably by biological bonds to the family center.

There is a very practical foundation to this focus on family. As with other traditional societies, it is "closed," and it is virtually impossible for a newcomer to enter economic or social life without an introduction. The family establishes one's station in life, which in turn sets boundaries for the aspirations of individuals. While these boundaries can be exceeded, social status is virtually impossible to change in just a generation or two and does not automatically follow material success. This "tribal" model requires that activities consonant with family-oriented goals be awarded the highest recognition.

The highest of these goals is clearly childbearing and rearing. Families devote themselves selflessly to caring for their young (and not so young), with a devotion that would be considered pathological in the West. Rather than temporary breeding grounds for children to grow up in before they move on to independence, families are like organisms that extend themselves by absorbing their young, and grow stronger or weaker based on the contributions of the new entrants. This is not just one model of life in Pakistan. It is not a choice: it is the *only* way of life. Individual love is recognized only in the context of this environment, and supported only if it furthers its development. This applies to marriages, which are usually arranged. Whether husband and wife get along with each other is far less important to to whether they breed well. If a husband takes care of his family's security needs and sires many children, what he does for personal sexual satisfaction is uninteresting to everyone involved, so long as he is discreet. It is certainly not discussed. It simply does not matter. It is quite irrelevant, and—so long as it is kept private—can be said to be "tolerated."

The "moral" issues of two men having sex do not arise in and of themselves as they do in the West. The "tolerance" of extramarital homosexual liaisons should not be taken to imply that there is ready, good-humored indulgence in this regard. To the contrary, homosexual behavior is derided in public discourse. Pragmatic accommodations to individual tastes must of necessity be worked out discreetly. From the standpoint of "family," it is less risky for men to have affairs with males than with females other than their wives. In most social situations, direct discussion of homosexuality is strictly discouraged. Homosexual behavior is proscribed in the *Qur'ān*; but infidelity with a woman may result in prescribed penalties that are far worse.

In this environment, homosexual sex is uninteresting since it neither creates children, nor adds the potential for children to the family's resource base (except to supplement the income of lower-class hustlers). In fact, sex in general is interesting primarily because of its impact on family, rather than its potential for individual pleasure or carnal fulfillment.

This interdependence between individuals and family is further exacerbated by the lack of widespread health insurance and social security benefits. The public health system is very poor, and private hospitals are expensive. While companies often pay for employee health coverage, the individual without a steady job and without family ties finds himself precariously alone. In Pakistan, family support is literally a matter of life and death.[2]

THE UN-GAY WAY

"Gay" implies a legitimation of a relationship that runs counter to family. Therefore gay life does not exist in Pakistan in general, or in Karachi in particular. From a practical standpoint, two lovers would find themselves without any social context. Unlike the fagbashing response to same-sex relationships in the West there is little such behavior here. There *is* no threat to family; it is, simply, irrelevant. At worst, there is ridicule, at best, willful blindness to the situation.

Two lovers from different social classes would have to explain their togetherness at every juncture. If from the same social class, they would have to invent a family-based "link" to justify their intimacy ("I know him because he went to school with my brother, and he needed a place to stay, so we are living together"). This might superficially appear to be the same as in the West; however, the closed and relatively immobile nature of society in Pakistan makes such simple solutions remarkably difficult to implement. Inevitably, the "cover" provided by the excuse would be blown, and the resulting embarrassment would "shame the family" and destroy the relationship.

Further, the lack of privacy in most living situations makes a personal relationship that is outside the norm impossible to maintain. In poorer households, space is shared. In wealthier families, servants provide a very effective monitoring system, making it impossible to maintain secrecy. Any secrecy that is crafted is so isolating that its maintenance corrodes the very relationship it was intended to protect.

Preventing "shame" or otherwise embarrassing the family is the most basic requirement for respectability. Respectability is the basic requirement for social acceptance and social acceptance is the oxygen without which life ceases to exist in any meaningful way. Therefore, the most enlightened Western-educated liberal-radical-gay liberationist finds himself immobilized on return to the Motherland. To agitate would be to bite the hand (family) that feeds him. To even attempt to launch a real revolution of gay liberation in Karachi is to tilt at windmills.

The most successful gay relationships in Karachi are quiet and heavily compromised. They are almost never the most important relationship for either partner; the family occupies that position. Deep affections do develop, though the long-term outcome is almost always a breakup, triggered by differences in family circumstances or demands. Human beings tend to develop emotional bonds, but in Pakistan these bonds either result in tragedy or in unacceptable (to a Westernized sensibility) compromises to steal private moments of tenderness or sexual release. To the gay Pakistani, this is simply another of life's compromises.

Meeting People

Pakistan is a male-dominated and very homosocial society. In Karachi, men congregate in parks, by the beach, on street corners. Contact is made in familiar ways: small talk, the determination of mutual interest, and the availability of privacy. During commute hours, most intersections are crowded with young men waiting for buses or open to an invitation.

A man drives by in a car and makes eye contact with another man on the lookout, standing separately from the crowd on a street corner. He gets in and is offered a ride. A quick pass and (if a private place is available) sex. There is no expectation of a relationship, though relationships between individuals based on continuing periodic sexual episodes are common.

Sexual Practices

Oral, anal, and manual sex occur. I have heard of no instance of sadomasochism or other physically brutal forms of lovemaking. Sexual activity is generally perceived as requiring tenderness, passion, good humor, and gracious permissiveness rather than harsh dominance.

In anal intercourse, the insertor tends to be older, the "man," while the insertee tends to be younger, or an available "queen" or masseur. In some encounters, kissing is unacceptable. In yet other encounters, a boy will willingly offer himself for anal penetration, but shyly refuse to allow the insertor to see or stimulate his genitals or to kiss him.

In some cases, the passive partner finds anal intercourse (acting as a "woman") more acceptable than fellating the man. (The derisive word *gandu* refers to the insertee in anal sex.) This is in part due to the special significance of rules of cleanliness that are part of the Muslim tradition; the genitals are "unclean," hence it would be improper to suck or swallow semen or ejaculate. However, this is not a general rule, and well-practiced fellators are readily available. Incidentally, such rules of cleanliness are practiced in relation to eating, as well as in routinely washing the anal area after defecation (rather than simply scraping the area with toilet paper, as in the Western method).

Availability of Sex

There are two classes of available men that bear special note. These are the *maalishis* (masseurs), and the *hijras.* Along many street corners, men sit and wait for customers to massage. Most customers are "legitimate," but it is commonly accepted that (for an additional fee) the masseurs will perform sexual services that include passive anal intercourse.

More interesting is the role of *hijras,* or hermaphrodites. This community consists of men who dress as women, including transvestites, castrati, and true hermaphrodites. It is a tradition in some communities to invite *hijras* to sing and dance at happy events, such as a wedding or the birth of a son. *Hijras* are also available as prostitutes, and it is well accepted that men (generally, unmarried men) may purchase their sexual services.[3]

Note that all sexual release is of the "pragmatic" variety, which assumes that the male (as a sexual animal) needs release before (or in addition to) marriage. Such needs are frowned upon, but accepted. What is totally unacceptable is for these outlets to act as a long-term substitute for the duty to bear children, or for a special feeling to develop between two men that precludes marriage and the bearing of children.

Love between men is, in fact, exalted, and tenderness, affection, and deep friendships are not uncommon. Unlike the macho backslap that passes for camaraderie in the West, men frequently hold hands while walking, and it is not uncommon to see men embracing. Poetry and popular song use the male gender as the object of affection. This is generally interpreted as a coy reference to women, but songs that talk of undying friendship between men are part of the repertoire of popular verse. There is a strong element of the Mediterranean pedagogical-Socratic love ideal that is seen as ennobling the soul. Men's affection for each other is generally seen as a good thing, and the fear that men in the West have of intimacy with one another is pointedly absent.

The high stature awarded to love between men is a continuation of a tradition that dates to the Mughal era and the traditions of Islamic mysticism (the Sufis). These traditions have been diluted with Hindu and (in the more recent past) Western influence in Pakistan. As mentioned earlier, notions of male bonding remain strong in most rural communities, including the fierce Pathan tribesmen.[4]

INDIVIDUAL ACCOMMODATIONS TO FAMILIAL DEMANDS

The bustling metropolis can be literally a "sex bazaar" for those seeking release. Local residents have found ways of accommodating family and love in pragmatic ways. The following reflect experiences reported to the author and are strictly anecdotal:

Case 1: Mohammad C. comes from a lower-middle-class family and lives in a modest apartment with his mother and two younger sisters in a high-rise near Karachi University. He went to the Middle East as a manual laborer when he was twenty-one, and saved up enough to buy a condominium, a car, and start a small business. Now thirty and financially stable, he is under pressure from his mother to get married soon.

He is fully aware of his attraction to men. He hangs around after work with friends to drink tea and talk, but after he leaves them to drive back home the young men waiting at bus stops and street corners inexorably draw his gaze. While his plans for a wife and family of his own are a source of immense satisfaction, it is these boys who arouse his flesh. Most often, this meant a quick trip to the loo to jerk off, stroke himself empty, and wash up. Somehow, this just doesn't satisfy. Recently, he had gotten into the habit of picking up Mumtaz, a student at nearby Islamia College. For a long time, Mumtaz was always at the roundabout near Karachi jail at 9 P.M., waiting for him.

One day Mumtaz was not there. However, his friend Ashraf—the one with the playful eyes, wide smile, and tight firm buns—was waiting for the bus. Mohammad pulled over:

He hopped in, and I think he knew I wasn't looking to give him just a ride. He said he was in no hurry. He lived on the other side of town near Malir, and everyone at home was going to be out. I was already hot, and when he reached down and stroked my hard cock, I just pushed the accelerator down all the way. There was nothing to talk about. He took me to his bedroom (which he shared with his brother) and we started embracing before he had locked the door. He wanted to be kissed and caressed and fucked, and he was not bashful about it. I stroked him, we embraced with much affection, on the bed, on the floor. I fucked him while he jerked off, and then we simply cuddled for a while. I reached home in time for bed. I went back after that to Mumtaz, my "regular," and never had sex with Ashraf again. I did, of course, occasionally pick up other boys for variety, but Mumtaz is so sweet, he never minds. We get along so well together.

Mohammad married his cousin the following year, and is now thirty-five with two children. He still picks up boys for sex, but, when asked whether he is homosexual, he is amused by the question. Yes, he says, he loves men. But he is not one for names and labels. He has a good relationship with his wife, but saves his love for his various lovers and occasional affairs. Mumtaz and he have broken up. No, he and his wife don't have recreational sex, but will start up again (unnatural though it is for him) when they are ready for a third child. He is happy with his life and the balance he has achieved.

Case 2: Tarik is gay. He has lived in London for several years and has had at least two major love affairs. He cheerfully calls himself a "slut," and grumbles that he had to come back to Karachi because his father (a wealthy industrialist) threatened to cut off his allowance since he had dropped out of school. Tarik is twenty-three and beautiful, with punk-cut wavy hair, a playful smile, and large sensuous eyes. His parents complain that he is irresponsible, he says, and they are right. He is gay, and he feels very trapped in Karachi. The only recreational sex available is with his family servants, whom he seduced shortly after his return. He has seduced a young Pathan boy who works in the garden and an older man who is the chauffeur. Both are quite willing to satisfy his needs (and he "tips" them generously for fucking him on a regular basis), but are concerned for their jobs. His parents sense that the servants are losing respect for him, and his decadence frightens them. He needs to get married!

He cannot really disagree with them, but is thoroughly frightened at the prospect. He has been to bed with two women, a disaster each time. While he was able to perform sexually on one of these instances, he finds satisfaction only with men. Then, he functions as insertee, and likes to, as he put it, "feel a man all the way inside me." Marriage to a woman is alien to his sensibilities and profoundly unnatural for him. He is trapped, though, and has little choice but to play along and hope for an exit. His mother is busy scouting around for eligible girls, and he is just as busy finding fault with every prospective candidate.

Case 3: Shah was visiting Karachi to see his family. He is a student in the Boston area, and a regular fixture at gay bars in Copley Square. In Karachi, he felt trapped. As he put it,

Being with my family was starting to get on my nerves, and the cute boys hanging around street corners and cruising me when I drove by gave me a perpetual erection. I took the family car for a spin. The roundabout near Clifton was almost empty. I cruised a guy standing on the road, and stopped to give him a lift. Our eyes met, and my spine tingled. He got into the car, and immediately put his hand on my leg, and then started stroking my crotch. No preliminaries, just a direct look and a soft stroke. The only question left was, where would we go? He had by now freed my swollen cock, which was erect in his hands. I was groping his crotch while trying to drive, at the same time trying to provide his hand cover by placing my jacket on my lap. We were both hot. We had no place to go the first time. . . . I really was poorly prepared! As I drove in circles, he bent over and started sucking me. . . . I was freaking out, but his soft lips and warm mouth were tantalizing. . . . I drove out to a remote area, and just drove in circles, literally, till I came! It was just too much, but what a memory! We met again, and this time we went to bed and had a proper session of affectionate lovemaking. He became my boyfriend for the rest of my visit, which passed very well indeed!

Case 4: Sex in public places, always a dangerous proposition, is sometimes necessary because of circumstances. Hamiduddin comes from a large lower-class family, and has no privacy at home. He really does not concern himself with feelings of guilt or a desire to understand his needs; he simply knows that he likes sex with men, and that the only feasible place to make contact is in public places. He has used friends' houses a couple of times, but generally has to accommodate his needs on the street. He reports that this is easy. Eye contact in public places at dusk, where men congregate just after the evening prayers, generally leads to readily available sex.

I was walking slowly in the park. It was getting dark. I was dressed in a well-ironed and loose *shalwar kameez* [loose pajama-like native dress] and the gentle sway of my hips was designed to coordinate with my open smile. I looked available! Occasionally, I would reach down and play with my genitals, as though scratching my balls. An older guy cruised me, then motioned me towards the bushes. I was horny. Why not!

As soon as we reached a dark spot near a clump of bushes, he silently stroked me, and I loosened my *shalwar*. For the next several minutes he gave me a slow and sweet blow job. Then he left, after we had exchanged a long and caring smile. He stroked my cheek gently with his hand and then disappeared.

In these situations, and others recounted to me, the notion of an exclusive relationship rarely came up. Though multiple sexual contacts with the same man may have been involved (rather than one-night stands) in some of the episodes related, the satisfaction did not extend beyond the sexual, despite desires that did.

Lesbians and Love

A lesbian orientation is in perfect harmony with family life, so long as the women are good mothers and wives. Rather, it is not in disharmony. To the extent that sex is an aspect of the relationship, it is a private matter. If a woman refuses to get married for whatever reason, she is effectively a pariah. If a married woman dallies with another woman, and if there is good reason for this personal interest other than sexuality (such as a family connection), there is again little problem. However, if she does anything to subvert her gender and social role, she risks retribution. As with a man, outward appearances count for a great deal.

At another level, however, lesbian love has always been incomprehensible. The notion of a woman preferring another woman to a suitable man is seen as absurd on the face of it. Sexual acts per se are not at issue; commitment to family is. There is little legal penalty: a woman can always be forcibly impregnated once married, and therefore her desires are of little concern. Two women asleep in an embrace causes no alarm: they are just friends. The thought that a woman could derive pleasure through sexual activity with another woman is interesting, but not particularly alarming. I know of no empirical way to verify the prevalence of lesbianism in Karachi, and have access only to limited anecdotal evidence.

Lesbian relationships continue to be heavily submerged, but one hears of a prominent teacher who lives with an ex-student . . . a woman who ran away from her husband to live with a "friend." In general, since women outside the context of family are viewed as being of little interest, such relationships do not cause hostility and often not even gossip. Gossip would damage the woman's marriage prospects and is therefore subdued. Anecdotes seem to involve older women, in part because they are presumably less concerned about such matters. This is in contrast to gay male anecdotes, which involve younger not yet married or "happily" married men, merely satisfying the imperatives of raging hormones.

PROGNOSIS

Karachi is a large and (by Pakistani standards) relatively Westernized city. If there is any "gay liberation" movement of any kind, its genesis will be in this urban center. Gay men who have lived abroad and returned to their families have already started to influence the rigid rules to some limited degree. In some instances, men have been bold enough to live away from their families. Some men have resisted marriage, or openly nurture quiet relationships with other men within the context of a marriage. These men can only come from families in upper-income brackets; their class of peers also includes men who have premarital sex with women, and men and women who have extramarital relationships. This upper crust operates as do upper classes everywhere, in a relatively "amoral" environment where personal desires are neither justified nor condemned by moral strictures.

The middle class, the great protector of public morality, continues to be frighteningly dominated by rules and restrictions, aided by interpretations of religion that are intended to provide the theoretical basis for shackles on behavior. The return to domination by religious doctrine (sometimes called "Islamic fundamentalism") spells trouble for freedom, and certainly limits the ability of men to be sexual. The police have been known to raid public places and scapegoat victims at random.

APPENDIX: SOME OTHER NATIVES' RESPONSES

After an earlier version of this chapter was published, I received (through the intermediacy of my editor) some comments by fellow Karachi-natives. The more extended and analytical ones reproduced below both seem to me to substantiate parts of my analysis, though conflicting with each other along predictable grounds (literally the ground where each lives). Predictably, neither wanted his name published.

From Ali H____ in London:

My family is originally from Karachi, we are settled in London, and I have traveled to Pakistan and to India, notably Bombay. There is gay life in Bombay. In Karachi, none!

I must say that I did not spend much time in Karachi, and most of the time was with family. Throughout my stay, I was horny as hell. There was no sex for a week, and when I went to Bombay, it was so open! There are magazines, and organizations, and clubs. People drink and socialize, and going to bed is so natural. Karachi is so closed by comparison. Alcohol is banned, and so people are inhibited and uptight.

One day I got so desperate that I walked the streets for almost three hours looking for someone. I do not speak Urdu very well anymore, but I met a handsome student. However, we did not get anywhere sexually, though I tried my best! I had to go home and jerk off, hardly very satisfying.

Pakistan is very conservative, and I think Muslim fundamentalism is on the rise. People are afraid. I have heard of extortion, and I did not want to try too hard. I was afraid of going out a lot of the time, because of reports of violence in the press. Sometimes I could hear gunfire in the distance, too.

I was happy to see the article. It is about time someone from a Muslim country like Pakistan spoke up! I would like to find more articles about gay life in Pakistan and other Muslim countries. Muslim gays are very closed with each other, but if we are going to start a movement or change things, it will have to be outside the country. Badruddin is right about that: nobody inside Pakistan can do anything about it because of family pressure. You cannot be free and open, you cannot be yourself. This has to change, and voices like his must be heard.

I cannot give you my real name, since I hope to go back to visit.

And from Mohammad Z_____ in Karachi itself:

Badruddin Khan's article about Karachi is interesting, but I beg to differ on some points. I currently live in Karachi, and I have sex almost every day. There is no shortage of men available for sex!

It is usually possible to go to a crowded place and pick up someone. Usually one look is enough. The other approach is to get close to someone, then "accidentally" touch their cock. Since it is so hot usually, most men do not wear underwear, and their dicks hang freely. I have even sometimes grabbed a cock at night in the dark, while standing in line waiting for the bus! Because it is so congested, this is usually not easy to see. If you pick a young guy who is obviously horny, there is never any problem. On a bus ride, it is nice to spend the time stroking cock. Once a guy was wearing a *langoti,* which can be opened from the front, and I was able to hold his cock and make him cum in my hands with people all round. His body was touching mine, and I could hear his breath in my ear. I saw his face, and the blissful look in his eyes, only when he got off the bus.

I love living here. I do not miss not being able to spend the night with a man. I am sexually satisfied, and, if we need privacy, we can always find a spot in a park at night. The emotional contact is very intense, and I have even been fucked by a man on the beach at Clifton at night. Even if you are caught in the act, people will rarely cause problems, and you can always walk away. The only big problem with anal sex this way is cleaning up afterwards.

I do not like the gay scene in the West. People are so artificial. Sex is sex, and it should not be confused with anything else. I live happily with my mother and brother, and have sex anytime I want. I usually go far away from my house. There is a saying: "You should not shit where you eat," and I think it is possible to have a happy home life but also plenty of sex. I am still only twenty-two, and I will marry before thirty. Until then, I expect to have many men, as many as I can. I saw a sign: "So many men, so little time!" I think this applies to me in Karachi. There is also so much variety. . . . I personally prefer Pathans, they are well built and usually without families. I spent one night with a Pathan on his cot near the construction site where he was working, and he was inside me most of the night. I have so many good memories, I should write a book!

Of course, a book about homosexual adventures could not be published in Pakistan today. The disjunction between ignoring what isn't publicly stated and virulently rejecting public "advocacy" are central to my analysis of Pakistan. I would also note that Mohammad is aware of other ways of living homosexuality, even if he says he prefers the way he knows best (very brief, anonymous encounters).

POSTSCRIPT: NOT-SO-GAY LIFE IN PAKISTAN IN THE 1990S

On my most recent extended visits to Karachi I was both saddened and encouraged by the changes I saw. My good friend Stephen Murray encouraged me to write a sequel to my article, to update readers and to deal with some issues I did not discuss in what I wrote in 1990.[5]

Obviously, Pakistan is not immune to the changes wrought in the nineties, where fax machines shape political events, and the internet enables people far away to remain in close contact. The country is inexorably being pulled along toward modern technology by a professional class, which remains a thin veneer over what is otherwise still fundamentally a feudal society. The ordered innocence of the past has dissipated. An ugly underside has developed, and people live in constant fear of political murders, kidnappings, and shootings, although in the midst of what seems to have become chronic low-grade civil war, they continue the traditions of the region. Pakistanis' urge to reach out and express affection, physical tenderness, and sexual love, continues unabated. Youthful loins are no less insistent because of endemic violence, and the birthrate continues to be high. While the ancient rituals of lovemaking that have given this region its reputation for romance and ritual may have succumbed to modern life, basic needs must still be attended to.

In this sequel I will touch upon the increasing terrors of Karachi, and I will also discuss gay life in cities other than Karachi, in particular areas of the Punjab province. What I write is not intended to be academic or pedantic. In my view, experience and experiment uncorrupted by analytic rubric can sometimes bring a broader cross section of readers closer to the action. I leave it to the theoreticians to ponder the meaning of it all. There is learning in experience, and to this I devote my energies.

Two memories stand out from this most recent visit to my homeland.

The first is that of a beautiful Pathan boy, perhaps twenty-one, standing at the side of the road while I was stopped at a traffic light on the way to the airport to leave, at the conclusion of my trip. It was a dark night, he was alone. I looked toward him with intensity. Our eyes locked, and his hard and blank gaze softened as he saw the frank desire in my eyes. His tight face relaxed into a smile. His right hand reached under his *kameez* and he started stroking himself slowly, all the while retaining eye contact with me. I looked away from his eyes toward his playful hands, then at his face. We both smiled at the same instant. For that moment, the not-to-be-consummated agenda was clear. His look embodied simple desire and deep longing. It was simple, straightforward, uncomplicated. Had I been accessible, had it been possible, I could have approached him, and we would have gone off together. I would have had his virginal body in my altogether lecherous clasp, and his youthful face would have been wet with my kisses. As it was, the light changed, the car started moving, and his face blurred into the crowd, just a memory of my homeland. My erection, disciplined by the weight of a twenty-pound carry-on bag, eventually withered into submission.

The second memory followed my return to Toronto. I picked up the local gay rag and read that students at a prominent school in Lahore had been harassing a student they had labeled "fag," and had threatened him with death. He had dropped out and gone into seclusion, to his family's protection. For him, there would be no return—ever—to school. He was banished from his community, excommunicated. Why? Had he refused favors to someone? Had he been caught being buggered in the toilets (a common pastime)? Why was this now being blown out of all proportion—with the poor chap as example?

I recalled incidents of death threats, and actual executions, of Iranian gay students who had gone back to Iran to visit family. In some instances, government spies in the United States had alerted the authorities, and people had been taken directly from the airport to jail, and been shot after being raped and sexually tortured. The fundamentalist trend is alive and thriving in the region, and Pakistan, long a bastion of relative freedom, seems to be the next frontier. There is little that is rational or defensible in this behavior, since Islam is by its very nature a very liberal religion in sexual matters, compared to Christianity and Judaism. The element of danger, however, is very real, and lurks everywhere. Pakistanis and Muslims abroad would be well advised to avoid making too big a show of "coming out." They could well be writing their death sentences, on some future return to their homeland. I do not mean to overstate the case, but at the same time it should not be understated. Sexual tolerance is at risk in previously tolerant countries like Pakistan, and natives abroad should beware.

CHANGES TO THE CITYSCAPE

Karachi is dirtier, more crowded, and more polluted than ever before. There are people everywhere, and most are still men. Some of them still congregate at bus stops, on street corners, or await a pickup by distancing themselves distinctively from the crowds. Men looking for men for love . . . an old story, and one that continues to be played out.

However, Karachi is in the midst of general lawlessness. As such, there is considerably less public expressiveness in same-sex relationships, and the meat-market action in the streets is more subdued than it was in the late 1980s. The main consequence is considerably less freedom for the visitor, whether Pakistani or foreigner, and the need for greater caution.

Ali's Dilemma

Ali told me that one evening he picked up a young man who was obviously waiting for action. As usual, the discourse was direct: the man got into his car, looked into his eyes and, as he drove off put his hand on Ali's crotch. "My name is Masood," he said, as he gently stroked Ali to erection, cupped his balls in his hand, and caressed his hard shaft with a tender grip. Ali's family was away that evening, nobody was home, so he told Masood to go slow, he had a place to go. "I will come if you continue like this," he whispered, his legs open wider while his feet alternated between brake and accelerator and his thighs squirmed under Masood's caressing fingertips.

Without turning the lights on, the two started to make love almost as soon as the door of the apartment was locked behind them. Masood had a very large penis, Ali told me, and it was hard. His legs, his thighs, and his peach-shaped ass were well muscled and responsive. His legs opened wide without much coaxing, and his buttocks seemed to relax in surrender as Ali caressed his inner thigh. Under his *shalwar*, which Ali quickly removed, his anus was relaxed and seemed to be pulsating in anticipation. Ali entered him slowly, taking care to put on a condom. Impaled, Masood quickly reversed roles. Mounting Ali, he sat on him, rhythmically coordinated his thrusts, holding back when he thought Ali was about to come. His hands caressed Ali's face. His large penis was erect, slapping against Ali's belly with each thrust. Masood was driving Ali into himself with passion. Twice he brought Ali to the point of ejaculation, twice he held Ali's cock tight and firm inside his ass till Ali's desire subdued. Held prisoner by Masood's vice-like ass, Ali was driven wild with desire, sweating, gasping, until finally Ali subdued Masood on the floor and got back on top of him. Almost instantly, he shot his load and Masood expertly squeezed every drop from his shaft with his ass-muscles. As Ali removed his sensitive and spent penis from Masood's warm enclosure, he saw Masood remove the condom carelessly, so that the warm semen dripped out onto their clothes. No matter, thought Ali, kissing Masood's neck and grasping his large penis, preparing to work on him so that he could come in turn. He was somewhat surprised to find that the hard appendage that had beat a fierce rhythm on his sweaty belly just moments before was now limp. The scrotum which moments before had been taut and tight between Ali's legs was now hanging low. Ali started to play gently with Masood's large testicles. The racehorse had hung his head for the moment, but Ali had both the skill, and a commitment to a tradition of reciprocity, to coax it up again, to do its wild thing. Besides, he wanted to admire Masood's organ. It was arguably one of the most beautiful he had seen for quite a while, and he wanted to feel it surge again.

Suddenly Masood jumped to his feet, and demanded money. Ali was shocked. He mildly offered him a few rupees. Nothing had been negotiated, and in the etiquette of the streets, this meant a *gratis* fuck. Ali was puzzled, and Masood wasted no time in defining the agenda:

"I want a thousand rupees, or I will tell everyone that you raped me," he said. "Give me the money now." His big flaccid penis swayed incongruously inviting beneath his pale and lightly haired belly. But there was no ambiguity in either his look or his voice. It was harsh, and he meant business. The musky smell of Ali's copious load of semen rose accusingly from his clothes.

"I will tell them that you brought me here and then took advantage of me. I am not going to put on my *shalwar.* I will go naked to your neighbors. I will run in the streets and let then examine my ass, to see that it has been fucked. I will bring them here. I will let them smell my clothes. I will bend over and show them my ass. It is still wide open. Then, I will point at you as my attacker. Give me the money now!"

Ali had only five hundred rupees, and he was thankful that Masood accepted this, put on his clothes, and ran away. For a long time after this incident, Ali refrained from picking up other men. This experience had traumatized him. He had no doubt that Masood had meant to carry out his threat. As he shared this episode with friends, he found that others had had similar experiences with recent pickups . . . the playful innocence of pleasure sullied by the desire for monetary gain . . . and the realization that the new environment had changed the power balance. This is one effect of the wave of regressive ideology that is sweeping the country.

Most writing about homosexuality in Muslim societies during the last few decades has been from the perspective of non-Muslim (generally white American or European) sex tourists or guest workers seeking sex with the locals during their stay. Steve Murray characterized the genre as "'He fucked me, so why wouldn't he kiss me?' plaints." I criticized the collection of such pieces of perplexed petulance edited by Schmitt and Sofer (1992) for ignoring class differences and for extrapolating intracultural conduct from foreigners' sexual experiences (Khan 1992).[6] An argument might be made that Ali's encounter with Masood exemplifies a similar (albeit entirely indigenous) confusion of romance (the upper class having its way while believing those they fuck are enjoying it as much as they are) with economic transactions (the poor renting their bodies).

While caution about assuming the social equality of sexual "partners" is in order, I reject the interpretation that Masood's interest in money precluded sexual desire on his part. Masood's erection was not necessary for Ali to penetrate him. The sight of Masood's erection slapping against his stomach enhanced Ali's pleasure, but it exceeded the complaisance required for the role. An erection cannot be faked. That is, Masood was turned on. Moreover, by squatting on Ali, Masood took a very active part in being penetrated, and gave every indication of enjoying it (including pre-cum, which also is not voluntarily controlled). And Masood gave much more pleasure than was necessary for threatening to reveal that Ali had "raped" him. Presumably, Masood could have lubricated himself and supplied his own semen to smear on his fundament. He certainly did not need to hold Ali's ejaculation back and build on it several times!

Ali and I both think that Masood would not have demanded money had he thought that Ali could not pay it, and note that Masood readily contented himself with what Ali had, half the amount he demanded. Consensual sex acts between men continue to take place routinely in Pakistan, without expectation of payment. I relate this story in some detail to show the degree of desperation to which some have been driven. As in many other places of endemic violence (not least U.S. cities), various kinds of shakedowns occur. Nonetheless, the quest for money and sexual desire are not mutually exclusive, even for those who say they are only having sex with men for the money they get.[7]

ISLAMIC PURITANISM AND GAY SEX

Islam is fundamentally sex-positive for men. Men are permitted up to four wives at any one time and concubines in addition under certain circumstances, such as when traveling away from home for extended periods. Sex between men is disapproved of and prohibited. Since neither activity results in children, the central role of family is unaffected. Islam is a wonderfully practical religion: divorce is permitted, women own their property free and clear irrespective of whether they are married. The stewardship of children is clearly spelled out in the event of separation or divorce. Under a certain age, the mother has all child custody rights. After that age, the child "belongs" to the father, as is to be expected in a patriarchal society. Sex *per se* is not considered to be undesirable, nor is denial of pleasure seen as a shortcut to heaven. In Arab societies, for instance, mothers routinely pacify their male children by playing with their genitals. . . .

Of course, AIDS has now entered the equation. AIDS is perceived by some as a Western disease, another symbol of the consequences of decadence. At the same time, as the social order has crumbled, a new and materialistic harshness has replaced the gentility and civility that accompanied the old order that was so pleasurable for upper-class men. Isn't this just retribution for economic oppression? If opportunists can make a buck by placing a tariff on the universal pleasure afforded by sex, and if the partner can afford it, what of it?

The problem, however, goes well beyond the economics of the deal. Placing a price on lovemaking transforms it into an economic transaction, and removes all semblance of play or tenderness. It is uncharacteristic of the Pakistani spirit to maximize returns by threatening exposure after intimacy. The same threat a decade ago would have been laughed off. But today, with the mullahs increasingly in charge, it must be taken seriously. It is just as likely for a lynch mob to dispense justice first and then ask whether the punishment fit the crime, or whether there was a crime committed at all. One can only hope that this is a temporary situation.

OTHER CITIES

Karachi is a cosmopolitan and multi-ethnic immigrant city made up of individual communities that share commercial and social interests. Other parts of the country, however, are far more homogeneous, with little in-migration. This homogeneity creates deep cultural roots that are widely shared, and a good-humored approach to sex. The inhabitants are simpler, with a direct approach that is sometimes veiled in cosmopolitan Karachi. However, outside Karachi it is far more difficult to get lost and become invisible, so picking up men or boys is a socially more dangerous activity. Gossip spreads and is impossible to reverse.

Lahore is the city of the fabled Anarkali bazaar, with its ancient walkways and crafty merchants. Behind the stalls are alleys and homes, and quiet shaded nooks that have undoubtedly seen their share of passion and lovemaking. Punjabis are generally tall, well built, good-humored, and very sensuous. They are hearty and good-humored, and have a reputation for passion and romance. They are *dil wale* (people with heart). Fundamentally agrarian, Lahoris know that hard work and pleasure both have a role in life.

The *hira munde* (literally, the market of jewels) is a famous red-light district in Lahore. It reportedly was already functioning when Alexander the Great marched through the Khyber Pass and down through Lahore. Nearby is the busy Mall Road, with its street corners and men idling nearby, scratching their genitals in anticipation of company.

Usman's parents live in Islamabad, but his uncle is in Lahore. He comes down from time to time. The *aya*'s son, Abdul, has taken a special fondness for him. This time, he has a private room and invites him in. The boy is barely nineteen, fresh from the fertile plains of Punjab, literally "the land of five waters."[8] The boy is naive, but quickly succumbs to the urgency of Usman's erection. Fucked once, he lost his inhibitions. Fucked twice, he lost his heart.

Abdul waited for Usman's every visit. With each visit, his longing grew. Between visits, he pined in silence. He could speak to no one about his feelings. He was not interested in finding some partner other than the man who had deflowered him. He wanted to live with Usman. "Take me as your servant," Abdul said. "Let me sleep on the floor by your bed. I am yours. Let me be with you forever." Usman laughed off this infatuation. This rural boy was so emotional! Usman was now growing up to become a young sophisticate, and to him the boy was simply a steady Lahore sex-toy. The boy lost weight. Alarmed, his mother got him married to a good girl from their village, a *deyhati,* a simple village girl. He joined the army, to escape. Usman lost track of him. Then he heard that the boy had left his wife and run away from the army. He had contacted his mother, and asked about Usman. Usman had no doubt that he wanted to see him again. Was this love? If not, what else?

In contrast to this tragic tale of what was play for Usman being grand passion to Abdul, the following incident demonstrates the healthy interest of Lahoris in matters sexual. I was walking along the canal bank, near the G.O.R. (Government Officers' Residences, an elegant area). It was a hot, dry day, and the canal was filled with water after a good rainy season. Boys were splashing in it, dashing out from behind verdant and colorful shrubbery to land, screaming, with a splash.

As I rounded a turn, I saw two boys standing about a foot apart, one a little higher on the bank than the other. They were both village boys, out for a swim. Their hair glistened wet in the sun, their warm brown skin and rippling wet muscles dripping water. The one standing on higher ground was older. They both had just shorts on. The older boy's shorts were wet, and he had the clear beginnings of an erection. It was a very large erection. I stopped to watch. The younger boy reached out, touched the wet cloth covering the older boy's penis, and giggled while he stroked it. I watched him hold it in his hand, gently, while the older boy's washboard belly contracted in pleasure, his chest heaving slightly. The younger boy looked up, and I could see their eyes meet. Their interchange was charged with sexual intensity, and I could observe the older boy's penis rise as the younger one held it, gently stroking. His own young organ, flaccid just moments before, was already hard under his skimpy shorts. I was just a few feet away behind a bush, watching this foreplay with increasing discomfiture.

Then, suddenly, there was a noise behind me. They looked in my direction and saw me. A look of panic mixed with guilt shadowed each of their faces. The older boy quickly turned away, covering his erection. They jumped into the canal and furiously swam away. I had interrupted some innocent lovemaking. While I yearned to be part of it, they clearly saw me as someone from a different class, someone to fear.

Fearful of what? This is where class distinctions play a part. Were I so inclined, I could have grabbed the boys by their ears, and marched them off, loudly proclaiming in good middle-class moralistic fashion that they had been playing with each other. Then they would have been punished by their parents, shamed in their circle, humiliated merely for being caught doing what most of their accusers had done themselves—and something I would have happily participated in, if invited. Social distance did not permit this, however.

THE FUTURE OF GAY LIFE IN PAKISTAN

As I mentioned in my earlier article, and above, there is no such thing as being "gay" in Pakistan. Men have sex with each other because of the need for human sexual contact, and in some cases this desire is fully satisfied only by men. Some brave souls declare their freedom from the tyranny of the majority ethic of traditional family and are consequently marginalized. In general, fully developed gay relationships are best seen in the highest and the lowest classes. The mass middle class is too deeply steeped in a false moralism. With the onset of violence and religious fundamentalism, the innocent search for sex in public places, a long-honored tradition, has become risky. Prostitution and blackmail have become more commonplace.

The bottom line is that there is now more overhead attached to the search, and more caution is required to avoid an unpleasant outcome like—or worse than—Ali's dalliance with Masood. This is unfortunate indeed. There is no question that rampant consensual sex continues, but it is now more discreetly presented, less flagrantly advertised. The notion of gay liberation, openly discussed in neighboring India, is a very distant possibility.

There is some reason to hope that, as the world draws closer in the coming decades, gay life in Karachi may yet develop in the inhospitable soil there. The long tradition of peaceful coexistence and generous and ample sexual expression that is typical of the region needs to be uncorked. I am optimistic that if the country can survive its current crisis, it will emerge a freer and more sympathetic nation, with wonderful and naturally lovable people.

Notes

1. My special thanks to Dr. Stephen Murray for making this possible, for publishing an earlier version of this chapter in *Society of Lesbian and Gay Anthropologists' Newsletter* 12, 1 (1990):10–19, for serving as a conduit for responses from readers, including the two reproduced here, and for patient editorial suggestions on all my writing. Rather than update my previous observations, which I think are accurate for an earlier time, I have appended criticisms from two fellow "natives" and added a separate update dealing with the increasing dangers of the Karachi streets.
2. See Murray for some comparative instances (1987:118–28; 1992; 1995:33–48).
3. See Nanda 1990 on this role in India.
4. This is the same ethnic group that is settled in Afghanistan and has fought off invaders for generations, including, more recently, the Russian invaders. Alexander the Great was unable to conquer them; so he married a tribeswoman to gain safe passage to the rich lands beyond.
5. I added what little I can say about lesbians above. I would again like to thank Stephen Murray for his ongoing encouragement and his questions that have helped me to clarify my thoughts and my writing.
6. Also see Manalansan 1991 and Murray 1991, 1996 for similar criticisms of extrapolations from sex tourism in other cultures.
7. I do not know that Masood would have contended this had I had the opportunity to elicit his version.
8. In the Punjabi language, *punj* is the number five, and *ab* means water, to refer to the five great tributary rivers to the great river Indus that meander through this province.

References

Khan, Badruddin. 1992. Review of *Sexuality and eroticism among males in Moslem societies. Society of Lesbian and Gay Anthropologists' Newsletter* 14(2):26–27.

Manalansan, Martin F. 1991. "Neo-colonial desire." *Society of Lesbian and Gay Anthropologists' Newsletter* 13,3:37–40.

Murray, Stephen O. 1987. *Male homosexuality in Central and South America*. New York: Gay Academic Union.

———. 1991. "Sleeping with natives as a source of data." *Society of Lesbian and Gay Anthropologists' Newsletter* 13:49–51.

———. 1992. "The 'underdevelopment' of 'gay' homosexuality in Mesoamerica, Peru, and Thailand." In *Modern homosexualities*, ed. Ken Plummer, 29–38. London: Routledge.

————. 1995. *Latin American male homosexualities*. Albuquerque: University of New Mexico Press.

————. 1996. "Male homosexuality in Guatemala: Possible insights and certain confusions from sleeping with natives." In *Lesbian and gay fieldwork*, ed. E. Lewin and W. Leap, 236–60. Urbana: University of Illinois Press.

Nanda, Serena. 1990. *Neither man nor woman: The hijras of India*. Belmont, CA: Wadsworth.

Schimmel, Annemarie. 1982. *Islam in India and Pakistan*. Leiden: Brill.

Schmitt, Arno and Jehoeda Sofer. 1992. *Sexuality and eroticism among males in Moslem societies*. Binghamton, NY: Harrington Park Press.

CHAPTER 21

Two Islamic AIDS Education Organizations

Stephen O. Murray and Eric Allyn

PINK TRIANGLE IN MALAYSIA

"There is no gay organization in Malaysia," Kit, Andrew, and Hong, the three Malaysian delegates to the Third Asian Gay and Lesbian Conference (held in Bangkok in August 1990) stressed. Pink Triangle, which Hong officially represented, is a registered AIDS-prevention and counseling organization "which happens to be made up of mostly gay people." Founded in 1987 by gay men in the capital city of Kuala Lumpur to provide AIDS-prevention information to gay men, it delivers safe sex information in fifteen Indian, Malay, and Chinese languages. Kit explained that the group has become known by the government as a "gay" group, despite its silence about its members' sexuality. With no official connection, the government provides some assistance. The group has been influential in altering objectionable material issued by the Ministry of Public Health. An early MPH booklet advised people to avoid homosexual sex (Malaysian Health Ministry 1988). "We convinced them to say instead, 'Avoid unsafe sex.' This took knocking on doors and talking with people, not writing letters," Kit said.

In addition to cautious support from the MPH, Pink Triangle has gained mass media attention for its work, and has been invited to make AIDS-prevention presentations at factories and schools. Funds from international agencies further legitimized the group. Janitex Condoms became the group's first commercial supporter, donating funds and condoms to the group. Kit noted that the group ran ads in mainstream publications as an "AIDS-information hotline," later changing the wording to "AIDS and sexual identity counseling."

According to Hong, it is illegal to "promote" homosexuality. Pink Triangle has been careful not to be publicly identified as a gay group. Licensing requirements for any publication that contains "news" has inhibited the formation of a gay press. Pink Triangle did, for a while, publish an in-house newsletter called *Pink news,* but now only issues an AIDS-education flyer called *Pink page.* It is also illegal to engage in "negligent sexual contacts that endanger the life of another."

Homosexual acts are illegal in Malaysia and under Islamic law, punishable by as much as twenty years' imprisonment, but according to Kit and Andrew the laws are not usually enforced.[1] Although homosexuality is generally not discussed, they say the government is quite relaxed about it. Though Malaysia is Islamic, they said, it is tempered by a venerable Malay cultural tolerance of private conduct.

Gay life has a low profile. There is only one gay bar in Kuala Lumpur, for instance. Friendship networks, cruising in parks and shopping centers, and discreet advertising for "male friends" in mainstream publications are common ways to meet each other.

Brettle notes the difficulty of interviewing at-risk populations "without fear of their arrest and detention" (1992:101). As Osteria and Sullivan put it, "It is difficult to identify members of high risk groups for HIV infection, and culturally inconsistent to be explicit in describing sexual behavior which exposes people to infection" (1991:134). They add,

Almost all of the responsibility for implementation of education programs is delegated to public health authorities at the state level, but the federal Ministry of Health Education Unit produced printed materials and advertising for distribution by the state authorities and arranged for the broadcast over national television networks of AIDS-education advertisements. Recently, the government has encouraged the establishment of non-governmental organizations to provide information to the public, especially high-risk groups, on the prevention and control of AIDS.

They mentioned Pink Triangle, as well as the Malaysian Medical Association. In Malaysia, as elsewhere in the world, some pragmatism and concern about reducing the costs of AIDS has led to slightly more open recognition of homosexuality than earlier.

THE NAZ PROJECT

Naz Project founder and chief executive Shivananda Khan wrote the following to an Imam to explain what he considers its (pragmatic but nonetheless orthodox) relationship to Islam:

The Naz Project is an HIV/AIDS and Sexual Health service for South Asian, Turkish, Arab and Irani communities with service agencies based in London and New Delhi. We are not a religiously based service. Our services and users of the service have a wide range of religious background . . . [and] different countries of origin, including India, Pakistan, Bangladesh, Sri Lanka, Middle-Eastern countries, North African countries such as Morocco, as well as Turkey and Iran. We provide HIV/AIDS awareness for our communities, provide confidential advice on prevention of HIV transmission to individuals, and also provide support for people from our communities living with HIV/ AIDS. . . . In our development since October 1991, we have not been able to find any specific religious advice on HIV/AIDS, whether Islamic, Hindu, Sikh, or Buddhist. Since none of these faiths have a centralized authoritative structure, what we have found have been different statements, not only from religion to religion, but also within specific faiths. For example, in the context of Islam, Imams from Indonesia and Malaysia have been saying different things from Imams in Iran, Saudi Arabia and Morocco. . . .

Most religious faiths, including Islam, vigorously condemn certain behaviors such as illegal drug use, premarital sex, homosexual behaviors, and so on. Such condemnations, however, historically have not completely stopped such behaviors which are most often carried out secretly and are invisible to the community from which these people come. In our cultures, however, we have clear distinctions between what is deemed public and what is deemed private. Very often, we have found that while public statements are made claiming that such behaviors do not exist within our communities, private practice does exist.

This leaves us with a dilemma. We can condemn behaviors that are not acceptable within specific religious faiths, and threaten such people with dire punishments. . . . Such an approach has been found to drive such behaviors even further underground and actually increases the risk of HIV infection spreading in our communities. We can provide accurate information to people who practice risky behaviors and leave the decision to them as to what they do. Or we can do nothing at all.

As a non-religious agency, we have chosen to provide practical information to people on a confidential basis, and ask the religious institutions to provide the moral approach. We have found that otherwise people will not come forward to ask questions about themselves. . . .

What we at Naz have had to do is understand the difference between religious practice and private practices.[2] Religious practice tends to be a public statement of one's faith, while sometimes a specific private practice may well be invisible, hidden, which can be publicly denied. . . .

I believe [that] for Islamic institutions, because of what the *Qur'ān,* the Hadith and the Sharia state, the Islamic response would be two-fold:

First, in regard to Muslim people living with AIDS, it is my understanding that the teaching of the Prophet was that when a person is ill in the community, it is the responsibility of that community to care for her or him. This is a religious duty. However, we have found many in the Muslim communities, including Imams (as well as those from other faiths) who do not accept this principle, and have rejected the person living with AIDS. Publicly humiliated them. Shamed them. And in the final statement refused to bury them as Muslims.

The second issue is much more difficult: the issue of HIV transmission. . . . Both [intravenous drug use and unprotected sexual intercourse] involve behaviors that are deemed by Islam to be sinful and punishable. They can be condemned, but can they be eradicated? . . . Religious institutions can increase the sense of condemnation, but this has not stopped behaviors. And, since in our cultures the majority of people who practice these behaviors are married, other people in our communities become at risk. . . . We at the Naz Project firmly believe that it is our responsibility to protect people's lives, to prevent the infection spreading even more in our communities. That is why we approach the issues in the way we do. (1995:3,20, reproduced with the author's permission; spelling and punctuation have been Americanized)

In the scanty literature on AIDS in Islamic countries,[3] the main theme is that the disease is exogenous and limited to those exposed directly or indirectly (via transfusions of blood purchased in foreign countries). Prostitution is mentioned, but male-male sex is not. Some gay-identified Muslims are nonetheless taking initiatives to help others protect themselves from HIV infection and to enhance the quality of services available to those living with AIDS. This last includes appealing to Islamic traditions as Khan does in his letter above.

Notes

An earlier version by Eric Allyn of the first part of this chapter appeared in the *Society of Lesbian and Gay Anthropologists' Newsletter* 13, 3 (October 1991): 52–53, © Bua Luang, 1990. Stephen Murray supplemented it with a review of the slender medical literature through 1994. Badruddin Khan passed on the Naz Project's Islamic rationale.

1. According to Osteria and Sullivan:

The Malaysian Penal Code punishes the offences of rape, incest, unnatural offence, gross indecency, and enticing a married woman. Such provisions apply to Muslims (Ahmad 1965). In [the states] of Selangor, Malacca, and Penang, any Muslim who is guilty of illicit intercourse, that is, sexual intercourse not amounting to rape between any male and any female who is not his wife or whom he is forbidden by Muslim Law to marry, shall be guilty of an offence, whether or not the other party to such illicit intercourse professes the Muslim religion. This offence is punishable with imprisonment for a term not exceeding six months, or with a fine not exceeding five hundred dollars. (1991:134)

Humana (1986) asserts that the laws are enforced diligently when offenses are brought to the attention of officials.

2. Khan's presentation of this distinction is quite different from that in the "West."

3. For example, Constantine 1990, Milder and Novelli 1992, Watts et al. 1993. Cf. Kandela 1993, Cohen 1995, Singh et al. 1994.

References

Ahmed, Ibrahim. 1965. *Islamic law in Malaysia*. Singapore: Malaysia Sociological Research Institute.

Brettle, R. P. 1992. "Observations on the problems of HIV infection in Malaysia." *Journal of Infection* 24:101–2.

Cohen, Lawrence. 1995. "Postcolonial India and the enormity of AIDS." *Chi Pukaar: The Newsletter of the Naz Project* 9:17–20.

Constantine N. T., et al. 1990. "HIV infection in Egypt: A two and a half year surveillance." *Journal of Tropical Medicine and Hygiene* 93:146–50.

Humana, Charles. 1986. *World human rights guide*. New York: Facts on File.

Kandela, Peter. 1993. "Arab nations: Attitudes to AIDS." *Lancet* 341 (3 April):884–85.

Khan, Shivananda. 1995. "The Naz Project and the Islamic viewpoint on AIDS?" *Chi Pukaar: The newsletter of the Naz project* 9:3,20.

Malaysian Health Ministry. 1988. *AIDS: Jawapan kepada kemusykilan anda* (*AIDS: Answers to your questions*). Kuala Lumpur: Health Education Unit.

Milder, J. E., and V. M. Novelli. 1992. "Clinical, social and ethical aspects of HIV-1 infections in an Arab Gulf State." *Journal of Tropical Medicine and Hygiene* 95:128–31.

Osteria, Trinidad, and Gerard Sullivan. 1991. "The impact of religion and cultural values on AIDS education programs in Malaysia and the Philippines." *AIDS Education and Prevention* 3:133–46.

Singh J., et al. 1994. "AIDS in Malaysia." *AIDS* 8, suppl. 2:99–103.

Watts D. M., et al. 1993. "Prevalence of HIV infection and AIDS in Egypt over four years of surveillance (1986–1990)." *Journal of Tropical Medicine and Hygiene* 96:113–17.

CHAPTER 22

Conclusion

Stephen O. Murray and Will Roscoe

IDIOMS OF ISLAMIC HOMOSEXUALITIES

As Murray notes in chapter 2, the dominant Arabic and southwest Asian discourse on pederasty has co-existed with attested (if less discussed and un-
celebrated) instances of gender-variant homosexuality, and at least some
relatively egalitarian relationships. While the major norm or cultural script of
homosexual roles in Islamic societies does not describe the extent of homosexual behavior or relations, conventions of discretion and covertness keep
even acted-upon illicit desires from challenging public norms.[1]

Pederasty has not been the only form of homosexuality in Arabic culture
(and still less so in other Islamic cultures—especially in the eastern reaches of
Islam), but it has long been the idealized form. It has not been generally supposed, however, that being anally penetrated by a Muslim sacralized the penetrated male or that it converted anyone to the True Religion.[2] The pleasure
of the man was and is the justification for Muslims to fuck boys, and the culturally appropriate basis for desiring boys is their beauty, not their incipient
masculinity. There is disagreement (both within and between Islamic cultures) about whether sexual relationships with older boys or men is harmful
to the development of the masculinity of those penetrated. Even where such
behavior is not seen as permanently stigmatizing or traumatic, there is no

attestation of a conception of insemination as necessary for maturation like that recorded for some highland New Guinea societies in which homosexual receptivity is a part of all boys' physical as well as social maturation (see Herdt 1984). In Islamic societies, being inseminated as a boy is a hindrance—if not always a bar—to attaining adult masculinity. It is no advantage to one's public reputation or individual self-conception as masculine. The boy in such sexual exchanges is quite clearly feminized, whether permanently (when *ubnah*, or effeminacy, is inculcated by adolescent receptive sexual conduct) or temporarily by being "used as a woman."

Lacking any rationale of pedagogical masculinization for men's sexual relations with boys, homoeroticism in medieval Islamic societies was more like that in ancient Rome than in ancient Greece or recent Melanesia.[3] In none of these societies, ancient, medieval, or modern, did the suitors express any interest in providing pleasure to anyone but themselves when they sought sexual relations with beautiful boys. Nor was the beloved (i.e., the one who is penetrated) always idealized. As in ancient Greece and Rome, some yearning suitors derided handsome boys as overly knowing, manipulative, and fickle.

Also like Greece and Rome, what a free adult did to slaves did not count (Lombard 1975:146). According to Lacey, the *ghulām*, the male slave kept for sexual purposes, was a Persian institution that became "naturalized" among the Arabs around the time of Harun al-Rashid in the late eighth century (1988:20). For more than a millennium thereafter, the choicest specimens were pale Christian boys, generally sold by their parents (but occasionally stolen), and often transported by Christian merchants to Egypt, Syria, or Turkey.[4] One reason William of Adam criticized trading with the enemy in the late thirteenth century was that Muslim merchants "take suitable boys, and fatten them up, and wash them often in all kinds of baths, and dress them in soft garments so that they are 'plumper and pinker and more delightful,' and so sell them as male prostitutes on a market where a man and an effeminate may live as man and wife" (*De modo Saracenas extirpandi* 2:523–25; quoted in N. Daniel 1975:224). This slave trade placed throngs of beautiful boys at the disposal of rich conquerors (M. Daniel 1977:4).

For their part, Muslim fathers often have been unconcerned about their sons' sexual receptivity and have even abetted the display of their availability.[5] Describing Damascus in 1395, the moralistic Ibn Sasrā wrote:

Each of them [the beardless youths] would like to be loved and promenades in the market, past the immoral people. Boys are more bashful than girls, matters are reversed and customs changed, what was hidden is revealed, until they have become like brides in finery and in dress. They commit immorality openly, and no one expresses disapproval; for most of the people have dressed in garments of shame and have boasted of sins, yet no one is indignant at his child's conduct. They have exchanged their honor for the passion of their desires. (1963:217)

Unlike Greece and Rome, however, the structural contrast organizing same-sex relations with aliens and slaves counterposed believers to non-believers, rather than citizens and non-citizens. Since fellow Muslims were not supposed to be enslaved, kept boys were in some real sense not part of Turkish or Arab societies.[6] Similarly, as chapters 9 and 10 show, *mamlūk* and *iç-oghlan* training was for foreign-born youth, not for those born within Islamic societies. Some (such as Abū Nuwās and jurists of the Maliki school) rationalized the practice of making non-believers submit to penetration by believers as a means of glorifying the superiority of Islam—a duty for Muslims rather than as a sin.[7]

The age-stratified idiom in Islamic societies has not been applied to those adults who continue to be sexually receptive, this is in contrast to Tokugawa Japan, where *nanshoku* (boy-love) was "legitimate whether or not a real man and real boy were involved, so long as one partner took the *role* of 'man' and the other the *role* of 'boy' in the relationship" (Schalow 1990:29; emphasis added). In the first and last samurai stories in the seventeenth-century *Nanshoku Okagami* by Saikaku Ihara, boys of the same age play the complementary older/younger roles. The penultimate story, concerning "two old cherry trees still in bloom," has a sixty-six-year-old still loving his sixty-three-year-old as a boy, even "though his hair was thinning and had turned completely white" (Schalow 1990:181). In contrast, there are terms in Arabic and other languages of Islamic societies for sexually receptive adult men distinct from those for sexually used boys (see chapter 2). The Moroccan *zāmel*, for instance, who continues to be available beyond his teens is called *hassās*.

Of all the societies in which age-stratified homosexuality has been described in some detail (including Greece, Melanesia, Japan, and Sudanic tribes), Islamic ones seem least to expect that the sexually used boy will grow up to be a man. Boys may outgrow being sexually used, but the expectation that they are junior warriors that existed in feudal Japan (and in ancient Greece and highland New Guinea until its recent pacification) is (and has been) missing in the pederasty of Arabic, Persian, and Turkish societies (outside military training schools). Azande and Mossi boy-wives in the Sudan, on the other hand, were also expected to leave sexual receptivity (and women's work) behind them and become warriors on reaching adulthood (Evans-Pritchard 1971:185; Tauxier 1912:569–70).[8] The military initiation aspects of Greek pederasty faded with time,[9] and too much enthusiasm (such as permitting more than intercrural intercourse or accepting payment for sexual service) by the *erastēs* could stigmatize him later.[10] Still, the cultural expectation was for the boy to outgrow sexual receptivity, not to enjoy it so much that he would continue to engage in it. In Islamic societies, childhood and adolescent sexual receptivity does not preclude adult masculinity, but it does not aid it either. Some pretty boys "graduate" to being husbands and fathers, but in the native view others are fated to continue being penetrated by men.

Sexual receptivity has, since early 'Abbāsid times (that is, beginning in 761), been assumed to be a "natural" concomitant of male beauty. Rowson (1991) shows that at the time of the Prophet and for some time after his death (throughout the Umayyad era), *mukhannathūn* were suspected of aiding or even committing heterosexual acts. By the ninth or tenth century, however, *mukhannath* meant a sexually receptive man. In the 'Abbāsid and later periods, *mukhannathūn* were assumed to desire being penetrated (i.e., to be *baghghā'un*, while continuing to display many of the distinctive traits for which they were known in the Umayyad period, such as wit and flippancy, association with music and certain musical instruments, activity as go-betweens, and (sometimes) cross-dressing. Their persona is summed up in the famous statement attributed to one of them: "We are the best of people: when we speak you laugh, when we sing you are enraptured, when we lie down you mount" (Rowson 1990:21).

The southern Arabian *khanith* and South Asian *hijra* discussed in chapters 16 and 18 directly continue the *mukhannath* role in such aspects as witty repartee, hennaed hands, distinctive (neither male nor female) dress, beardlessness, elaborate jewelry, singing while pounding tambourines, and sexual receptivity. Indeed, in northwest India, *hijra* in the late nineteenth century were also called *mukhanna* (Crooke 1896:495). The major difference today from earlier roles seems to be direct payment for entertainment, whether sexual or otherwise. The most important continuity is voluntarily giving up masculine gender and dignity. Still, these men do not give up all male prerogatives; they retain or even surpass the general male freedom of movement.[11]

Alongside the sexual use of boys and the sexual availability of low-class, gender-mixing entertainers, there has long been the recognition that some men who are neither effeminate nor young are eager to be penetrated. Age- and gender-stratified homosexualities and the sexual receptivity of eunuchs reaffirm and reproduce the masculinist sex/gender hierarchy. The existence of sexually receptive masculine adults, on the other hand, would be subversive of it, should such practices become generally known.

The dominant idiom of homosexuality at least as far east as Bangladesh remains age-stratified, although sexual receptivity is an expected part of effeminate male roles, which co-exists with the general valuation of boy-love. In Indonesia and the southern Philippines, there is something of a fusion of age- and gender-stratified homosexuality, as chapter 17 relates. Boy-love was the only kind of homosexuality that Muslim men could appropriately discuss (albeit often obscured by spiritual metaphors). With females segregated and tightly controlled, young and/or effeminate males available for sexual pene-tration were tacitly accepted—and carefully not discussed.

There are only glimmers and not much lexicalization of egalitarian male homosexuality. What has been written about female homosexuality provides little information about roles, but taking turns is sometimes mentioned. Egal-itarian (or "gay") male homosexuality is largely (though not entirely) missing from historical Muslim societies and from contemporary ones—with minor exceptions in the capitals of the relatively secular states of Turkey and Paki-stan. Turkey is the only Islamic society with any open gay liberation move-ment, one which is associated with the Radical Democratic Green Party (Yüzgün 1986, 1993; Sofer 1992b). Beginning in the late 1980s, the party's magazine *Yesil Baris* included discussions of egalitarian homosexuality. Tapnic, for example, believes that the modern "gay" type of homosexuality,

in which the traditional distinction between "active" and receptive sexuality disap-pears, is found widely among urban, young, educated, and middle-class homosexu-als. Most gays in Turkey regard themselves as "real men," differentiating themselves from the so-called feminine homosexuals by adopting a male identity in the urban arena. They represent a new sexually conscious stratum of the homosexual popula-tion in society, and have introduced the word "gay" with which to identify them-selves. . . . In contrast to Western experiences, gay politics in Turkey emerged within a "political party." (1992:46–47)

Although waves of puritanism have risen and fallen before, neither tradi-tional nor modern Islamic states have attempted to remove homosexual behavior or its practitioners from society (for a review of current legislation, see Sofer 1992a). As chapters from both Murray ("The will not to know") and Khan show, so-called Islamic "tolerance" depends on *not* making any claims for acceptance of a homosexual way of life or pursuing ongoing same-sex erotic relationships that compete or interfere with family responsibilities.

RELIGIOUS TEACHINGS AND ATTITUDES TOWARD SEXUALITY

Any attempt to account for the diversity, longevity, and "tolerance" of homo-sexuality in Islamic societies must consider its written guide, the *Qur'ān*, supposedly the source of all that believers need to know for right living.[12] Although there are many continuities between Islam and the earlier southwestern Asian scriptural religions of Judaism and Christianity, Islamic laws relating to marriage, divorce, and other aspects of sexual behavior derive more from pre-Islamic Arabic attitudes than from the Talmudic-Christian tradition (Bullough 1976:205; Pellat 1983:776). Bullough argues that the Arabic tradition regarded sex as good, and that Mohammad did not alter that basic valuation (see also Bouhdiba 1985). Although there is some basis for such a characterization, positive valuation of male sexuality in Islamic societies is frequently offset by acute anxiety and more-than-sporadic puritanism (Crapanzano 1980; Yüzgün 1993). Moreover, as Sabbah remarked, "You have to be a man and a man with a special political conception of woman and her place in society, to decode the quranic message as a positive one regarding sex" (1984:110).

In Mohammad's homeland of Arabia, male-male sexual relations apparently were ridiculed, but not formally sanctioned. Poetry celebrated heterosexuality, while proverbs and ritual insults stigmatized men "acting like women" by being sexually receptive to other men.[13] As Marc Daniel concludes, "Mohammad shared the contempt of his countrymen towards homosexuality" (1977:3). Despite the Prophet's familiarity with the Talmudic tradition, and his view that sodomy ran contrary to God's will (fāsiq), he did not include it among the "abominations" offensive to Allah for which he related specific punishments. Nor did subsequent Islamic commentators draw on accounts of Sodom and Gomorrah (which are not mentioned by name in the Qur'ān) to condemn homosexuality, as did biblical commentators.

Within Islamic cosmology, male sexual pleasure is "good-in-itself" not merely as a means to procreation, but as prefiguring paradise, which, according to the Qur'ān, is staffed with beautiful serving boys (al-fatā) as well as girls (the term houri includes both) (56.17ff; 52.24; 76.19).[14] In marked contrast to the many later stories of the Prophet (the hadīth) in which male-male sex is condemned, there is the famous tale in which Mohammad saw God in the form of a beautiful youth (Schimmel 1982:67–68; Ritter 1955:445–46), the tradition that the Prophet loved a man (Arberry 1956:53n24), and the report of al-Jāhiz (ca. 776–ca. 868) concerning the ease with which early companions of the Prophet discussed sexuality in the introduction of Kitab Mufakharat al-jawari wa-al-ghulman (A book of the debate comparing the advantages of [sex with] women and young men; see AbuKhalil 1993:33).

Still, loving without touching (let alone penetrating) remains the ideal—even for men (Giffen 1971:99–115; Mauzalaoui 1979:43–44). Muslim men are expected to be aim-inhibited, noble martyrs to a male love kept pure from any physical contact, let alone consummation. Even permitted gazes tend to lead to the "tasting of forbidden pleasures" and, even when they do not lead there, they distract men from focusing on God and what He said to His Prophet. Consequently, religious leaders skeptical of men's capacity for self-control have condemned looking and yearning at female or male objects of desire (Giffen 1971:10–11, 118–20; Bell 1979:127–44; Mauzalaoui 1979). Those who came to be called "orthodox,"

cautiously tried to minimize the risks to the social and moral fabric of the community. Profoundly distrusting the self-possession and self discipline of the average Muslim, they wished, by hedging against every possible slip due to weak human nature, to insure that there was no danger of transgressing the precepts of Holy Law. They were surer that sin would almost necessarily result from the activity of the wandering eye and the temptations of face-to-face encounters. (Giffen 1971:123)

How much (if any) effect on actual practice puritanical moralists had is open to question, however. Scholars such as Norman Roth (1991:159) and Franz Rosenthal (in Marsot 1979:37) believe that there was no effect.

Rather than "sex-positive" or "sex-negative," the Arab sexual morality of Mohammad's time, as inscribed in the *Qur'ān*, is best described as restrictive but not ascetic (Greenberg 1988:173; see also Wafer infra). Naim provides a native perspective on Islamic attitudes toward sexuality:

[Most Western analyses] tend to oppose the negative valuation of homosexuality in the West with what they see as a a positive one in the East, particularly in the Islamic societies. It would be more correct, however, to posit for the latter an in-between state of indifference which can, given sufficient impetus of one kind or another, turn into either salaciousness or harsh disapproval. In other words, if the European response to homosexual love has been totally antagonistic, the Islamic East has neither celebrated in an unequivocal fashion nor looked at it with total impassivity. [Samuel] Klausner's phrase, "tolerant jocularity" comes closest to describing the latter's response, but only at one end of the scale; at the other end, religious condemnation always remains a viable threat. (1979:120)

Male sexual pleasure, not just procreation, was viewed as good, and irresistible male sexual urges that required release of accumulated semen were and continue to be taken for granted in Islamic societies (Wikan 1977:315, 1982:181; Crapanzano 1980:108–9).[15] Most Islamic religious leaders marry; they are not segregated into monasteries of celibate religious adepts. Moreover, as Schmitt contends, "for North Africans and Southwest Asians it is self-evident that men like to sodomize all kinds of objects [and] it is understandable that men prefer boys over women" (1985:54). Boys are much more available, and their sexual use less serious than the expropriation of women's bodies to which some other man might have the rights or responsibility for conserving (especially the virginity of unmarried females and the clear paternity of their children).

After the death of the Prophet, rapid Arab conquest spread the faith to ethnically diverse areas where previous civilizations had exalted pederastic love and sacralized some forms of gender variance, as Roscoe discusses in chapter 3. Egyptian, Syrian, and Carthaginian civilizations all mixed indigenous traditions with later Greek and/or Roman cultural influences, homosexual and other, and there is a long-standing Arab tradition dating back to Al-Jāhiz that pederasty came from Persia with the 'Abbāsid army in the mid-eighth century (Mez 1937:358n2; Ritter 1955:351). Although there was no clean revolutionary break (with an epistemic rupture à la Foucault), between the Umayyad patrimonial state and the administration by relatively permanent officials of the 'Abbāsid dynasty, major changes in finance and administration occurred in the eighth century, beginning before the 'Abbāsid triumph. Practices changed and a literati arose in intimate connection with 'Abbāsid administrative practices (Grunebaum 1952:338, 1955:155–57; Hourani 1991:34–35).

In Islamic Persia, as elsewhere, mystic writers like Rūmī produced a rhetoric in which sexual union between two males was a metaphor for ecstatic union with God.[16] In the middle of the eighth century, with the rise of the 'Abbāsid caliphate, Muslim mystics generally adopted the vocabulary of boy-love poetry to signify love for God, although, as Marc Daniel points out, "They never succeeded in integrating it into their conception of the relationship between man and God"(1977:10). However, because the focus of Orientalist research has been on written texts rather than the relationship between spiritual masters and their disciples, there may have been more "integration" than outsiders have noticed. As Trix observes, "Previous Islamic studies have preserved the poetry of *murshids* and certain biographical details but have tended to take for granted the process of teaching" (1993:147).[17] Naim explains, "A Sufi seeker [*tālib*] should first direct all his love toward his mentor (*murshid*), who is always a male; only later, through the help of the mentor, can he reach his true love, God, who is again always referred to in the masculine" (1979:123).[18]

Perhaps, the real gulf is between legalists and antinomian mystics. While rigorists (Hanbalite in particular) sought to proscribe even glances at beautiful boys (and at any women outside the household), some Sufis considered beauty a manifestation of God and love of beauty equivalent to love of God. As Bell observes, "The mystic who claimed to see all things in the moment of ecstatic union only as God sees them—as divine acts and therefore good—could justify any [conventionally] unlawful deed." In other words, "The distinction between good and evil is an illusion and does not exist for the mystic who sees the world from God's perspective," from which it is a short step to inferring that "if God's love is identical with his will, then if it is granted that he wills all that occurs, it must likewise be admitted that he loves all that occurs" (Bell 1979:203). Both the legalists and the mystics considered themselves to be good Muslims, even as they reached quite contrary interpretations of the Qur'ān and selected *hadīths*.[19]

SOCIAL AND HISTORICAL FACTORS

Bullough considers widespread Islamic homoeroticism a "natural outgrowth of a sex-positive, sex-segregating religion in which women had little status or value" (1976:238). Similarly, Dickemann argues that man-boy love "is predictable from a few variables: social stratification with a controlling patrilineal elite and a large poverty class, seclusion of women, [a] decentralized political system involving individual political networks, absence of formal education" (1993:62). Patrilineal inheritance, rather than open political competition, is the cause in her account, resulting "in intense paternity concern, with the seclusion and devaluation of women as household workers and childbearers, dangerous to men." Polygamy further alienates the sexes. Wikan sees the acceptance of homosexual prostitution as the state's recognition of the utility of a sexual "safety valve" for men in a social system in which access to women is rigorously restricted (1977:314). The sexual availability of boys and effeminate men thus protects female virtue.[20] (So little is known about Islamic female homosexualities that generalizations about its presence and nature cannot yet be offered.)

Patrilineal practices and social stratification also account for the all-male institutions in which homosexual relations frequently occurred, as Murray discusses in his chapters on the *mamlūks* and Ottoman slave elites (to which can be added the use of eunuchs to fill state offices that Roscoe discusses). Efforts by Islamic rulers to create one-generation elites to fill military and bureaucratic posts who would not be able to foster dynastic aspirations of their own resulted in a form of "situational" homosexuality. The single-sex environment in which these retainers functioned and their segregation from the larger population facilitated the formation of homosexual relations among them; in some cases these were the only form of personal relations, sexual or emotional, open to them. Such relationships, in turn, proved to be advantageous for various reasons, and so they persisted. As Murray argues in chapters 9 and 10, the possibility of same-sex relations in these cases again is related to inheritance practices (specifically, its blockage). In Islamic societies, non-reproductivity automatically disqualifies a male from adult masculine status. Normally this is a highly marginal, if not proscribed, position within tribal patrilineal systems, but in the urban societies of the Oikoumene region, with their need for state and religious specialists, such males were found quite useful precisely because they were not "players" in the politics of patrilineal descent and inheritance. At the same time, their social and conceptual segregation from the mainstream of Islamic societies decreased the likelihood that the kinds of same-sex relations fostered in these institutions would spread beyond them.

Historical continuities in both status-differentiated homosexuality and gender-variant social roles in this region predating the rise of Islam must also be considered in accounting for their presence in Islamic societies. Both patterns, as the earlier evidence of them suggests, were closely associated with city-state institutions—military and educational in the case of Greek *paiderastia*, religious and administrative in the case of alternative gender roles in Mesopotamia. Since Islamic conquerors did not alter the fundamental socioeconomic structure of the agrarian-based, urban societies they conquered, it is not surprising that same-sex patterns so long connected to the urban cultures of the Oikoumene should continue. Here future studies in history and archaeology may clarify the precise historical links and the socio-structural reasons for them.

The evidence on Islamic homosexualities, as we argued in the Introduction, also allows us to revisit the question of modern homosexual identity and its origins. Why did this transformation in human sexuality occur in the industrialized, urban societies of northern Europe and North America? Are these, indeed, the only kinds of societies in which a dichotomized heterosexual/homosexual organization of sexuality could develop? Are identity, lifestyle, and subculture completely unique features of modern Euro-American homosexuality, which no other pattern (status-differentiated or gender-defined) can produce? Recent scholarship in the study of sexuality has tended to reinscribe European exceptionalism and unilinear evolution onto the study of the history of sexuality. Many social constructionists would indeed claim that the "modern homosexual" is the product of an epistemological break that sharply distinguishes that role from all other same-sex patterns (Foucault 1978; Halperin 1990).

The issue of lexicalization provides a good means of testing this assumption. The exceptionalist argument on modern homosexuality would lead us to hypothesize that in no other society except those of northern Europe in the late nineteenth century would we find terminology that labels individuals in terms of sexual object choice. Nor should we expect to find terms that refer to an ongoing state of being equivalent to "orientation" or to a character trait or type of personality, but rather only terms that identified specific sexual desires and acts (the argument of Schmitt 1992). As Murray showed in chapter 2, however, evidence from Islamic societies seriously questions such a hypothesis. Homosexual roles, both age- and gender-defined, were and are lexicalized in Arabic, Farsi, Turkish, Urdu, and other languages. These are not terms for acts without actors. At the same time, speakers and writers of these languages were well aware that the boundaries of these categories are not always observed.

In fact, there appears to be a recurrent tendency for the distinctions between roles in status- and gender-differentiated homosexuality to become blurred and for a *de facto* recognition of a general category of homosexuality and even homosexual inclination, to develop—still not quite the same as, but much closer to the contemporary Western category of homosexuality. This can occur whenever partners switch roles in sexual intercourse, when the penetrating partner is nonmasculine or the receptive partner masculine, when the age or status difference between partners are not sharply differentiated, or when the penetration of a youth is linked to the expectation that he will become an effeminate adult who desires penetration. The latter expectation, as Murray shows in chapter 2, was common in Islamic societies and explicit terminology existed to name and describe such men.

In fact, the emergence of modern homosexuality may be best characterized as a breakdown of these traditional distinctions between status-differentiated and gender-variant patterns, rather than a break with them. As Islamic examples reveal, the more these distinctions are blurred, the more same-sex relations come to resemble the organization, conceptualization, and subjectivity of so-called modern homosexuality.[21] While the penetrator/penetrated distinction had a long history in the West, remaining relevant in legal and religious treatment of same-sex acts until quite recently, it does not appear in the biblical injunctions on which the Judeo-Christian condemnation of sodomy is based. Indeed, a proclivity to lump all forms and practitioners of same-sex acts together into a general category is incipient within Judeo-Christian theology. Once it is acknowledged that the penetrated partner desires penetration and undergoes it willingly, any basis for treating either partner differently vanishes—both are guilty of sodomy. Medical discourse, which defines and categorizes types of persons based on ongoing inclinations and motivational patterns, in this sense was not a break with Christian discourse on sodomy but fully compatible with it—the missing element, as it were, of a complete apparatus for the social control of a population. In this regard, the speculations on the "disease" that causes homosexual desire in medieval Arabic medical treatises are quite comparable to the initial speculations of Western medical writers in the mid-nineteenth century, who began with physical causes of the "disease" of gender variation before proceeding to the psychology of same-sex desire.

Had Europe not been converted to a centralized monotheism with some capability of regulating social behavior through local agents (a capability vastly supplemented with the emergence of the nation-state), status-differentiated and gender-defined patterns might have flourished in the pre-modern era with the same diversity and visibility that they had in Islamic societies. Conversely, should modern Islamic "fundamentalist" movements seize control of the state, as they did in Iran, new opportunities to enforce rigorist interpretations of religious law may lead to concerted attempts to extirpate all forms of same-sex relations, such as have not been seen before in Islamic history. (Ironically, recent denunciations of homosexuality by fundamentalists betray the influence of the Western category of "homosexuality" by no longer distinguishing penetrating and penetrated roles, and by their consciousness of Western contempt for endemic Muslim involvement in homosexuality.)

The evidence in this collection suggests that there is no reason that the status-differentiated and gender-defined patterns found in Islamic societies could not have become "modern" homosexualities. In many non-Western urban centers around the world this is precisely what we see: men adopting the new terminology and self-conceptions of a gay identity under the influence of Western examples, while continuing to observe traditional distinctions of older/younger, active/passive, and even masculine/non-masculine in their personal relationships (see Murray and Arboleda 1995; Murray 1992b; Jackson 1995). One lexical set replaces another, but the traditional categories (distinctions of age or gender-definition) do not disappear. Rather, they become subsidiaries of the new, overarching category of "homosexuality." Individuals identify as homosexuals first and secondarily as "tops" or "bottoms" (North America, Europe) or "queens" or "kings" (Thailand). Moreover, much homosexual behavior in Western societies is not tied to any identity. Closeted men, who engage in anonymous sex with other males, and post-identity "queers," who celebrate sexual "fluidity," reject the gay label and identity. What might be termed "pre-modern," "modern," and "post-modern" homosexualities actually co-exist in contemporary societies, Western and non-Western.

This discussion leads to the conclusion that a much more complex model of historical change is needed to account for the "modern homosexual" than

Foucault's notion of epistemological rupture and the unilineal causation of social constructionist theory, which credits elite discourse with the power to construct social roles and identities *de novo* and co-opt state power to enforce these discursive entities. Contradictions within every system of human relations and categories are, from another perspective, incipient forms of other relations and other categories. No system is ever purely itself and none other. Because of the inherent ambiguities of categories and the failure of humans to follow rules and conventions, cultural systems are always on the verge of becoming some other system.

The difference between modern, Western homosexualities and the forms of same-sex relations we find in Islamic societies past and present is not a function of one single, categorical factor or development but of a series of small, sometimes minor differences, in religion, socioeconomic structures, state organizations, labeling practices, kinship systems and family structure, and others. Many of the factors credited with fostering the emergence of modern Western homosexual patterns such as sexual labeling practices, the popular belief that homosexuality is a character trait, the association of non-masculinity with homosexual desire, and the possibility of urban networks or subcultures were present in historical Islamic societies. Any account of the emergence of Western homosexuality consequently needs to consider all relevant factors, instead of giving inordinate weight to just one or two, such as psychiatric labeling practices or "capitalism." It must consider as well the historical context of ancient same-sex patterns throughout the Mediterranean basin, the same context in which Islam emerged. The appearance of homosexual identity first in the northern part of Europe may reflect coincidence as much as social determination. At the same time, the assumption that the emergence of "gay" homosexuality in contemporary non-Western societies is a function of diffusion from the West can and should be questioned. As in so many other inquiries into history and culture, we find the "Other" homosexualities of Islamic societies are really less different than they have been constructed in our discourse, past and present (both sets of societies, for example, recognize and label individuals based on sexual behavior), while at the same time radically different in ways that previously have been overlooked—reflecting, in particular, the role of patrilineal kinship practices, the centrality of siring sons in the construction of masculinity, beliefs about the body, the social and religious "will not to know" about private sexual behavior, and other factors in Islamic societies that lack counterparts in the West.

Notes

1. As discussed in the conclusion of that chapter, these forms of sexuality are part of a comparative (etic) model, not seen as part of "the same thing" within Islamic societies (i.e., not an emic domain).

2. As Wafer suggests in chapter 4, a rationale for training is submission to God's will (which is what all Muslims of all ages should do), but there are no attested examples of a native view justifying boys' sexual submission as such training. Indeed, it is the beloved who is a synecdoche of the beauty and inscrutability of God, not the lover.

3. On ancient sexual practices, the analogies between the penetrability of adolescents and slaves, and anxieties over similarities in the sexual use of young future citizens and slaves, see Roscoe's chapter above; Dynes (1982); Golden (1984); Richlin (1993); and Verstraete (1980).

4. See chapters 9–11. Sons of Christian merchants resident in Muslim cities were also prime objects of desire. Mez (1937:360–61) relates an instance from Danaubari (d. 945) of a Syrian book dealer named Sa'd expiring from unrequited longing for one named Isa in Edessa.

5. Not all fathers were delighted to have their sons sodomized by those with wealth and power. Herbert recounted the Persian "king" (presumably Shah 'Abbās) allowing a poor father to punish (i.e., cut off) the parts of a duke that had offended the father/patriline by sodomizing the man's son "against the Boyes will, his parents knowledge and the Law of Nature" ([1626] 1971:99). Surieu related a similar case of an officer in the service of Shah Safi "fain to ravish any handsome boy whom he encountered," who was also castrated by a boy's father with royal consent (1967:171–72). Rape and fathers' rights to the property of the boy's body seem to have been more salient than the boys' feelings in both these cases.

6. Exceptions were commonly made for new converts, especially with the Islamicization of the Mongol Golden Horde's territory (the Kipchak Khannate). With the connivance of slave dealers some fair-skinned boys who had been born Muslim were passed off as steppe-bred pagans. Some of the latter were discovered and ousted from *mamlūk* positions.

7. This view continues, for example, Edi: "If the Arabs would have had war with the Israelis using cocks, we would have defeated them easily. The Israelis are a bunch of feminine males who want and should be fucked by the Arabs" (1970 interview quoted by Sofer 1992c:109). Schmitt generalized that "fucking Westerners, whether male or female, is seen as a well deserved revenge . . . and as an expression of physical and moral superiority over a decaying West" (1992:125). See also Bowman 1989.

8. What happened to the young caravan wives (*zun'i-sāfāri*) of Afghanistan when they became adults no one seems to have inquired.

9. The dominant English-language view, most authoritatively argued by Dover 1988, is that the view of proto-Indo-European pederastic initiation is somewhere between dubious and a twentieth-century fantasy.

10. As Roscoe argues in chapter 3, the Romans jettisoned the (by-then faded) pedagogical rationale (or rationalization) for pederasty, and, like the Arab and later the Ottoman conquerors, had many aliens (not sharing citizenship in the case of Rome, not sharing their faith in the case of Islamic societies) to use sexually. As in Islamic societies, along with pederasty, there were gender-defined homosexual roles in both ancient Greece and Rome. There was no expectation of a progression from *erastēs* to *kinaidos*, although fear of such a possibility is evident in the pejorative use of the term *kinaidos*. In ancient Rome, the predominant discourse about same-sex sexuality centered on effeminacy.

11. Roscoe has described some of these roles as "third genders" (1993, 1996, and herein). The distinction needs to be made, however, between native cosmologies that

actually recognize three genders and those that recognize two genders with failures (in which case, gender equals zero, rather than three: see Murray 1994). For elaboration of the few recurrent types that are the primary idiom (i.e., dominant organization) of homosexuality in human societies, see the introduction to Murray 1992a and the first chapter of Murray 1995.

12. However, ignoring polities and classes, it is, as Kessler put it, "sociologically deficient" (1978:210).

13. For relatively recent examples of the ritual insult genre, see Dundes, Leach, and Özkök 1972; Glazer 1976; and Murray 1983.

14. The *houri* are generally believed to be reserved for those who forswore forbidden pleasures in their terrestrial life—"no man being allowed both the pleasures of forbidden women or boys in this world and the delights of the houris in the next" (Bell 1979:136). The Qur'ān does not explicitly indicate that *houri* provide sexual service. See Bouhdiba (1985:75) and Wendel 1974 on the tradition of assuming so.

15. In the major Hanbalite treatise on love, *Rawdat al-muhibbīn*, Ibn Qayyim al-Jawzīya (1292–1350) contended that, in contrast to food, men can survive without sexual intercourse (Bell 1979:132).

16. See Lane 1975; Schimmel 1975, 1982; M. Daniel 1977; Chittick 1983; Southgate 1984:428; Bouhdiba 1985:119; and Wafer's and Murray's discussions in this volume of Persian and Turkish love poetry. Although there is a considerable tradition of what one might label aim-inhibited boy-gazing, there is also plenty of ardent celebration of union. As the sixteenth-century Turkish poet Pir Sultan Abdul wrote (with no specification of the sex of the beloved):

Love is not fulfilled with glances.

Who flees from love is not a man.

(quoted and translated in Trix 1993:153)

17. An exception she explicitly notes is Lings 1971.

18. At least metaphorically, this makes the adult male the object of love and the boy the agent, that is, the lover, though he imbibes the *murshid*'s essence (spiritual wisdom) both actively and passively.

19. Alternately, one could say that (some) Sufis considered proscriptions as good for the masses, but not applicable to spiritual virtuosi such as themselves. That is, "they held the religious law to be merely an exoteric science intended for the common people, while they reserved esoteric knowledge to themselves" (Bell 1979:43), or, more properly, they believed that God chose only a few saints to understand the deepest mysteries.

20. As detailed in chapter 16, the local type Wikan studied, Sohari women's circles, seem to accept the *khanith*, nor does the far-from-libertarian masculinist state of Oman interfere with them.

21. It bears reiterating that a considerable amount of homosexuality, even in cities such as Amsterdam and San Francisco in the 1990s, involves persons who do not consider themselves gay or lesbian. The predominant conception/organization of homosexuality is never the only one.

References

AbuKhalil, As'ad. 1993. "A note on the study of homosexuality in the Arab/Islamic civilization." *Arab Studies Journal* 1(2):32–34, 48.

Arberry, Arthur J. 1956. *The mystical poems of Ibn al-Farid*. Dublin: Emery Walker.

Bell, Joseph Norment. 1979. *Love theory in later Hanbalite Islam*. Albany, NY: State University of New York Press.

Bouhdiba, Adelwahab. 1985. *Sexuality in Islam*. London: Kegan Paul.

Bowman, Glenn. 1989. "Fucking tourists: Sexual relations and tourism in Jerusalem's Old City." *Critiques of Anthropology* 9:77–93.

Bullough, Vern L. 1976. *Sexual variance in society and history.* New York: Wiley.

Chittick, William C. 1983. *The Sufi path of love: The spiritual teachings of Rumi.* Albany, NY: State University of New York Press.

Crapanzano, Vincent. 1980. *Tuhami: Portrait of a Moroccan.* University of Chicago Press.

Crooke, William. 1896. *The popular religion and folk-lore of northern India.* London: A. Cosntable.

———. 1911. "Indian charms and amulets." Vol. 3, *Encyclopaedia of religion and ethics,* ed. James Hastings. New York: Scribner's.

Daniel, Marc. 1977. "Arab civilization and male love." *Gay Sunshine* 21:1–11,27.

Daniel, Norman. 1975. *The Arabs and medieval Europe.* London: Longman.

Dickemann, Mildred. 1993. "Reproductive strategies and gender construction: An evolutionary view of homosexuality." *Journal of Homosexuality* 24:55–71.

Dover, Kenneth J. 1988. *The Greeks and their legacy.* New York: Basil Blackwell.

Dundes, Alan, Jerry W. Leach, and Bora Özkök. 1972. "The strategy of Turkish boys' verbal dueling rhymes." In *Directions in sociolinguistics: The ethnography of communication,* ed. John Gumperz and Dell Hymes, 130–60. New York: Holt, Rinehart and Winston.

Dynes, Wayne R. 1982. "Homosexuality in ancient Rome." In *Cultural diversity and homosexualities* by Stephen Murray, 27–44. San Francisco: Instituto Obregón.

Evans-Pritchard, E. E. 1971. *The Azande.* Oxford: Clarendon Press.

Foucault, Michel. 1978. *The history of sexuality.* New York: Pantheon.

Giffen, Lois Anita. 1971. *Theory of profane love among the Arabs: The development of the genre.* New York: New York University Press.

Glazer, Mark. 1976. "On verbal dueling among Turkish boys." *Journal of American Folklore* 89:88–91.

Golden, Mark. 1984. "Slavery and homosexuality at Athens." *Phoenix* 38:308–24.

Greenberg, David F. 1988. *The construction of homosexuality.* Chicago: University of Chicago Press.

Grunebaum, Gustave E. von. 1952. "The aesthetic foundation of Arabic literature." *Comparative Literature* 4:323–40.

———. 1955. *Unity and variety in Muslim civilization.* Chicago: University of Chicago Press.

Halperin, David. 1990. *One hundred years of homosexuality.* New York: Routledge.

Herbert, Thomas. [1626] 1971. *A relation of some yeares travaile into Afrique, Asia, and the Indies.* Reprint. New York: Capo.

Herdt, Gilbert H. 1984. *Ritualized homosexuality in Melanesia.* Berkeley: University of California Press.

Hourani, Albert. 1991. *A history of the Arab peoples.* Cambridge: Harvard University Press.

Ibn Sasrā, Muhammad ibn Muhammad. 1963. *A chronicle of Damascus, 1389–1397.* Berkeley: University of California Press.

Jackson, Peter A. 1995. *Dear Uncle Go: Male homosexuality in Thailand.* Bangkok: Bua Luang.

Kessler, Clive S. 1978. *Islam and politics in a Malay state.* Ithaca, NY: Cornell University Press.

Lacey, Edward A. 1988. *The delight of hearts: Or what you will not find in any book.* San Francisco: Gay Sunshine Press.

Lane, Enskine. 1975. *In praise of boys: Moorish poems from al-Andalus.* San Francisco: Gay Sunshine Press.

Lings, Martin. 1971. *A Sufi saint of the twentieth century: Shaikh Ahmad al-Alawi.* London: Allen and Unwin.

Lombard, Maurice. 1975. *The golden age of Islam.* Amsterdam: North Holland.

Marsot, Afaf Lutfi al-Sayyid. 1979. *Society and the sexes in medieval Islam*. Malibu, CA: Undena.

Mauzalaoui, M. A. 1979. "Tragic ends of lovers: Medieval Islam and the Latin West." *Comparative Criticism* 1:37–52.

Mez, Adam. 1937. *The renaissance of Islam*. Patna: Jubilee.

Murray, Stephen O. 1983. "Ritual insults in stigmatized subcultures." *Maledicta* 7: 189–211.

———. 1992a. *Oceanic homosexualities*. New York: Garland.

———. 1992b. "The 'underdevelopment' of gay homosexuality in urban Mesoamerica, Peru and Thailand." In *Modern homosexualities*, ed. Ken Plummer, 29–38. London: Routledge.

———. 1994. "Subordinating native cosmologies to the empire of gender." *Current Anthropology* 35:59–61.

———. 1995. *Latin American male homosexualities*. Albuquerque: University of New Mexico Press.

Murray, Stephen O., and Manuel A. Arboleda G. 1995. "Stigma transformation and relexification in the diffusion of *gay* in Latin America." In *Latin American male homosexualities*, by Stephen O. Murray, 138–44. Albuquerque: University of New Mexico Press.

Naim, C. M. 1979. "The theme of homosexual (pederastic) love in pre-modern Urdu poetry." In *Studies in Urdu gazal and prose fiction*, ed. Umar Memon, 120–42. Madison: University of Wisconsin Press.

Pellat, Charles. 1983. "Liwāt." *Encyclopedia of Islam* 5:776–79. Leiden: Brill.

Richlin, Amy. 1993. "Not before homosexuality: The materiality of the *cinaedus* and the Roman law against love between men." *Journal of the History of Sexuality* 3:523–73.

Ritter, Hellmut. 1955. *Das Meer der Seele*. Leiden: Brill.

Roscoe, Will. 1993. "How to become a berdache: Toward a unified analysis of multiple genders." In *Third sex, third gender: Beyond sexual dimorphism in culture and history*, ed. Gilbert Herdt, 329–72. New York: Zone Books.

———. 1996. "Priests of the goddess: Gender transgression in ancient religion." *History of Religions* 35(3):295–330.

Roth, Norman. 1991. "Fawn of my delights: Boy-love in Hebrew and Arabic verse." In *Sex in the middle ages*, 157–72. New York: Garland.

Rowson, Everett K. 1990. "Gender irregularity as entertainment: Transvestism at the early 'Abbāsid court." Unpublished ms.

———. 1991. "The effeminates of early Medina." *Journal of the American Oriental Society* 111:671–93.

Sabbah, Fatna A. 1984. *Woman in the Muslim unconscious*. New York: Pergammon.

Schalow, Paul G. 1990. *The great mirror of male love*. Stanford: Stanford University Press.

Schimmel, Annemarie. 1975. *Mystical dimensions of Islam*. Chapel Hill: University of North Carolina Press.

———. 1982. *As through a veil: Mystical poetry in Islam*. New York: Columbia University Press.

Schmitt, Arno. 1985. "Some reflections on male-male sexuality in Muslim society." In *Klein Schriften zu zwischmeannlicker sexualitat und Erotik in der muslimischen Gesellschaft*, by G. De Martino and A. Schmitt, 54–58. Berlin: privately printed.

———. 1992. "Sexual meetings of East and West: Western tourism and Muslim immigrant communities." In *Sexuality and eroticism among males in Moslem societies*, ed. Arno Schmitt and Jehoeda Sofer, 125–29. Binghamton, NY: Harrington Park Press.

Schmitt, Arno, and Jehoeda Sofer. 1992. *Sexuality and eroticism among males in Moslem societies*. Binghamton, NY: Harrington Park Press.

Sofer, Jehoeda. 1992a. "Sodomy in the law of Muslim states." In *Sexuality and eroticism among males in Moslem societies*, ed. Arno Schmitt and Jehoeda Sofer, 131–49. Binghamton, NY: Harrington Park Press.

———. 1992b. "The dawn of a gay movement in Turkey." In *Sexuality and eroticism among males in Moslem societies*, ed. Arno Schmitt and Jehoeda Sofer, 77–78. Binghamton, NY: Harrington Park Press.

———. 1992c. "Testimonies from the Holy Land: Israeli and Palestinian men talk about their sexual encounters." In *Sexuality and eroticism among males in Moslem societies*, ed. Arno Schmitt and Jehoeda Sofer, 105–19. Binghamton, NY: Harrington Park Press.

Southgate, Minoo S. 1984. "Men, women, and boys: Love and sex in the works of Saʻdī." *Iranian Studies* 17:413–52.

Surieu, Robert. 1967. *Sarve naz: An essay on love and the representation of erotic themes in ancient Iran*. Geneva: Nagel.

Tapnic, Huseyin. 1992. "Masculinity, femininity, and Turkish male homosexuality." In *Modern homosexualities*, ed. Ken Plummer, 39–49. London: Routledge.

Tauxier, Lovis. 1912. *Les noirs du Soudan: Pays Mossi et bouraunni*. Paris: Émile LaRose.

Trix, Frances. 1993. *Spiritual discourse: Learning with an Islamic master*. Philadelphia: University of Pennsylvania Press.

Verstraete, Bert. 1980. "Slavery and social dynamics of male homosexual relations in ancient Rome." *Journal of Homosexuality* 5:227–36.

Wendel, Charles. 1974. "The denizens of paradise." *Humaniora Islamica* 2:29–59.

Wikan, Unni. 1977. "Man becomes woman: Transsexualism in Oman as a key to gender roles." *Man* 12:304–19.

———. 1982. *Behind the veil in Arabia: Women in Oman*. Baltimore: Johns Hopkins University Press.

Yüzgün, Arslan. 1986. *Turkiyede escinselik, dün bügün*. Istanbul: Hüryüz.

———. 1993. "Homosexuality and police terror in Turkey." *Journal of Homosexuality* 24(3/4):159–69.

Appendix

Key Dates in Early Islamic History[1]

622	Muhammad's Hejira from Mecca to Medina; beginning of Muslim calendar
630	Mecca conquered by Muhammad
632	Death of Muhammad
636	Palestine and Syria conquered; victory over Byzantines at Yarmuk river
641	Egypt conquered
643	Persia overrun
644	'Umar, first Caliph, murdered
656	'Uthmān, second Caliph, murdered
650	Arab rule established in Mesopotamia
661	'Ali murdered; Umayyad dynasty founded
662–762	Umayyad capital at Damascus
711	Muslim invasion of Spain
712	Sindh falls to Muslims
718	Siege of Constantinople repulsed
750	'Abbāsid caliphate founded
762	Capital moved to Baghdad

MAJOR CENTRAL AND SOUTHWESTERN ASIAN DYNASTIES
AFTER THE DEATH OF MUHAMMAD

Dynasty	Duration	Major areas ruled
Umayyad caliphs	661–750	Claimed to rule all Muslims, from Damascus
'Abbāsid caliphs	749–1258	Claimed to rule all Muslims from Baghdad
Umayyads of Cordoba	756–1031	Claimed to be caliphs, ruled most of Iberia
Almoravid	1056–1147	Maghrib, Iberia
Ayyūbid	1169–1260	Egypt, Syria, western Arabia
Golden Horde (Kipchak Khannate)	1242–1370	Crimea, Kazan, Astrakhan
Mamlūk	1250–1517	Egypt, Syria, Judea, western Arabia (Kipchak/Qipchaqi mamlūks at first; Circassian mamlūk sultans from 1382 onward)
Ilkhānid	1256–1353	Persia, Iraq
Ottoman	1281–1922	Turkey, North Africa, Syria, Iraq, Armenia, Cyprus, Crete, Greece, Albania, Bulgaria, Serbia, Bosnia-Herzegovinia
Timurid	1370–1506	Central Asia, Persia, northern India
Saffarid/Safavid	1501–1732	Persia
Mughal	1526–1858	India
Sa'ūdî	1746–present	Central, then western Arabia

Note

1. Not all dates are clear-cut. For a more extensive list see *The Cambridge Encyclopedia of the Middle East and North Africa* (1988:59).

Authors

ERIC ALLYN is a Bangkok-based publisher, the author of *Trees in the Same Forest: Thailand's Culture and Gay Subculture,* and the editor of two volumes of Thai men's same-sex sexual experiences: *The Dove Coos* I and II.

LOUIS CROMPTON, professor emeritus of English at the University of Nebraska is the author of *Byron and Greek Love*. He is completing *Homosexuality and Civilization*, a massive history of pre-modern homosexuality in Europe, China, and Japan from which the chapter here on Arab Spain is drawn.

MILDRED DICKEMANN is professor emerita of anthropology at Sonoma State University.

BADRUDDIN KHAN is the pen-name of a Pakastani-Canadian business-man. He is completing an autobiography.

HASAN MUJTABA and NAUMAN NAQVI are journalists in Karachi, Pakistan.

STEPHEN O. MURRAY is a San Francisco-based sociologist and public health consultant. His books include *Latin American Male Homosexualities, American Gay, Social Theory/Homosexual Realitie*s, and *Oceanic Homosexualities*.

WILL ROSCOE is an anthropologist and historian. He is the author of *The Zuni Man-Woman* and *Queer Spirits: A Gay Men's Myth Book*, and the editor of *Living the Spirit: A Gay American Indian Anthology* and *Radically Gay: Gay*

Liberation in the Words of Its Founder by Harry Hay. He has taught at San Francisco State University and the University of California, Berkeley.

JIM WAFER is a senior lecturer at the University of Newcastle in Australia. He is the author of *The Taste of Blood: Spirit Possession in Brazilian Candomblé* and has published on Australian Aboriginal cultures. His current projects include application of queer theory to ethnographic fieldwork and writing, and the study of gay and lesbian alternative religious movements.

SIGRID WESTPHAL-HELLBUSCH is the author of *Die Ma'dan: Kultur und Geschichte der Murschenbewohner im Süd-Iraq, The Jat of Pakistan, Muntzen aus Zentralasien und Persien* and other works.

Index

AIDS: unawareness of dangers of, 224, 292; organizations, 297–301
Abbāsid dynasty, 110, 133, 164n. 2, 309
Abru, Najmuddīn, 23
Abu Bakr, 90, 143, 150
Abū-Nuwās, 45n. 21, 92, 103n. 4, 115, 118
Abu Tamman, 22
actresses, male, 256–61
addiction, to penetration, 18, 20, 30, 161, 250, 251, 305, 312
adultery, 102
Afghanis, 28, 206–7, 215, 219n. 8, 269
Africa: sub-Saharan, 4, 40–41, 213, 219n. 6, 222–29, 304; North, 212–13, 217–18. *See also* Algerians; Egyptians; Moroccans
agriculture, 8, 55
Ajami, 250
ajemi-ohglan, 174–77
al-Amin, 24, 45n. 20, 103n. 4
Albanians, 187–89, 197–202
al-Baqqāli, 217
al-Daylami, 108
al-Din, 119, 120
Alexander the Great, 213, 295n. 4
al-Farid, 113, 115–17, 129n. 13
al-Farra', 152–53
al-Fath, 154
Algerians, 35, 44n. 13, 181
al-Ghazzāli, 108, 117–18

al-Hakam II, 23, 151
al-Hamadhani, 115
al-Hariri, 23
al-Hilli, 47n. 38
Ali, 143
Ali Pasha, 189–95
al-Irrīsi, 99
al-Jawzī, 111
al-Morginani, 47n. 38
al-Mulk, 153
al-Nasir, 165–66, 171nn. 15, 16
al-Rāzī, 29
al-Tabni, 148
al-Tha'alibi, 45n. 18
al-Tibari, 47n. 38
al-Tifashi, 23, 35, 44n. 13
"Amazons," 98, 103n. 2
Andalusian poetry, 151–55
Ansārī, 117
antagonistic acculturation, 15
'Arabī, 112, 129n. 8
Arabian Nights, 9, 23, 115, 214, 216, 218–19; Burton's "Terminal Essay" to, 211–17
Arabic: language, 28–33, 48n. 41, 242; mystical literature, 113, 115–17, 140n. 1, 164
Arabs, 6–7, 14–18, 22, 28–36, 41–42, 48n. 47–50, 164, 204, 222, 226, 231–55, 303, 305, 307–9, 317n. 7. *See also* Egyptians; Iraqis; Libyans; Omanis

325